ECONOMICS & SOCIETY

THIRD EDITION

EDWIN G. DOLAN
Ph.D. Yale University

HORIZON
TEXTBOOK PUBLISHING

P.O. Box 494658 • Redding, CA 96049-4658

TEXT DESIGN AND COMPOSITION: Archetype Book Composition

COVER DESIGN: Walker Printing

ISBN: 1-59602-852-1
Copyright © 2008 by Horizon Textbook Publishing, LLC

The views and opinions of each author do not necessarily reflect the views and opinions of the other authors.

TABLE OF CONTENTS

PREFACE

AS THE ECONOMY changes, teaching materials must change, too. Many such changes are incorporated in this third edition of *Economics & Society* from Horizon Textbook Publishing.

Many of the changes reflect the increased globalization of economic life. Years ago, international topics were confined to one or two chapters, usually tucked in at the end of textbooks, and usually skipped over in the rush to complete the semester. That approach is no longer suitable today. In the macroeconomics volume, discussion of the balance of payments, net exports, exchange rates, international financial flows, and related topics are fully integrated into the chapters where the related theory and policy issues are discussed. There is no separate international macro chapter at all. In the microeconomics volume, there is still a separate chapter at the end covering international trade and trade policy, but this is no longer the first introduction to these topics. Instead, it is a capstone chapter that pulls together individual threads of international economics that have been introduced chapter by chapter, starting in Chapter 1.

The globalization of this text is not confined to discussion of the big issues, like exchange rates or comparative advantage. It is also reflected in a wide variety of small boxed cases and examples incorporated throughout the text. These not drawn exclusively from U.S. experience, as was the case in textbooks of the past, and why should they be? Principles such as supply and demand, marginal cost, and the effects of expansionary monetary policy apply as much in Russia or Malawi as they do in Kansas or California. The inclusion of examples from many places around the world will make the presentation of economic principles more vivid both for increasingly outward-looking American students and for the large number of students from abroad who come to the United States for an education.

Other changes reflect trends in economics itself. Neoclassical models of rational choice remain the foundation of microeconomics, but they are increasingly supplemented by expanded approaches that incorporate insights of other social sciences. Users of the microeconomics volume will find these expanded approaches incorporated at many points. Similarly, recent years have seen a restoration of balance in the teaching of macroeconomics between long-run and short-run perspectives, and between the real and monetary sectors of the economy. The macroeconomics chapters of this new edition begin with an introduction to the theory of economic growth before introducing short-run business cycle considerations. Also, the chapters on money, banking, and monetary policy are moved to an earlier place in the book in keeping with their importance. The short-run "Keynesian cross" income determination model no longer receives chapter-length treatment, although it is still included in a shorter form.

As was the case with the first edition, it has been a pleasure for me to work with such an innovative publisher.

Acknowledgments

My first thanks must go to my long-time co-author, David E. Lindsey, with whom I worked on earlier editions of this text over a period of many years. During his years as Deputy Director of the Division of Monetary Affairs of the Board of Governors of the Federal Reserve System, David was able to find the ideal balance between the theory and practice of economics. Although he did not contribute to preparation of this new edition, his strong influence can still be seen in both the macroeconomic and microeconomic chapters.

Second, I thank the entire publishing and editorial staff of Horizon Textbook Publishing for introducing me to this great new concept in college publishing. I hope you, the user, benefit as much as I have.

Finally, I would like to acknowledge the support and inspiration of Jere Calmes who encouraged me to try my hand at textbook writing more than 30 years ago. Without his energy and commitment over many years, this book would never have been written.

EDWIN G. DOLAN
Lopez Island, Washington

Features of This Edition

- *State of the art pedagogy*. An abundance of case studies introduce and illustrate the subject matter of every chapter.
- *Integrated international economics*. As the world economy itself comes closer together, international economics must be more closely integrated into the principles course. Accordingly, topics in international economic theory and policy, ranging from balance of payments accounts to the foreign exchange operations of the Fed, are introduced in the chapters in which they occur naturally, rather than presented separately in a single chapter.

Supplements

Test Bank

The accompanying Test Bank contains over 2,000 questions in a variety of formats including multiple choice, true/false, and essay questions.

Instructor's Manual

The expanded Instructor's Manual contains material which can be easily included in lectures. The manual also includes all of its traditional elements, including instructional objectives, lecture notes, and suggestions.

Study Guide

The Study Guide has hands-on applications and self-testing programs. It is available in two versions, *Macroeconomics*, and *Microeconomics*. Students can gain an advantage by reinforcing their reading and lecture notes with the following study guide features:

- *Where You're Going*. The objectives and terms for each chapter are recapped to tie concepts together.
- *Walking Tour*. The "Walking Tour" section provides a narrative summary of the chapter and incorporates questions on key points. Answers are given in the margin.
- *Hands On*. Geographical and numerical exercises clarify concepts and better prepare students for tests and quizzes.
- *Economics in the News*. A news item illustrates how concepts covered in the chapter can appear in the real world. Questions and answers reinforce the concepts.
- *Questions for Review*. These questions and answers follow the key chapter concepts, preparing students for the self-test.
- *Self-Test*. Extra test preparation increases a student's understanding and ability to succeed.
- *Careers in Economics*. Formerly an appendix in the text, this material provides students with an understanding of where the study of economics could lead them.

Online Student Tutorial

Created to support and enhance the student's comprehension of the economic principles discussed in the textbook. The online tutorial includes chapters objectives and study questions. To access the tutorial please visit our Students section on our Web site www.htpublishing.com.

Economic PowerPoint Transparencies

This PowerPoint slide set combines graphics and text to further illustrate the economic principles discussed in the text.

About the Author

EDWIN G. DOLAN was born in Oklahoma and grew up in a small town in Oregon. He attended Earlham College and Indiana University, where he majored in Russian Studies and received the Certificate of Indiana University's famed Russian and East-European Institute. After earning a doctorate in economics from Yale University, he taught at Dartmouth College, the University of Chicago, George Mason University and Gettysburg College. In 1990, he began teaching in Moscow, Russia, where he and his wife founded the American Institute of Business and Economics, an independent, not-for-profit MBA program. Since retiring as President of that institution in 2001, he has taught global macroeconomics, managerial economics and public policy in Latvia, Hungary, Croatia, Bulgaria, and the Czech Republic. When not lecturing abroad, he makes his home in Washington's San Juan Islands.

PART I

CHAPTER 1

The Economic Way of Thinking

After reading this chapter, you will understand:

1. The subject matter of economics
2. The considerations underlying four fundamental economic choices:
   – What an economy will produce
   – How goods and services will be produced
   – Who will produce which goods and services
   – For whom goods will be produced
   – How to coordinate economic choices
3. How economists use theory, graphs, and evidence in their work

---

2 005 WAS A tough one for General Motors, the world's largest carmaker. In the first three months of the year alone, it lost $1.1 billion as sales of its largest SUVs plunged. On Wall Street, the company's bonds were downgraded to "junk" status, as were those of rival Ford Motor Company, which was also heavily reliant on sales of large SUVs and pickups. Meanwhile, sales of fuel-efficient hybrids made by Toyota and Honda were booming. The cause of all this turmoil? Soaring gasoline prices and record-high world prices for the crude oil from which gasoline is refined.

Rising gasoline prices and falling SUV sales are examples of **scarcity** and the choices people make when there is not enough of something to meet everyone's wants. In this case the scarce resource is energy. American consumers want to use a lot of the world's scarce energy resources to run the large cars they love so much. But consumers in rapidly growing China and India want energy to build a lifestyle based

Scarcity

A situation in which there is not enough of a resource to meet all of everyone's wants.

Economics

The social science that seeks to understand the choices people make in using scarce resources to meet their wants.

on refrigerators, air conditioners, and motor transport, too. There is not enough oil in the world to satisfy all wants at once, so choices must be made. Scarcity and the way people deal with it are the central topics of **economics**, which can be defined as the social science that seeks to understand the choices people make in using scarce resources to meet their wants.

Economics, as the definition makes clear, is a study not of things or money or wealth but of *people*. Economics is about people because scarcity itself is a human phenomenon. Deposits of crude oil lay undisturbed in the ground for millions of years before they became the object of human wants. Only at that point did they become *scarce* in the sense that economists understand the term. It is the focus on the human dimension of scarcity and choice that makes economics a social science rather than a branch of engineering or mathematics.

Microeconomics

The branch of economics that studies the choices of individuals, including households, business firms, and government agencies.

Scarcity and choice, the ideas that unify all of economics, have many different applications. The example of gasoline prices and vehicle choices are applications from **microeconomics**. The prefix *micro,* meaning "small," indicates that this branch of economics deals with the choices of small economic units such as households, firms, and government agencies. Although microeconomics studies individual behavior, its scope can be worldwide. When households, firms, and government agencies conduct worldwide trade in such goods as cars and crude oil, that trade and the policies regulating it fall within the scope of microeconomics.

Macroeconomics

The branch of economics that studies large-scale economic phenomena, particularly inflation, unemployment, and economic growth.

Economics also has another branch, known as **macroeconomics**. The prefix *macro,* meaning "large," indicates that this branch deals with larger-scale economic phenomena. Typical problems in macroeconomics include how to maintain conditions in which people who want jobs can find them, how to protect the economy against the distortions caused by widespread price increases (inflation), and how to provide for a continued increase in living standards over time. Choices studied by macroeconomics include those made by governments, for example, choices among alternative policies concerning taxes, expenditures, budget deficits, and the financial system. However, because macroeconomic phenomena, such as inflation, represent the end result of millions of individual choices regarding the prices of particular goods and services, macroeconomics ultimately rests on a microeconomic foundation.

Whether one is dealing with microeconomics or macroeconomics, and whether with domestic or international economic relationships, all economic analysis comes down to a special way of thinking about how people choose to use scarce resources.

WHAT? HOW? WHO? FOR WHOM?

In every economy certain basic choices must be made. Among these, the most important are what goods will be produced, how they will be produced, who will do which jobs, and for whom the results of economic activity will be made available. Each of these choices is made necessary because of scarcity, and each can be used to introduce key elements of the economic way of thinking.

Deciding What to Produce: Opportunity Cost

The first basic choice is that of what goods to produce. In any real economy the number of goods and services that could be produced is immense. The key features of the choice of what goods to produce, however, can be illustrated using an economy in which there are just two alternative goods, say, cars and education. For many students, going without a car (or driving an older, used car instead of a new one) is a sacrifice that must be made in order to get a college education. The same trade-off that is faced by an individual student is also faced by the economy as a whole: Not enough cars and education can be produced to satisfy everyone's wants. Somehow it must be decided how much of each good to produce.

The impossibility of producing as much of everything as people want reflects a scarcity of the productive resources that are used to make all goods. Many scarce productive resources must be combined to make even the simplest of goods. For example, making a table requires lumber, nails, glue, a hammer, a saw, the work of a carpenter, and that of a painter. For convenience, productive resources are often grouped into three basic categories, called **factors of production**: labor, capital, and natural resources. **Labor** includes all of the productive contributions made by people working with their minds and muscles. **Capital** includes all the productive inputs created by people, including tools, machinery, buildings, and intangible items, such as computer programs. **Natural resources** include anything that can be used as a productive input in its natural state—for example, farmland, building sites, forests, and mineral deposits.

Productive resources that are used to satisfy one want cannot be used to satisfy another at the same time. Steel, concrete, and building sites used for automobile factories cannot also be used for classrooms. People who are employed as teachers cannot spend the same time working on an automobile assembly line. Even the time students spend in class and studying for tests represents use of a factor of production that could otherwise be used as labor in an auto plant. Because production uses inputs that could be used elsewhere, the production of any good entails forgoing the opportunity to produce something else instead. In economic terms, everything has an **opportunity cost**. The opportunity cost of a good or service is its cost in terms of the forgone opportunity to pursue the best possible alternative activity with the same time or resources.

Let's go back to the example of an economy that has only two goods, cars and education. In such an economy, the opportunity cost of producing a college graduate can be stated in terms of the number of cars that could have been produced by using the same labor, capital, and natural resources. Suppose that the opportunity cost of educating a college graduate might be four Toyota Camrys. Such a ratio

Factors of production

The basic inputs of labor, capital, and natural resources used in producing all goods and services.

Labor

The contributions to production made by people working with their minds and muscles.

Capital

All means of production that are created by people, including tools, industrial equipment, and structures.

Natural resources

Anything that can be used as a productive input in its natural state, such as farmland, building sites, forests, and mineral deposits.

Opportunity cost

The cost of a good or service measured in terms of the forgone opportunity to pursue the best possible alternative activity with the same time or resources.

(graduates per car or cars per graduate) is a useful way to express opportunity cost when only two goods are involved. More typically, though, we deal with situations in which there are many goods. Having more of one means giving up a little bit of many others.

In an economy with many goods, opportunity costs can be expressed in terms of a common unit of measurement, money. For example, rather than saying that a college education is worth four Camrys or that a Camry is worth one-fourth of a college education, we could say that the opportunity cost of a car is $20,000 and that of a college education is $80,000.

Useful as it is to have a common unit of measurement, great care must be taken when opportunity costs are expressed in terms of money, because not all out-of-pocket money expenditures represent the sacrifice of opportunities to do something else. At the same time, not all sacrificed opportunities take the form of money spent. *Applying Economic Ideas 1.1*, which analyzes both the out-of-pocket expenditures and the opportunity costs of a college education, shows why.

The importance of opportunity cost will be stressed again and again in this book. The habit of looking for opportunity costs is one of the distinguishing features of the economic way of thinking.

Deciding How to Produce: Efficiency and Entrepreneurship

A second basic economic choice is that of how to produce. There is more than one way to produce almost any good or service. Cars, for example, can be made in highly automated factories using a lot of capital equipment and relatively little labor, or they can be built one by one in small shops, using a lot of labor and only a few general-purpose machines. Toyota Camrys are built the first way, Ferraris and Rolls Royces the second way. The same kind of thing could be said about education. Economics can be taught in a small classroom with one teacher and a blackboard serving 20 students, or it can be taught in a large lecture hall in which the teacher uses projectors, computers, and TV monitors to serve hundreds of students.

Economic efficiency
___
A state of affairs in which it is impossible to make any change that satisfies one person's wants more fully without causing some other person's wants to be satisfied less fully.

EFFICIENCY Efficiency is a key consideration in deciding how to produce. In everyday speech, efficiency means producing with a minimum of expense, effort, and waste. Economists use a more precise definition. **Economic efficiency**, they say, refers to a state of affairs in which it is impossible to make any change that satisfies one person's wants more fully without causing some other person's wants to be satisfied less fully.[1]

Although this formal definition of economic efficiency may be unfamiliar, it is actually closely related to the everyday notion of efficiency. If there is some way to make you better off without making me worse off, it is wasteful (inefficient) to pass up the opportunity. If I have a red pen that I am not using, and you need one just for a minute, it would be wasteful for you to buy a red pen of your own. It is more efficient

APPLYING ECONOMIC IDEAS 1.1

THE OPPORTUNITY COST OF A COLLEGE EDUCATION

How much does it cost you to go to college? If you are a resident student at a typical four-year private college in the United States, you can answer this question by making up a budget like the one shown in Figure A. This can be called a budget of out-of-pocket costs, because it includes all the items—and only those items—that you or your parents must actually pay for in a year.

Your own out-of-pocket costs may be much higher or lower than these averages. Chances are, though, that these are the items that come to mind when you think about the costs of college. As you begin to think like an economist, you may find it useful to recast your college budget in terms of opportunity costs. Which of the items in Figure A represent opportunities that you have forgone in order to go to college? Are any forgone opportunities missing? To answer these questions, compare Figure A with Figure B, which shows a budget of opportunity costs.

Some items are both opportunity costs and out-of-pocket costs. The first three items in Figure A show up again in Figure B. To spend $14,000 on tuition and fees and $1,200 on books and supplies, you must give up the opportunity to buy other goods and services—to buy a car or rent a ski condo, for instance. To spend $1,100 getting to and from school, you must pass up the opportunity to travel somewhere else or to spend the money on something other than travel. Not all out-of-pocket costs are also opportunity costs, however. Consider the last two items in the out-of-pocket budget. By

spending $7,000 on room, board, and personal expenses during the year, you are not really giving up the opportunity to do something else. Whether or not you were going to college, you would have to eat, live somewhere, and buy clothes. Because these are expenses that you would have in any case, they do not count as opportunity costs of going to college.

Finally, there are some items that are opportunity costs without being out-of-pocket costs. Think about what you would be doing if you were not going to college. If you were not going to college, you probably would have taken a job and started earning money soon after leaving high school. As a high-school graduate, your earnings would be about $16,000 during the nine months of the school year. (You can work during the summer even if you are attending college.) Because this potential income is something that you must forgo for the sake of college, it is an opportunity cost even though it does not involve an outlay of money.

Which budget you use depends on the kind of decision you are making. If you have already decided to go to college and are doing your financial planning, the out-of-pocket budget will tell you how much you will have to raise from savings, a job, parents' contributions, and scholarships to make ends meet. But if you are making the more basic choice between going to college and pursuing a career that does not require a college degree, the opportunity cost of college is what counts.

Figure A	Budget of Out-of-Pocket Costs	Figure B	Budget of Opportunity Costs
Tuition and fees	$14,000	Tuition and fees	$14,000
Books and supplies	1,200	Books and supplies	1,200
Transportation to and from home	1,100	Transportation to and from home	1,000
Room and board	7,000	Forgone income	16,000
Personal expenses	1,400		
Total out-of-pocket costs	**$24,700**	**Total opportunity costs**	**$32,200**

for me to lend you my pen; it makes you better off and me no worse off. If there is a way to make us both better off, it would be all the more wasteful not to take advantage of the opportunity. You lend me your bicycle for the afternoon and I will lend you my volleyball. If I do not ride a bicycle very often and you do not play volleyball very often, it would be inefficient for us both to own one of each item.

Efficiency in production

A situation in which it is not possible, given available knowledge and productive resources, to produce more of one good without forgoing the opportunity to produce some of another good.

The concept of economic efficiency has a variety of applications: one such application centers on the question of *how* to produce. **Efficiency in production** refers to a situation in which it is not possible, given available productive resources and existing knowledge, to produce more of one good without forgoing the opportunity to produce some of another good. The concept of efficiency in production, like the broader concept of economic efficiency, includes the everyday notion of avoiding waste. For example, a grower of apples finds that beyond some certain quantity, using more fertilizer per tree does not increase the yield of apples. To use more than that amount would be wasteful. Better to transfer the extra fertilizer to the production of, say, peaches. That way more peaches can be grown without any reduction in the apple crop.

The economist's definition also includes more subtle possibilities for improving the efficiency of production in cases where the waste of resources is less obvious. For example, it is possible to grow apples in Georgia. It is also possible, by selecting the right tree varieties and using winter protection, to grow peaches in Vermont. Some hobbyists do grow both fruits in both states. However, doing so on a commercial scale would be inefficient even if growers in both states followed the most careful cultivation practices and avoided any obvious "waste." To see why, suppose that initially apple and peach trees were planted in equal numbers in the two states. Then compare this with a situation in which 500 fewer struggling peach trees had been planted in Vermont, and 500 thriving apple trees had been planted instead. At the same time, suppose 500 fewer heat-stressed apple trees had been planted in Georgia, and their place had been taken by peaches. The second alternative would increase the output of both fruits without increasing the total land, labor, and capital used in fruit production. This shows that the original distribution of trees was inefficient.

HOW TO INCREASE PRODUCTION POTENTIAL   Once efficiency has been achieved, more of one good can be produced only by forgoing the opportunity to produce something else, assuming that productive resources and knowledge are held constant. But over time, production potential can be expanded by accumulating more resources and finding new ways of putting them to work.

In the past, discovery of new supplies of natural resources has been an important way of increasing production potential. Population growth has always been, and still is, another source. However, as the most easily tapped supplies of natural resources are depleted and as population growth slows in the most developed countries, capital will increasingly be the factor of production that contributes most to the expansion of production potential.

Investment

The act of increasing the economy's stock of capital—that is, its supply of means of production made by people.

The act of increasing the economy's stock of capital—that is, its supply of productive inputs made by people—is known as **investment**. Investment involves a trade-off of present consumption for future consumption. To build more factories, roads, and computers, we have to divert resources from the production of bread, movies, haircuts, and other things that satisfy immediate wants. In return, we put ourselves in a better position to satisfy our future wants.

Increased availability of productive resources is not the only source of economic growth, however. Even more important are improvements in human knowledge—the invention of new technology, new forms of organization, new ways of satisfying wants. The process of looking for new possibilities—making use of new ways of doing things, being alert to new opportunities, and overcoming old limits—is called **entrepreneurship.** It is a dynamic process that breaks down the constraints imposed by existing knowledge and limited supplies of factors of production.

Entrepreneurship does not have to mean inventing something or starting a new business, although it sometimes does. It may mean finding a new market for an existing product—for example, convincing people in New England that tacos, long popular in the Southwest, make a quick and tasty lunch. It may mean taking advantage of price differences between one market and another—for example, buying hay at a low price in Pennsylvania, where growing conditions have been good in the past year, and reselling it in Virginia, where the weather has been too dry.

Households can be entrepreneurs, too. They do not simply repeat the same patterns of work and leisure every day. They seek variety—new jobs, new foods, new places to visit. Each time you try something new, you are taking a step into the unknown. In this sense you are an entrepreneur.

Entrepreneurship is sometimes called the fourth factor of production. However, entrepreneurship differs from the three classical factors of production in important ways. Unlike labor, capital, and natural resources, entrepreneurship is intangible and difficult to measure. Although entrepreneurs earn incomes reflecting the value that the market places on their accomplishments, we cannot speak of a price per unit of entrepreneurship; there are no such units. Also, unlike human resources (which grow old), machines (which wear out), and natural resources (which can be used up), the inventions and discoveries of entrepreneurs are not depleted as they are used. Once a new product or concept, such as gasoline-electric hybrid power for cars, text messaging on cell phones, or the limited-partnership form of business, has been invented, the required knowledge does not have to be created again (although, of course, it may be supplanted by even better ideas). All in all, it is more helpful to think of entrepreneurship as a process of learning better ways of using the three basic factors of production than as a separate factor of production in itself.

Deciding Who Will Do Which Work: The Division of Labor

The questions of what will be produced and how to produce it would exist even for a person living in isolation. Even the fictional castaway Robinson Crusoe had to decide whether to fish or hunt birds, and if he decided to fish, he had to decide whether to do so with a net or with a hook and line. In contrast, the economic questions of who will do which work and for whom output will be produced exist only for people living in a human society—another reason economics is considered one of the social sciences.

Entrepreneurship

The process of looking for new possibilities—making use of new ways of doing things, being alert to new opportunities, and overcoming old limits.

The question of who will do which work is a matter of organizing the social division of labor. Will everyone do everything independently—be a farmer in the morning, a tailor in the afternoon, and a poet in the evening? Or will people cooperate—work together, trade goods and services, and specialize in one particular job? Economists answer these questions by pointing out that it is more efficient to cooperate. Doing so allows a given number of people to produce more than they could if each of them worked alone. Three things make cooperation worthwhile: teamwork, learning by doing, and comparative advantage.

First consider *teamwork*. In a classic paper on this subject, Armen Alchian and Harold Demsetz use the example of workers unloading bulky crates from a truck.[2] The crates are so large that one worker alone can barely drag them along or cannot move them at all without unpacking them. Two people working independently would take hours to unload the truck. If they work as a team, however, they can easily pick up the crates and stack them on the loading dock. This example shows that even when everyone is doing the same work and little skill is involved, teamwork pays.

A second reason for cooperation applies when there are different jobs to be done and different skills to be learned. In a furniture plant, for example, some workers operate production equipment, others use office equipment, and still others buy materials. Even if all the workers start out with equal abilities, each gets better at a particular job by doing it repeatedly. *Learning by doing* thus turns workers of average productivity into specialists, thereby creating an even more productive team.

A third reason for cooperation comes into play after the process of learning by doing has developed different skills and also applies when workers start out with different talents and abilities. It is the principle of division of labor according to *comparative advantage*. **Comparative advantage** is the ability to do a job or produce a good at a relatively lower opportunity cost than someone else.

Comparative advantage
___

The ability to produce a good or service at a relatively lower opportunity cost than someone else.

An example will illustrate the principle of comparative advantage. Suppose two clerical workers, Bill and Jim, are assigned the job of getting out a batch of personalized letters to clients. Jim is a whiz. Using the latest office productivity software, he can prepare a letter in 5 minutes and stuff it into an envelope in 1 minute. Working alone, he can finish ten letters in an hour. Bill is clumsy. It takes him 10 minutes to prepare a letter and 5 minutes to stuff it into the envelope. Alone, he can do only four letters an hour. In summary form:

Jim: Prepare 1 letter 5 min.
       Stuff 1 envelope 1 min.

Bill: Prepare 1 letter 10 min.
      Stuff 1 envelope 5 min.

Without cooperation, the two workers' limit is 14 letters per hour between them. Could they do better by cooperating? It depends on who does which job. One idea might be for Jim to prepare all the letters while Bill does all the stuffing, because that way they can just keep up with each other. But at 5 minutes per letter, that kind of cooperation cuts their combined output to twelve letters per hour. It is worse than not cooperating at all.

Instead, they should divide the work according to the principle of comparative advantage. Even though Bill is slower at preparing the letters, he has a *comparative advantage* in preparation because the opportunity cost of that part of the work is lower for him: The 10 minutes he takes to prepare a letter is equal to the time he needs to stuff two envelopes. For Jim, the 5 minutes he takes to prepare a letter could be used to stuff five envelopes. For Bill, then, the opportunity cost of preparing one letter is to forgo stuffing *two* envelopes, whereas for Jim the opportunity cost of preparing one letter is to forgo stuffing *five* envelopes.

Because Bill gives up fewer stuffed envelopes per letter than Jim, the principle of comparative advantage says that Bill should spend all his time preparing letters. If he does, he can produce six letters per hour. Meanwhile Jim can spend 45 minutes of each hour preparing nine letters, and the last 15 minutes of each hour stuffing all 15 envelopes. By specializing according to comparative advantage, the two workers can increase their total output to 15 letters per hour, their highest possible joint productivity.

In this example the principle of comparative advantage points the way toward an efficient division of labor between two people working side by side. But the principle also has broader implications. It can apply to a division of labor between individuals or business firms working far apart—even in different countries. In fact, the earliest application of the principle was to international trade (see *Who Said It? Who Did It? 1.1*). Today comparative advantage remains one of the primary motivations for mutually beneficial cooperation, whether on the scale of the workplace or on that of the world as a whole.

Whatever the context, the principle of comparative advantage is easy to apply provided one remembers that it is rooted in the concept of opportunity cost. Suppose there are two tasks, A and B, and two parties, X and Y (individuals, firms, or countries), each capable of doing both tasks, but not equally well. First ask what is the opportunity cost for X of doing a unit of task A, measured in terms of how many units of task B could be done with the same time or resources (the opportunity cost). Then ask the same question for Y. The party with the lower opportunity cost for doing a unit of task A has the comparative advantage in doing that task. To check, ask what is the opportunity cost for each party of doing a unit of task B, measured in terms how many units of task A could be done with the same time or resources. The party with the lower opportunity cost for doing a unit of task B has the comparative advantage in doing that task.

Deciding for Whom Goods will be Produced: Positive and Normative Economics

Together, the advantages of team production, learning by doing, and comparative advantage mean that people can produce more efficiently by cooperating than they

---

 WHO SAID IT? WHO DID IT? 1.1

DAVID RICARDO AND THE THEORY OF COMPARATIVE ADVANTAGE

David Ricardo was born in London in 1772, the son of an immigrant who was a member of the London stock exchange. Ricardo's education was rather haphazard, and he entered his father's business at the age of 14. In 1793, he married and went into business on his own. These were years of war and financial turmoil. The young Ricardo developed a reputation for remarkable astuteness and quickly made a large fortune.

In 1799, Ricardo read Adam Smith's *The Wealth of Nations* and developed an interest in political economy (as economics was then called). In 1809, his first writings on economics appeared. These were a series of newspaper articles on "The High Price of Bullion," which appeared during the following year as a pamphlet. Several other short works added to his reputation in this area. In 1814, he retired from business to devote all his time to political economy.

Ricardo's major work was *Principles of Political Economy and Taxation*, first published in 1817. This work contains, among other things, a pioneering statement of the principle of comparative advantage as applied to international trade. Using a lucid numerical example, Ricardo showed why, as long as wool can be produced *comparatively* less expensively in England, it was to the advantage of both

countries for England to export wool to Portugal and to import wine in return, even though both products could be produced with fewer labor hours in Portugal.

But international trade is only a sideline of Ricardo's *Principles*. The book covers the whole field of economics as it then existed, beginning with value theory and progressing to a theory of economic growth and evolution. Ricardo held that the economy was growing toward a future "steady state." At that point economic growth would come to a halt and the wage rate would be reduced to the subsistence level. This gloomy view and the equally pessimistic views of Ricardo's contemporary, Thomas Malthus, gave political economy a reputation as "the dismal science."

Ricardo's book was extremely influential. For more than half a century thereafter, much of the writing on economic theory published in England consisted of expansions and commentaries on Ricardo's work. Economists as different as Karl Marx, the revolutionary socialist, and John Stuart Mill, a defender of liberal capitalism, took Ricardo's theories as their starting point. Even today there are "neo-Ricardian" and "new classicist" economists who look to Ricardo's works for inspiration.

---

could if each worked in isolation. But cooperation raises yet another issue: For whom will goods be produced? The question of the distribution of output among members of society has implications in terms of both efficiency and fairness.

EFFICIENCY IN DISTRIBUTION   Consider first a situation in which production has already taken place and the supply of goods is fixed. Suppose, for example, that 30 students get on a bus to go to a football game. Bag lunches are handed out. Half the bags contain a ham sandwich and a root beer; the other half contain a tuna sandwich and a cola. What happens when the students open their bags? They do not just eat whatever they find—they start trading. Some swap sandwiches; others swap drinks. Maybe there is not enough of everything to give each person his or her first choice. Nevertheless, the trading makes at least some people better off than they were when they started. Moreover, no one ends up worse off. If some of the students do not want to trade, they can always eat what was given to them in the first place.

This example shows one sense in which the "for whom" question is partly about efficiency: Starting from any given quantity of goods, the allocation can be improved through trades that result in better satisfaction of some people's preferences. As long as it is possible to trade existing supplies of goods in a way that permits some people

Efficiency in distribution

A situation in which it is not possible, by redistributing existing supplies of goods, to satisfy one person's wants more fully without causing some other person's wants to be satisfied less fully.

to satisfy their wants more fully without making others worse off, **efficiency in distribution** can be improved even while the total quantity of goods remains fixed.

Efficiency in distribution and efficiency in production are two aspects of the general concept of economic efficiency. When both aspects are taken into account, the relationship between distribution and efficiency is not restricted to situations in which the total amount of goods is fixed in advance. That is so because the rules for distribution affect the patterns of production. For example, the rules for distribution affect the supply of productive resources, because most people earn their incomes by providing labor to business firms, and the amount they supply is affected by the wages they are promised. Another reason is that rules for distribution affect incentives for entrepreneurship. Some people may work hard to discover new ways of doing things even if they expect no material reward, but that is not true of everyone.

FAIRNESS IN DISTRIBUTION   Efficiency is not the whole story when it comes to the question of for whom goods will be produced. One can also ask whether a given distribution is fair. Questions of fairness often dominate discussions of distribution.

One widely held view judges fairness in distribution in terms of equality. This concept of fairness is based on the idea that all people, by virtue of their shared humanity, deserve a portion of the goods and services turned out by the economy. There are many versions of this concept. Some people think that all income and wealth should be distributed equally. Others think that people have an equal right to a "safety net" level of income but that inequality in distributing any surplus beyond that level is not necessarily unfair. Still others think that certain goods, such as health care, food, and education, should be distributed equally but that it is fair for other goods to be distributed less equally.

An alternative view, which also has many adherents, judges fairness primarily in terms of the procedures through which a given distribution is carried out. In this view, fairness requires that certain rules and procedures be observed, such as respect for private property or nondiscrimination on grounds of race and gender. As long as those rules are followed, any resulting distribution of income is viewed as acceptable. In this view, equality of opportunity is emphasized more than equality of outcome.

Positive economics

The area of economics that is concerned with facts and the relationships among them.

Normative economics

The area of economics that is devoted to judgments about whether economic policies or conditions are good or bad.

POSITIVE AND NORMATIVE ECONOMICS   Many economists make a sharp distinction between the question of efficiency and that of fairness. Discussions of efficiency are seen as part of **positive economics**, the area of economics that is concerned with facts and the relationships among them. Discussions of fairness, in contrast, are seen as part of **normative economics**, the area of economics that is devoted to judgments about whether particular economic policies and conditions are good or bad.

Normative economics extends beyond the question of fairness in the distribution of output. Value judgments also arise about the fairness of the other three basic choices faced by every economy. In choosing what will be produced, is it fair to permit production of alcohol and tobacco but to outlaw production of marijuana? In choosing how to produce, is it fair to allow people to work under dangerous or unhealthy conditions, or should work under such conditions be prohibited? In choosing who does which work, is it fair to limit access to specific jobs according to age, gender, race, or union membership? As you can see, normative issues extend to every corner of economics.

Positive economics, rather than offering value judgments about outcomes, focuses on understanding the processes by which the four basic economic questions are or could be answered. It analyzes the way economies operate, or would operate if certain institutions or policies were changed. It traces relationships between facts, often looking for regularities and patterns that can be measured statistically.

Most economists consider positive economics their primary area of expertise, but normative considerations influence the conduct of positive economics in several ways. The most significant of those influences is the selection of topics to investigate. An economist who sees excessive unemployment as a glaring injustice may study that problem; one who sympathizes with victims of job discrimination may take up a different line of research. Also, normative views are likely to affect the ways in which data are collected, ideas about which facts can be considered true, and so on.

At one time it was thought that a purely positive economics could be developed, untouched by normative considerations of values and fairness. Within its framework, all disputes could be resolved by reference to objective facts. Today that notion is less widely held. Nevertheless, it remains important to be aware that most major economic controversies, especially those that have to do with government policy, have normative as well as positive components, and to be aware of the way each component shapes the way we think about those controversies.

COORDINATING ECONOMIC CHOICES

To function effectively, an economy must have some way of coordinating the choices of millions of individuals regarding what to produce, how to produce it, who will do each job, and for whom the output will be produced. This section discusses how households, businesses, and the government interact in the coordination of economic choices.

A Noneconomic Example

You, like almost everyone, have probably had the experience of shopping at a supermarket where there are several long checkout lines. In such a situation, you and other shoppers want to get through the checkout process as fast as possible. The store would like to speed your way through as well and to avoid a situation in which some lines have a long wait for service while the cashiers in other lines stand idle for lack of customers. How can this be done?

One way would be for the store to direct certain customers to certain lines. The store could use a standard rule, such as customers with names starting with A–D go to line 1, E–H go to line 2, and so on. Or the store could hire an employee to sit in a special booth and direct shoppers to one line or another.

Such a system is sometimes used to control lines. For example, the U.S. Customs service at New York's busy Kennedy International Airport has an employee on duty to direct arriving passengers to the next available agent. But supermarkets do not work that way. Instead, supermarkets leave shoppers to decide for themselves what line to join, based on information from their own observations. As you approach the checkout area, you first look to see which lines are the shortest. You then make allowance for the possibility that some shoppers may have carts that are heaped full, while others have only a few items. Using your own judgment, you head for the line you think will be fastest.

The coordination system used by the Customs Service at JFK airport is an example of coordination by **hierarchy.** Hierarchy is a way of achieving coordination in which individual actions are guided by instructions from a central authority. The approach used in supermarkets is an example of coordination by **spontaneous order.** Under this system, coordination is achieved when individuals adjust their actions in response to cues received from their immediate environment. It is *orderly* because it achieves an approximately equal waiting time in each checkout line. It is spontaneous in that coordination is achieved without central direction. Even though no shopper has the specific goal of equalizing the lines, that is the end result.

Spontaneous Order in Markets

In economics, markets are the most important example of the coordination of decisions through spontaneous order. A **market** is any arrangement people have for trading with one another. Some markets have formal rules and carry out exchanges at a single location, such as the New York Stock Exchange. Other markets are more informal, such as the word-of-mouth networks through which teenage babysitters get in touch with people who need their services. Despite the wide variety of forms that markets take, they all have one thing in common: They provide the information and incentives people need to coordinate their decisions.

Just as shoppers need information about the length of checkout lines to coordinate their efforts, participants in markets need information about the scarcity and opportunity costs of various goods and factors of production. Markets rely primarily on prices to transmit this information. If a good or factor of production becomes more scarce, its price is bid up. The increase in the price tells people it is worth more and signals producers to make greater efforts to increase supplies. For example, when platinum first began to be used in catalytic converters to reduce pollution from auto-

Hierarchy

A way of achieving coordination in which individual actions are guided by instructions from a central authority.

Spontaneous order

A way of achieving coordination in which individuals adjust their actions in response to cues from their immediate environment.

Market

Any arrangement people have for trading with one another.

mobile exhaust, new buyers entered the market. As automakers began to compete with makers of jewelry and other traditional users, platinum became more difficult to acquire. Competition for available supplies bids up the price of platinum. This provided buyers with a cue that the value of platinum had increased and provided an incentive to be careful with its use. At the same time, producers learned that, where possible, they should increase the quantity of platinum mined.

Instead, suppose a new technology were to reduce the cost of producing platinum, for example, by allowing extraction of platinum from mine wastes that used to be discarded. Information about the reduced cost would be transmitted by markets in the form of a lower price. People could then consider increasing the quantity of platinum they use.

In addition to knowing the best use for resources, people must also have incentives to act on that information. Markets provide incentives to sell goods and productive resources where they will bring the highest prices and to buy them where they can be obtained at the lowest prices. Profits motivate business managers to improve production methods and to design goods that match consumer needs. Workers who stay alert to opportunities and work where they are most productive receive the highest wages. Consumers are motivated to use less expensive substitutes where feasible.

Adam Smith, often considered the father of economics, saw the achievement of coordination through markets as the foundation of prosperity and progress. In a famous passage in *The Wealth of Nations*, he called markets an "invisible hand" that nudges people into the economic roles they can play best (see *Who Said It? Who Did It? 1.2*). To this day, an appreciation of markets as a means of coordinating choices remains a central feature of the economic way of thinking.

The Role of Hierarchy

Important as markets are, they are not the only means of achieving economic coordination. Some decisions are guided by direct authority within organizations, that is, by the mechanism of hierarchy. Decisions made by government agencies are one important example. Government decisions are made not through the spontaneous choices of individuals, but via directives issued by a central authority. Business firms, especially large corporations, are another important example of the hierarchical form of organization. The Toyota Motor Corporation uses directives from a central authority to make many important decisions, for example, the decision to build the new hybrid version of its popular Camry in Kentucky rather than in Japan.

Although governments and corporations use hierarchical methods to make choices within their organizations, they deal with one another and with individual consumers through markets. Markets and hierarchies thus play complementary roles in achieving economic coordination. Some economies rely more on markets,

⌐ **WHO SAID IT? WHO DID IT? 1.2**
ADAM SMITH ON THE INVISIBLE HAND

Adam Smith is considered to have been the founder of economics as a distinct field of study, even though he wrote only one book on the subject: *The Wealth of Nations*, published in 1776. Smith was 53 years old at the time. His friend David Hume found the book such hard going that he doubted that many people would read it. But Hume was wrong—people have been reading it for more than 200 years.

The wealth of a nation, in Smith's view, was not a result of the accumulation of gold or silver in its treasury, as many contemporary theorists believed. Rather, it was the outcome of the activities of ordinary people working and trading in free markets. To Smith, the remarkable thing about the wealth produced by a market economy is that it is not a result of any organized plan, but rather the unintended outcome of the actions of many people, each of whom is pursuing the incentives the market offers with his or her own interests in mind. As he put it:

It is not from the benevolence of the butcher, the brewer, or the baker that we expect our dinner, but from their regard to their own interest. . . . Every individual is continually exerting himself to find out the most advantageous employment for whatever capital he can command. . . . By directing that industry in such a manner as its produce may be of the greatest value, he intends only his own gain, and he is in this, as in many other cases, led by an invisible hand to promote an end which was no part of his intention.*

Much of the discipline of economics as it has developed over the past two centuries consists of elaborations on ideas found in Smith's work. The idea of the "invisible hand" of market incentives that channels people's efforts in directions that are beneficial to their neighbors remains the most durable of Smith's contributions to economics.

*Adam Smith, *The Wealth of Nations* (1776), Book 1, Chapter 2.

others on government or corporate planning. At one extreme, the centrally-planned economy of North Korea places heavy emphasis on government authority. Market economics, such as that of the United States, make greater use of markets. But no economy uses one means of coordination to the exclusion of the other. Government regulatory agencies in the United States establish laws to control pollution or protect worker safety; on the other hand, North Korea uses small-scale markets to distribute some goods. Large corporations use commands from higher authority to make many decisions, but they also often subcontract with outsiders through the market, and they sometimes encourage their own divisions to deal with one another on a market basis.

In short, wherever one turns in economics, the question of coordination arises. Understanding economic coordination means understanding the complementary roles of markets, on the one hand, and of government and corporate hierarchies, on the other.

ECONOMIC METHOD

The economic way of thinking is a very broad concept; economic method is a somewhat narrower idea having to do with the way economists go about their work. The chapter would be incomplete without a few comments about method.

Theories and Models

Economists are always trying to understand how the choices people make are related to the situations in which the choices are made.

Theory

A representation of the way in which facts are related to one another.

Model

A synonym for theory; in economics, often applied to theories that are stated in graphical or mathematical form.

Any representation of the way in which facts are related can be called a **theory** or a **model**. The terms are synonyms, although economists tend to use the term *theory* to refer to more general statements about economic relationships and the term *model* to refer to more particular statements, especially those that take the form of graphs or mathematical equations.

Economics needs theories and models because facts do not speak for themselves. Take, for example, the fact that in 2005, for the first time in more than a decade, people bought fewer large SUVs and more ordinary passenger cars. Why did they do that? Economists have a theory. They relate the change in car-buying choices to the 50 percent rise in the retail price of gasoline over the preceding two years. The relationship between the price of gasoline and the choice of cars is seen as a particular instance of a broader theory according to which an increase in the price of any good, other things being equal, leads consumers to seek ways to reduce their consumption of the good.

The theory as stated is a simple one. It relates car choices to just one other fact, the price of gasoline. A more complete theory would bring in other factors that influence consumer choice, such as the prices of goods other than gasoline, consumers' incomes, changes in the social image of SUV owners, and so on. Where does one draw the line? How much detail does it take to make a good theory?

There is no simple answer to this question, because adding detail to a theory involves a trade-off. On the one hand, if essential details are left out, the theory may fail altogether to fit the facts. On the other hand, adding too much detail defeats the purpose of understanding because key relationships may become lost in a cloud of complexity. The only real guideline is that a theory should be just detailed enough to suit the purpose for which it is intended, and no more.

By analogy, consider the models that aircraft designers use. The wind-tunnel models made to test the aerodynamics of a new design need to represent the shapes of the wings, fuselage, and control surfaces accurately, but they do not need to include tiny seats with tiny tables and magazine racks. On the other hand, a full-scale model built for the purpose of training flight attendants to work on the new plane would need seats and magazine racks, but it would not need wings.

In much the same way, the theories and models presented in this book are designed to highlight a few key economic relationships. They are helpful in understanding economics in the same way that playing a flight simulation game on a computer is helpful in understanding the basics of flying. Professional economists use more detailed models, just as professional pilots train with complex flight simulators rather than with simple computer games. Nevertheless, the basic principles learned from the simple models do not contradict those that apply to the more complex ones.

In the simple games, just as in the complex simulators, adjusting the rudder makes the plane turn and adjusting the elevators makes it climb or dive.

The Use of Graphs[3]

The theories introduced so far have been stated in words. Words are a powerful tool for developing understanding, but they are even more powerful when they are supplemented by pictures. Economists support their words with pictures called graphs. An example will illustrate how economists use graphs to represent theories.

THE PRODUCTION POSSIBILITY FRONTIER   Recall our earlier discussion of the trade-off between education and cars. Figure 1.1 shows the trade-off in graphical form for an economy in which only those two goods are produced. The horizontal axis measures the quantity of education in terms of the number of college graduates produced per year; the vertical axis measures the production of cars. Any combination of education and cars can be shown as a point in the space between the two axes. For example, production of 10 million graduates and 5 million cars in a given year would be represented by point E.

In drawing this graph, supplies of productive resources and the state of knowledge are assumed to remain constant. Even if all available resources are devoted to education, there is a limit to the number of graduates that can be produced in a year: 20 million. The extreme possibility of producing 20 million graduates and no cars is shown by point A. Likewise, the maximum number of cars that would be produced if no resources were put into education is 18 million cars, shown by point B. Between those two extremes is a whole range of possible combinations of education and cars. Those intermediate possibilities are shown by points such as C and D, which fall along a smooth curve. The curve is known as a **production possibility frontier**.

EFFICIENCY AND ECONOMIC GROWTH   The production possibility frontier is a boundary between the combinations of education and cars that can be produced and those that cannot, using given knowledge and productive resources. As such, it serves nicely to illustrate the concept of efficiency in production. Points inside the frontier, such as point E, represent inefficient production. Beginning from such a point, more cars can be made without cutting the output of education (shown by a vertical move toward the frontier); more education can be produced without cutting the output of cars (a horizontal move toward the frontier); or the output of both goods can be increased (a move up and to the right toward the frontier).

Points such as A, B, C, and D that are on the frontier represent efficient production. Starting from any of those points, it is not possible to produce more of one good without producing less of the other. For example, in moving from C to D, output of education is increased but output of cars falls. Points such as F that lie outside the

Production possibility frontier

A graph that shows possible combinations of goods that can be produced by an economy given available knowledge and factors of production.

FIGURE 1.1 **PRODUCTION POSSIBILITY FRONTIER**

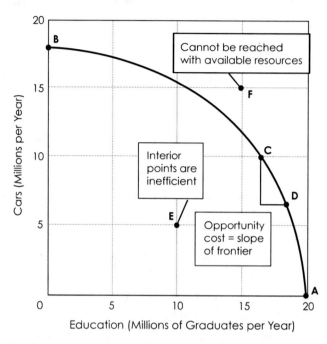

This figure shows combinations of cars and education that can be produced in a simple economy in which they are the only two products. Quantities of available factors of production and the state of existing knowledge are assumed to be fixed. If all factors are devoted to education, 20 million college graduates can be produced each year (point A). If all factors are devoted to making cars, 18 million cars can be produced each year (point B). Other combinations of the two goods that can be produced using available factors efficiently, such as those represented by points C and D, lie along a curve called a production possibility frontier. The slope of the frontier indicates the opportunity cost of education in terms of cars. Interior points, such as E, represent inefficient use of resources. Beginning from such a point, more of one good can be produced without producing less of the other. Points outside the frontier, such as F, cannot be reached using available factors of production and knowledge.

---

frontier cannot be reached even when the currently available knowledge and factors of production are used efficiently.

Over time, however, economic growth can stretch the production possibility frontier outward so that points such as F become possible. As mentioned earlier, the discovery of new ways of using available factors of production is one source of growth. So are additions to the total stock of factors of production—for example, through growth of the labor force. The case under discussion points to still yet another source of growth: Over time, the educational process itself improves the quality of the labor force, thus making a given number of people capable of producing more.

OPPORTUNITY COST AND COMPARATIVE ADVANTAGE The production possibility frontier can also be used to represent the concept of opportunity cost. As we have seen, once the economy is producing efficiently at a point on the frontier, choosing to make more of one good means making less of the other. For example, suppose we start at point C, where 16 million students graduate each year and 10 million cars are being made. If we want to increase the output of graduates to 18 million per year, we must give up some cars and use the labor, capital, and natural resources freed in this way to build and staff classrooms. In moving from point C to point D, we trade off production of 4 million cars for the extra 2 million graduates. Over that range of the frontier, the opportunity cost of each extra graduate is about two cars. The opportunity cost of graduates, measured in terms of cars, is shown by the slope of the frontier.

As more graduates are produced, and the economy moves down and to the right along the frontier, the frontier becomes steeper and the opportunity cost of producing graduates increases. A major reason is that not all factors of production—especially not all workers—are alike. Suppose we start all the way up at point B, where no education is produced, and transfer enough resources to education to open one small college. The first people we would pull off the assembly line to staff the classrooms would be those who have a comparative advantage in teaching. By the time enough resources have been transferred to education from the auto industry to reach point D, the most suitable recruits for academic life have already been used. Increasingly, to produce still more education we have to take some of the best production workers with no assurance that they will be good teachers. The opportunity cost of increasing the output of education (shown by the slope of the frontier) is correspondingly greater.

Theory and Evidence

Theories are of no use in explaining relationships among facts unless they fit those facts. Theory building is a matter of constantly comparing proposed explanations with evidence gleaned from observations of the actual choices people make—that is, with **empirical** evidence. When empirical evidence is consistent with the relationships proposed in a theory, confidence in the validity of the theory is increased. When evidence is not consistent with the theory, the theory needs to be reexamined. The relationships proposed in it may be invalid, or they may be valid only under circumstances different from those that prevailed when the observations were made. The theory then needs to be modified by changing the proposed relationships or adding detail.

Government agencies and private firms generate mountains of empirical data on economic activity. Economists constantly examine those data in an effort to confirm theories or find inconsistencies that point the way to better theories. Statistical analysis of empirical economic data is known as **econometrics**—literally, the science of economic measurement.

Empirical

Based on experience or observation.

Econometrics

The statistical analysis of empirical economic data.

Theories and Forecasts

Economic theories can help us understand things that happened in the past—trends in gasoline consumption since the 1970s, the effects of the information revolution of the 1990s, and so on. But understanding the past is not always enough. People also want forecasts of future economic events.

Within limits, economic theory can be useful here, too. Any theory that purports to explain a relationship between past events provides a basis for predicting what will happen under similar circumstances in the future. To put it more precisely, economic theory can be used to make **conditional forecasts** of the form "If A, then B, other things being equal." Thus, an economist might say, "If gasoline prices rise, and if at the same time consumer incomes and the prices of other goods do not change, purchases of low-mileage vehicles will fall."

Thousands of economists make a living from forecasting. Decision-makers in business and government use economic forecasts extensively. Forecasts are not perfect, however, and forecasters sometimes make conspicuous mistakes. There are at least three reasons for the mistakes.

First, insufficient attention is sometimes paid to the conditional nature of forecasts. The news might report, for example, that "economists predict a drop in SUV sales," yet people keep right on buying big vehicles. In such a case the news report may have failed to note the forecasters' precautionary comments. The forecasters may have said that SUV sales would drop in response to a gas price increase if consumer incomes and technology remained the same, but consumers got richer and new technology made SUVs less gas-hungry, so SUV sales did not fall after all.

Second, a forecast may be invalid because the theory on which it is based is incorrect or incomplete. Economists do not always agree on what theory best fits the facts. Some theories give more weight to one fact, others to different facts. The competing theories may imply conflicting forecasts under some conditions. At least one of the forecasts will then turn out to be wrong. Finding out which theories yield better forecasts than others is an important part of the process through which valid theories are distinguished from inadequate ones.

Third, economic forecasts can go wrong because some of the things that business managers and government officials most want to know are among the hardest to predict. For example, a competent economist could produce a fairly accurate forecast of vehicle sales, making certain assumptions about incomes and the prices of gasoline and other goods. However, what the marketing people at General Motors would like to know is what will happen to the social image of SUVs—will they continue to be a symbol of high status, or will they become an embarrassment in a more environmentally conscious society? Social attitudes are not among the variables that economists can forecast accurately.

Despite these limitations, most economists take the view that well-founded conditional forecasts, for all their limitations, are a better basis for business and public policy decisions than whims and guesswork. Still, they caution against relying too heavily on forecasts.

Conditional forecast

A prediction of future economic events in the form "If A, then B, other things being equal."

Theory and Policy

Economists are often asked to use their theories to analyze the effects of public policies and forecast the effects of policy changes. The government may, for example, be considering new measures to aid unemployed workers, new approaches to improving air quality, or new measures to regulate international trade. How will the effects of such policies be spread through the economy? How will they affect people's lives?

Economists have their own characteristic way of thinking about public policy, just as they have their own way of thinking about other topics. In particular, economists are concerned with identifying both the direct and indirect effects of policy, as well as any indirect or unintended consequences. They are also constantly alert to both the long-run and short-term effects of policy. For example:

- Unemployment compensation has the intended effect of aiding unemployed workers, but it also has the unintended effect of increasing the number of workers who are unemployed, because workers receiving compensation can afford to take their time finding just the right new job. Many observers see generous unemployment compensation in Germany and other European countries as one reason unemployment rates there are higher than in the United States.

- Regulations intended to improve the fuel efficiency of automobiles encourage production of cars that weigh less, but the lighter cars are somewhat less safe. Increased highway deaths among drivers of the lighter cars may thus be an unintended consequence of efforts to save fuel.

- After widespread banking failures in the 1980s, U.S. regulators made rule changes intended to strengthen the balance sheets of commercial banks. Those regulations also raised the cost of bank loans relative to loans from other sources outside the banking system. As an unintended consequence, banks lost their most credit-worthy customers to other lenders and ended up with balance sheets that held higher percentages of risky loans than before.

While policies may have unintended consequences, public policy still plays an important role in the economy. It would be wrong to conclude that the government should never act simply because its actions may do some harm as well as some good. Rather, economists simply urge that policy makers look at the whole picture, not just part of it, before they make a decision. As Henry Hazlitt once put it, the whole of economics can be reduced to a single lesson:

The art of economics consists in looking not merely at the immediate but at the longer effects of any act or policy; it consists in tracing the consequences of that policy not merely for one group but for all groups.[4]

As you progress through your study of economics—both the macro and micro branches—you will encounter repeated examples of the way economic theory can help understand the choices people make and the complex effects of policies intended to regulate those choices.

～

SUMMARY

1. **What is the subject matter of economics?** Economics is a social science that seeks to understand the choices people make in using scarce resources to meet their wants. Scarcity is a situation in which there is not enough of something to meet everyone's wants. *Microeconomics* is the branch of economics that studies choices that involve individual households, firms, and markets. *Macroeconomics* is the branch of economics that deals with large-scale economic phenomena, such as inflation, unemployment, and economic growth.

2. **What considerations underlie the choice of what an economy will produce?** Producing more of one good requires producing less of something else because productive resources that are used to produce one good cannot be used to produce another at the same time. Productive resources are traditionally classified into three groups, called *factors of production. Labor* consists of the productive contributions made by people working with their hands and minds. *Capital* consists of all the productive inputs created by people. *Natural resources* include anything that can be used as a productive input in its natural state. The *opportunity cost* of a good or service is its cost in terms of the forgone opportunity to pursue the best possible alternative activity with the same time or resources.

3. **What considerations underlie the choice of how to produce?** Goods and services can be produced in many different ways, some of which are more efficient than others. *Economic efficiency* refers to a state of affairs in which it is impossible to make any change that satisfies one person's wants more fully without causing some other person's wants to be satisfied less fully. *Efficiency in production* refers to a situation in which it is not possible, given the available productive resources and existing knowledge, to produce more of one good or service without forgoing the opportunity to produce some of another good or service. Once efficiency has been achieved, production potential can be expanded by increasing the availability of resources or by improving knowledge. The process of increasing the economy's stock of capital is known as *investment.* The process of looking for new possibilities—making use of new ways of doing things, being alert to new opportunities, and overcoming old limits—is known as *entrepreneurship.*

4. **What considerations underlie the choice of who will do which work?** Although a person can survive apart from all human contact, economic efficiency is greatly enhanced by cooperation with others. Three things make cooperation worthwhile: teamwork, learning by doing, and comparative advantage. Teamwork can enhance productivity even when there is no specialization. Learning by doing improves productivity even when all workers start with equal talents and abilities. Comparative advantage comes into play when people have different innate abilities or, after learning by doing, have developed specialized skills. Having a *comparative advantage* in producing a particular good or service means

being able to produce it at a relatively lower opportunity cost than someone else.

5. **What considerations underlie the choice of for whom goods will be produced?** In part, deciding for whom goods will be produced revolves around issues of efficiency. *Efficiency in distribution* refers to a state of affairs in which, with a given quantity of goods and services, it is impossible to satisfy one person's wants more fully without satisfying someone else's less fully. Efficiency is part of *positive economics,* the area of economics that is concerned with facts and the relationships among them. *Normative economics* is the area of economics that is devoted to judgments about which economic conditions and policies are good or bad.

6. **What mechanisms are used to coordinate economic choices?** The two principle methods of coordinating choices are *hierarchy* and *spontaneous order.* Markets are the most important example of spontaneous order. The internal decisions made by large corporations and units of government are the most important examples of hierarchy.

7. **How do economists use theory, graphs, and evidence in their work?** A *theory* or *model* is a representation of the ways in which facts are related to one another. Economists use graphs to display data and make visual representations of theories and models. For example, a *production possibility frontier* is a graph that shows the boundary between combinations of goods that can be produced and those that cannot, using available factors of production and knowledge. Economists refine theories in the light of *empirical* evidence, that is, evidence gleaned from observation of actual economic decisions. The economic analysis of empirical evidence is known as *econometrics.* Economic models are often used to make *conditional forecasts* of the form "If A, then B, other things being equal."

KEY TERMS

Scarcity	Efficiency in
Economics	distribution
Microeconomics	Positive economics
Macroeconomics	Normative economics
Factors of production	Spontaneous order
Labor	Hierarchy
Capital	Market
Natural resources	Theory
Opportunity cost	Model
Economic efficiency	Production possibility
Efficiency in production	frontier
Investment	Empirical
Entrepreneurship	Econometrics
Comparative advantage	Conditional forecast

PROBLEMS AND TOPICS FOR DISCUSSION

1. **Opportunity cost.** Gasoline, insurance, depreciation, and repairs are all costs of owning a car. Which of these can be considered opportunity costs in the context of each of the following decisions?

    a. You own a car and are deciding whether to drive 100 miles for a weekend visit to a friend at another university.

    b. You do not own a car but are considering buying one so that you can get a part-time job located 5 miles from where you live.

    In general, why does the context in which you decide to do something affect the opportunity cost of doing it?

2. **Comparative advantage in international trade.** Suppose that in the United States a car can be produced with 200 labor hours, while a ton of rice requires 20 labor hours. In Japan, it takes 150 labor hours to make a car and 50 labor hours to

grow a ton of rice. What is the opportunity cost of producing rice in each country, stated in terms of cars? What is the opportunity cost of cars, stated in terms of rice? Which country has a comparative advantage in cars? Which in rice?

3. **Efficiency in distribution and the food stamp program.** The federal food stamp program could have been designed so that every low-income family would receive a book of coupons containing so many bread coupons, so many milk coupons, and so on. Instead, it gives the family an allowance that can be spent on any kind of food the family prefers. For a given cost to the federal government, which plan do you think would better serve the goal of efficiency in distribution? Why?

Now consider a program that would allow families to trade their food stamps for cash (some such trading does occur, but it is restricted by law) or one in which poor families are given cash, with which they can buy whatever they want. Compare these alternatives with the existing food stamp program in terms of both positive and normative economics.

4. **Spontaneous order in the cafeteria.** Suppose that your college cafeteria does not have enough room for all the students to sit down to eat at once, so it stays open for lunch from 11:30 A.M. to 1:30 P.M. Consider the following three methods of distributing diners over the two-hour lunch period in such a way that everyone can have a seat.

a. The administration sets a rule: Freshmen must eat between 11:30 and 12:00, sophomores between 12:00 and 12:30, and so on for juniors and seniors.

b. The lunch period is broken up into half-hour segments, with green tickets for the first shift, blue tickets for the second, and so on. An equal number of tickets of each color is printed. At the beginning of each semester an auction is held in which students bid for the ticket color of their choice.

c. Students can come to the cafeteria whenever they want. If there are no empty seats, they have to stand in line.

Compare the three schemes in terms of the concepts of (i) spontaneous order and hierarchy; (ii) information and incentives; and (iii) efficiency.

5. **A production possibility frontier.** Bill Swartz has four fields spread out over a hillside. He can grow either wheat or potatoes in any of the fields, but the low fields are better for potatoes and the high ones are better for wheat. Here are some combinations of wheat and potatoes that he could produce:

Number of Fields Used for Potatoes	Total Tons of Potatoes	Total Tons of Wheat
All 4	1,000	0
Lowest 3	900	400
Lowest 2	600	700
Lowest 1	300	900
None	0	1,000

Use these data to draw a production possibility frontier for wheat and potatoes. What is the opportunity cost of wheat, stated in terms of potatoes, when the farmer converts the highest field to wheat production? What happens to the opportunity cost of wheat as more and more fields are switched to wheat?

CASE FOR DISCUSSION

Zimbabwe's Land Questions

HARARE, November 2003—President Mugabe continued seizure of primarily white-owned land in urban areas. The country's white farmers own much of the country's best agricultural land; according to government figures, 4,400 whites owned 32% of Zimbabwe's agricultural land, while about one million black peasant families farmed 38%. Furthermore, whites own a disproportionate share of the country's most fertile land. The situation was created in colonial times when blacks were forced off their ancestral lands. "The land question" was the source of discontent among the majority of Zimbabweans and a major cause of the guerrilla war that led to Zimbabwe's independence in 1980. When Mugabe came to power in 1980, he promised to balance the scales for black farmers through land reform.

Land reform and redistribution is expensive. Not only does the government need to compensate farmers giving up their property, but it also needs to provide infrastructure—such as roads, schools, and hospitals—for land redistribution to be beneficial. There is also the difficulty of taking large, sophisticated farms and then subdividing them into plots to give to people without the means to farm them effectively.

President Mugabe says Britain should pay because the British government colonized the region, seizing land from African farmers in the late 19th century. While the U.K. and others have provided some aid to help the government purchase land from "willing" white farmers, donors have refused further support unless President Mugabe's land program is more clearly defined.

The white farmers themselves do not see why they should have to pay because of what happened in the past. Many say they bought their farms at market rates since Zimbabwe's independence and reject arguments rooted in colonization. While Zimbabwe's government has paid some farmers, a new law requires farmers to leave their farms before receiving compensation.

Despite promises to target the seizure of the least-productive farms, many of those on the so-called "hit-list" have been the most efficient growers of tobacco. President Mugabe's opponents accuse him of exploiting the land question to win support amid Zimbabwe's current economic crisis.

The threat of land seizures has led to a steep decline in agricultural production on white-owned farms, exacerbating food shortages and unemployment in Zimbabwe. This coupled with two years of drought threaten a famine in which up to six million of Zimbabwe's citizens could go hungry. Aid agencies estimate over one-third of the population will be unable to feed themselves by the end of the year.

Consider the following hypothetical situations involving individuals and the government in Zimbabwe:

- Shekan currently owns 100 hectares of land that he uses for tobacco farming. On this land he has hired several hands to assist in harvesting and curing the tobacco leaves. He owns capital equipment to assist in curing the tobacco leaves. Shekan pays his workers 5 Zimbabwean dollars per pound of tobacco. Shekan then sells tobacco at the market price of 7 Zimbabwean dollars per pound.
- Amadika is a middle-aged woman who works on Shekan's farm. Using Shekan's curing equipment, she gathers and cures 50 pounds of tobacco each year.
- Tatenda is a young woman who was able to gather and cure 60 pounds of tobacco on Shekan's farm. She has decided to leave the farm and attend college in the United States. Tatenda has received a full scholarship and financing from the school to cover her expenses.
- Dakarai is a young man who currently works on Shekan's farm. He is able to gather and cure 75 pounds of tobacco each year using the available capital equipment. Instead of giving all 75 pounds to Shekan, he sells 25 pounds of tobacco illegally to a cigarette manufacturer for 6 Zimbabwean dollars per pound.

QUESTIONS

1. What might explain why Shekan pays his workers 5 Zimbabwean dollars per pound of cured tobacco while he sells it for 7 Zimbabwean dollars? What is Shekan's contribution to the tobacco production process?

2. Under President Mugabe's land management plan, Amadika is to receive 10 hectares of Shekan's property, but she receives none of the capital equipment she currently uses on Shekan's farm. When Amadika receives 10 hectares of land from Shekan's farm, will she be able to gather and cure the same amount of tobacco? Why or why not?

3. In terms of Zimbabwean dollars, what is Tatenda's opportunity cost of attending college? Why is there still a cost, even though Tatenda receives a scholarship? If she were to receive land under President Mugabe's plan, how might this affect her decision to attend school?

4. Assume that a gallon of milk costs 2 Zimbabwean dollars. What is the cost of a gallon of milk in terms of pounds of tobacco?

5. Suppose Zimbabwe's government decides that 2 dollars is too expensive for milk, and imposes a law that sets the price of milk at 1 Zimbabwean dollar per gallon. How will this affect the availability of milk in Zimbabwe?

6. Why might Dakarai sell some of his tobacco crop to Shekan at 5 Zimbabwean dollars per pound, when he can receive 6 dollars from an illegal trader?

7. President Mugabe recently denounced people, such as Dakarai, who engage in illegal trade. The government, and many Zimbabweans, see people like Dakarai as an exploiter who robs from Shekan. Discuss this issue in terms of fairness and efficiency.

END NOTES

1. Efficiency, defined this way, is sometimes called *Pareto efficiency* after the Italian economist Vilfredo Pareto.
2. Armen A. Alchian and Harold Demsetz, "Production, Information Cost, and Economic Organization," *American Economic Review* (December 1972): 777–795.
3. Some basic graphical concepts—axes, points and number pairs, slopes, and tangencies—are discussed in the appendix to this chapter.
4. Henry Hazlitt, *Economics in One Lesson* (New York: Arlington House, 1979), 17.

Appendix to Chapter 1:
WORKING WITH GRAPHS

Graphs are an invaluable aid in learning economics precisely because they make use of these three special abilities of the human brain. Graphs are not used to make economics harder, but to make it easier. All it takes to use graphs effectively as a learning tool is the inborn human skill in working with pictures plus knowledge of a few simple rules for extracting the information that graphs contain. This appendix outlines those rules in brief. Additional details and exercises can be found in the *Study Guide* that accompanies this textbook.

Pairs of Numbers and Points

The first thing to master is how to use points on a graph to represent pairs of numbers. The table in Figure 1A.1 presents five pairs of numbers. The two columns are labeled "x" and "y." The first number in each pair is called the *x value* and the second the *y value*. Each pair of numbers is labeled with a capital letter. Pair A has an *x* value of 2 and a *y* value of 3; pair B has an *x* value of 4 and a *y* value of 4; and so on.

The diagram in Figure 1A.1 contains two lines that meet at the lower left-hand corner; they are called *coordinate axes*. The horizontal axis is marked off into units representing the *x* value and the vertical axis into unit representing the *y* value. In the space between the axes,

FIGURE 1A.1   NUMBER PAIRS AND POINTS

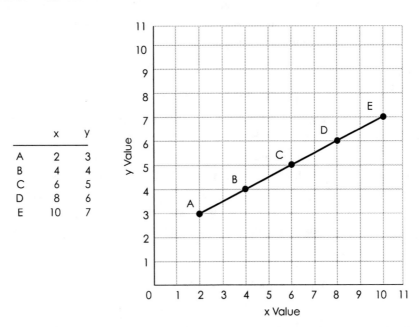

Each lettered pair of numbers in the table corresponds to a lettered point on the graph. The x value of each point corresponds to the horizontal distance of the point from the vertical axis; the y value corresponds to its vertical distance from the horizontal axis.

FIGURE 1A.2   SLOPES OF LINES

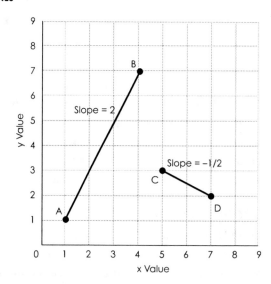

The slope of a straight line drawn between two points is defined as the ratio of the change in the y value to the change in the x value as one moves from one point to the other. For example, the line between points A and B in this Figure has a slope of +2, whereas the line between points C and D has a slope of −1/2.

each pair of numbers from the table can be shown as a point. For example, point A is found by going two units to the right along the horizontal axis and then three units straight up, parallel to the vertical axis. That point represents the x value of 2 and the y value of 3. The other points are located in the same way.

The visual effect of a graph usually can be improved by connecting the points with a line or a curve. By doing so, the relationship between x values and y values can be seen at a glance: as the x value increases, the y value also increases.

Slopes and Tangencies

The lines or curves used in graphs are described in terms of their slopes. The **slope** of a straight line between two points is defined as the ratio of the change in the y value to the change in the x value between the two points. In Figure 1A.2, for example, the slope of the line between points A and B is 2. The y value changes by six units between these two points, whereas the x value changes by only three units. The slope is the ratio 6/3 = 2.

The slope of a line between the points (x_1, y_1) and (x_2, y_2) can be expressed in terms of a simple formula that is derived from the definition just given:

$$\text{Slope} = (y_2 - y_1)/(x_2 - x_1)$$

Applied to the line between points A and B in Figure 1A.2, the formula gives the following result:

$$\text{Slope} = (7 - 1)/(4 - 1) = 6/3 = 2$$

A line such as that between A and B in Figure 1A.2 is said to have a **positive slope**, because the value of its slope is a positive number. A positively sloped line represents a **direct relationship** between the variable represented on the x axis and that represented on the

Slope

For a straight line, the ratio of the change in the y value to the change in the x value between any two points on the line.

Positive slope

A slope having a value greater than zero.

Direct relationship

A relationship between two variables in which an increase in the value of one variable is associated with an increase in the value of the other.

y axis—that is, a relationship in which an increase in one variable is associated with an increase in the other. The relationship of the age of a tree to its height is an example of a direct relationship. An example from economics is the relationship between family income and expenditures on housing.

When a line slants downward, such as the one between points C and D in Figure 1A.2, the *x* and *y* values change in opposite directions. Going from point C to point D, the *y* value changes by –1 (that is, decreases by one unit) and the *x* value changes by +2 (that is, increases by two units). The slope of this line is the ratio –1/2.

When the slope of a line is given by a negative number, the line is said to have a **negative slope**. Such a line represents an **inverse relationship** between the *x* variable and the *y* variable—that is, a relationship in which an increase in the value of one variable is associated with a decrease in the value of the other variable. The relationship between the temperature in the room and the time it takes the ice in your lemonade to melt is an example of an inverse relationship. To give an economic example, the relationship between the price of gasoline and the quantity consumers purchase, other things being equal, is an inverse relationship.

The concepts of positive and negative slopes, and of direct and inverse relationships, apply to curves as well as to straight lines. However, the slope of a curve, unlike that of a straight line, varies from one point to the next.[1] We cannot speak of the slope of a curve in general, but only of its slope at a given point. The slope of a curve at any given point is defined as the slope of a straight line drawn tangent to the curve at that point. (A **tangent** line is one that just touches the curve without crossing it.) In Figure 1A.3, the slope of the curve at point A is 1 and the slope at point B is –2.

---

[1] Economists try to be consistent, but in talking about lines and curves, they fail. They have no qualms about calling something a "curve" that is a straight line. For example, later we will encounter "demand curves" that are as straight as a stretched string. Less frequently, they may call something a line that is curved.

Negative slope

A slope having a value less than zero.

Inverse relationship

A relationship between two variables in which an increase in the value of one variable is associated with a decrease in the value of the other.

Tangent

A straight line that touches a curve at a given point without intersecting it.

FIGURE 1A.3 SLOPES OF CURVES

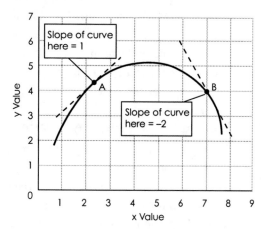

The slope of a curve at any point is defined as the slope of a straight line drawn tangent to the curve at that point. A tangent line is one that just touches the curve without crossing it. In this figure, the slope of the curve at point A is 1 and the slope at point B is –2.

Using Graphs to Display Data

Graphs are used in economics for two primary purposes: for visual display of quantitative data and for visual representation of economic relationships. Some graphs are primarily designed to serve one purpose, some the other, and some a little of both. We begin with some common kinds of graphs whose primary purpose is to display data.

Figure 1A.4 shows three kinds of graphs often used to display data. Part (a) is *pie chart*. Pie charts are used to show the relative size of various quantities that add up to a total of 100 percent. In this case, the quantities displayed are the percentages of U.S. foreign trade accounted for by various trading partners. In the original source, the graph was drawn as part of a discussion of U.S. trade with Canada, Japan, and Western Europe. The author wanted to make the point that trade with these countries is very important. Note how the graph highlights Canadian, Japanese, and Western European trade with the U.S., and at the same time omits details not relevant to the discussion by lumping together the rest of Europe, Africa, the rest of Asia, and many other countries under the heading "rest of the world." In reading graphs, do not just look at the numbers, but ask yourself, "What point is the graph trying to make?"

Part (b) of Figure 1A.4 is a *bar chart*. Bar charts, like pie charts, are used to display numerical data (in this case, unemployment rates) in relationship to some nonnumerical classification of cases (in this case, educational attainment). Bar charts are not subject to the restriction that data displayed must total 100 percent. What point do you think the author of this graph was trying to make?

Part (c) of Figure 1A.4 is an example of a data display graph very common in economics—the *time-series graph*. A time-series graph shows the values of one or more economic quantities on the vertical axis and time (years, months, or whatever) on the horizontal axis. This graph shows the ups and downs of the U.S. unemployment rate by month over the period 1980 through 1991.

Note one feature of this time-series graph: the scale on the vertical axis begins from 3 percent rather than from 0. By spreading out the data points in the range 3 to 11 percent, one can show the trend of unemployment in greater detail. The advantage of greater detail has an offsetting danger, however. Careless reading of the graph could cause one to exaggerate the amount by which unemployment rises during a recession. For example, the unemployment line is more than three times higher above the horizontal axis in 2003 than in 2000. However, careful reading of the graph shows that the unemployment rate in December 1991 was actually only about half again as high (6% vs. 4%) in 2003 as in 2000. The moral of the story: Always examine the vertical and horizontal axes of a graph carefully.

Using Graphs to Display Relationships

Some graphs, rather than simply recording observed facts, attempt to represent theories and models—that is, to show the relationships among facts. Figure 1A.5 shows two typical graphs whose primary purpose is to display relationships.

Part (a) of Figure 1A.5 is the production possibility frontier that we encountered in Chapter 1. The graph represents the inverse relationship between the quantity of cars that can be produced and the quantity of education that can be produced, given available knowledge and productive resources.

FIGURE 1A.4   USING GRAPHS TO DISPLAY DATA

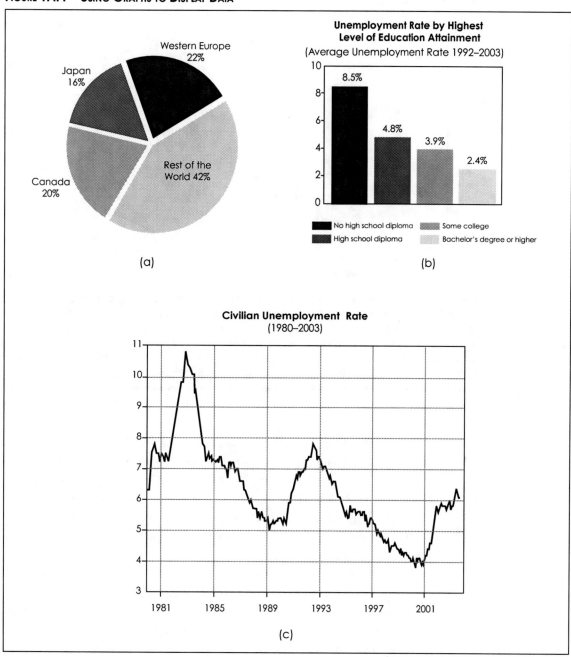

(a)

(b)

(c)

This figure shows three common kinds of data display graphs. The *pie chart* in part (a) is used when the data items sum to 100 percent. The *bar chart* in part (b), like the pie chart, is used when reporting numerical data that are associated with nonnumerical categories (in this case educational attainment). The bar chart does not require data items to sum to 100 percent. The *time-series graph* in part (c) shows the values of one or more economic quantities on the vertical axis and time on the horizontal axis.

Source: Part (a), U.S. Council of Economic Advisers, *Economic Report of the President* (Washington, D.C.: Government Printing Office, 2002), Table B-105, 397; part (b), Bureau of Labor Statistics, *Current Population Survey*; and part (c), Bureau of Labor Statistics, *The Employment Situation*.

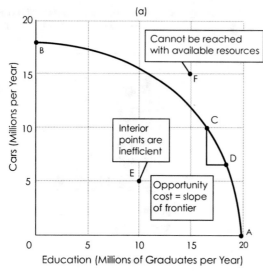
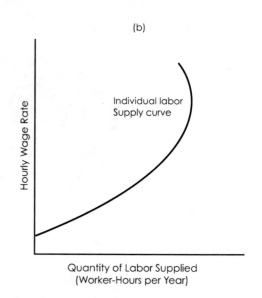

Relational graphs are visual representations of theories, that is, of relationships among facts. Two typical relational graphs are shown here. Part (a) is the production possibility frontier discussed in Chapter 1. It relates quantities of cars to quantities of education that can be produced with given factors of production and knowledge. Part (b) represents a theory of individual labor supply, according to which an increase in the hourly wage rate, after a point, will cause a person to reduce the quantity of labor supplied. Part (b) is an abstract graph in that it shows only the general nature of the relationship, with no numbers on either axis.

Part (b) of Figure 1A.5 represents a relationship between the quantity of labor that a person is willing to supply (measured in worker-hours per year) and the wage rate per hour the person is paid. According to the theory portrayed by the graph, raising the wage rate will, up to a point, induce a person to work more hours. But beyond a certain point (according to the theory), a further increase in the wage will actually cause the person to work fewer hours. Why? Because the person is so well off, he or she prefers the luxury of more leisure time to the reward of more material goods.

Note one distinctive feature of this graph: There are no numbers on the axes. It is an abstract graph that represents only the qualitative relationships between the hours of labor supplied per year and the wage rate. It makes no quantitative statements regarding how much the number of hours worked will change as a result of any given change in wage rate. Abstract graphs are often used when the point to be made is a general one that applies to many cases, regardless of quantitative differences from one case to another.

Packing Three Variables into Two Dimensions

Anything drawn on a flat piece of paper is limited to two dimensions. The relationships discussed so far fit a two-dimensional framework easily, because they involve just two variables. In the case of the production possibility frontier, the two are the quantity of education (horizontal axis) and the quantity of cars (vertical axis). In the case of the labor supply, they are hours worked per year (horizontal axis) and wage rate per hour (vertical axis). But reality does not always cooperate with geometry. Often one must take three or more variables into account in order to understand relationships among facts.

A number of methods have been devised to represent relationships involving three or more variables. For example, a map of the United States might use coordinates of latitude and longitude to indicate position, contour lines to indicate altitude, and shadings of various colors to indicate vegetation. An architect might use a perspective drawing to give the illusion of three dimensions—height, width, and depth—on a flat piece of paper. This section deals with one simple method of packing three variables into two dimensions. Although the method is a favorite of economists—it will be used in dozens of graphs in this book—we will show its generality by beginning with a noneconomic example.

A NONECONOMIC EXAMPLE   The example concerns heart disease, the leading cause of death in the United States. In recent years, medical researchers have discovered that the risk of heart disease is closely linked to the quantity of cholesterol in a person's blood. Studies have indicated, for example, that a 25 percent reduction in cholesterol can cut the risk of death from heart attack by nearly 50 percent. Knowing this, millions of people have had their cholesterol levels tested, and if they were found to be high, have undertaken programs of diet, exercise, or drug therapy to reduce their risk of heart disease.

Important though cholesterol is, however, just knowing your cholesterol level is not enough to tell you your risk of dying of a heart attack in the coming year. Other variables also enter into the risk of heart disease. One of the most important of these variables is age. For example, for men aged 20 with average cholesterol levels, the mortality rate from heart disease is only about 3 per 100,000. For men aged 60, the mortality rate rises to over 500 per 100,000, still assuming average cholesterol. We thus have three variables to deal with: mortality, cholesterol, and age. How can we represent these three variables using only two-dimensional graphs?

A possible approach would be to draw two separate graphs. One would show the relationship between age and heart disease for the male population as a whole, without regard to differences in cholesterol counts. The other would show the relationship between cholesterol and heart disease for the male population as a whole, without regard to age. By looking from one diagram to the other, we could get an idea of the three-variable relationship as a whole.

However, such a side-by-side pair of graphs would be clumsy. There must be a better way to represent the three variables in two dimensions. The better way, shown in Figure 1A.6, is to use cholesterol and mortality as the *x* and *y* axes, and to take age into account by plotting separate lines for men of various ages. That chart is far easier to interpret than the side-by-side pair would be. If you are a man and know your age and cholesterol count, you just pick out the appropriate line and read off your risk of mortality. If you do not like what you see, you go on a diet.[2]

The multi-curve graph is a lovely invention. One of the great things about it is that it works for more than three variables. For example, we could add a fourth variable, gender, to the graph by drawing a new set of lines in a different color to show mortality rates for women

---

[2]We could instead have started with the age-mortality chart and drawn separate lines for men with different cholesterol levels. Such a chart would show exactly the same information. We could even draw a chart with cholesterol and age on the axes, and separate contour lines to represent various levels of mortality. The choice often depends on what one wants to emphasize. Here, we emphasize the cholesterol-mortality relationship because cholesterol is something you can do something about. You cannot do anything about your age, so we give age slightly less emphasis by not placing it on one of the two axes.

FIGURE 1A.6   THREE VARIABLES IN TWO DIMENSIONS

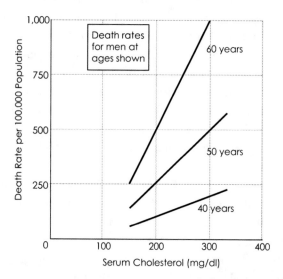

This graph shows a common way of representing a three-variable relationship on a two-dimensional graph. The three variables in this case are serum cholesterol (a measure of the amount of cholesterol in the blood), age, and death rate from heart disease for the U.S. male population. The relationship among the three variables is most easily interpreted, if all three variables are included in one graph, by drawing separate cholesterol-death rate lines for each age group. As a man ages, his cholesterol-death rate line shifts upward.

of various ages. Each line for women would have a positive slope similar to the men's lines, but would lie somewhat below the corresponding line for men of the same age, because women, other things being equal, experience lower mortality from heart disease.

SHIFTS IN CURVES AND MOVEMENTS ALONG CURVES   Economists use three-variable, multi-curve graphs often enough that it is worth giving some attention to the terminology used in discussing them. How can we best describe what happens to a man as he ages, given the relationship shown in Figure 1A.6?

One way to describe the effects of aging would be to say, "As a man ages, he moves from one curve to the next higher one on the chart." There is nothing at all wrong with saying that, but an economist would tend to phrase it a bit differently, saying "As a man ages, his cholesterol-mortality curve shifts upward." The two ways of expressing the effects of aging have exactly the same meaning. Preferring one or the other is just a matter of habit.

If we express the effects of aging in terms of a shift of the cholesterol-mortality curve, how should we express the effects of a reduction in cholesterol for a man of a given age? An economist would say it this way: "Cutting a man's cholesterol count through diet or exercise will move him down along his cholesterol-mortality curve."

Before you finish this book, you will see the phrases "shift in a curve" and "movement along a curve" a great many times. How can you keep them straight? Nothing could be easier.

- If you are talking about the effect of a change in a variable that is shown on one of the coordinate axes of the diagram, the effect will be shown as a movement along one of the curves.

- If you are talking about the effect of a change in a variable that is not shown on one of the coordinate axes of the diagram, the effect will be shown by a shift in one of the curves.

Study Hints

So much for the basic rules of graphics. Once you master them, how should you study a chapter that is full of graphs?

The first—and most important—rule is to avoid trying to memorize graphs as patterns of lines. In every economics course, at least one student comes to the instructor after failing an exam and exclaims, "But I learned every one of those graphs! What happened?" The reply is that the student should have learned economics instead of memorizing graphs. Following are some hints for working with graphs.

After reading through a chapter that contains several graphs, go back through the graphs one at a time. Cover the caption accompanying each graph, and try to express the graph's "picture" in words. If you cannot say as much about the graph as the caption does, reread the text. Once you can translate the graph into words, you have won half the battle.

Next, cover each graph and use the caption as a guide. Try to sketch the graph on a piece of scratch paper. How are the graph's axes labeled? How are the curves labeled? What are the slopes of various curves? Are there important points of intersection or tangencies? If you can go back and forth between the caption and the graph, you will find that the two together are much easier to remember than either one separately.

Finally, try going beyond the graph that is shown in the book. If the graph illustrates the effect of an increase in the price of butter, try sketching a similar diagram that shows the effect of a decrease in the price of butter. If the graph shows what happens to the economy during a period of rising unemployment, try drawing a similar graph that shows what happens during a period of falling unemployment. This is a good practice that may give you an edge on your next exam.

MAKING YOUR OWN GRAPHS   For some students, the hardest test questions to answer are ones that require original graphs as part of an essay. Suppose the question is, "How does a change in the number of students attending a university affect the cost per student of providing an education?" Here are some hints for making your own graph.

1. Write down the answer to the question in words. If you cannot, you might as well skip to the next question. Underline the most important quantities in your answer, such as "The larger the *number of students* who attend a college, the lower the *cost per student* of providing them with an education, because fixed facilities, such as libraries, do not have to be duplicated."

2. Decide how you want to label the axes. In our example, the vertical axis could be labeled "cost per student" and the horizontal axis "number of students."

3. Do you have specific numbers to work with? If so, the next step is to construct a table showing what you know and use it to sketch your graph. If you have no numbers, you must draw an abstract graph. In this case, all you know is that the cost per student goes down when the number of students goes up. Your graph would thus be a negatively sloped line.

4. If your graph involves more than one relationship between quantities, repeat steps 1 through 3 for each relationship you wish to show. When constructing a graph with more than one curve, pay special attention to points at which you think the curves should intersect.

(Intersections occur whenever both the *x* and *y* values of the two relationships are equal.) Also note the points at which you think two curves ought to be tangent (which requires that their slopes be equal), the points of maximum or minimum value, if any, and so on.

5. When your graph is finished, try to translate it back into words. Does it really say what you want it to?

A REMINDER   As you read this book and encounter various kinds of graphs, turn back to this appendix now and then. Do not memorize graphs as meaningless pictures; if you do, you will get lost. If you can alternate between graphs and words, the underlying point will be clearer than if you rely on either one alone. Keep in mind that the primary focus of economics is not graphs; it is people and the ways in which they deal with the challenge of scarcity.

CHAPTER 2

Supply and Demand: The Basics

After reading this chapter, you will understand:	1. How the price of a good or service affects the quantity demanded by buyers
	2. How other market conditions affect demand
	3. How the price of a good affects the quantity supplied by sellers
	4. How other market conditions affect supply
	5. How supply and demand interact to determine the market price of a good or service
	6. How market prices and quantities change in response to changes in market conditions
	7. How price supports and price ceilings affect the operations of markets
Before reading this chapter, make sure you know the meaning of:	1. Spontaneous order
	2. Markets
	3. Opportunity cost
	4. Law of unintended consequences

WE BEGAN THE preceding chapter with an example of the way rising gasoline prices affected sales of gas-guzzling SUVs in 2005. Automobiles are just one category among millions of goods and services for which prices, quantities sold, and other market conditions vary from day to day and from year to year. Whether they are goods that we ourselves buy and sell, or goods that our employers, neighbors, or family members buy and sell, the changing market conditions affect our lives in many ways. The factors determining market prices and quantities are thus a good starting point for any discussion of economics.

This chapter outlines a model of price determination in a market economy, the supply-and-demand model. Economists use the term **supply** to refer to sellers' willingness and ability to provide goods for sale in a market. **Demand** refers to buyers' willingness and ability to purchase goods.

Supply

The willingness and ability of sellers to provide goods for sale in a market.

Demand

The willingness and ability of buyers to purchase goods.

Law of demand

The principle that an inverse relationship exists between the price of a good and the quantity of that good that buyers demand, other things being equal.

DEMAND

The **law of demand**, one of the foundation stones of economics, can be stated formally as follows: In any market, other things being equal, an inverse relationship exists between the price of a good and the quantity of the good that buyers demand—that is, the amount they are willing and able to buy. Thus, the quantity demanded tends to rise as the price falls and to fall as the price rises.

We expect this to happen for two reasons. First, if the price of one good falls while the prices of other goods stay the same, people are likely to substitute the cheaper good. Second, when the price of one good falls while incomes and other prices stay the same, people feel a little richer. They use their added buying power to buy a bit more of many things, including, in most cases, a little more of the good whose price went down.

The terms *demand* and *quantity demanded,* as used in economics, are not the same as *want* or *need.* For example, I think a Porsche is a beautiful car. Sometimes when I see one on the street, I think, "Hey, I want one of those!" Alas, my income is limited. Although in the abstract I might want a Porsche, there are other things I want more. Thus, the quantity of Porsches I demand at the going price is zero.

On the other hand, I might *need* dental surgery to avoid losing my teeth. But suppose I am poor. If I cannot pay for the surgery or find someone to pay for it on my behalf, I am out of luck. The quantity of dental surgery I demand, therefore, would be zero, however great my need for that service. Demand, then, combines both willingness and ability to buy. It is not desire in the abstract, but desire backed by the actual intent to buy.

The Demand Curve

The law of demand states a relationship between the quantity of a good that people are willing and able to buy, other things being equal, and the price of that good. Figure 2.1 represents this one-to-one relationship for a familiar consumer good, chicken. It would be possible to discuss the demand for chicken of a single consumer, but more frequently, as in the following discussion, we focus on the total demand for the good by all buyers in the market.

The figure shows the demand relationship in two different ways. First look at part (a). The first row of the table shows that when the price of chicken is $3.00 a pound, the quantity demanded per year is 1 billion pounds. Reading down the table, we see

FIGURE 2.1   A DEMAND CURVE FOR CHICKEN

(a)	
Price of Chicken (Dollars per Pound)	Quantity of Chicken Demanded (Billions of Pounds per Year)
$3.50	0.5
$3.00	1
$2.50	1.5
A $2.00	2
$1.50	2.5
B $1.00	3
$0.50	3.5

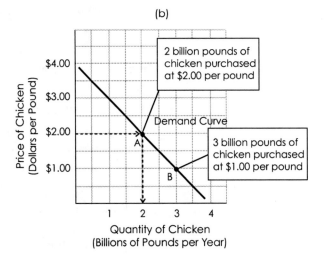

(b)

Both the table and the chart show the quantity of chicken demanded at various prices. For example, at a price of $2.00 per pound, buyers are willing and able to purchase 2 billion pounds of chicken per year. This price-quantity combination is shown by row A in part (a) and point A in part (b).

Demand curve

A graphical representation of the relationship between the price of a good and the quantity of that good that buyers demand.

Change in quantity demanded

A change in the quantity of a good that buyers are willing and able to purchase that results from a change in the good's price, other things being equal; shown by a movement from one point to another along a demand curve.

that as the price falls, the quantity demanded rises. At $2.50 per pound, buyers are willing and able to purchase 1.5 billion pounds per year; at $1.50, 2.5 billion pounds; and so on.

Part (b) of Figure 2.1 presents the same information in graphical form. The graph is called a **demand curve** for chicken. Suppose we want to use the demand curve to find out what quantity of chicken will be demanded at a price of $2.00 per pound. Starting at $2.00 on the vertical axis, we move across, as shown by the arrow, until we reach the demand curve at point A. Continuing to follow the arrow, we drop down to the horizontal axis. Reading from the scale on that axis, we see that the quantity demanded at a price of $2.00 per pound is 2 billion pounds per year. That is the quantity demanded in row A of the table in part (a).

The effect of a change in the price of chicken, other things being equal, can be shown as a movement from one point to another along the demand curve for chicken. Suppose that the price drops from $2.00 to $1.00 per pound. In the process, the quantity that buyers plan to buy rises. The point corresponding to the quantity demanded at the new, lower price is point B (which corresponds to row B of the table). Because of the inverse relationship between price and quantity demanded, the demand curve has a negative slope.

Economists speak of a movement along a demand curve as a **change in quantity demanded**. Such a movement represents buyers' reaction to a change in the price of the good in question, other things being equal.

Shifts in the Demand Curve[1]

The demand curve in Figure 2.1 represents a relationship between two variables: the price of chicken and the quantity of chicken demanded. But changes in other variables can also affect people's purchases of chicken. In the case of chicken, the prices of beef and pork would affect demand. Consumer incomes are a second variable that can affect demand. Changes in expectations about the future are a third, and changes in consumer tastes, such as an increasing preference for foods with a low carbohydrate content, are a fourth. The list could go on and on—the demand for ice is affected by the weather; the demand for diapers is affected by the birthrate; the demand for baseball tickets is affected by the won-lost record of the home team; and so on.

How are all these other variables handled when drawing a demand curve? In brief, two rules apply:

1. When drawing a single demand curve for a good, such as the one in Figure 2.1, all other conditions that affect demand are considered to be fixed or constant under the "other things being equal" clause of the law of demand. As long as that clause is in force, the only two variables at work are quantity demanded (on the horizontal axis) and price (on the vertical axis). The effect of a change in price on quantity demanded thus is shown by a *movement along* the demand curve.

2. When we look beyond the "other things being equal" clause and find that there is a change in a variable that is not represented on one of the axes, such as the price of another good or the level of consumer income, the effect is shown as a *shift* in the demand curve. In its new position, the demand curve still represents a two-variable price-quantity relationship, but it is a slightly different relationship than before because one of the "other things" has changed.

These two rules for graphical representation of demand relationships are crucial to understanding the theory of supply and demand as a whole. It will be worthwhile to expand on them through a series of examples.

CHANGES IN THE PRICE OF A RELATED GOOD   We have already noted that the demand for chicken depends on what happens to the price of beef, as well as what happens to the price of chicken. Figure 2.2, which shows demand curves for both goods, provides a closer look at this relationship.

Suppose that the price of beef is initially $3.00 per pound and then increases to $4.50 per pound. The effect of this change on the quantity of beef demanded is shown in part (a) of Figure 2.2 as a movement along the beef demand curve from point A to point B. Part (b) of the figure shows the effect on the demand for chicken. With the price of beef higher than before, consumers will tend to buy more chicken *even if the price of chicken does not change.* Suppose the price of chicken is $2.00 per pound. When beef was selling at $3.00 a pound, consumers bought 2 billion pounds of

Figure 2.2   Effects of an Increase in the Price of Beef on the Demand for Chicken

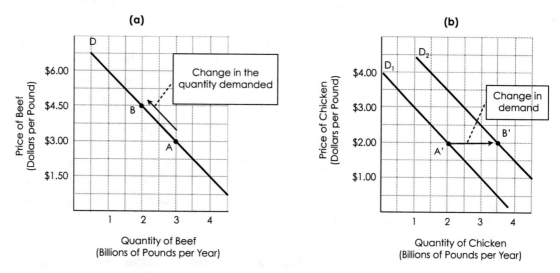

An increase in the price of beef from $3.00 to $4.50 per pound, other things being equal, causes a movement from point A to point B on the beef demand curve—a decrease in the quantity of beef demanded. With the price of chicken unchanged at $2.00 per pound, consumers will substitute chicken for beef. That will cause an increase in the demand for chicken, which is shown as a shift in the chicken demand curve from D₁ to D₂.

chicken a year (point A′ on demand curve D₁). After the price of beef goes up to $4.50 a pound, they will buy 3.5 billion pounds of chicken a year, assuming that the price of chicken does not change (point B′ on demand curve D₂).

A rise in the price of beef would cause consumers to buy more chicken regardless of the initial price of chicken. If the price of chicken had started out at $3.00 a pound and remained there while the price of beef went up, consumers would have increased their chicken consumption from 1 billion pounds a year to 2.5 billion pounds a year. At a price of $1.00 a pound for chicken, the quantity would have risen from 3 billion pounds to 4.5 billion pounds, and so on. We see, then, that a change in the price of beef causes the entire demand curve for chicken to shift. The "other things being equal" clause of the new demand curve, D₂, incorporates a price of $4.50 a pound for beef, rather than the price of $3.00 a pound assumed in demand curve D₁.

Earlier we explained that economists refer to a movement along a demand curve as a "change in quantity demanded." The corresponding term for a shift in a demand curve is a **change in demand**. A change in quantity demanded (a movement along the curve) is caused by a change in the price of the good in question (the variable on the vertical axis). In contrast, a change in demand (a shift in the demand curve) is caused by a change in some variable other than the price of the good in question (one that does not appear on either axis).

In the example in Figure 2.2, people bought more chicken when the price of beef went up, replacing one meat with the other in their dinners. Economists call such

Change in demand

A change in the quantity of a good that buyers are willing and able to purchase that results from a change in some condition other than the price of that good; shown by a shift in the demand curve.

which an increase
in the price of one
causes an increase
in demand for the
other.

Complementary goods

A pair of goods for which an increase in the price of one results in a decrease in demand for the other.

pairs of goods **substitutes**, because an increase in the price of one causes an increase in the demand for the other—a rightward shift in the demand curve.

Consumers react differently to price changes when two goods tend to be used together. One example is cars and gasoline. When the price of gasoline goes up, people's selection of cars will be affected. In particular, they will buy fewer low-mileage, large SUVs even if there is no change in the price of those vehicles. An increase in the price of gasoline thus causes a movement upward along the gasoline demand curve and a *leftward* shift in the demand curve for SUVs. Pairs of goods that are related in this way are known as **complements**.

Whether a given pair of goods are substitutes or complements depends on buyers' attitudes toward those goods; these terms do not refer to properties of the goods themselves. Some people might regard cheese and beef as substitute sources of protein in their diets; others, who like cheeseburgers, might regard them as complements.

One more point regarding the effects of changes in the prices of other goods is also worth noting: In stating the law of demand, it is the price of a good *relative to those of other goods* that counts. During periods of inflation, when the average level of all prices rises, distinguishing between changes in *relative prices* and changes in *nominal prices*—the number of dollars actually paid per unit of a good—is especially important. When the economy experiences inflation, a good can become relatively less expensive even though its nominal price rises, provided that the prices of other goods rise even faster.

Consider chicken, for example. Between 1950 and 2005 the average retail price of a broiler rose by almost 40 percent, from $.59 per pound to $1.05 per pound. Over the same period, however, the average price of all goods and services that consumers bought rose by about 600 percent. The relative price of chicken thus fell during the period even though its nominal price rose. The drop in the relative price of chicken had a lot to do with its growing popularity on the dinner table.

CHANGES IN CONSUMER INCOMES   The demand for a good can also be affected by changes in consumer incomes. When their incomes rise, people tend to buy larger quantities of many goods, assuming that the prices of those goods do not change.

Figure 2.3 shows the effect of an increase in consumer incomes on the demand for chicken. Demand curve D_1 is the same as the curve shown in Figure 2.1. Suppose now that consumer incomes rise. With higher incomes, people become choosier about what they eat. They do not just want calories, they want high-quality calories from foods that are tasty, fashionable, and healthful. These considerations have made chicken increasingly popular as consumer incomes have risen.

More specifically, suppose that after their incomes rise, consumers are willing to buy 2.5 billion pounds of chicken instead of 1 billion pounds at a price of $3.00 per pound. The change is shown as an arrow drawn from point A to point B in Figure 2.3. If the initial price of chicken had been $2.00 per pound, even more chicken would be

FIGURE 2.3 **EFFECTS OF AN INCREASE IN CONSUMER INCOME ON THE DEMAND FOR CHICKEN**

Quantity of Chicken
(Billions of Pounds per Year)

Demand curve D₁ assumes a given level of consumer income. If their incomes increase, consumers will want to buy more chicken at any given price, other things being equal. That will shift the demand curve rightward to, say, D₂. If the prevailing market price at the time of the demand shift is $3.00 per pound, the quantity demanded increases to 2.5 billion pounds (B) from 1 billion (A); if the prevailing price is $2.00 per pound, the quantity demanded will increase to 2 billion pounds (D) from 3.5 billion (C); and so on.

bought at the new, higher level of income. At the original income level and a price of $2.00, the amount purchased would be 2 billion pounds, as shown by point C. After the increase in incomes, buyers would plan to purchase 3.5 billion pounds, shown by the arrow from point C to point D.

Whatever the initial price of chicken, the effect of an increase in consumer incomes is shown by a shift to a point on the new demand curve, D₂. The increase in demand for chicken that results from the rise in consumer incomes thus is shown as a shift in the entire demand curve. If consumer incomes remain at the new, higher level, the effects of any changes in the price of chicken will be shown as movements along the new demand curve. There is, in other words, a chicken demand curve for every possible income level. Each represents a one-to-one relationship between price and quantity demanded, given the assumed income level.

In the example just given, we assumed that an increase in income would cause an increase in the demand for chicken. Experience shows that this is what normally happens. Economists therefore call chicken a **normal good,** meaning that when consumer incomes rise, other things being equal, people will buy more of it.

There are some goods, however, that people will buy less of when their incomes rise, other things being equal. For example, among your classmates, those with higher

Normal good

A good for which an increase in consumer incomes results in an increase in demand.

incomes are likely to go out for pizza more often than those with lower incomes. On nights when they eat pizza, they do not eat in the cafeteria, so the demand for cafeteria food falls as income rises. Similarly, when their incomes rise, people tend to buy less flour for baking at home and to buy more baked goods instead. People tend to buy fewer shoe repair services when their incomes rise; instead, they buy new shoes. Goods such as cafeteria food, flour, and shoe repair services are termed **inferior goods**. When consumer incomes rise, the demand curve for an inferior good shifts to the left instead of to the right. As in the case of substitutes and complements, the notions of inferiority and normality arise from consumer choices; they are not inherent properties of the goods themselves.

Inferior good

A good for which an increase in consumer incomes results in a decrease in demand.

CHANGES IN EXPECTATIONS   Changes in buyers' expectations are a third factor that can shift demand curves. If people expect the price of a particular good to rise relative to the prices of other goods, or expect something other than a price increase to raise the opportunity cost of acquiring the good, they will step up their rate of purchase before the change takes place.

For example, suppose that in May, consumers rush to buy airline tickets in response to a series of news reports indicating that prices will be raised for tickets ordered after June 1. The people who buy their tickets in May will probably include many who were planning to travel late in the summer and ordinarily would have waited several more weeks before making their purchase. Thus, many more tickets will be sold in May than would have been sold at the same price if consumers had not anticipated the June price rise. We can interpret the surge in ticket sales in May as a temporary rightward shift in the demand curve.

CHANGES IN TASTES   Changes in tastes are a fourth source of changes in demand. Sometimes these changes occur rapidly, as can be seen, for example, in such areas as popular music, clothing styles, and fast foods. The demand curves for these goods and services shift often. In other cases, changes in tastes take longer to occur but are more permanent. For example, in recent years consumers have been more health conscious than they were in the past. The result has been reduced demand for cigarettes and foods with high content of refined carbohydrates, along with increased demand for fish, whole grain foods, and exercise equipment.

SUPPLY

The Supply Curve

We now turn from the demand side of the market to the supply side. As in the case of demand, we begin by constructing a one-to-one relationship between the price of a good and the quantity that sellers intend to offer for sale. Figure 2.4 shows such a relationship for chicken.

FIGURE 2.4　A SUPPLY CURVE FOR CHICKEN

(a)

	Price of Chicken (Dollars per Pound)	Quantity of Chicken Demanded (Billions of Pounds per Year)
	$4.00	4
	$3.50	3.5
A	$3.00	3
	$2.50	2.5
B	$2.00	2
	$1.50	1.5
	$1.00	1

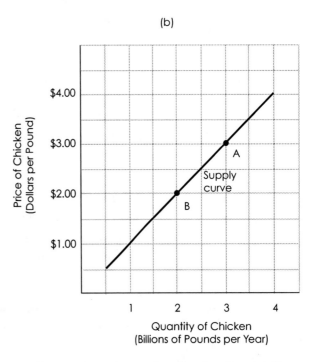

(b)

Parts (a) and (b) of this figure show the quantity of chicken supplied at various prices. As the price rises, the quantity supplied increases, other things being equal. The higher price gives farmers an incentive to raise more chickens, but the rising opportunity cost of doing so limits the supply produced in response to any given price increase.

Supply curve

A graphical representation of the relationship between the price of a good and the quantity of that good that sellers are willing to supply.

The positively sloped curve in Figure 2.4 is called a **supply curve** for chicken. Like demand curves, supply curves are based on an "other things being equal" condition. The supply curve for chicken shows how sellers change their plans in response to a change in the price of chicken, assuming that there are no changes in other conditions—the prices of other goods, production techniques, input prices, expectations, or any other relevant condition.

Why does the supply curve have a positive slope? Why do sellers, other things being equal, plan to supply more chicken when the prevailing market price is higher than they plan to supply when the price is lower? Without going too deeply into a discussion of microeconomic theory, we can consider some common-sense explanations here.

One explanation is that the positive slope of the supply curve represents *producers' response to market incentives*. When the price of chicken goes up, farmers have an incentive to devote more time and resources to raising chickens. Farmers who raise chickens as a sideline may decide to make chickens their main business. Some people may enter the market for the first time. The same reasoning applies in every market. If parents are finding it hard to get babysitters, what do they do? They offer to pay more.

If a sawmill cannot buy enough timber, it raises the price it offers to loggers, and so on. Exceptions to this general rule are rare.

Another explanation is that the positive slope of the supply curve reflects *the rising cost of producing additional output in facilities of a fixed size.* A furniture factory with a fixed amount of machinery might be able to produce more chairs only by paying workers at overtime rates to run the machinery for more hours. A farmer who is trying to grow more wheat on a fixed amount of land could do so by increasing the input of fertilizer and pesticides per acre, but beyond a certain point each unit of added chemicals yields less additional output.

Finally, the positive slope of the supply curve can be explained in terms of *comparative advantage and opportunity cost.* Figure 2.5a shows a production possibility frontier for an economy in which there are only two goods, tomatoes and chicken. Farmers can choose which product they will specialize in, but some farmers have a comparative advantage in growing tomatoes, others in raising chickens. Beginning from a situation in which only tomatoes are produced, farmers with the strongest

FIGURE 2.5   THE PRODUCTION POSSIBILITY CURVE AND THE SUPPLY CURVE

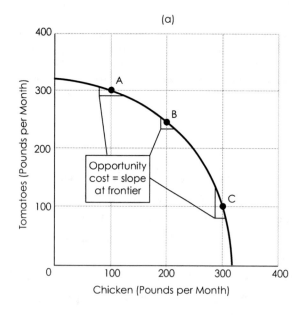
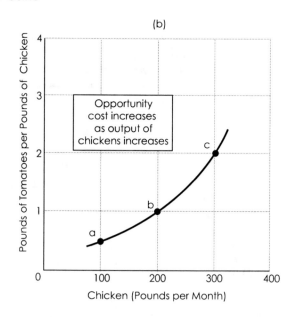

This figure offers an interpretation of the supply curve in terms of the production possibility frontier for an economy in which two goods are produced, tomatoes and chicken. Part (a) shows a production possibility frontier. The slope of the frontier at any point shows the opportunity cost of producing an additional pound of chicken measured in terms of the quantity of tomatoes that could have been produced using the same factors of production. The frontier curves because some operators have a comparative advantage in producing tomatoes and others have a comparative advantage in producing chicken. As more chicken is produced, those with the greatest comparative advantage in producing chicken are the first to stop producing tomatoes. Because the frontier gets steeper as more chicken is produced, the opportunity cost rises, as shown in part (b). The curve in part (b) can be interpreted as a supply curve, in the sense that an incentive, in the form of a higher price, will cause factors of production to be shifted from tomatoes to chicken despite the rising opportunity cost of producing chicken.

comparative advantage in raising chickens—that is, those who are able to produce chicken at relatively the lowest opportunity cost—will switch from tomatoes to chicken even if the price of chicken is low. As the point of production moves along the frontier, the price of chicken must rise to induce farmers with relatively higher opportunity costs to make the switch. The slope of the frontier at any point represents the opportunity cost of producing more chicken for a farmer who finds it worthwhile to switch from tomatoes to chicken just at that point.

In Figure 2.5 the slopes at points A, B, and C in part (a) are graphed on a new set of axes in part (b). The graph can be interpreted as a supply curve if it is noted that the price of chicken must rise relative to the price of tomatoes to induce more farmers to switch to chicken as the opportunity cost rises.

Each of these common-sense explanations fits certain circumstances. Together, they provide an intuitive basis for the positive slope of the supply curve.

Shifts in the Supply Curve

As in the case of demand, the effects of a change in the price of chicken, other things being equal, can be shown as a movement along the supply curve for chicken. Such a movement is called a **change in quantity supplied**. A change in a condition other than the price of chicken can be shown as a shift in the supply curve. Such a shift is referred to as a **change in supply**. Four sources of change in supply are worth noting. Each is related to the notion that the supply curve reflects the opportunity cost of producing the good or service in question.

CHANGES IN TECHNOLOGY   A supply curve is drawn on the basis of a particular production technique. When entrepreneurs reduce the opportunity costs of production by introducing more efficient techniques, it becomes worthwhile to sell more of the good than before at any given price. Figure 2.6 shows how an improvement in production technology affects the supply curve for chicken.

Supply curve S_1 is the same as the one shown in Figure 2.4. It indicates that farmers will plan to supply 3 billion pounds of chicken per year at a price of $3.00 per pound (point A). Now suppose that the development of a faster-growing bird reduces the amount of feed used in raising chickens. With lower costs per unit, farmers will be willing to supply more chicken than before at any given price. They may, for example, be willing to supply 4 billion pounds of chicken at $3.00 per pound (point B). The move from A to B is part of a shift in the entire supply curve from S_1 to S_2. Once the new techniques are established, an increase or decrease in the price of chicken, other things being equal, will result in a movement along the new supply curve.

CHANGES IN INPUT PRICES   Changes in input prices are a second item that can cause supply curves to shift. An increase in input prices, other things being equal, increases the opportunity cost of producing the good in question, and hence it tends to reduce the quantity of a good that producers plan to supply at a given price. Refer

---

Change in quantity supplied

A change in the quantity of a good that suppliers are willing and able to sell that results from a change in the good's price, other things being equal; shown by a movement along a supply curve.

Change in supply

A change in the quantity of a good that suppliers are willing and able to sell that results from a change in some condition other than the good's price; shown by a shift in the supply curve.

FIGURE 2.6 SHIFTS IN THE SUPPLY CURVE FOR CHICKEN

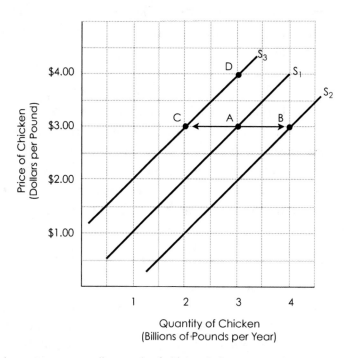

Several kinds of changes can cause the supply of chicken to increase or decrease. For example, a new production method that lowers costs will shift the curve to the *right*, from S_1 to S_2. The shift is to the right because, taking into account the new, lower cost of production per unit, producers will be willing to supply more chicken at any given price. An increase in the price of inputs, other things being equal, will shift the curve to the *left*, from S_1 to S_3. The shift is to the left because, taking into account the new, higher price of inputs, producers will be willing to supply less chicken at any given price. Changes in sellers' expectations or in the prices of competing goods can also cause the supply curve to shift.

again to Figure 2.6. Suppose that starting from point A on supply curve S_1, the price of chicken feed increases and no offsetting changes occur. Now, instead of supplying 3 billion pounds of chicken at $3.00 per pound, farmers will supply, say, just 2 billion pounds at that price (point C). The move from A to C is part of a leftward shift in the supply curve, from S_1 to S_3.

If the price of feed remains at the new level, changes in the price of chicken will cause movements along the new supply curve. For example, farmers could be induced to supply the original quantity of chicken—3 billion pounds—if the price of chicken rose enough to cover the increased cost of feed. As you can see in Figure 2.6, that would require a price of $4.00 per pound for chicken (point D).

CHANGES IN THE PRICES OF OTHER GOODS Changes in the prices of other goods that could be produced using the same factors of production can also produce a shift in the chicken supply curve. In our earlier example, farmers could use available resources to produce either chickens or tomatoes. Suppose that the price of tomatoes rises while the price of chicken stays at $3.00. The rise in the price of tomatoes gives some farmers who would otherwise have produced chickens an incentive to shift the use of their labor, land, and capital to the production of tomatoes. Thus, the effect of an increase in the price of tomatoes can be shown as a leftward shift in the chicken supply curve.

CHANGES IN EXPECTATIONS　　　Changes in expectations can cause supply curves to shift in much the same way that they cause demand curves to shift. Again, we can use farming as an example. At planting time, a farmer's selection of crops is influenced not so much by current prices as by the prices expected at harvest time. Expectations over a time horizon longer than one growing season also affect supply. Each crop requires special equipment and know-how. We have just seen that an increase in the price of tomatoes gives farmers an incentive to shift from chicken to tomatoes. The incentive will be stronger if the price of tomatoes is expected to remain at the higher level. If it is, farmers are more likely to buy the special equipment needed for that crop and to learn the necessary production techniques.

THE INTERACTION OF SUPPLY AND DEMAND

Markets transmit information, in the form of prices, to people who buy and sell goods and services. Taking these prices into account, along with other knowledge they may have, buyers and sellers make their plans.[2] As shown by the demand and supply curves, buyers and sellers plan to buy or sell certain quantities of a good at any given price.

Each market has many buyers and sellers, each making plans independently. When they meet to trade, some of them may be unable to carry out their plans on the terms they expected. Perhaps the total quantity of a good that buyers plan to purchase is greater than the total quantity that suppliers are willing to sell at the given price. In that case, some of the would-be buyers must change their plans. Or, perhaps planned sales exceed planned purchases at the given price. In that case, some would-be sellers will be unable to carry out their plans.

Equilibrium

A condition in which buyers' and sellers' plans exactly mesh in the marketplace, so that the quantity supplied exactly equals the quantity demanded at a given price.

Market Equilibrium

Sometimes no one is surprised: The total quantity of a good that buyers plan to purchase exactly matches the total quantity that producers plan to sell. When buyers' and sellers' plans mesh when they meet in the marketplace, no buyers or sellers need to change their plans. Under these conditions, the market is said to be in **equilibrium**.

Supply and demand curves, which reflect the plans of sellers and buyers, can be used to give a graphical demonstration of market equilibrium. Figure 2.7 uses the same supply and demand curves as before, but this time both curves are drawn on the

Figure 2.7   Equilibrium in the Chicken Market

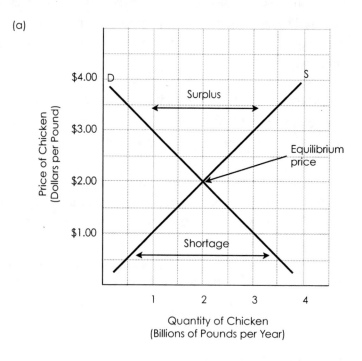

(a)

(b)

Price (per Pound)	Quantity Demanded (Billions of Pounds)	Quantity Supplied (Billions of Pounds)	Shortage (Billions of Pounds)	Surplus (Billions of Pounds)	Direction of Pressure on Price
$3.50	0.5	3.5	—	3	Downward
$3.00	1	3	—	2	Downward
$2.50	1.5	2.5	—	1	Downward
$2.00	2	2	—	—	Equilibrium
$1.50	2.5	1.5	1	—	Upward
$1.00	3	1	2	—	Upward
$0.50	3.5	0.5	3	—	Upward

This figure shows the supply and demand curves for chicken presented earlier in graphical and numerical form. The demand curve shows how much buyers plan to purchase at a given price. The supply curve shows how much producers plan to sell at a given price. At only one price—$2.00 per pound—do buyers' and sellers' plans exactly match. That is the equilibrium price. A higher price causes a surplus of chicken and puts downward pressure on price. A lower price causes a shortage and puts upward pressure on price.

same diagram. If the quantity of planned sales at each price is compared with the quantity of planned purchases at that price (either the table or the graph can be used to make this comparison), it can be seen that there is only one price at which the two sets of plans mesh. That price—$2.00 per pound—is the equilibrium price. If all buyers and sellers make their plans with the expectation of a price of $2.00, no one will be surprised and no plans will have to be changed.

Shortages

But what will happen if for some reason people base their plans for buying or selling chicken on a price other than $2.00 a pound?[3] Suppose, for example, that they base their plans on a price of $1.00. Figure 2.7 shows that at that price buyers will plan to purchase chicken at a rate of 3 billion pounds per year, but farmers will plan to supply only 1 billion pounds. When the quantity demanded exceeds the quantity supplied, as in this example, the difference is an **excess quantity demanded** or, more simply, a **shortage**. In Figure 2.7 the shortage is 2 billion pounds of chicken per year when the price is $1.00 per pound.

Excess quantity demanded (shortage)

A condition in which the quantity of a good demanded at a given price exceeds the quantity supplied.

Inventory

A stock of a finished good awaiting sale or use.

In most markets the first sign of a shortage is a drop in the **inventory**, that is, in the stock of the good in question that has been produced and is waiting to be sold or used. Sellers plan to hold a certain quantity of goods in inventory to allow for minor changes in demand. When they see inventories dropping below the planned level, they change their plans. Some may try to rebuild their inventories by increasing their output, if they produce the good themselves; or, if they do not make it themselves, they may order more from the producer. Some sellers may take advantage of the strong demand for their product to raise the price, knowing that buyers will be willing to pay more. Many sellers will do a little of both. If sellers do not take the initiative, buyers will—they will offer to pay more if sellers will supply more. Whatever the details, the result will be an upward movement along the supply curve as both price and quantity increase.

As the shortage puts upward pressure on price, buyers will change their plans too. Moving up and to the left along their demand curve, they will cut back on their planned purchases. As both buyers and sellers change their plans, the market will move toward equilibrium. When the price reaches $2.00 per pound, both the shortage and the pressure to change buying and selling plans will disappear.

In the markets for most goods, sellers have inventories of goods ready to be sold. There are exceptions, however. Inventories are not possible in markets for services—haircuts, tax preparation, lawn care, and the like. Also, some goods, such as custom-built houses and machine tools that are designed for a specialized need, are not held in inventories. Sellers in these markets do not begin production until they have a contract with a buyer.

In markets in which there are no inventories, the sign of a shortage is a queue of buyers. The queue may take the form of a line of people waiting to be served or a list of names in an order book. The queue is a sign that, given the prevailing price, buyers would like to purchase the good at a faster rate than that at which producers have planned to supply it. However, some plans cannot be carried out—at least not right away. Buyers are served on a first-come, first-served basis.

The formation of a queue of buyers has much the same effect on the market as a decrease in inventories. Sellers react by increasing their rate of output, raising their prices, or both. Buyers react by reducing the quantity they plan to purchase. The result is a movement up and to the right along the supply curve and, at the same time, up and to the left along the demand curve until equilibrium is reached.

Surpluses

Having considered what happens when buyers and sellers initially expect a price below the equilibrium price, we now turn to the opposite case. Suppose that for some reason buyers and sellers of chicken expect a price that is higher than the equilibrium price—say, $2.50 per pound—and make their plans accordingly. Figure 2.7 shows that farmers will plan to supply 2.5 billion pounds of chicken per year at $2.50, but their customers will plan to buy only 1.5 billion pounds. When the quantity supplied exceeds the quantity demanded, there is an **excess quantity supplied**, or a **surplus**. As Figure 2.7 shows, the surplus of chicken at a price of $2.50 per pound is 1 billion pounds per year.

> **Excess quantity supplied (surplus)**
>
> A condition in which the quantity of a good supplied at a given price exceeds the quantity demanded.

When there is a surplus of a product, sellers will be unable to sell all that they had hoped to sell at the planned price. As a result, their inventories will begin to grow beyond the level they had planned to hold in preparation for normal changes in demand.

Sellers will react to the inventory buildup by changing their plans. Some will cut back their output. Others will lower their prices to induce consumers to buy more and thus reduce their extra stock. Still others will do a little of both. The result of these changes in plans will be a movement down and to the left along the supply curve.

As unplanned inventory buildup puts downward pressure on the price of chicken, buyers change their plans too. Finding that chicken costs less than they had expected, they buy more of it. In graphical terms, they move down and to the right along the demand curve. As that happens, the market is restored to equilibrium.

In markets in which there are no inventories, surpluses lead to the formation of queues of sellers looking for customers. Taxi queues at airports are a case in point. At some times of the day the fare for taxi service from the airport to downtown is more than high enough to attract a number of taxis that is equal to the demand. A queue of cabs waiting for passengers then forms. In some cities drivers who are far back in the queue try to attract riders by offering cut-rate fares. Often, though, there are rules against fare cutting. The queue then grows until the next peak period, when a surge in demand shortens it.

Changes in Market Conditions

On a graph, finding the equilibrium point looks easy. In real life, though, it is a moving target. Market conditions, by which we mean all the items that lie behind the "other things being equal" clause, change frequently. When they do, both buyers and sellers revise their plans, and market prices and quantities adjust.

RESPONSE TO A SHIFT IN DEMAND   We will first consider a market's response to a shift in demand. Suppose, for example, that television news broadcasts a warning that eating chicken meat might transmit a new virus. The result would be an immediate decrease in demand for chicken. Part (a) of Figure 2.8 interprets this case in terms of the supply-and-demand model.

As the figure is drawn, the chicken market is initially in equilibrium at E_1. There the price is $3.00 per pound and the quantity produced is 2 billion pounds per year. Now the temporary change in tastes caused by the health warning shifts the demand curve to the left, from D_1 to D_2. (There is a shift in the demand curve rather than a movement along it, because a change in tastes is not one of the items represented by the axes of the diagram.) What will happen next?

At the original price of $3.00 per pound, there will be a surplus of chicken. The supply curve shows that at that price chicken farmers will plan to produce 2 billion pounds per year. However, according to the new demand curve, D_2, consumers will no longer buy that much chicken at $3.00 per pound. Instead, given their new tastes, they will buy only 1billion pounds at that price.

But the price does not stay at $3.00 for long. As soon as the demand curve begins to shift and the surplus begins to develop, chicken inventories rise above their planned levels, putting downward pressure on the price. As the price falls, producers revise their plans. They move down and to the left along their supply curve, reducing

FIGURE 2.8 EFFECTS OF CHANGING CONDITIONS IN THE CHICKEN MARKET

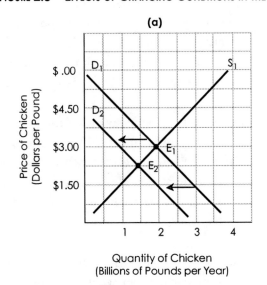
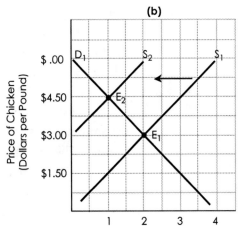

Part (a) of this figure shows the effects of a decrease in demand for chicken caused by a health warning about the safety of eating chicken. Initially the market is in equilibrium at E_1. The change in tastes causes a shift in the demand curve. At the original equilibrium price of $3.00 per pound, there is a temporary surplus of chicken. This causes inventories to start to rise and puts downward pressure on the price. As the price falls, producers move down along their supply curve to a new equilibrium at E_2. There both the price and quantity of chicken are lower than before the shift in demand. Part (b) shows the effects of a decrease in supply caused by a drought, which raises the price of corn used to feed chicken. The shift in the supply curve causes a shortage at the initial price of $3.00 per pound. The shortage puts upward pressure on price. As the price rises, buyers move up and to the left along the demand curve until a new equilibrium is reached at E_2. In each case, note that only one curve needs to shift to bring about the new equilibrium.

the quantity supplied. (There is a movement along the supply curve, not a shift in the curve, because the producers are responding to a change in the price of chicken, the variable shown on the vertical axis. Nothing has happened to change the "other things being equal" condition, such as technology, input prices, and so on, which could cause the supply curve to shift.)

As farmers move downward along their supply curve in the direction shown by the arrow in part (a) of Figure 2.8, they eventually reach point E_2, where their plans again mesh with those of consumers. At that point the price has fallen to $2.25 per pound and production to 1.5 billion pounds. Although health-conscious consumers would not have bought that much chicken at the old price, they will do so at the new, lower price. E_2 thus is the new equilibrium point. Later, if the health scare proves to be baseless, the demand curve will shift back D_1 and the market price and quantity will return to their original values.

RESPONSE TO A SHIFT IN SUPPLY   The original equilibrium might be disrupted by a change in supply rather than by a change in demand. For example, beginning from a condition of equilibrium, a drought in the Midwest might result in a higher price for grain for chicken feed. That would shift the supply curve to the left while the demand curve remained unchanged, as shown in part (b) of Figure 2.8.

Given the new supply curve, there will be a shortage of chicken at the original price. Inventories will decline and the prices will rise in response. As the price increases, producers will move upward and to the right along their new supply curve, S_2, and consumers will move upward and to the left along their demand curve, D_1, which remains in its original position. A new equilibrium is established when the price reaches $4.50 per pound.

One of the most frequent mistakes people make in learning the supply-and-demand model is to think that *both* curves always must shift in order to restore equilibrium. The examples given in Figure 2.8 show clearly that this is not the case. In part (a), after the demand curve shifts, a movement along the supply curve is enough to establish the new equilibrium. No shift in the supply curve is needed. Similarly, in part (b), after the supply curve shifts, the demand curve does not need to shift to reach the new equilibrium.

However, in the turmoil of real-world markets, cases can be found in which both curves do shift at once. This will happen when two separate changes in conditions occur at the same time, one acting on the supply curve and the other on the demand curve. *Economics in the News 2.1* provides a real-world example. It shows how beef prices were pushed upward in 2003 by two simultaneous changes in market conditions. One was a swing in consumer tastes toward beef because of the popularity of low-carbohydrate, high-protein diets. That shifted the demand curve to the right. At the same time a cutoff of beef imports from Canada shifted the supply curve to the left. Either change acting alone would have been enough to raise the price. Both changes acting together had an especially sharp impact.

BEEF PRICES UP; FAST FOOD CHAINS SWITCH TO CHICKEN

Stock up the freezer if you like steak because beef prices at the supermarket are on their way up. And they're likely to stay there for a while.

U.S. cattle prices are at a record high, say economists with the U.S. Department of Agriculture . They've increased 34% since July, and this month the benchmark price of Nebraska choice steers went from $90 to $116 per 100 pounds. A year ago, the price per 100 pounds was $64.

"We've seen increases in the last 10 days," said Jim Robb, director of the Livestock Marketing Information Center in Denver. "Choice T-bone steak and New York strip steak, those prices are double what they were three weeks ago."

"Those prices will ease off a little bit but not much," said David Kay of *Cattle Buyers Weekly*. "We look as if we're going to have even tighter cattle supplies for slaughter in 2004 and even into 2005."

Prices are up because of a set of circumstances that Robb calls "completely unprecedented." First, consumer demand for beef has increased nearly 10% since 1998 after declining for 20 years.

Recent increases in consumption may be due in part because of the increasing popularity of high-protein diets, such as this summer's blockbuster South Beach diet, and the venerable Atkins diet.

Second, as Wayne Purcell of the Research Institute on Livestock Pricing at Virginia Tech points out, the U.S. banned imports of Canadian cattle and beef five months ago. The ban was imposed because of the discovery of a case of mad cow disease there last spring and reduced cattle and meat imports to the United States by 9%.

Consumers already may be feeling the impact, whether they're eating out or at home. U.S. restaurant chains such as McDonald's and Wendy's have been hyping salads and lean chicken pieces lately, and industry observers say it's no coincidence that the switch coincides with rising beef prices. Experts expect cost-cutting by other restaurant companies to offset rising food prices.

It is not clear how long it will take for the impact of the price increases to be felt at local meat counters. Retail beef prices typically trail the price paid at the stockyard anywhere from two weeks to two months. So last week's increase will not show up at supermarkets until the first weeks of November or until Christmas.

If grocers think the price hike is temporary, they may eat the difference rather than risk aggravating customers. But if grocers do raise prices, "they'll raise their everyday prices only a little, but they will keep them up for a year or so. And we just won't see beef featured in sales very much," Kay said.

Source: Elizabeth Weise, "Beef Prices On the Way Up," *USA Today*, October 24, 2003.

Equilibrium as Spontaneous Order

The way that markets move toward a new equilibrium following a disturbance is an example of economic coordination through spontaneous order. In the case we have been following, the disturbance began either with a change in health consciousness among consumers or with a change in the weather. To make the adjustment to new conditions, the decisions of thousands of farmers, wholesalers, retailers, as well as that of millions of consumers, must somehow be coordinated. How can that be done?

In a market economy, no central planning agency or regulatory bureaucracy is needed. The required shift in the use of scarce resources is brought about through information and incentives transmitted in the form of changing market prices. The trend toward low-carbohydrate, high-protein diets in the early 2000s is a typical example. As demand for beef, chicken, and other high-protein foods rose, farmers responded to higher prices by raising more chickens and cattle. Labor, capital, natural resources, and entrepreneurial energy flowed into chicken and beef production without any central authority giving an order. At the same time, investments in donuts, a high-carb food that had boomed in the 1990s, slowed substantially.

The process was remarkably smooth for so vast a shift in resource use. Behind the scenes, surpluses and shortages nudged choices in the needed directions, but at no time did shortages occur in the acute form of empty meat coolers at the supermarket or lines of chicken-hungry consumers stretching down city streets. Similarly, slack demand for donuts signaled entrepreneurs to turn away from building new outlets, but it did not give rise to mountains of rotting donuts that had to be dumped into landfills.

No one *intended* this process of adjustment. Equilibrium is not a compromise that must be negotiated by a committee of consumers and producers. Just as shoppers manage to equalize the length of supermarket checkout lines without the guidance of a central authority, markets move toward equilibrium spontaneously, through the small, local adjustments that people make in their efforts to serve their own interests. As Adam Smith might have put it, we have not the benevolence of Frank Perdue or the Beef Industry Council to thank for our dinner; instead it is their self-interest that puts the right food on our table.

PRICE FLOORS AND CEILINGS: AN APPLICATION

Economics—both macro and micro—encompasses a great many applications of the concepts of supply and demand. Although each situation is unique, each to some extent draws on ideas developed in this chapter. This section, which uses the model to analyze the effects of government-imposed price floors and ceilings, provides some examples. Many more will be added in later chapters.

Price Supports: The Market for Milk

In our earlier example of the market for beef, a decrease in demand caused a surplus, which in turn caused the price to decrease until the surplus was eliminated. Markets are not always free to respond by adjusting prices, however. The market for milk is a case in point.

Figure 2.9 shows the market for milk in terms of supply and demand curves. The quantity of milk is measured in hundredweight, the unit used for bulk milk sales, equal to roughly 12 gallons. Suppose that initially the market is in equilibrium at point E_1. The wholesale price of milk is $13 per hundredweight, and 110 million hundredweight is produced per year. Then suppose that a trend in taste away from high-cholesterol foods shifts the demand curve for milk to the left. The result would be a surplus of milk at the $13 price, as shown by the arrow in Figure 2.9.

At this point a new factor comes into operation that was not present in our earlier discussion of the chicken market. In that case, chicken prices were free to fall in response to a surplus, but in the milk market they are not. Instead, an elaborate set of

FIGURE 2.9   PRICE SUPPORTS FOR MILK

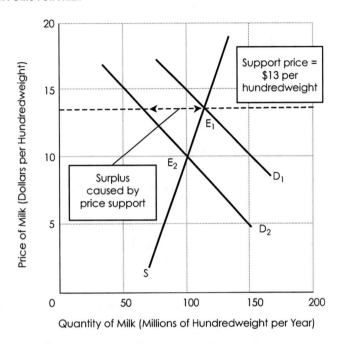

Quantity of Milk (Millions of Hundredweight per Year)

Suppose that initially the market for milk is in equilibrium at E_1. A shift in tastes away from high-cholesterol foods then shifts the demand curve to D_2. If the price were free to fall, there would be a temporary surplus that would push the price down to a new equilibrium at $10 per hundredweight. Instead, suppose that the government maintains a support price for milk at a level higher than the equilibrium price, as it did for many years ($13 per hundredweight in this example). The government would then need to buy the surplus milk and stores it in the form of powdered milk, butter and cheese to keep the price from falling.

government-imposed controls and subsidies puts a floor under the price of milk. As part of the controls, the government agrees to pay a minimum price for all milk that cannot be sold at that price on the open market. In our example, the support price is assumed to be $13.

With the demand curve in its original position D_1, there was no surplus and the government did not need to buy any milk. But with the demand curve in position D_2, there is a surplus of 40 million hundredweight per year. Under the price support law the government must buy this surplus and store it in the form of powdered milk, cheese, butter, and other products with long shelf lives.

Without price supports, the shift in demand would cause the price of milk to fall to the new equilibrium price of $10 per hundredweight. When price supports are applied to a product at a level higher than the equilibrium price, however, the result is a persistent surplus. The effects of the price support can be understood in terms of conflicting signals sent to producers and consumers. To consumers, the price of $13 says, "Milk is scarce. Its opportunity cost is high. Hold your consumption down." To producers, it says, "All is well. Incentives are unchanged. Feel free to continue using scarce resources to produce milk." Without price supports, a drop in the price to $10 would send a different set of messages. Consumers would hear: "Milk is cheaper and more abundant. Although it is not cholesterol free, give in to temptation! Drink more of it!" Producers would hear: "The milk market is not what it once was. Look at your opportunity costs. Is there perhaps some better use for your labor, capital, and natural resources?"

During the 1980s and 1990s, the government's price support was consistently higher than the equilibrium price. The program became very expensive, more than $1,000 per U.S. family by some estimates, enough to buy each family its own cow. From time to time the government has tried to eliminate the milk surplus by shifting the supply curve to the left so that it would intersect the demand curve near the support price. Under one program, for example, farmers were encouraged to sell their cows to be slaughtered for their meat, thereby reducing the size of dairy herds. But such programs have failed to eliminate the milk surplus. The chief reason is the dairy farmers' entrepreneurial response to the high price of milk. The government's efforts to cut the size of herds were largely offset by increased output per cow as a result of genetic improvements and better farm management practices. The government accumulated mountains of surplus dairy products.

Then, during the early years of the 21st century, conditions in the milk market changed. By 2005, the support price had fallen below the market price and the surplus had disappeared. This, too, had unintended consequences for public policy. Under the U.S. Department of Agriculture's Commodity Supplemental Food Program, as many as 100,000 mothers, children, and elderly people had received packages of free milk powder drawn from government surpluses. Suddenly these vast stocks were threatened with exhaustion, and officials were left scrambling to find other ways to aid needy citizens. Meanwhile, across the Atlantic, the European Union continues to operate a price support system that produces an ongoing surplus of more than 30 million tons per year. The European milk market is still in a position much like that shown in Figure 2.9.

Price Ceilings: The Case of Rent Control

In the milk market, the government maintains a support price that has often been above the equilibrium price. In certain other markets, a price ceiling below the equilibrium price is imposed. An example of the latter situation is rent control in housing markets.

Rent control in one form or another has been used in several major U.S. cities, including New York, Washington, D.C., San Francisco, and Los Angeles. The controls vary from one city to another, but in all cases maximum rents, at least for some categories of apartments, are established by law. The purpose of rent control is to aid tenants by preventing landlords from charging "unreasonably high" rents. What is unreasonably high is determined by the relative political strength of landlords and tenants rather than by the forces of supply and demand.

INTENDED EFFECTS   Figure 2.10 interprets the effects of rent control in terms of supply and demand. For the sake of simplicity it is assumed that the supply of rental housing consists of units of equal size and rental value. Part (a) of the figure shows the effects of rent control in the short run. Here the short run means a period that is too short to permit significant increases or decreases in the supply of rental housing. (The short-run supply curve, which is drawn as a vertical line, indicates that a change in price will not result in any change in the quantity of apartments supplied in the short run.[4])

Under the conditions shown, the equilibrium rent per standard housing unit is $1,250 per month for each of the 200,000 units in the city. Now suppose that a rent ceiling of $500 is imposed. The result is a gain to tenants of $750 per unit per month. The total sum transferred to tenants (that is, the benefit to them from below-market rents) is $750 per unit times 200,000 units, or $150 million, in all. In graphical terms,

FIGURE 2.10   EFFECTS OF RENT CONTROL

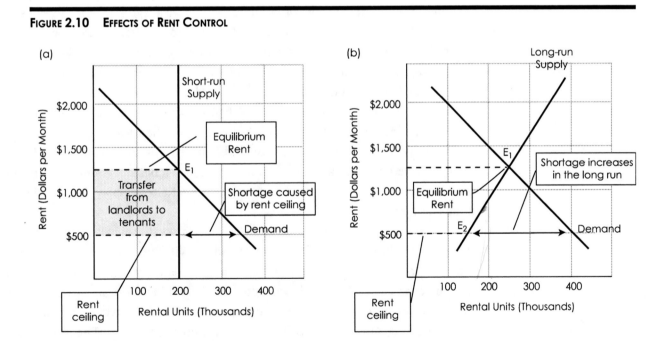

Part (a) shows the short-run effects of rent control. In the short run, the supply of rental apartments is considered to be fixed. The equilibrium rent is $1,250 per month. A rent ceiling of $500 per month is then put into effect. One possible outcome is that landlords will charge disguised rent increases, which will bring the true price back to $1,250 per month. If such disguised increases are prohibited, there will be a shortage of 350,000 units at the ceiling price. Part (b) shows the long-run effects when there is time to adjust the number of units in response to the price. If the ceiling price is enforced, landlords move down their supply curve to E₂. The shortage then becomes even more severe than in the short run.

that sum is equal to the area of the shaded rectangle in Figure 2.10. The benefit to tenants at the expense of landlords is the principal intended effect of rent control.

UNINTENDED EFFECTS The policy of rent control, which does accomplish its goal of benefiting tenants at the expense of landlords, provides a classic illustration of the law of unintended consequences. In the short run, when the stock of apartments is fixed, the unintended consequences stem from the apartment shortage created by the controls. The shortage occurs because the quantity demanded is greater at the lower ceiling price than at the higher equilibrium price.

The greater quantity demanded has several sources. First, people who would otherwise own a house or condominium may now want to rent. Second, people who would otherwise live in non–rent-controlled suburbs may now seek rent-controlled units in the city. Third, each tenant may want more space, which results in a demand for more of the standardized units shown in Figure 2.10.

The shortage creates a problem for both landlords and tenants: How will the limited supply of apartments be rationed among those who want them? Both landlords and tenants devise a number of creative responses—*entrepreneurial* responses, as an economist would say.

One response on the part of landlords is to seek disguised rent increases. These may take the form of large, nonrefundable "key deposits" or security deposits. As an alternative, they may sell old, used furniture or drapes at inflated prices as a condition for renting the apartment. Finally, the costs of certain maintenance or security services that the landlord might otherwise have paid for may be transferred to tenants.

Tenants too may get into the act. When they decide to move, they may sublet their apartments to other tenants rather than give up their leases. Now it is the tenant who collects the key money or sells the old drapes to the subtenant. The original tenant may have moved to a distant city but maintains a bank account and a post office box for use in paying the rent. The subtenant is instructed to play the role of a "guest" if the landlord telephones.

Advocates of rent control view these responses as cheating and often try to outlaw them. If prohibitions are enforced, the landlord will find that there are many applicants for each vacant apartment. In that case, the landlord must decide to whom to rent the apartment. The result will often be discrimination against renters who are from minority groups, who have children, or who have unconventional lifestyles.

In the long run, rent control has other unintended effects. The long run in this case means enough time for the number of rental units to grow through construction of new units or shrink through abandonment of old ones (or their conversion to condominiums). Other things being equal, the higher the rent, the greater the rate of construction, and the lower the rent, the greater the rate of abandonment or conversion. This is reflected in the positively sloped long-run supply curve in part (b) of Figure 2.10.

If rent controls are enforced in such a way that there are no disguised charges by landlords, the number of rental units shrinks and the market moves from E_1 to E_2. At E_2, the unintended effects that appeared in the short run become more pronounced. The intensity of housing discrimination increases relative to the short-run case, because the difference between the number of units available and the number sought by renters increases. Graphically, that difference is shown by the horizontal gap between the supply and demand curves at the ceiling price. In the short run, there is a shortage of 50,000 units; in the long run, the shortage increases to 75,000 units.

Rent controls are often defended as being beneficial to the poor. But when all of the unintended effects of rent control are taken into account, one may question whether poor families really benefit. In cases in which disguised rent increases are possible, the true cost of rental housing is not really decreased. Further, it is hard to believe that landlords' tendency to discriminate against minority group members, single-parent families, and tenants with irregular work histories will benefit the poor. The most likely beneficiaries of rent control are stable, middle-class families who work at the same jobs and live in the same apartments for long periods.

Why does rent control persist as a policy, given its many seemingly perverse unintended consequences? Some economists explain the popularity of rent control in terms of the political power of the middle-class tenants who are most likely to benefit from rent controls and who see helping the poor as nothing more than a convenient cover for simple self-interest. Some explain their popularity in terms of the short time horizon of government officials: The adverse effect on tenants of ending rent control would appear very quickly, whereas such benefits as increased construction of new apartments would materialize only long after the next election. And some attribute the popularity of rent control to the simple fact that many voters do not give much thought to the policy's unintended consequences. Whatever the reason, it appears that very gradually rent control is weakening its hold, even in New York, long home of the strongest controls. In the past decade, more than 10 percent of the 1 million apartments once covered by New York's rent controls have left the system, and the trend is expected to continue.

THIS CHAPTER HAS covered the basics of the supply-and-demand model and described a few applications of that model. There are many more applications in both macro- and microeconomics. In macroeconomics, the supply-and-demand model can be applied to financial markets, labor markets, and the problem of determining the rate of inflation and real output for the economy as a whole. In microeconomics, the model can be applied to product markets, markets for productive resources, and policy issues ranging from pollution to farm policy to international trade, to name just a few. As the great economist Alfred Marshall once put it, nearly all of the major problems of economics have a "kernel" that reflects the workings of supply and demand (see *Who Said It? Who Did It? 2.1*).

⁓ **WHO SAID IT? WHO DID IT? 2.1**

ALFRED MARSHALL ON SUPPLY AND DEMAND

Alfred Marshall, often considered to have been the greatest economist of his day, was born in London in 1842. His father was a Bank of England cashier who hoped the boy would enter the ministry. Young Marshall had other ideas, however. He turned down a theological scholarship at Oxford to study mathematics, receiving his M.A. from Cambridge in 1865.

While at Cambridge, Marshall joined a philosophical discussion group. There he became interested in promoting the broad development of the human mind. He was soon told, however, that the harsh realities of economics would prevent his ideas from being carried out. Britain's economic potential as a country, it was said, could never allow the masses sufficient leisure for education. This disillusioning episode appears to have triggered Marshall's fascination with economics.

At the time, British economics was dominated by the classical school founded by Adam Smith and David Ricardo. Marshall had great respect for the classical writers. Initially he saw his own work as simply applying his mathematical training to strengthen and systematize the classical system. Before long, however, he was breaking new ground and developing a system of his own. By 1890, when he brought out his famous *Principles of Economics*, he had laid the foundation of what we now call the neoclassical school.

In an attempt to explain the essence of his approach, Marshall included the following passage in the second edition of his *Principles*:

> In spite of a great variety in detail, nearly all the chief problems of economics agree in that they have a kernel of the same kind. This kernel is an inquiry as to the balancing of two opposed classes of motives, the one consisting of desires to acquire certain new goods, and thus satisfy wants; while the other consists of desires to avoid certain efforts or retain certain immediate enjoyment . . . in other words, it is an inquiry into the balancing of the forces of demand and supply.

Marshall's influence on economics—at least in the English-speaking world—was enormous. His *Principles* was the leading economics text for several decades, and modern students can still learn much from it. As a professor at Cambridge, Marshall taught a great many of the next generation's leading economists. Today his neoclassical school continues to dominate the profession. It has received many challenges, but so far it has weathered them all.

When one takes a detailed look at the underpinnings of the model, it appears to fit some kinds of markets more closely than others. The fit is best for markets in which there are many producers and many customers, the goods sold by one producer are much like those sold by others, and all sellers and buyers have good information on market conditions. Markets for farm commodities, such as wheat and corn, and financial markets, such as the New York Stock Exchange, meet these standards reasonably well.

However, even in markets that do not display all of these features, the fit is often close enough so that the supply-and-demand model provides useful insights into what is going on. The rental housing market is an example: Not all rental units are, in fact, alike, even when measurement is standardized for objective characteristics such as floor space. Nevertheless, most economists would agree that valid conclusions about the effects of rent control can be arrived at by applying the supply-and-demand model to that market. Thus, the supply-and-demand model serves a precise analytical function in some cases and a broader, more metaphorical function in others. That flexibility makes the model one of the most useful items in the economist's tool kit.

SUMMARY

1. **How does the price of a good or service affect the quantity of it that buyers demand?** Economists use the term *demand* to refer to the willingness and ability of buyers to purchase goods and services. According to the *law of demand,* there is an inverse relationship between the price of a good and the quantity of it that buyers demand. The *quantity demanded* is the quantity that buyers are willing and able to pay for. The law of demand can be represented graphically by a negatively sloped *demand curve.* A change in the quantity demanded is shown by a movement along the demand curve.

2. **How do other market conditions affect demand?** A change in any of the variables covered by the "other things being equal" clause of the law of demand causes a shift in the demand curve; this is known as a *change in demand.* Examples include changes in the prices of goods that are *substitutes* or *complements* of the good in question as well as changes in consumer incomes, expectations, and tastes.

3. **How does the price of a good affect the quantity supplied by sellers?** *Supply* refers to sellers' willingness and ability to offer products for sale in a market. In most markets an increase in the price of a good will increase the quantity of the good that sellers are willing to supply. This relationship can be shown as a positively sloped *supply curve.* The higher price gives producers an incentive to supply more, but rising opportunity costs set a limit on the amount they will supply at any given price.

4. **How do changes in other market conditions affect supply?** A change in any of the items covered by the "other things being equal" clause of the supply curve will shift the curve. Examples include changes in technology, changes in the prices of inputs, changes in the prices of other goods that could be produced with the same resources, and changes in expectations.

5. **How do supply and demand interact to determine the market price of a good or service?** In a market with a positively-sloped supply curve and a negatively-sloped demand curve, there is only one price at which the quantity of a good that sellers plan to supply will exactly match the quantity that buyers plan to purchase. That is known as the *equilibrium* price. At any higher price there will be a *surplus,* and at any lower price there will be a *shortage.*

6. **Why do market prices and quantities change in response to changes in market conditions?** A change in any market condition that shifts the supply or demand curve will change the equilibrium price and quantity in a market. For example, the demand curve may shift to the right as a result of a change in consumer incomes. This causes a shortage at the old price, and the price begins to rise. As the price rises, suppliers move up along the supply curve to a new equilibrium. No shift in the supply curve is required. On the other hand, better technology may shift the supply curve to the right. In that case, there is a surplus at the old price, and the price will fall. As the price decreases, buyers will move down along their demand curve to a new equilibrium. No shift in the demand curve is required.

7. **How do price supports and price ceilings affect the operation of markets?** A price support prevents the market price from falling when the demand curve shifts to the left or the supply curve shifts to the right. The result may be a lasting surplus. A price ceiling prevents the price from rising to its equilibrium level. The result may be a permanent shortage. The total quantity supplied may then be less than the quantity that buyers would like to purchase at the ceiling price or even at the equilibrium price.

KEY TERMS

Supply

Demand

Law of demand

Demand curve

Change in quantity
demanded

Change in demand

Substitute goods

Complementary goods

Normal good

Inferior good

Supply curve

Change in quantity
supplied

Change in supply

Equilibrium

Excess quantity
demanded (shortage)

Inventory

Excess quantity supplied
(surplus)

PROBLEMS AND TOPICS FOR DISCUSSION

1. **A shifting demand curve.** A vending machine company has studied the demand for soft drinks sold in cans from machines. On a 70-degree day consumers in the firm's territory will buy about 2,000 cans at a price of $0.75. For each $.05 rise in price, the quantity sold falls by 200 cans per day; for each 5-degree rise in the temperature, the quantity sold rises by 150 cans per day. The same relationships hold for decreases in price or temperature. Using this information, draw a set of curves showing the demand for soft drinks on days when the temperature is 60, 70, and 85 degrees. Then draw a separate diagram with temperature on the vertical axis and quantity on the horizontal axis. Draw a line representing the relationship between temperature and quantity when the price is $0.75. Next draw additional temperature-quantity lines for prices of $0.50 and $1.00. Do the two diagrams give the same information? Discuss. (Note: If you have any trouble with this exercise, review the appendix to Chapter 1, "Working with Graphs," especially the section entitled "Packing Three Variables into Two Dimensions.")

2. **Demand and the relative price of motor fuel in the 1980s.** In 1979 and 1980 the nominal price of motor fuel rose much more rapidly than the general price level, pushing up the relative price of motor fuel. As we would expect, the quantity sold decreased. In 1981 and 1982 the relative price leveled off and then began to fall, but the quantity sold continued to fall. Which one or more of the following hypotheses do you think best explains the behavior of motor fuel sales in 1981 and 1982? Illustrate each hypothesis with supply and demand curves.

   a. In the 1970s the demand curve had the usual negative slope. However, in 1981 and 1982 the demand curve shifted to an unusual positively sloped position.

   b. The demand curve had a negative slope throughout the period. However, the recession of 1981 and 1982 reduced consumers' real incomes and thus shifted the demand curve.

   c. The demand curve has a negative slope at all times, but the shape depends partly on how much time consumers have to adjust to a change in prices. Over a short period, the demand curve is fairly steep because few adjustments can be made. Over the long term, it has a somewhat flatter slope because further adjustments, such as buying more fuel-efficient cars or moving closer to the job, can be made. Thus, the decreases in fuel sales in 1981 and 1982 were delayed reactions to the price increases that occurred in 1979 and 1980.

3. **Shortages, price controls, and queues.** During the late 1980s and early 1990s, economic reforms initiated by Soviet President Mikhail Gorbachev began to raise consumer incomes, but the Soviet government continued to impose price ceilings

on basic goods like food, clothing, and household goods. As a result, there were severe shortages of many goods and long lines at all kinds of stores became common. Then, in January 1992, the new Russian government, under President Boris Yeltsin, removed retail price controls on most goods. Within a month, prices more than doubled on average and lines disappeared. Analyze these events using the supply and demand model. First draw a supply and demand diagram for some common good, say, toilet paper, showing the market in equilibrium before the beginning of the Gorbachev reforms. Next, use shifts of the appropriate curves to show why the combination of rising incomes plus price ceilings produced shortages and lines. Finally, show what happened when price controls were removed in 1992.

4. **Eliminating queues through flexible pricing.** You are a member of the Metropolitan Taxi Commission, which sets taxi fares for your city. You have been told that long lines of taxis form at the airport during off-peak hours. At peak hours, on the other hand, few taxis are available and there are long lines of passengers waiting for cabs. It is proposed that taxi fares from the airport to downtown be cut by 10 percent during off-peak hours and raised by 10 percent during peak hours. How do you think these changes would affect the queuing patterns of taxis and passengers? Do you think the proposal is a good one from the passengers' point of view? From the cabbies' point of view? From the standpoint of economic efficiency? Discuss.

5. **Rent control.** Turn to part (b) of Figure 2.10, which shows the long-run effects of rent control. If the controls are enforced and there are no disguised rent charges, landlords move down the supply curve to E_2. Buildings are abandoned or converted because of the low rent they bring in. Now consider some alternative possibilities.

a. Suppose that the controls are poorly enforced so that landlords, through key deposits, furnishcharge as much as the market will bear. What will the resulting equilibrium price and quantity be, taking both open and disguised rental charges into account?

b. Now suppose that the controls are enforced so that landlords really cannot collect more than $500 per month. However, the controls are not enforced against tenants who sublet. What will the equilibrium quantity and price be, including both the rent paid to landlords and the disguised rental payments made by subtenants to their subleasors?

CASE FOR DISCUSSION

The hottest topic at a recent exposition for suppliers and users of off-road heavy equipment was tire shortages. Booming Chinese demand for raw materials meant that mining companies in China, Russia, and Indonesia were stocking up on new earth moving equipment and wearing tires our faster on equipment they already owned.

While demand soared, supply had a hard time keeping up. Building a new production line for large tires can take more than two years. The *Financial Times* reported that some tire makers were reactivating mothballed production lines for old-fashioned bias-ply tires. While not as good as modern radial tires, they were good enough to satisfy demand from customers who just wanted something "black and round," according to Prashant Prabhu, president of the earth-mover and industrial tire business of Michelin, the French tire maker. Prabhu also said his company was revising its pricing for large tires to take the shortage into account.

According to *Light and Medium Truck Magazine*, the shortages of huge off-road tires were spilling over into the market for heavy-duty truck tires. In addition to sharply increased demand, it blamed rising prices for materials, including both natural and synthetic rubber. The magazine predicted that the shortage would last two years or more.

Expectations, based on past experience, were a significant factor slowing the adjustment of supply to the shortage. In 2000–2003, demand for heavy-duty tires from equipment makers had dropped by more than 50%, leaving some tire makers with serious overcapacity. The fear that recent high demand might not last was leading some manufacturers to take a "wait-and-see" attitude.

Sources: *Financial Times*, Materials squeeze leads to tire shortage, By James Mackintosh Published: April 28 2005 03:00; *Light and Medium Truck Magazine*, May 2005, http://www.ttnews.com/lmt/May05/tire.asp (May 22, 2005); and *Rental Management Online*, http://www.rentalmanagementmag.com/newsart.asp?ARTID=1776, May 22, 2005.

QUESTIONS

1. Beginning from a position of equilibrium, use supply and demand curves to show how the tire market is affected by an increase in demand for earth-moving equipment. Does the supply curve shift? The demand curve? Both? Explain.

2. Using a scheme similar to Figure 2.10, distinguish between long-run and short-run supply in the tire market. What do you expect to happen to the price and quantity of tires in the short run? The long run?

3. Why are expectations a factor determining the position of the supply curve? How would the path of price and quantity over time differ with and without the element of supplier caution based on the experience of 2000–2003?

END NOTES

1. Before continuing, the reader may want to review the Chapter 1 appendix "Working with Graphs," especially the section entitled "Packing Three Variables into Two Dimensions."

2. The "plans" referred to need not be formal or thought out in detail, and are subject to change. A consumer might, for example, make out a shopping list for the supermarket based on the usual prices for various foods, but then revise it to take into account unexpected price increases or sales on certain items. On specific occasions, consumer decisions may even be completely impulsive, with little basis in rational calculation. The model of supply and demand does not require that every decision be based on precise analysis, but only that consumer intentions, on the average, are influenced by prices and other economic considerations.

3. Why might buyers and sellers enter the market expecting a price other than the one that permits equilibrium? It may be, for example, that market conditions have caused the supply or demand curve to shift unexpectedly, so that a price that formerly permitted equilibrium no longer does so. It may be that buyers or sellers expect conditions to change, but they do not change after all. Or, it may be that government policy has established a legal maximum or minimum price that differs from the equilibrium price. Later sections of the chapter will explore some of these possibilities.

4. This is a fairly restrictive assumption. In practice, a small number of housing units can move into or out of the rental market quickly in response to changing conditions. "Mother-in-law apartments" in private homes are an example. If conditions in the rental market are unfavorable, the owners of such units may simply leave them vacant. Allowing for such fast-reaction units means that the short-run supply curve, while still quite steep, would not be vertical. However, a vertical short-run curve simplifies the geometry while capturing the essential features of the situation.

CHAPTER 3

Supply, Demand, and Elasticity

After reading this chapter, you will understand:

1. How the responsiveness of quantity demanded to a price change can be expressed in terms of elasticity
2. How elasticity applies to situations other than the responsiveness of the quantity of a good demanded to a change in its price
3. How elasticity is useful in interpreting issues of taxation and other public policies

Before reading this chapter, make sure you know the meaning of:

1. Supply and demand
2. Demand, quantity demanded
3. Supply, quantity supplied
4. Substitutes and complements
5. Normal and inferior goods

How much did you pay for this textbook? Was it more expensive or less expensive than the books you buy for other courses? As a student, you probably have a strong desire to pay less for your books if you can. Have you ever wondered why your professor sometimes chooses books that are so expensive?

This chapter will help you understand the effect of price on choices that people make among alternative goods, like different textbooks, different foods, or different modes of transportation. It will focus on the concept of *elasticity*, a word economists use to say how sensitive such choices are to price. As a student, your choice of textbook is probably very sensitive to price—your demand is *elastic*, to use the economist's term. However, your professor, who does not pay for the books, cares less about how much they cost. Your professor's demand may be *inelastic*. In the following pages you will learn how to define, measure, and apply the important concept of elasticity.

ELASTICITY

The responsiveness of quantity demanded to a change in price can be expressed in many ways, depending on the units of measurement that are chosen. Consider the demand for chicken, an example used in the preceding chapter. A study of the budget of a single American household might find that an increase of ten cents per pound would decrease consumption by 1 pound per week. A study done in France might find that a price increase of 1 euro per kilogram decreased consumption of all consumers in the city of Lille by 25,000 kilos per month. Are the findings of these studies similar? It is hard to tell, because the units used are different. It would require more information, and some calculations, to know whether the sensitivity of demand to price as measured in different countries using different currencies, are the same. The same would be true of two studies in one country if one measured price in dollars per ton and tons per year, while the other used dollars per pound and pounds per week.

To avoid confusion arising from the choice of different units of measurement, it is useful to standardize. One common way of doing so is to express all changes as percentages. Suppose, for example, that the studies of both American and French consumers found that a 20 percent increase in price was associated with a 10 percent decrease in quantity demanded. These percentages would stay the same regardless of whether the original data were stated in dollars per pound, euros per kilo, or any other measurement.

The use of percentages to express the response of one variable to a change in another is widespread in economics. The term **elasticity** is used to refer to relationships expressed in percentages. Like equilibrium, elasticity is a metaphor borrowed from physics. Much as equilibrium calls to mind a pendulum that has come to rest hanging straight down, elasticity conjures up the image of a rubber band that stretches by a certain proportion of its length when the force applied to it is increased by a given percentage. This chapter introduces several applications of elasticity in economics.

Price Elasticity of Demand

We begin with the relationship between price and quantity demanded. The **price elasticity of demand** is the ratio of the percentage change in the quantity of a good demanded to a given percentage change in its price. Figure 3.1 presents five demand curves showing different degrees of price elasticity of demand. In part (a), the quantity demanded is strongly responsive to a change in price. In this case, a decrease in price from $5 to $3 causes the quantity demanded to increase from

Elasticity

A measure of the response of one variable to a change in another, stated as a ratio of the percentage change in one variable to the associated percentage change in another variable.

Price elasticity of demand

The ratio of the percentage change in the quantity of a good demanded to a given percentage change in its price, other things being equal.

FIGURE 3.1 **PRICE ELASTICITY OF DEMAND**

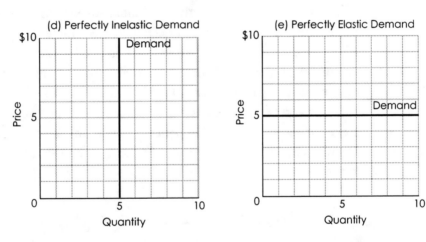

This figure shows five examples of demand curves with various degrees of elasticity over the indicated range of variation of price and quantity. The examples illustrate elastic, inelastic, unit elastic, perfectly inelastic, and perfectly elastic demand. For the first three cases, the revenue change associated with a change in price is shown. When demand is elastic, a price decrease causes revenue to increase. When demand is inelastic, a price decrease causes revenue to decrease. When demand is unit elastic, revenue does not change when price changes.

Revenue

Price times quantity sold.

three units to six. Because the percentage change in quantity demanded is greater than the percentage change in price, the drop in price causes total revenue from sales of the good to increase. **Revenue** is the price times the quantity sold. On a supply-and-demand diagram, revenue can be shown as the area of a rectangle drawn under the demand curve, with a height equal to price and a width equal to quantity demanded. In this case comparison of the shaded rectangles representing revenue before the price reduction ($5 per unit × 3 units = $15) and afterward ($3 per unit × 6 units = $18) shows that revenue is greater after the price has been reduced. When the quantity demanded changes by a greater percentage than price, so that a price decrease causes total revenue to increase, demand is said to be **elastic**.

Part (b) of Figure 3.1 shows a case in which the quantity demanded is only weakly responsive to a change in price. Here, a $2 decrease in price, from $5 to $3 per unit, causes the quantity demanded to increase by just one unit—from three to four. This time the percentage change in quantity demanded is less than that in price. As a result, the decrease in price causes total revenue to fall (again note the shaded rectangles). In such a case demand is said to be **inelastic**.

Part (c) shows a case in which a change in price causes an exactly proportional change in quantity demanded, so that total revenue does not change at all. When the percentage change in quantity demanded equals the percentage change in price, demand is said to be **unit elastic**.

The final two parts of Figure 3.1 show two extreme cases. Part (d) shows a vertical demand curve. Regardless of the price, the quantity demanded is five units—no more, no less. Such a demand curve is said to be **perfectly inelastic**. Part (e) shows a demand curve that is perfectly horizontal. Above a price of $5, no units of the good can be sold; but as soon as the price drops to $5, there is no limit on how much can be sold. A horizontal demand curve like this one is described as **perfectly elastic**. The law of demand, which describes an inverse relationship between price and quantity, does not encompass the cases of perfectly elastic and inelastic demand, and we do not expect market demand curves for ordinary goods and services to fit these extremes. Nevertheless, we will see that perfectly elastic and inelastic curves sometimes provide useful reference points for theory building, even though they do not resemble real-world market demand curves.

Calculating Elasticity of Demand

In speaking of elasticity of demand, it is often enough to say that demand is elastic or inelastic, without being more precise. At other times, though, it is useful to give a numerical value for elasticity. This section introduces the most common method used to calculate a numerical value for elasticity of demand.

The first step in turning the general definition of elasticity into a numerical formula is to develop a way to measure percentage changes. The everyday method for calculating a percentage change is to use the initial value of the variable as the denominator and the change in the value as the numerator. For example, if the quantity of California lettuce demanded in the national market is initially 10,000 tons per week and then decreases by 2,500 tons per week, we say that there has been a 25 percent change (2,500/10,000 = .25). The trouble with this convention is that the same change in the opposite direction gives a different percentage. By everyday reasoning, an increase in the quantity of lettuce demanded from 7,500 tons per week to 10,000 tons per week is a 33 percent increase (2,500/7,500 = .33).

Elastic demand

A situation in which quantity demanded changes by a larger percentage than price, so that total revenue increases as price decreases.

Inelastic demand

A situation in which quantity demanded changes by a smaller percentage than price, so that total revenue decreases as price decreases.

Unit elastic demand

A situation in which price and quantity demanded change by the same percentage, so that total revenue remains unchanged as price changes.

Perfectly inelastic demand

A situation in which the demand curve is a vertical line.

Perfectly elastic demand

A situation in which the demand curve is a horizontal line.

Decades ago the mathematical economist R. G. D. Allen proposed an unambiguous measure of percentage changes that uses the midpoint of the range over which change takes place as the denominator. Allen's formula is not the only possible one, but it caught on and remains the most popular.

To find the midpoint of the range over which a change takes place, we take the sum of the initial value and the final value and divide by 2. In our example, the midpoint of the quantity range is $(7,500 + 10,000)/2 = 8,750$. When this is used as the denominator, a change of 2,500 units becomes (approximately) a 28.6 percent change $(2,500/8,750 = .286)$. Using Q_1 to represent the quantity before the change and Q_2 to represent the quantity after the change, the midpoint formula for the percentage change in quantity is

$$\text{Percentage change in quantity} = \frac{Q_2 - Q_1}{(Q_1 + Q_2)/2}$$

The same approach can be used to define the percentage change in price. In our case, the price of lettuce increased from about $250 per ton to about $1,000 per ton. Using the midpoint of the range, or $625, as the denominator $[(\$250 + \$1,000)/2 = \$625]$, we conclude that the $750 increase in price is a 120 percent increase $(\$750/\$625 = 1.2)$. The midpoint formula for the percentage change in price is

$$\text{Percentage change in price} = \frac{P_2 - P_1}{(P_1 + P_2)/2}$$

THE MIDPOINT FORMULA FOR ELASTICITY   Defining percentage changes in this way allows us to write a useful formula for calculating elasticities. With P_1 and Q_1 representing price and quantity before a change, and P_2 and Q_2 representing price and quantity after the change, the midpoint formula for elasticity is

$$\text{Price elasticity of demand} = \frac{(Q_2 - Q_1)/(Q_1 + Q_2)}{(P_2 - P_1)/(P_1 + P_2)} = \frac{\text{Percentage change in quantity}}{\text{Percentage change in price}}$$

Here is the complete calculation for the elasticity of demand for lettuce when an increase in price from $250 per ton to $1,000 per ton causes the quantity demanded to fall from 10,000 tons per day to 7,500 tons per day:

P_1 = price before change = $250
P_2 = price after change = $1,000
Q_1 = quantity before change = 10,000
Q_2 = quantity after change = 7,500

$$\text{Elasticity} = \frac{(7,500 - 10,000)/(7,500 + 10,000)}{(\$1,000 - \$250)/(\$1,000 + \$250)}$$

$$= \frac{-2{,}500/17{,}500}{\$750/\$1{,}250}$$

$$= \frac{-.142}{.6}$$

$$= -.24$$

Because demand curves have negative slopes, this formula yields a negative value for elasticity. The reason is that the quantity demanded changes in the direction opposite to that of the price change. When the price decreases, $(P_2 - P_1)$, which appears in the denominator of the formula, is negative, whereas $(Q_2 - Q_1)$, which appears in the numerator, is positive. When the price increases, the numerator is negative and the denominator is positive. However, in this book we follow the widely used practice of dropping the minus sign when discussing price elasticity of demand. Thus, the elasticity of demand for lettuce would be stated as approximately .24 over the range studied.

A numerical elasticity value such as .24 can be related to the basic definition of elasticity in a simple way. That definition stated that price elasticity of demand is the ratio of the percentage change in quantity demanded to a given percentage change in price. Thus, an elasticity of .24 means that the quantity demanded will increase by .24 percent for each 1 percent change in price. An elasticity of 3 would mean that quantity demanded would change by 3 percent for each 1 percent change in price, and so on.[1]

ELASTICITY VALUES AND TERMINOLOGY   Earlier in the chapter we defined *elastic, inelastic, unit elastic, perfectly elastic,* and *perfectly inelastic* demand. Each of these terms corresponds to a numerical value or range of values of elasticity. A perfectly inelastic demand curve has a numerical value of 0, since any change in price produces no change in quantity demanded. The term *inelastic* (but not perfectly inelastic) *demand* applies to numerical values from 0 up to, but not including, 1. *Unit elasticity,* as the name implies, means a numerical value of exactly 1. *Elastic demand* means any value for elasticity that is greater than 1. *Perfectly elastic* demand, represented by a horizontal demand curve, is not defined numerically; as the demand curve becomes horizontal, the denominator of the elasticity formula approaches 0 and the numerical value of elasticity increases without limit.

Varying- and Constant-Elasticity Demand Curves

The midpoint formula shows elasticity of demand over a certain range of prices and quantities. Measured over some other range, the elasticity of demand for the same good may be the same or different, depending on the shape of the demand curve, as shown in Figure 3.2.

Part (a) of Figure 3.2 shows a demand curve that, like most of those in this book, is a straight line. The elasticity of demand is not constant for all ranges of price and quantity along this curve. For example, when measured over the price range $8 to $9, the elasticity of demand is 5.66; when measured over the range $2 to $3, it is .33. (The calculations are shown in the figure.)

The calculations illustrate the general rule that elasticity declines as one moves downward along a straight-line demand curve. It is easy to see why. With such a demand curve, a $1 reduction in price always causes the same absolute increase in quantity demanded. At the upper end of the demand curve, a $1 change is a small percentage of the relatively high price, while the change in quantity is a large percentage of the relatively low quantity demanded at that price. At the lower end of the curve, however, the situation is reversed: A $1 change is now a large percentage of the relatively low price, while the increase in quantity is smaller in relation to the relatively larger quantity demanded. Because it is percentages, not absolute amounts, that matter in elasticity calculations, a linear demand curve is less elastic near the bottom than near the top.

If the demand curve is not a straight line, other results are possible. There is an important special case in which the demand curve has just the curvature needed to keep elasticity constant over its entire length. Such a curve is shown in part (b) of Figure 3.2. As can be seen from the calculations in the figure, elasticity is 1.0 at every

FIGURE 3.2   ELASTICITY AT VARIOUS POINTS ALONG A DEMAND CURVE

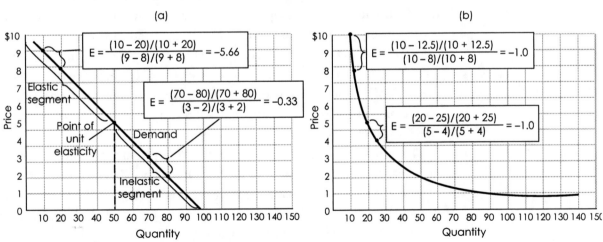

Elasticity varies along a straight-line demand curve, as part (a) of this figure illustrates. At the upper end of the curve, where the price is relatively high, a $1 change in price is a relatively small percentage change, and, because the quantity demanded is low, the corresponding change in quantity is relatively large in percentage terms. Demand is thus elastic near the top of the demand curve. At the lower end of the curve, the situation is reversed: a $1 change in price is now a relatively large change in percentage terms, whereas the corresponding change in quantity is smaller in percentage terms. Thus demand is inelastic. As part (b) shows, a curved demand curve can be drawn such that elasticity is constant for all ranges of price and quantity change.

point on that curve. It is possible to construct demand curves with constant elasticities of any value. Econometric studies of demand elasticity often look for the constant-elasticity demand curve that most closely approximates buyers' average sensitivity to price changes as revealed by market data over time.

Determinants of Elasticity of Demand

The fact that elasticity often varies along the demand curve means that care must be taken in making statements about *the* elasticity of demand for a good. In practice, what such statements usually refer to is the elasticity, measured by the midpoint formula or some alternative method, over the range of price variation that is commonly observed in the market for that good. With this understanding, we can make some generalizations about what makes the demand for some goods relatively elastic and the demand for others relatively inelastic.

SUBSTITUTES, COMPLEMENTS, AND ELASTICITY One important determinant of elasticity of demand is the availability of substitutes. When a good has close substitutes, the demand for that good tends to be relatively elastic, because people willingly switch to the substitutes when the price of the good goes up. Thus, for example, the demand for corn oil is relatively elastic, because other cooking oils can usually be substituted for it. On the other hand, the demand for cigarettes is relatively inelastic, because for a habitual smoker there is no good substitute.

This principle has two corollaries. One is that the demand for a good tends to be more elastic the more narrowly the good is defined. For example, the demand for lettuce in the numerical example given earlier was relatively inelastic. This could be because many people are in the habit of eating a salad with dinner and do not think of spinach or coleslaw as completely satisfactory substitutes. At the same time, however, it could be that the demand for any particular variety of lettuce is relatively elastic. If the price of Boston lettuce rises while the prices of iceberg, romaine, and red-leaf lettuce remain unchanged, many people will readily switch to one of the other varieties, which they see as close substitutes.

The other corollary is that demand for the product of a single firm tends to be more elastic than the demand for the output of all producers operating in the market. As one example, the demand for cigarettes as a whole will be less elastic than the demand for any particular brand. The reason is that one brand can be substituted for another when the price of a brand changes.

The complements of a good can also play a role in determining its elasticity. If something is a minor complement to an important good (that is, one that accounts for a large share of consumers' budgets), demand for it tends to be relatively inelastic. For example, the demand for motor oil tends to be relatively inelastic, because it is a complement to a more important good, gasoline. The price of gasoline has a greater effect on the amount of driving a person does than the price of motor oil.

PRICE VS. OPPORTUNITY COST   Elasticity measures the responsiveness of quantity demanded to the monetary price of a good. In most cases, the price, in money, is an accurate approximation of the opportunity cost of choosing a good, but that is not always the case. We mentioned one example at the beginning of the chapter: The price of a textbook is an opportunity cost to the student who buys it, but it is not an opportunity cost to the professor who assigns it, because the students pay for the book, not the professor. As a result, publishers have traditionally assumed that professors will pay little attention to the price of the text, and demand will be highly inelastic. However, in recent years students have increasingly been making their influence felt, so that price-elasticity of demand for textbooks may be increasing.

The textbook market is a relatively small one, but there are other much more important markets where the responsibility for choice does not lie with the party who bears the opportunity cost. Medical care provides many examples. Doctors choose what drug to offer to patients, but either the patient or the patient's insurance company pays for the drug. As a result, demand for drugs is very inelastic, and doctors sometimes prescribe expensive brand-name drugs when cheaper generic drugs are available to do the same job.

Business travel is still another example of the separation of price and opportunity cost. Business travelers do not pay for their own airline tickets, hotels, and meals, so their demand for these services tends to be inelastic. When vacationers purchase the same services, they bear the full opportunity cost themselves. Not surprisingly, business travelers often choose more expensive options. In many cases airlines and hotels take advantage of the separation of price and opportunity cost by charging different rates to business and vacation travelers.

TIME HORIZON AND ELASTICITY   One of the most important considerations determining the price elasticity of demand is the time horizon within which the decision to buy is made. For several reasons, demand is often less elastic in the short run than in the long run.

One reason is that full adjustment to a change in the price of a good may require changes in the kind or quantity of many other goods that a consumer buys. Gasoline provides a classic example. When the price of gasoline jumped in the early 2000s, many people's initial reaction was to cut out some nonessential driving, but the total quantity of gasoline demanded was not much affected. As time went by, though, consumers began adjust in many ways. One important adjustment, as mentioned in Chapter 1, was to buy fewer fuel-hungry SUVs and more higher-mileage cars. If this trend continues, the total amount of gasoline purchased could fall substantially.

Another reason elasticity tends to be greater in the long run than in the short run is that an increase in the price of one good encourages entrepreneurs to develop substitutes—which, as we have seen, can be an important determinant of elasticity. To take an example from history, consider the response to what has been called America's first energy crisis, a sharp increase in the price of whale oil, which was used as lamp fuel in the early nineteenth century. At first candles were the only substitute for whale-oil lamps, and not a very satisfactory one. People therefore cut their use of whale oil only a little when the price began to rise. But the high price of whale oil spurred entrepreneurs to develop a better substitute, kerosene. Once kerosene came onto the market, the quantity of whale oil demanded for use as lamp fuel dropped to zero.

A final reason for greater elasticity of demand in the long run than in the short run is the slow adjustment of consumer tastes. The case of beef and chicken, featured in the preceding chapter, provides an example. Chicken, originally the more expensive meat, achieved a price advantage over beef many years ago, but eating lots of beef was a habit. Gradually, though, chicken developed an image as a healthy, stylish, versatile food, and finally it overtook beef as the number-one meat in the United States.

Income Elasticity of Demand

Determining the response of quantity demanded to a change in price is the most common application of the concept of elasticity, but it is by no means the only one. Elasticity can also be used to express the response of demand to any of the conditions covered by the "other things being equal" assumption on which a given demand curve is based. As we saw in the preceding chapter, consumer income is one of those conditions.

Income elasticity of demand

The ratio of the percentage change in the quantity of a good demanded to a given percentage change in consumer incomes, other things being equal.

The **income elasticity of demand** for a good is defined as the ratio of the percentage change in the quantity of that good demanded to a percentage change in income. In measuring income elasticity, it is assumed that the good's price does not change. Using Q_1 and Q_2 to represent quantities before and after the change in income, and y_1 and y_2 to represent income before and after the change, the midpoint formula for income elasticity of demand can be written as follows:

$$\text{Income elasticity of demand} = \frac{(Q_2 - Q_1)/(Q_1 + Q_2)}{(y_2 - y_1)/(y_1 + y_2)} = \frac{\text{Percentage change in quantity}}{\text{Percentage change in income}}$$

For a normal good, an increase in income causes demand to rise. Because income and demand change in the same direction, the income elasticity of demand for a normal good is positive. For an inferior good, an increase in income causes demand to decrease. Because income and demand change in opposite directions, the income elasticity of demand for an inferior good is negative.

Some of the considerations that determine price elasticity also affect income elasticity. In particular, whether a good is considered to be normal or inferior depends on how narrowly it is defined and on the availability of substitutes. For example, a study by Jonq-Ying Lee, Mark G. Brown, and Brooke Schwartz of the University of Florida looked at the demand for frozen orange juice.[2] Orange juice considered as a broad category is a normal good; people tend to consume more of it as their income rises. However, when the definition is narrowed so that house-brand and national-brand frozen orange juice are treated as separate products, the house-brand product turns out to be an inferior good. As their incomes rise, consumers substitute the higher-quality national brands, which have a positive income elasticity of demand.

Cross-Elasticity of Demand

Cross-elasticity of demand

The ratio of the percentage change in the quantity of a good demanded to a given percentage change in the price of some other good, other things being equal.

Another condition that can cause a change in the demand for a good is a change in the price of some other good. The demand for chicken is affected by changes in the price of beef, the demand for SUVs by changes in the price of gasoline, and so on. Such relationships can be expressed as elasticities: The **cross-elasticity of demand** for a good is defined as the ratio of the percentage change in the quantity of that good demanded to a given percentage change in the price of another good. The midpoint formula for cross-elasticity of demand looks just like the one for price elasticity of demand, except that the numerator shows the percentage change in the quantity of one good while the denominator shows the percentage change in the price of some other good.

Cross-elasticity of demand is related to the concepts of substitutes and complements. Because lettuce and cabbage are substitutes, an increase in the price of cabbage causes an increase in the quantity of lettuce demanded; the cross-elasticity of demand is positive. Because SUVs and gasoline are complements, an increase in the price of gasoline causes a decrease in the quantity of SUVs demanded; the cross-elasticity of demand is negative. The previously mentioned study of frozen orange juice found a positive cross-elasticity of demand between house-brand and national-brand juices, indicating that the two are substitutes.

Price Elasticity of Supply

Price elasticity of supply

The ratio of the percentage change in the quantity of a good supplied to a given percentage change in its price, other things being equal.

Elasticity is not confined to demand; it can also be used to indicate the response of quantity supplied to a change in price. Formally, the **price elasticity of supply** of a good is defined as the percentage change in the quantity of the good supplied divided by the percentage change in its price. The midpoint formula for calculating price elasticity of supply looks like the one for determining price elasticity of demand, but the Qs in the numerator of the formula now refer to quantity *supplied* rather than quantity *demanded*. Because price and quantity change in the same direction along a positively sloped supply curve, the formula gives a positive value for the elasticity of supply. Figure 3.3 applies the elasticity formula to two supply curves, one with constant elasticity and the other with variable elasticity.

In later chapters we will look in detail at the considerations that determine the elasticity of supply for various products. Two of those considered are especially important, however, and deserve some discussion here.

One determinant of the elasticity of supply of a good is the mobility of the factors of production used to produce it. As used here, *mobility* means the ease with which factors can be attracted away from some other use, as well as the ease with which they can be reconverted to their original use. The trucking industry provides a classic example of mobile resources. As a crop such as lettuce or watermelons comes to har-

FIGURE 3.3   CALCULATING PRICE ELASTICITY OF SUPPLY

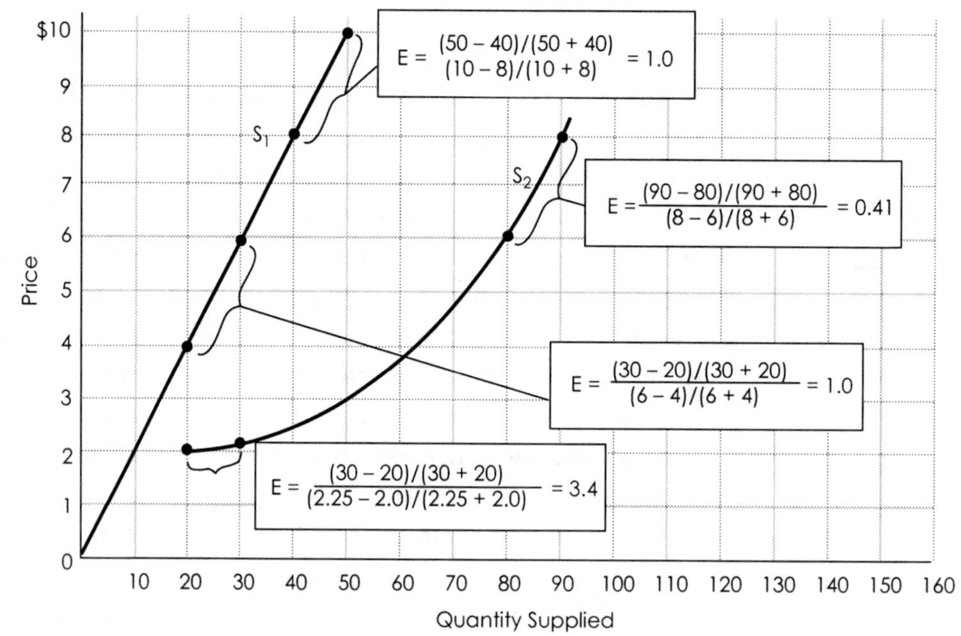

This figure gives four examples of the way price elasticity of supply is calculated. Price elasticity of supply is shown for two ranges on each of the two supply curves. Supply curve S_1 which is a straight line passing through the origin, has a constant elasticity of 1.0. Supply curve S_2, which is curved, is elastic for small quantities and inelastic for larger ones.

vest in a particular region of a country, hundreds of trucks are needed to haul it to market. Shippers compete for available trucks, driving up the price paid to truckers in the local market. Independent truckers throughout the country learn—from their own experience, from trucking brokers, and from Internet sites—where they can earn the best rates for hauling produce. It takes only a modest rise in the price for hauling a load of Georgia watermelons to attract enough truckers to Georgia to haul the crop to market. When the harvest is over, the truckers will move elsewhere to haul peaches, tomatoes, or whatever.

In contrast, other products are produced with resources that are not so mobile. Petroleum provides a good example. When oil prices rise, producers have an incentive to drill more wells. However, given limited numbers of drilling rigs and other highly specialized equipment, not to mention limited numbers of sites worth exploring, even a doubling of oil prices has only a small effect on oil output. Factor mobility in this industry is limited in the other direction, too. Once a well has been drilled, the investment cannot be converted to a different use. Thus, when world demand falls, as it did in 1998, prices fall sharply but the quantity of oil produced falls by much less than price.

A second determinant of elasticity of supply is time. As in the case of demand, price elasticity of supply tends to be greater in the long run than in the short run. In part, the reason for this is connected with mobility of resources. In the short run, the output of many products can be increased by using more of the most flexible inputs—for example, by adding workers at a plant or extending the hours of work. Such short-run measures often mean higher costs per unit for the added output, however, because workers added without comparable additions in other inputs (such as equipment) tend to be less productive. If a firm expects market conditions to warrant an increase of supply in the long run, it will be worthwhile to invest in additional quantities of less mobile inputs such as specialized plants and equipment. Once those investments have been made, the firm will find it worthwhile to supply the greater quantity of output at a lower price than in the short-run case because its costs per unit supplied will be lower. The Case for Discussion at the end of Chapter 2, which discussed the market for heavy-duty tires, provides an example of the difference between short-run and long-run elasticity of supply.

APPLICATIONS OF ELASTICITY

Elasticity has many applications in both macro- and microeconomics. In macroeconomics, it can be applied to money markets, to the aggregate supply and demand for all goods and services, and to foreign-exchange markets, to name just a few. In microeconomics, elasticity plays a role in discussions of consumer behavior, the profit-maximizing behavior of business firms, governments' regulatory and labor policies, and many other areas. To further illustrate elasticity, we conclude this chapter with applications featuring the problems of tax incidence and drug policy.

Elasticity and Tax Incidence

Who pays taxes? One way to answer this question is in terms of *assessments*—the issue of who bears the legal responsibility to make tax payments to the government. A study of assessments would show that property owners pay property taxes, gasoline companies pay gasoline taxes, and so on. However, looking at assessments does not always settle the issue of who bears the economic burden of a tax—or, to use the economist's term, the issue of **tax incidence**.

Tax incidence

The distribution of the economic burden of a tax.

The incidence of a tax does not always coincide with the way the tax is assessed, because the economic burden of the tax, in whole or in part, often can be passed along to someone else. The degree to which the burden of a tax may be passed along depends on the elasticities of supply and demand. Let's consider some examples.

INCIDENCE OF A GASOLINE TAX　　First consider the familiar example of a gasoline tax. Specifically, suppose that the state of Virginia decides to impose a tax of

$1 per gallon on gasoline beginning from a situation in which there is no tax. The tax is assessed against sellers of gasoline, who add the tax into the price paid by consumers at the pump.

Figure 3.4 uses the supply-and-demand model to show the effects of the tax. Initially, the demand curve intersects supply curve S_1 at E_1, resulting in a price of $2 per gallon. The supply curve is elastic in the region of the initial equilibrium. The elasticity of supply reflects the fact that we are dealing with the gasoline market in just one state; only a slight rise in the price in Virginia is needed to divert additional quantities of gasoline from elsewhere in the nation, because of the wide geographic reach of the wholesale gasoline market. The retail gasoline market is more local. If the price in Virginia rises, some consumers living near the border may cross a state line to fill up in Maryland or North Carolina, but most people will continue to fill up in Virginia. In the short run, they have only limited ways to save gas, such as cutting back on nonessential trips. As a result, demand for gasoline is less elastic than the supply in the region of the initial equilibrium.

The effect of the tax is to shift the supply curve to the left until each point on the new supply curve is exactly $1 higher than the point for the corresponding quantity

FIGURE 3.4   INCIDENCE OF A TAX ON GASOLINE

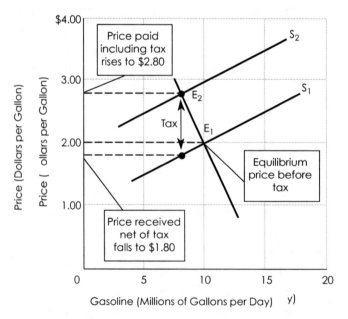

S_1 and D are the supply and demand curves before imposition of the tax. The initial equilibrium price is $2 per gallon. A tax of $1 per gallon shifts the supply curve to S_2. To induce sellers to supply the same quantity as before, the price would have to rise to $3. However, as the price rises, buyers reduce the quantity demanded, moving up and to the left along the demand curve. In the new equilibrium at E_2, the price rises only to $2.80. After the tax is paid, sellers receive only $1,80 per gallon. Thus, buyers bear $.80 of the tax on each gallon and sellers the remaining $.20. Buyers bear the larger share of the tax because demand, in this case, is less elastic than supply.

on the old supply curve. (We could instead say that the supply curve shifts *upward* by $1.) Because sellers must now turn over $1 to the state government for each gallon of gas sold, they would have to get $3 per gallon to be willing to sell the same quantity (10 million gallons per day) as initially. However, when sellers attempt to pass the tax on to motorists, motorists respond by reducing the amount of gas they buy. As the quantity sold falls, sellers move down and to the left along supply curve S_2 to a new equilibrium at E_2.

In the new equilibrium, the price is $2.80 per gallon—just $.80 higher than the original price. The new price includes the $1 tax, which sellers add to their net price of $1.80 per gallon—a net price that is $.20 less than before. The amount of the tax—$1 per gallon—is shown by the vertical gap between the supply and demand curves. The economic burden of the tax is divided between buyers and sellers, but in this case it falls more heavily on the buyers.

INCIDENCE OF A TAX ON APARTMENT RENTS   In the preceding example, the incidence of the gasoline tax falls more heavily on buyers than on sellers because demand is less elastic than supply. If the elasticities are reversed, the results will also be reversed, as can be seen in the case of a tax on apartment rents.

In Figure 3.5, the market for rental apartments in Ogden, Utah (a small city) is initially in equilibrium at $500 per month. The supply of rental apartments is inelastic. An increase in rents will cause a few new apartments to be built, whereas a reduction will cause a few to be torn down, but in either case the response will be moderate. On the other hand, demand is fairly elastic, because potential renters consider houses or condominiums a fairly close substitute for rental apartments.

Given this situation, suppose that the local government decides to impose a tax of $250 per month on all apartments rented in Ogden. This tax, like the gasoline tax, is assessed against landlords, who include the tax payment in the monthly rental they charge to tenants. As in the previous example, the tax shifts the supply curve to the left until each point on the new supply curve lies above the corresponding point on the old supply curve by the amount of the tax. (Again, we could instead say the supply curve shifts upward by the amount of the tax.) After the shift, the market reaches a new equilibrium at E_2. There the rental price paid by tenants rises to only $550 per month, as indicated by the intersection of the new supply and demand curves. Landlords succeed in passing only $50 of the $250 monthly tax along to tenants. Their net rental income, after turning over the tax receipts to the town government, is now just $300, down from $500 before imposition of the tax. In this case, because supply is inelastic and demand is elastic, suppliers bear most of the incidence of the tax and buyers only a little.

INCIDENCE AND TAX REVENUE   When the government considers imposing a tax on gasoline, cigarettes, apartments, or any other item, the price elasticity of demand and supply is important not only for how the burden is shared between buyers

FIGURE 3.5 INCIDENCE OF A TAX ON APARTMENT RENTS

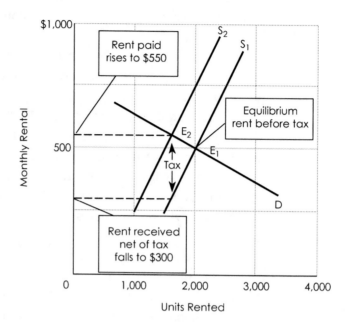

This figure shows the incidence of a tax imposed in a market in which supply is less elastic than demand. Initially, the equilibrium rent is $500 per month. A $250-per-month tax on apartment rents shifts the supply curve to S_2. The new equilibrium is at E_2. Landlords end up absorbing all but $50 of the tax. If they tried to pass more of the tax on to renters, more renters would switch to owner-occupied housing, and the vacancy rate on rental apartments would rise.

and sellers, but also for how much tax revenue the government collects. When buyers or sellers are more responsive to changes in price (when demand or supply is more elastic), a tax will generate less revenue for the government.

Figure 3.6 compares the markets for two items: milk and pork. The elasticities of supply are similar, but the price elasticities of demand differ. Pork has many obvious substitutes—beef, chicken, turkey, and other meats. Milk has few substitutes, so its demand is more inelastic. The markets for milk and pork are shown in Figure 3.6. The equilibrium price of milk is $0.50 per gallon and 12 million gallons are sold each year at this price. The milk market equilibrium is point E_1 on the left panel of Figure 3.6. The equilibrium (shown by the point E_1 on the right panel of Figure 3.6) is $0.75 per pound and 12 million pounds are sold each year.

Suppose now that the government imposes a $1.00 tax on each product. In the milk market, where demand is inelastic, the tax leads to a small decrease in the quantity, from 12 to 10 million gallons. The government collects $1.00 on each gallon of milk sold, for a tax revenue of $10 million on the 10 million gallons sold after the tax. In the market for pork, the tax leads to a larger reduction in the quantity people buy, from 12 to 6 million pounds. The government will collect a total of $6 million from the

FIGURE 3.6

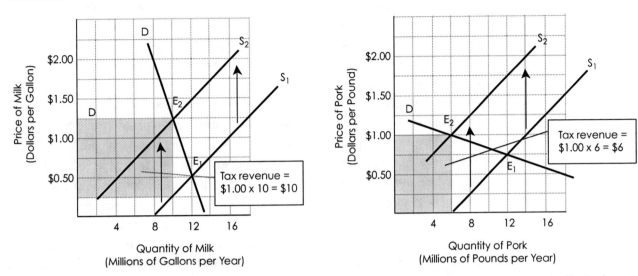

A tax imposed on a good that has an inelastic demand will generate more tax revenue than a tax on a good with elastic demand, assuming similar supply conditions. The diagrams above compare the effects of a $1.00 tax on the markets for milk (inelastic demand) and pork (elastic demand). In the market for milk, the tax reduces the equilibrium quantity by 2 million gallons, from point E_1 (12 million gallons) to E_2 (10 million gallons). Therefore, the government collects a total of $10 million from the milk tax. The same $1.00 tax on pork causes a large reduction in the quantity sold, from 12 million pounds (point E_1) to 6 million pounds (point E_2). This means the government will only collect $6 million, as only 6 million pounds of pork are sold at the new equilibrium.

tax on pork, collecting $1.00 on each of the 6 million pounds sold. When comparing the two taxes, the government collects more revenue from the tax on milk. Today, governments rely for most of their revenue on broad-based taxes like income taxes, sales taxes, and value-added taxes. In past centuries, however, taxes on individual goods were more important than they are now. In those days, taxes on goods with highly inelastic demand, like salt, tobacco, and matches, were especially popular.

Elasticity and Prohibition

In the case of gasoline and apartment rents, a tax led to a reduction in the quantity consumed, which we characterized as an unintended consequence of the tax. In a few cases, the reduction in quantity consumed may be an *intended* consequence of the tax. Modern taxes on tobacco products are one example: because tobacco is regarded as harmful, a reduction in quantity consumed is seen as desirable. Taxes on environmentally harmful products, such as the chemicals responsible for ozone depletion, are another example.

Prohibition is a more extreme policy aimed at reducing the quantity of a product consumed. Alcoholic beverages were subject to prohibition in the United States during the 1920s, and drugs like marijuana, heroin, and cocaine are subject to prohibition today. Prohibition is a common method of environmental regulation as well, with the pesticide DDT and lead additives for gasoline serving as examples.

On the surface, a policy of prohibition may seem very different from a tax, since unlike a tax, prohibition raises no tax revenue for the government. However, if we use economic analysis to look below the surface, we see some similarities as well as differences between taxation and prohibition.

First, passage of a law prohibiting production and sale of a good does not make it impossible to supply the good, but simply more expensive. After the prohibition is in effect, the supplier must consider not only the direct costs of production, but the extra costs of covert transportation and distribution systems, the risk of fines or jail terms, the costs of hiring armed gangsters to protect illegal laboratories, and so on. From the law-breaking supplier's point of view, these costs can be seen as an implicit tax. If the price rises by enough to cover them, the good will still be supplied. Thus, the effect of prohibition of a good is to shift its supply curve to the left until each point on the new supply curve lies above the corresponding point on the old curve by a distance equal to the extra costs associated with evading the prohibition.

Second, the effects of the prohibition, like those of a tax, depend on the elasticities of demand and supply. This is illustrated in Figure 3.7, which compares the effects of prohibition on the U.S. markets for DDT and cocaine. The demand for DDT is shown as relatively elastic, because fairly effective substitutes are available at a price only a little higher than the banned pesticide. The demand for cocaine is shown as relatively inelastic, in part because once people become addicted, they will be very reluctant to curtail their use of the drug even if its price rises sharply.

In the case of elastic demand for DDT (Figure 3.7a), even a weakly enforced prohibition, which raises costs of illegal supply only a little, will sharply reduce the quantity sold. Such a weak prohibition, represented by a shift in the supply curve from S_1 to S_2, is already enough to reduce the total revenue (price times quantity sold) earned by producers from $14,000 per week to $8,500 per week. A more vigorously enforced prohibition, as represented by supply curve S_3, raises the cost of supply by enough to eliminate use of the product altogether.

In the of case cocaine, with its inelastic demand, even a strongly enforced prohibition has relatively little effect on quantity sold. This case is represented in Figure 3.7b by a shift in the supply curve to S_2. Because quantity demanded is not much affected by the price increase, total revenue from the sale of cocaine rises substantially, from $130,000 per week at equilibrium E_1 to $300,000 per week at equilibrium E_2. As long as demand is inelastic, increasing strictness of enforcement, which drives the supply curve still higher, will make the sales revenue of drug suppliers increase still further.

Elasticity of demand is important in understanding the intended and unintended consequences of prohibition. The intended consequence, of course, is to reduce or eliminate use of the product. As we see, the more elastic the demand for the product, the more successful is the policy of prohibition in achieving its intended effects. The unintended effects of prohibition are those associated with

FIGURE 3.7 **ELASTICITY AND THE EFFECTS OF PROHIBITION**

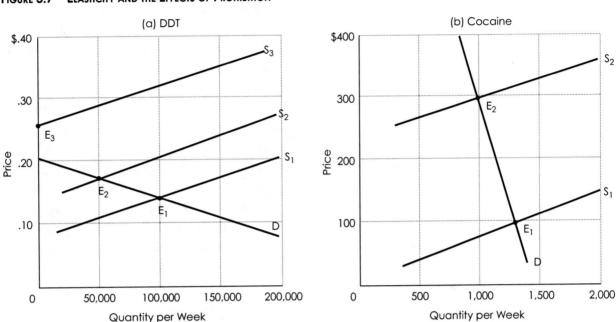

A law prohibiting production and sale of a good, like a tax on the good, shifts its supply curve to the left. The new supply curve will lie above the old supply curve at any given quantity by a distance equal to the cost of evading the prohibition. The effects on price, quantity, and revenue depend on the elasticity of demand. Part (a) uses DDT to illustrate prohibition of a good with elastic demand. A weakly enforced prohibition (S_2) raises the price, reduces the quantity, and reduces total revenue earned by producers from sale of the product. A strongly enforced prohibition reduces quantity and revenue to zero (S_3). Part (b) uses cocaine to illustrate prohibition of a good with inelastic demand. In this case, even strong efforts to enforce prohibition do not reduce quantity sold to zero. Because quantity sold increases by a smaller percentage than price increases, there is an increased total revenue and expenditure on the good.

the change in revenue that the policy produces. These are very different in the case of elastic and inelastic demand.

Where demand is elastic, the unintended consequences are a loss of profit to DDT producers, and a small rise in the cost of growing crops as farmers switch to more expensive pesticides. Neither has major social consequences. The loss of profit from producing DDT will be offset by profits from production of substitutes, very likely by the same companies. And the increased cost of growing crops is offset by the benefits of a cleaner environment.

On the other hand, where demand is inelastic, prohibition increases total expenditure on the banned product. The social consequences of this are severe. First, users of cocaine must spend more to sustain their habit. At best this means impoverishing themselves and their families; at worst it means an increase in muggings and armed robberies by users desperate for cash. Second, the impact of the prohibition on suppliers must be considered as well. For suppliers, the increase in revenue does not just mean an increase in profit (although profits may increase), but also an increase in expenditures devoted to evading prohibition. In part, the result is simply wasteful, as when drug suppliers buy an airplane to make a single one-way flight rather than using normal transportation methods. Worse, another part of suppliers' increased expenditures take the form of hiring armies of thugs to battle the police and other suppliers, further raising the level of violence on city streets, or bribing government officials, thereby corrupting the quality of government.

The issue of drug prohibition, of course, involves many normative issues that reach far beyond the concept of elasticity. One such issue is whether people have a right to harm themselves through consumption of substances such as tobacco, alcohol, or cocaine, or whether, instead, the government has a duty to act paternalistically to prevent such harm. Another concerns the relative emphasis that should be placed on prohibition versus treatment in allocating resources to reduce drug use. The analysis given here cannot answer such questions. However, it does suggest that the law of unintended consequences applies in the area of drug policy as elsewhere, and that elasticity of demand is important in determining the nature and severity of those consequences.

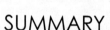

SUMMARY

1. **How can the responsiveness of quantity demanded to a price change be expressed in terms of elasticity?** *Elasticity* is the responsiveness of quantity demanded or supplied to changes in the price of a good (or changes in other factors), measured as a ratio of the percentage change in quantity to the percentage change in price (or other factor causing the change in quantity). The *price elasticity of demand* between two points on a demand curve is computed as the percentage change in quantity demanded divided by the percentage change in the good's price.

2. **How is the elasticity of demand for a good related to the revenue earned by its seller?** If the demand for a good is elastic, a decrease in its price will increase total revenue. If it is inelastic, an increase in its price will increase total revenue. When the demand for a good is unit elastic, revenue will remain constant as the price varies.

3. **How can elasticity be applied to situations other than the responsiveness of the quantity of a good demanded to a change in its price?** The concept of elasticity can be applied to many situations besides movements along demand curves. The *income elasticity of demand* for a good is the ratio of the percentage change in quantity demanded to a given percentage change in income. The *cross-elasticity of demand* between goods A and B is the ratio of the percentage change in the quantity of good A demanded to a given percentage change in the price of good B. The *price elasticity of supply* is the ratio of the percentage change in the quantity of a good supplied to a given change in its price.

4. **What determines the distribution of the economic burden of a tax?** The way in which the economic burden of a tax is distributed is known as the *incidence* of the tax. The incidence depends on the relative elasticities of supply and demand. If supply is relatively more elastic than demand, buyers will bear the larger share of the tax burden. If demand is relatively more elastic than supply, the larger share of the burden will fall on sellers. If the good is subject to prohibition rather than to a tax, elasticity of demand will determine how many resources are likely to be devoted to enforcement and evasion of the prohibition.

KEY TERMS

Elasticity

Price elasticity of
  demand

Revenue

Elastic demand

Inelastic demand

Unit elastic demand

Perfectly inelastic
  demand

Perfectly elastic demand

Income elasticity of
  demand

Cross-elasticity of
  demand

Price elasticity of supply

Tax incidence

PROBLEMS AND TOPICS FOR DISCUSSION

1. **Time horizon and elasticity.** Suppose a virus infects the California lettuce crop, cutting production by half. Consider three time horizons: (a) The "very short" run means a period that is too short to allow farmers to change the amount of lettuce that has been planted. No matter what happens to the price, the quantity supplied will be the amount already planted, less the amount destroyed by the virus. (b) The "intermediate" run means a period that is long enough to allow farmers to plant more fields in lettuce, but not long enough to permit them to develop new varieties of lettuce, introduce new methods of cultivation, or acquire new specialized equipment. (c) The "long" run means a period that is long enough to allow farmers to develop new varieties of virus-resistant lettuce and improve cultivation techniques. Discuss these three time horizons in terms of the price elasticity of supply. Sketch a figure showing supply curves for each of the time horizons. Which time horizon or horizons are relevant to the story at the beginning of the chapter?

2. **Calculating elasticity.** Draw a set of coordinate axes on a piece of graph paper. Label the horizontal axis from 0 to 50 units and the vertical axis from $0 to $20 per unit. Draw a demand curve that intersects the vertical axis at $10 and the horizontal axis at 40 units. Draw a supply curve that intersects the vertical axis at $4 and has a slope of 1. Make the following calculations for these curves, using the midpoint formula:

   a. What is the price elasticity of demand over the price range $5 to $7?

   b. What is the price elasticity of demand over the price range $1 to $3?

   c. What is the price elasticity of supply over the price range $10 to $15?

   d. What is the price elasticity of supply over the price range $15 to $17?

3. **Elasticity and revenue.** Look at the demand curve given in Figure 2.1 of the preceding chapter. Make a third column in the table that gives revenue for each price-quantity combination shown. Draw a set of axes on a piece of graph paper. Label the horizontal axis as in Figure 2.1, and label the vertical axis from 0 to $5 billion of revenue in increments of $1 billion. Graph the relationship between quantity and revenue using

the column you added to the table. Discuss the relationship of your revenue graph to the demand curve, keeping in mind what you know about elasticity and revenue and about variation in elasticity along the demand curve.

4. **Elasticity of demand and revenue.** Assume that you are an officer of your campus film club. You are at a meeting at which ticket prices are being discussed. One member says, "What I hate to see most of all is empty seats in the theater. We sell out every weekend showing, but there are always empty seats on Wednesdays. If we cut our Wednesday night prices by enough to fill up the theater, we'd bring in more money." Would this tactic really bring in more revenue? What would you need to know in order to be sure? Draw diagrams to illustrate some of the possibilities.

5. **Cross-elasticity of demand.** Between 1979 and 1981 the price of heating oil rose by 104 percent. Over the same period, use of fuel oil fell slightly while use of LP gas, another heating fuel, rose. Assuming that there was no change in the price of LP gas, what does this suggest about the cross-elasticity of demand for LP gas with respect to the price of fuel oil? Draw a pair of diagrams to illustrate these events. (Suggestion: Draw upward-sloping supply curves for both fuels. Then assume that the supply curve for heating oil shifts upward while the supply curve for LP gas stays the same.)

CASE FOR DISCUSSION

VP Asks Cigarette Firms for Sacrifice

Rendi A. Witular, *The Jakarta Post*, Jakarta, Indonesia, June 1, 2005

The lower profits cigarette-makers were likely to experience when the government raised the retail price on cigarettes should be viewed as a sacrifice to the state, [Indonesian] Vice President Jusuf Kalla said on Tuesday.

"The tobacco industry is one of the most profitable sectors in [Indonesian] business. Raising the (retail) rate won't affect tobacco firms much, since they will still be able to make a profit. Remember that cigarette prices here are still the lowest in the world," Kalla said.

By increasing the retail price of cigarettes the government planned to make more money on the excise duty it charged manufacturers, which was calculated on the final retail price.

The amount of the increase has not been finalized but last week the Minister of Finance Jusuf Anwar suggested it would be in the range of 15 to 20 percent. This extra revenue would help plug the state budget deficit that has increased in line with the rising costs of the government's fuel subsidy.

PT H. M. Sampoerna, the country's second-largest cigarette maker by sales, said that more than a 10 percent increase in the cigarette prices could hurt producers as it would affect sales.

Sampoerna is 98 percent-owned by U.S. cigarette giant Philip Morris International.

"Less than a 10 percent increase in the price is likely to be OK, but more (than that) could disturb sales," Sampoerna director Angky Camaro said after meeting Kalla earlier in the day.

Angky said the industry had not yet fully recovered from the aggressive excise rate hikes in 2002 and 2003, which had resulted in declines in the volumes of cigarette produced and lower profits across the board.

Last year, local cigarette company profits rose on increased consumption spurred on by higher general economic growth and the absence of any increases in excise duty.

The Indonesian Cigarette Producer Union (Gappri) estimates that some 141 million of the country's 220 million people are smokers.

Source: Rendi A. Witular, *The Jakarta Post*, Jakarta, Indonesia, June 1, 2005 (Downloaded June 5, 2005 from http://www.the jakartapost.com/yesterdaydetail.asp?field=20050601.L04).

QUESTIONS

1. On the basis of this article, do you think that price elasticity of demand for cigarettes in Indonesia is elastic, inelastic, unit elastic, perfectly elastic, or perfectly inelastic? Cite the specific passages supporting your conclusion, and note any apparent contradictions in the article.

2. According to the article, 64 percent of the people of Indonesia, where cigarette prices are among the lowest in the world, are smokers, compared to less than 25 percent in the United States, where prices are higher. What does this suggest about the price elasticity of demand for tobacco in the long run? Why might the long-run elasticity of demand for cigarettes be greater than the short-run demand?

3. According to Angky Camaro of Sampoerna, a tax increase that reduced quantity sold would hurt producers. Using a diagram similar to Figure 3.4, explain why this would be true even if the percentage decrease in quantity were less than the percentage increase in price.

4. According to the article, in 2004, cigarette sales increased as income increased, while taxes were unchanged. What does this tell you about the income elasticity of demand?

END NOTES

1. As we have said, the midpoint formula (also sometimes called *arc-elasticity*) is not the only one for calculating elasticity. A drawback of this formula is that it can give misleading elasticity values if applied over too wide a variation in price or quantity. Because of this limitation, it is often suggested that the midpoint formula be used only over fairly small ranges of variation in price or quantity. Following this reasoning to its logical conclusion, there is an alternative formula for calculating elasticity for a single point on the demand curve. For a linear demand curve having the formula $q = a - bp$ (with q representing quantity demanded, p the price, and a and b being constants), the *point formula* for elasticity of demand (stated, as elsewhere, as a positive number) is

$$\text{Elasticity} = bp/(a - bp).$$

2. Jonq-Ying Lee, Mark G. Brown, and Brooke Schwartz, "The Demand for National Brand and Private Label Frozen Concentrated Orange Juice: A Switching Regression Analysis," *Western Journal of Agricultural Economics* (July 1986): 1–7.

CHAPTER 4

Economic Theory, Markets, and Government

After reading this chapter, you will understand:

1. The basic structure of economic theory
2. Why rationality is of central importance in economics
3. The meaning of market performance and market failure
4. Some alternative theories of the economic role of government

Before reading this chapter, make sure you know the meaning of:

1. Positive and normative economics
2. Entrepreneurship
3. Law of unintended consequences
4. Supply and demand

T HE PRECEDING TWO chapters introduced the theory of supply and demand. The theory is a useful one, with immediate applications not only to microeconomics but to macroeconomics as well. However, before seeking further practical applications, or developing some of the more detailed theories that lie behind the deceptively simple concepts of supply and demand, it will be worth taking the time to ask some more general questions about the structure of economic theory, the reliability with which markets work, and the nature of the individuals and organizations that populate the economist's world. That will be the job of this chapter.

THE STRUCTURE OF ECONOMIC THEORY

To *analyze* something means to break it down into its component parts. A literary critic might analyze a novel in terms of such basic components as plot, character, and dialog. A detective might analyze a murder in terms of motive, means, and opportunity. Similarly, economists look for certain common elements when they analyze the choices people make in using scarce resources to meet their wants.

Objectives, Constraints, and Choices

The elements of which every economic theory is composed are three types of statements: statements about objectives, statements about constraints on opportunities, and statements about choices.

STATEMENTS ABOUT OBJECTIVES   An *objective* is anything people want to achieve. A business owner may have the objective of earning the greatest possible profit. A consumer may strive for the greatest possible material satisfaction with a given income. People in any situation may blend their pursuit of narrowly "economic" objectives with family values, social responsibilities, and so on. Terms such as *aims, goals,* and *preferences* are interchangeable with *objectives.*

STATEMENTS ABOUT CONSTRAINTS ON OPPORTUNITIES   A key part of every economic theory is a statement of the constraints on the set of opportunities that are available to choose among in a given situation. In a world of scarcity, alternatives are never unlimited, and constraints are universal. Some constraints relate to what is physically possible, given available resources and knowledge. Only so many bales of hay can be loaded into a truck that can hold 1,000 cubic feet of cargo. Only so many pounds of iron can be smelted from a ton of ore of a given quality.

Other constraints take the form not of physical limits but of opportunity costs, often defined in terms of prices. For example, there is no physical limit to the number of pairs of shoes a person can own, but if shoes cost $60 a pair and sweaters cost $30 apiece, each pair of shoes purchased means forgoing the opportunity to buy two sweaters (or something else of equal value).

Still other constraints take the form of legal rules. For example, it may be physically possible and worthwhile, in terms of costs and benefits, for a farmer to control insect pests by spraying DDT; however, it is illegal to do so. A particularly important set of legal constraints are those that define *property rights.* **Property rights** are legal rules that establish what things a person may use or control and the conditions under which that use or control may be exercised. In short, they establish what a person *owns.*

As an everyday example, consider the property rights that establish a person's ownership of a house. Those rights include the right to live in the house, to modify its structure, and to control the arrangement of furniture in its rooms. In some communities, ownership may include the right to park a boat trailer in the driveway and to have a swing set on the front lawn. In others, those particular rights may be limited by zoning laws or restrictive covenants.

Property rights

Legal rules that establish what things a person may use or control, and the conditions under which such use or control may be exercised.

Property rights extend to more abstract relationships as well. For example, ownership of a share of common stock in ConocoPhillips Corporation gives the stockholder a complex package of rights, including the rights to vote on issues affecting the firm and to share in the firm's profits. As another example, a software firm's copyright on a program it has produced gives it control over the conditions under which the program may be licensed for use by others.

STATEMENTS ABOUT CHOICES   The final component of an economic theory is a statement of the choice that is most likely to be made, given particular objectives and constraints on opportunities. For example, the next chapter will look at the choices that underlie the law of demand. There, consumers will be seen as having the objective of obtaining the greatest possible satisfaction, given the constraints placed on their opportunities by their budgets, the range of goods available, and the prices of those goods. Given those objectives and constraints, the law of demand states that people can be expected to choose to increase their purchases of a good when its price is reduced, other things being equal.

Economic Theory and Rationality

Although all economic theories contain the three types of statements just listed, a successful theory is more than just a list—its elements need to form a coherent whole. Our understanding of the structure of economic theory would be incomplete without a discussion of a key assumption that serves to hold the three elements of a theory together: the assumption that people choose the *best* way of accomplishing their objectives, given the constraints they face. In other words, people are *rational*.

Rationality

Acting purposefully to achieve an objective, given constraints on the opportunities that are available.

Rationality means acting purposefully to achieve an objective, given constraints on available opportunities. The concept of rationality is built into the definition of economics given at the beginning of this book, which speaks of choosing the best way to use scarce resources to meet human wants. To say that some ways of using scarce resources are better than others, and that those are the ones people tend to choose, is to express the essence of rationality.

The assumption of rationality, so central to economics, is sometimes misunderstood as a psychological or philosophical assertion about human nature—an assertion that people are always coolly calculating, not emotional or impulsive. A critic once ridiculed economists for seeing the human individual as a "lightning calculator of pleasures and pains, who oscillates like a homogeneous globule of desire under the impulse of stimuli . . . [who] spins symmetrically about his own spiritual axis until the parallelogram of forces bears down upon him, whereupon he follows the line of the resultant. "[1] But as used in economics, the rationality assumption has nothing to do with that sort of caricature of "economic man."

The rationality assumption, properly understood, is simply a tool for giving structure to theories about the choices people make. Economists then fill in the specifics of the structure by observing what people do in various situations, that is, what choices they make when faced with certain opportunities.

Consider a very simple example. Suppose Bundy Hall, a dormitory, and Carpenter Hall, where economics classes are held, are located at opposite corners of a grassy quadrangle in the middle of a college campus. Across the diagonal of the quad between Bundy and Carpenter, a well-worn path has been beaten into the grass. Why is the path there, even though there are perfectly good sidewalks around all four sides of the quad?

If you ask an economist that question, the answer you get will probably be something like this: "The student's objective is to minimize the time it takes to get to class so that they can sleep as late as possible. Of the alternative routes to class, the diagonal path is the shortest one, so that's the path they choose to take."

Most people would probably accept that theory as a reasonable explanation of the path across the quad. Why? First and most important, because it is consistent with the observation that the path is there and students use it. Second, adding to its appeal, the theory corresponds with our intuition about what we would do in the given situation. Although economists are wary of relying too heavily on their own experience to verify their theories, in practice introspection plays a significant role. Finally, our theory about the path across the quad is likely to be accepted partly because it is simple. Economists, like their colleagues in other social and natural sciences, tend to prefer simple theories to complex ones when both are consistent with given observations. (The preference for simple theories over complex ones is known as **Ockham's razor**, after a fourteenth-century philosopher who urged its use to "shave away" unnecessary theoretical complexities.)

Ockham's razor

The principle that simpler theories are to be preferred to more complex ones when both are consistent with given observations.

So far, so good. But suppose now that a transfer student arrives from another campus and says, "At Treelined University there is a big quad just like this one, and there is no diagonal path across it. Here's a picture to prove it. What do you say to that, O Wise Economist?"

This is not a far-fetched possibility. Observations that are inconsistent with previously accepted theories cross economists' desks frequently. When that happens, they look for a way to modify the theory so that it provides a rational basis for the new observation. Given the structure of economic theory, we can expect the search to take one of two directions.

First, closer investigation will often show that the original theory failed to allow for some *constraint* on the opportunities available to people in the situation under study. For example, it might be that the campus police at Treelined University have a nasty practice of slapping a $20 fine on any student caught walking on the grass. A modified theory is then formulated that takes this constraint into account: "Even when the shortest distance to class is a diagonal across the quad, a fine for walking on the grass will induce a certain percentage of students to take the sidewalk. The percentage taking the sidewalk will increase as the fine increases, so that with a sufficiently large fine, not enough students will take the shortcut to wear a path in the grass." This more general theory is consistent with observations made on both campuses.

Second, if closer investigation fails to turn up some previously unnoticed constraint on opportunities, it may turn out that the original theory was based on a mistaken understanding of the *objectives* of the people involved. In the case under discussion, it was assumed that students on both campuses placed a high priority on getting to class on time. However, perhaps the students of Treelined University take great pride in the appearance of their campus. They would rather be late to class than trample on the grass. Thus, there is a path on one campus and not on the other because students at the two schools rank their objectives differently.

Clearly differing choices can sometimes properly be attributed to differing objectives. For example, if Marcia buys pistachio ice cream while Mark buys chocolate ice cream, and the two flavors cost the same, we are comfortable concluding that their choices differ because their preferences do. However, as a rule, economists like first to see whether an explanation of different choices can be framed in terms of differing constraints on opportunities—prices, regulations, climate, and so on. If constraints are not checked first, explaining things in terms of differing preferences is simply too easy. Take, for example, the fact that people in the United States drive larger cars, on average, than people in Italy. Who would be satisfied just to say that Italians prefer little cars, without noting that drivers in Italy face different constraints—narrower streets, more expensive gasoline, and so on?

Something similar can be said about the rationality assumption. Just as economists are wary of relying too much on differences in preferences to explain choices, they are also wary of explaining choices in nonrational terms. Suppose, for example, that an economist sees a student, obviously late for class, who, instead of cutting across the quad or even hurrying around by the sidewalk, is walking slowly in circles in the middle of the grass. The economist questions the student, seeking a rational explanation. "Have you lost a contact lens? Are you exercising?" If an explanation cannot be found in terms of constraints and the rational pursuit of objectives, the economist is faced with a dilemma. One alternative would be to give up on studying this particular aspect of human behavior and call in some other specialist, perhaps a psychotherapist. The other would be to consider whether the concept of rationality itself needs to be rethought in order to understand what is going on. Increasingly, economists are choosing the alternative of rethinking the concept of rationality.

Full and Bounded Rationality

Full rationality

The assumption that people make full use of all available information in calculating how best to meet their objectives.

One way in which the rationality assumption can be modified is to distinguish full and bounded rationality.

Theories based on **full rationality** assume that people make full use of all available information in calculating how best to meet their objectives. The cost of making decisions, the possibility of error, and often, the cost of acquiring information are put to one side in theories based on full rationality.

Bounded rationality

The assumption that people intend to make choices that best serve their objectives, but have limited ability to acquire and process information.

On the other hand, some theories assume *bounded* rather than full rationality. To assume **bounded rationality** means to assume that people *intend* to make choices that best serve their objectives, but that they have limited ability to acquire and process information. They typically have to rely on partial information and use rules of thumb that do not make full use of the information they have.

For example, consider the task of choosing which university to attend. If college applicants strictly followed the assumption of full rationality, they would make full use of all sources of information available. They would carefully study the information on the Web site of every college in the country. On the basis of the information, they would outline preferred four-year programs of study at each school. They would systematically interview people who had attended all of the schools that rated near the top of their list and would perhaps visit those schools. Only when all information was in hand would they make a choice; in doing so, they might weigh such factors as the probable grades they would earn at each school, the influence of grades and choice of school on their lifetime incomes, and so on.

On the other hand, if applicants followed the assumptions of bounded rationality, they would conduct a more limited search. Perhaps they would arbitrarily limit their search in advance to schools from a certain region. They would listen to what friends and relatives said about schools they had attended and perhaps visit the nearest schools. Their final choice might be based more on advice from people they trusted and less on systematic balancing of objective information.

In the chapters that follow, we will encounter examples of theories based both on full and on bounded rationality.

Self-Regarding Versus Other-Regarding Preferences

Self-regarding preferences

A set of objectives that depend only on the material welfare of the decision maker.

Other-regarding preferences

A set of objectives that includes not only the material welfare of the decision maker, but also the material welfare of others and their attitudes toward the decision maker.

Another way to modify the assumption of rationality is to expand the definition of objectives to include human feelings like fairness, altruism, trust, spite, and envy. These feelings can be captured by distinguishing between **self-regarding** and **other-regarding** preferences. People who are concerned only with their own material welfare are said to have self-regarding preferences. People who balance considerations of their own material welfare with the welfare of others and also take into account what others think about them are said to have other-regarding preferences.

One simple example of other-regarding preferences is revealed in the "ultimatum game" described in *Applying Economic Ideas 4.1*. Results from repeated experiments around the world suggest that people often behave in ways that are better explained on the basis of other-regarding rather than strictly self-regarding preferences. Somewhat more controversial is the issue of whether to describe choices based on altruism, envy, and similar feelings as rational. The tendency in economics today seems to be toward expanding the concept of rationality in a way that allows for other-regarding preferences.

⇆ APPLYING ECONOMIC IDEAS 4.1

ULTIMATUMS, DICTATORS, AND OTHER GAMES

In recent years, games have become increasingly popular as a tool of economic research. One game that consistently produces results that contradict narrow definitions of economic rationality is the so-called *ultimatum game*.

The game works like this. Player A is given a sum of money, say $10. She is then asked to offer some share of the money to Player B. Next Player B has the option of accepting the offer or rejecting it. If B rejects A's offer, neither player gets to keep anything. If player B accepts, they divide the money according to the terms that A proposed. The name of the game comes from the fact that there is only one offer and only one chance to refuse—no extended bargaining is allowed, no repeated play during which an objective of developing a reputation or building trust might come into play.

Under the assumption of full rationality and self-regarding preferences, the outcome of the game is easy to predict. First, we conclude that Player B will never rationally reject any nonzero offer. To do so would give up a certain (although perhaps small) reward in favor of getting nothing at all. Second, we conclude that Player A, knowing that B will never reject any nonzero offer, no matter how small, will rationally make the smallest offer allowed. (Sometimes the rules might say this is one cent, sometimes one dollar, or whatever.)

But that is not at all what happens when the game is actually played. In practice, Player A typically offers a substantial amount, say 30 to 50 percent of the total. Furthermore, B typically rejects offers that are too low, with the frequency of rejection rising sharply for offers below 20 percent or so of the total. The experiment has been repeated thousands of times, not only with American college students but with African hunter-gatherers, Wall Street brokers, residents of Mongolia, and almost any group one can think of.

The average amount offered and the threshold for rejection differ somewhat from one society to another, but it seems that the narrowly rational result is never observed.

What is going on? One hypothesis is that, when placed in the Player A position, people behave altruistically. They take pleasure from pleasing Player B. Another hypothesis is that Player A is not altruistic, but rather, strategically motivated by the fear that a too-low offer will be rejected. But if so, what motivates Player B? Why are low offers rejected when there is nothing material to gain by doing so? Is B motivated by some innate aversion to inequality? By a spiteful desire to draw pleasure from punishing an insufficiently generous Player A?

One way to try to sort out the motives is to play the related *dictator game* with a similar group of subjects. In the dictator game, Player A gets to keep her share regardless of whether B accepts or rejects the offer. Since there is no fear of rejection, any nonzero offer must be motivated purely by altruism. Interestingly, although the dictator game typically produces smaller offers than the ultimatum game, the offers are still substantially above zero. Seemingly, both altruism and fear of rejection play a role.

There are many, many variants of the games. Sometimes the players are known to each other, sometimes anonymous. Sometimes the game is played in a "double-blind" form where neither the players nor the experimenter knows the individual identities of the players or amount specific individuals offer or reject. (The double-blind variant is supposed to eliminate the possibility that Player A might be ashamed of appearing "too selfish" in the eyes of the experimenter.) No matter what, the offers never fall to zero. Human behavior is stubbornly more complex than narrowly rational, self-regarding preferences can account for!

Richard H. Thaler of the University of Chicago suggests that including ideas like bounded rationality and other-regarding preferences will once again make economics more of a social science, as it was in the past. In the 19th and early 20th centuries, economists seemed comfortable with discussing emotional and psychological elements of economic behavior. As a preference for rigorous mathematical modeling came to dominate economics in the second half of the 20th century, these elements were eliminated. Almost all models of the period were based on full rationality and self-regarding preferences. While admitting that it is harder to construct models that incorporate the full range of human behavior, Thaler is hopeful that today's generation of economists are up to the task.[2]

MARKET PERFORMANCE AND MARKET FAILURE

Economic choices are not made in a vacuum. They are made within the context of a set of institutions, of which markets and government are two of the most important. This section offers a preview of what coming chapters will have to say about markets, especially the key concepts of *market performance* and *market failure*. The next section will preview the role of government in the economy.

Market Performance

Earlier, we defined a *market* as any arrangement that people have for trading with one another. When economists speak of **market performance**, then, they are referring to how efficiently markets do their job of providing arrangements for mutually beneficial trade.

Ideally, markets would make it possible to carry out every exchange that is to the mutual benefit of the parties involved. Suppose we are talking about the market for peaches. The parties to peach trading are farmers and consumers. An exchange will benefit consumers if the satisfaction they get from a peach is at least as great as the satisfaction they would get from spending the same amount on the next most attractive good (say, an apple). The exchange will benefit producers if the price paid for a peach is at least high enough to cover the opportunity cost of producing it. If there is a price that makes the trade beneficial both to consumers and to producers, then carrying out the trade will be *efficient* inasmuch as it will leave at least one party better off and neither worse off.

Although the details will require several chapters to work out, a simple diagram can give an intuitive idea of efficient market performance. Figure 4.1 shows two curves that represent the market for peaches. The demand curve represents the benefit of peaches to consumers as reflected by their willingness to buy peaches, given the price of peaches, the prices of alternative goods, and so on. The supply curve represents the opportunity costs of producing an additional peach as reflected by the willingness of farmers to produce and sell the product under given conditions.

At any point to the left of the intersection of the two curves, the price consumers would willingly pay for a peach (as indicated by the height of the demand curve) is greater than the minimum needed to cover farmers' costs (as indicated by the height of the supply curve). Thus, to the left of the intersection, trades carried out at any price between the two curves are mutually beneficial to consumers and producers. However, to the right of the intersection, the maximum consumers would find it worthwhile to pay for still more peaches is less than what is needed to cover farmers' costs. There is no price at which further trades would benefit both parties, and therefore production beyond the intersection point would not be efficient.

Market performance

The degree to which markets work efficiently in providing arrangements for mutually beneficial trade.

FIGURE 4.1 **PERFORMANCE OF THE MARKET FOR PEACHES**

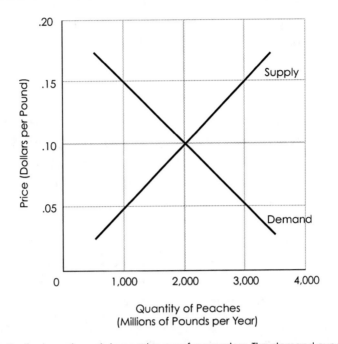

Quantity of Peaches
(Millions of Pounds per Year)

This exhibit shows hypothetical supply and demand curves for peaches. The demand curve reflects the willingness of consumers to buy peaches, given the price of peaches and the prices of alternative goods. The supply curve represents the willingness of farmers to sell peaches, given the price of peaches and the opportunity costs of production. At any point to the left of the intersection of the curves, the price that consumers would willingly pay for a peach (as indicated by the height of the demand curve) is greater than the minimum needed to cover farmers' costs (as indicated by the height of the supply curve). Thus, up to that point, exchanges carried out at a price between the two curves are mutually beneficial to consumers and producers. At any point to the right of the intersection, the maximum amount that consumers would be willing to pay for still more peaches is less than the amount needed to cover farmers' costs. Thus, production beyond the intersection point would not be efficient. It follows, then, that a market in which production is carried out just up to but not beyond the intersection point performs efficiently.

It follows, then, that a market in which production is carried out just up to but not beyond the intersection point performs efficiently. At a lower quantity, some mutually beneficial exchanges would not occur. At a higher quantity, no price could be found that would benefit both parties. Not only is the quantity indicated by the intersection of the two curves just right, but the price is, too. Any higher price would lead to a wasteful surplus of peaches, whereas any lower price would lead to a shortage in which some consumers' wants would not be satisfied.

It is hard to exaggerate the enthusiasm that economists have for markets that generate such efficient outcomes. From those pursuing economic reform in the nations of the former Soviet Union to candidates touting new solutions to problems of American capitalism, there is widespread agreement that within large areas of economic life, markets can be an efficient means of solving basic economic problems. Yet even the most enthusiastic fans of markets recognize that they do not always function perfectly. Several conditions must be met before markets reach a stable equilibrium exactly at the intersection of the supply and demand curves. Let's look briefly at some of the situations in which market performance falls short of the ideal, again leaving details to later chapters.

Market Failure

Market failure

A situation in which a market fails to coordinate choices in a way that achieves efficient use of resources.

A **market failure** is a situation in which a market fails to coordinate choices in a way that achieves efficient use of resources. Of the many possible sources of market failure, three deserve special attention. We will discuss them under the headings of *externalities, public goods,* and *insufficient competition.* Other sources of market failure will be mentioned more briefly.

EXTERNALITIES   One type of market failure is failure to transmit information about scarcity in the form of prices. For markets to perform their job efficiently, prices should reflect the opportunity costs of producing the goods or services in question. Ordinarily, market prices do reflect at least a reasonable approximation of opportunity costs. However, situations arise in which producers' (and consumers') actions have effects on third parties, that is, people other than the buyer and seller who carry out a transaction. These third-party effects, which are not reflected in prices, are known as **externalities**. When externalities are present, the price system does not transmit accurate information about opportunity costs.

Externalities

The effects of producing or consuming a good whose impact on third parties other than buyers and sellers of the good is not reflected in the good's price.

The classic example of an externality is pollution. Suppose a utility burns coal in its boilers to generate electricity. The costs of fuel, capital, and labor come to $.05 per kilowatt hour of electricity produced. They are called *internal costs* because they are borne by the utility itself. Those costs are reflected in market transactions—payments to coal producers, workers, stockholders and bondholders, and so on. Internal costs are part of the opportunity cost of making electricity because they represent the forgone opportunities of using the same natural resources, capital, and labor in some other industry. To stay in business, the utility must receive a price of at least $.05 per kilowatt hour, that is, a price at least equal to the internal opportunity costs.

But the internal costs are not the only costs of making electricity, as we saw in the case study at the beginning of the chapter. In the process of burning coal, the utility spews out clouds of sulfur dioxide, soot, and other pollutants. The pollution damages health, kills trees, and corrodes buildings in areas downwind from the plant. Those effects are referred to as *external costs* of generating electricity because they are borne by third parties—people who are neither buyers nor sellers of electricity or any of the inputs used in making it. From the viewpoint of the economy as a whole, external costs are also part of the opportunity cost of generating power. They represent the value of the factors of production that are destroyed by the pollution (such as dead trees or workers in other firms taking extended sick leave) or required in order to repair its effects (repainting houses, treating pollution-related diseases).

Suppose that pollution damage of all kinds comes to $.02 per kilowatt hour of power produced. Added to the $.05 in internal costs, the $.02 of external costs brings the overall opportunity cost of steel to $.07 per kilowatt hour. This figure reflects the value of the factors of production used directly by the utility plus those that are destroyed or diverted from other uses by the pollution.

If the price of electric power is set by supply and demand, its equilibrium value will tend toward the level of $.05 per kilowatt hour that just covers internal costs. But this sends a false signal to users of electricity: It tells them that producing a kilowatt hour puts a smaller drain on the economy's scarce factors of production than is really the case. Thus, electricity users will use more power than they should. They will be less inclined to buy new, more efficient machinery, to design products so as to use less electricity, to shift to cleaner natural gas, and so on. In short, the market will fail to achieve efficient resource allocation because prices will have sent users the wrong information.

In a later chapter, in which we return to the economics of pollution, we will see that externalities can be interpreted as defects in the economy's system of property rights. For example, air pollution arises because no one has clear ownership rights to air. If landowners had the right to control the use of air above their property, they could, in principle, prevent utilities and other pollution sources from using their airspace to dispose of wastes unless they were paid appropriate compensation. Following this reasoning, some economists advocate restructuring property rights to control pollution.

PUBLIC GOODS   The goods and services discussed in all the examples used to this point—chicken, cars, apartments, and so on—share two characteristics or *properties:* (1) The supplier can decide to supply the good to some people and to exclude others; this is termed the *property of exclusion.* (2) Use of a unit of the good by one person limits the possibility of use of that unit by other people; this is termed the *property of rivalry.* Some goods do not possess the properties of exclusion and rivalry, however. These are known as **public goods.** Lacking the property of exclusion, they cannot be provided for one person without also being provided for others. Lacking the property of rivalry, once they are provided for one person, they can be provided for others at no extra cost. Public goods, like externalities, are a potential source of market failure.

Perhaps the closest thing to a pure public good is national defense. One person cannot be protected against nuclear attack or invasion without the protection being extended to everyone. Also, it costs no more to protect a single resident of an area than to safeguard an entire city or region. Although pure public goods are rare, other goods may lack the properties of exclusion or rivalry to some extent. These can be called impure public goods. Police protection provides one example: In their functions of promoting public safety in general and deterring street crime, the police are providing a public good. But in their function of solving an individual crime, such as a burglary,

Public goods

Goods that (1) cannot be provided for one person without also being provided for others and (2) when provided for one person can be provided for others at zero additional sum.

they are providing a private good to the person who hopes to recover the stolen property. Maintenance of urban streets, the provision of parks, even the space program have been cited as examples of goods that are neither purely public nor purely private.

Private firms have difficulty making a profit selling products that, once they are provided to one customer, become available to others at no additional cost. To see why the market may fail in such cases, imagine that someone tries to set up a private missile defense system—call it Star Wars, Inc.—to be paid for by selling subscriptions to people who want protection from a nuclear attack. There are two reasons I might choose not to subscribe. First, I know that if my neighbors subscribed and got their homes protected, my home would be protected too, even if I did not pay; I could take a *free ride* on a public good paid for by others. Second, I might be willing to contribute if I had *assurance* that at least, say, 1,000 of my neighbors did so. That would raise enough money to buy at least one missile. But I would not contribute without the assurance that this minimum would be met. Contributing along with just 500 neighbors would buy only half a missile, which would be useless, and my contribution would be completely wasted.

Economists have long argued that the *free-rider problem* and the *assurance problem*, which make people reluctant to contribute voluntarily to the support of public goods, mean that government may have to provide those goods if they are to be provided at all. (We say *may* because, as *Applying Economic Ideas 4.2* illustrates, some things that have the characteristics of public goods are provided by private firms.) However, many goods and services that are provided at public expense are public goods only to a small extent, if at all. Take education, for example. The principal beneficiaries of public education are students. It is not impossible to exclude students from the schools. Only a few schools, public or private, operate on an "open admission" basis. Others select their students according to neighborhood, ability to pay, or scholastic achievement. Moreover, education clearly has the property of rivalry in consumption. Students cannot be added to a school without some additional expense. The more students a school admits, the more teachers, classrooms, laboratories, and other facilities it must provide. Thus, education fits the definition of a public good, if at all, only to the extent that it has some overall benefit such as promoting good citizenship.

INSUFFICIENT COMPETITION   A third source of market failure is insufficient competition. As we have seen, market prices should reflect opportunity costs if they are to guide resource allocation efficiently. In the case of harmful externalities, market failure occurs because prices fall below opportunity costs. Where competition is insufficient, however, market failure can occur because prices are too high.

As an extreme case, consider a market in which there is only a single seller of a good or service; such a market is termed a **monopoly**. Residential electric service is a frequently cited example. Suppose that Metropolitan Electric can generate power at an opportunity cost of $10 per kilowatt hour. Selling electric power at that price would guide customers in choosing between electricity and other energy sources,

Monopoly

A situation in which there is only a single seller of a good or service.

❧ APPLYING ECONOMIC IDEAS 4.2
PRIVATE PROVISION OF PUBLIC GOODS

Many economists argue that private firms cannot supply public goods because of the assurance and free rider problems that arise whenever goods have the properties of non-exclusion and nonrivalry. In practice, however, private firms and voluntary organizations often do find methods of providing goods that have these properties. Examples include broadcast radio and television, computer software, and amenities like streets and parks in residential neighborhoods.

In some cases private firms simply alter the product in a way that makes it possible to exclude free riders. Thus, television signals can be scrambled so that they can be received only by subscribers who rent a decoder; computer software can be copy protected so that the original purchasers cannot make free copies for their friends; and streets can be equipped with toll booths. In this case, the good ceases to be a public good, even though it continues to have the property of nonrivalry.

Exclusion has its disadvantages, however. The necessary technology may be expensive and less than fully reliable, and the attempt to exclude may be offensive to customers the firm would like to attract. To avoid these disadvantages, private firms and voluntary organizations often use other techniques to provide public goods.

- One approach is to link the public good to an ordinary good, offering the two as a package deal. Thus, public radio stations send their contributors magazines with movie reviews and program guides; computer software companies provide advice via telephone to legitimate registered purchasers; and real estate developers find it worthwhile to build residential streets as part of a package included with the sale of private homes.

- Another approach is to build on the psychological satisfaction of contributing to a good cause or the psychological discomfort of being recognized as a free rider. This works best in small communities where everyone knows everyone else. But organizations like public radio stations can achieve something of the same effect by publicly thanking contributors over the air.

- Still another device is the "assurance contract." Sometimes people hesitate to contribute to a good cause because they fear their contribution will be in vain unless others join them. In such a case, the provider can accept pledges of support that will be activated only if an agreed minimum of support is received. Thus, families might be asked to contribute checks to a fund to build a neighborhood playground on the understanding that the checks will be returned uncashed if the necessary minimum is not raised.

As these examples show, the economic category of "public good" does not always mean a good that must be provided by the government.

such as oil or coal, and in undertaking energy-saving investments, such as home insulation and high-efficiency lighting.

If homeowners could buy electricity from anyone they chose the way they buy eggs or gasoline, the forces of competition, acting through supply and demand, would push the market price toward the level of opportunity costs. The utility would not sell power at a price below opportunity costs because doing so would put it out of business. Further, in a competitive market any seller that tried to raise prices much above opportunity costs would be undercut by others.

However, utilities do not compete in selling to residential customers. Every home, after all, is connected to only one set of power lines. In this case, if not restrained by government regulation, a utility could substantially increase its profits by charging a price higher than opportunity costs. Of course, raising the price would mean that less power would be sold as customers moved up and to the left along their demand curves. But up to a point, the greater profit per kilowatt hour sold would more than outweigh the effects of the reduction in quantity demanded.

If too high a price is charged, homeowners will get a false message regarding the opportunity cost of electricity. They may make substitutions that are not economically justified. For example, they may switch from electricity to oil for heat even in regions where cheap hydroelectric power is available, or from electric air conditioning to gas air conditioning even in areas where the opportunity cost of electricity is below that of gas.

Market failures due to insufficient competition are not necessarily limited to the extreme case of monopoly. Under some circumstances, competition among a small number of firms may also lead to prices that are above opportunity costs, especially if the firms engage in collusion. The circumstances under which competition is or is not sufficient to ensure the efficient operation of markets is the subject of an enormous body of economic research and of more than a few controversies, as we will see in coming chapters.

OTHER MARKET FAILURES   Some economists would list other sources of market failure in addition to the three just discussed. For example, the macroeconomic phenomena of inflation and cyclical unemployment are sometimes considered to be market failures. Certainly, an economy that is subject to excessive inflation and unemployment provides a poor environment in which to coordinate the actions of buyers and sellers of individual goods and factor services. However, the effects of inflation and unemployment, together with policies intended to keep them under control, lie outside the scope of the microeconomics course.

As we have defined it, market failure means failure to achieve an *efficient* allocation of scarce resources. In addition, the market may or may not achieve an *equitable* allocation of resources. Whether unfairness, inequality, and economic injustice in a market economy should be given the label *market failure* is more a matter of terminology than of substance. In this book, market failure is defined in a way that makes it an issue of efficiency alone. But this definition is not meant to deny the importance of issues of economic justice. Such issues will be discussed extensively at several points in the following chapters, although not under the heading of market failure.

THE ECONOMIC ROLE OF GOVERNMENT

Although markets play an enormous role in answering the key questions of who, what, how, and for whom, not all economic decisions are made in markets. Some important economic decisions are made in hierarchies. Allocation of resources within a business firm is one example of hierarchical decision making; we will focus on that later. Here we are concerned with the role of government, the other major example of hierarchy in economics.

If we want to understand the microeconomic role of government, a good place to begin is by asking, Why does government play any role in the economy at all? Why, that is, cannot all decisions be made by households and private firms coordinating their actions through markets? Economists offer two answers, one based on the notion of market failure, the other on that of *rent seeking*. The answers are partly contradictory and partly complementary. Each will figure prominently in coming chapters, and each deserves a brief preview here.

The Market Failure Theory of Government

According to the market failure theory of government, the principal economic role of government is to step in where markets fail to allocate resources efficiently and fairly. Each type of market failure calls for a particular type of governmental intervention.

Take the case of pollution. Earlier we gave the example of a utility whose contribution to air pollution caused $.02 worth of damage for every kilowatt hour of electricity. Government can do a number of things to correct the resulting market failure, for example, it can require the utility to install pollution control equipment that will prevent poisonous gas from escaping into the atmosphere.

When markets fail to supply public goods, government also is called in. Often, as in the case of national defense, the government simply becomes the producer of the public good. In other cases, such as education, which some economists consider to be in part a public good, the government need not be the sole producer. Private schools and colleges are encouraged with subsidies and tax benefits to add to the supply of education produced by public institutions.

Government has attempted to remedy market failures arising from insufficient competition in a variety of ways. In some cases government uses *antitrust laws* to preserve competition by preventing mergers of competing firms, or even by breaking large firms up into a number of smaller ones. In other cases, such as the electric power industry, *regulation* is used to control prices charged by a monopoly firm. In a few cases, such as the Tennessee Valley Authority's electric power facilities, the government itself may become a monopoly producer of a good or service.

The Public Choice Theory of Government

The market failure theory of government is sometimes criticized for being more of a theory about what the government ought to do than about what it actually does. The problem, say the critics, is that too many government programs, rather than correcting market failures, seem to promote inefficiency or inequality in markets that would function well without government intervention. Price supports for milk are an example. That program holds the price of milk above its equilibrium level, thus causing persistent surpluses. That is hardly efficient. Further, although some benefits go to farmers who are in financial difficulty, thus serving the goal of fairness, many of the subsidies go to farmers who are financially well off.

Critics of the market failure theory maintain that government policies should be understood not in terms of broad social goals like efficiency and fairness but in terms

Public choice theory

The branch of economics that studies how people use the institutions of government in pursuit of their own interests.

Economic rent

Any payment to a factor of production in excess of its opportunity cost.

Political rent seeking (rent seeking)

The process of seeking and defending economic rents through the political process.

of how people use the institutions of government to pursue their own self-interest. This approach to policy analysis is known as **public choice theory**.

RENTS AND RENT SEEKING   One of the key concepts of public choice theory is *economic rent*. In everyday language, a *rent* is simply a payment made for the use of something, say, an apartment or a car. Public choice theorists use the term in a more specialized sense, however. An **economic rent** is any payment to a factor of production in excess of its opportunity cost. An example is the huge income a popular author like J. K. Rowling or Dan Brown earns from a new novel—an income much higher than the author could earn working the same amount time in any other line of work.

When rents are earned through competition in markets, they are called *pure economic profits*. Entrepreneurs are always on the lookout for earning such profits, for example, by introducing a new product superior to that of rival firms, or by being the first to implement a cost-saving production method. When they are successful, the income they earn may be substantially higher than what others are able to earn by employing similar factors of production in less imaginative ways.

Pure economic profit that entrepreneurs earn through private market activity is not the only category of economic rents, however. Firms, workers, and resource owners often turn to government in search of rents, rather than trying to outwit their rivals in the marketplace. A dollar earned through a government program that raises the price at which a firm sells its output or lowers the prices at which it buys its inputs is worth just as much as a dollar of profit earned through purely private efforts at innovation. In some cases it may even be better. Profits earned from innovation in a competitive market may be short lived because rivals will soon come out with an even better product or introduce an even cheaper production method. However, government regulations can not only create opportunities to earn rents but also shield those opportunities from competitors. Obtaining and defending rents through government action is known as **political rent seeking**, or often simply as **rent seeking**, with the political aspect implied.[3]

Consider the case of milk price supports, which, as we saw earlier, are hard to explain in terms of the market failure theory of government. Public choice theorists see this policy as a classic case of *political rent seeking*. Because a large portion of the benefits of price supports go to farmers who are not in trouble, broad-ranging programs generating rents for all farmers will draw much wider political support than programs more narrowly targeted only on needy farmers. Without the political support of the relatively prosperous farmers who draw the bulk of the subsidies, say public choice theorists, programs for farmers in trouble would not get the votes they need in Congress.

Government restrictions on competition are another way of generating rents. For example, tariffs and import quotas on clothing, cars, sugar, steel, and other products shield domestic firms and their employees from foreign competition. The firms thus are able to earn rents by raising prices above the competitive market level, and the employees are able to earn rents in the form of higher wages. Examples of government restrictions on competition can be found within the domestic economy as well. For example, licensing fees and examinations restrict the number of competitors who can enter such professions as law and medicine and often even such occupations as manicuring and hair styling.

FROM THE LAW OF UNINTENDED CONSEQUENCES TO GOVERNMENT FAILURE   The notion that government policies do not always promote efficiency and equity is not new. Economists have long been aware of the law of unintended consequences—the tendency of government policies to have effects other than those desired by their proponents. But public choice theory goes beyond the notion of unintended consequences, which could be traced simply to incomplete analysis on the part of policy makers. Rather, the element of rent seeking in the formulation of government policy suggests that there is a systematic tendency for government programs to cause rather than to cure economic inefficiencies—a tendency, that is, toward **government failure**.

In introducing the notion of government failure, public choice theorists do not intend to imply that government always makes a mess of things or that the market always functions perfectly; rather, they demonstrate that both the market and government are imperfect institutions. In deciding whether a given function is better performed by government or the market, the possibilities of government failure must be weighed against those of market failure.

Government failure

A situation in which a government policy causes inefficient use of resources.

ꙮ

SUMMARY

1. **What is the basic structure of economic theory?** Economic theories are constructed from statements about people's objectives, aims, and preferences; statements about the constraints on available opportunities; and statements about how people choose among the available opportunities so as to best meet their objectives.

2. **Why is rationality of central importance to economics?** To be rational means to act purposefully to achieve one's objectives, given the available opportunities. In some cases, economists assume *full rationality*, which means that they assume that people make full use of all available information in calculating how best to meet their objectives. In other cases, they assume *bounded rationality*, which means that they assume that people intend to make the choices that best serve their objectives, but have limited ability to acquire and process information. The assumption of rationality is sometimes further modified to allow for other-regarding as well as self-regarding preferences.

3. **What is the meaning of market performance and market failure?** *Market performance* refers to how efficiently markets do their job of providing arrangements for mutually beneficial trade. Ideally, markets would make it possible to carry out

every possible mutually beneficial trade, in which case they would operate perfectly efficiently. Sometimes, however, *market failure* occurs, in which case markets fail to carry out their job efficiently. *Externalities, public goods,* and insufficient competition (leading to *monopoly*) are among the most widely discussed sources of market failure.

4. **What are some alternative theories of the economic role of government?** According to the market failure theory of government, everything that markets can do efficiently should be left to them. Government should intervene only to correct market failures, whether narrowly or broadly defined. Another theory maintains that many government policies are not efforts to correct market failure but, instead, result from *political rent seeking*. Rent seeking refers to the process of seeking payments in excess of opportunity costs.

KEY TERMS

Property rights

Rationality

Ockham's razor

Full rationality

Bounded rationality

Self-regarding
   preferences

Other-regarding
   preferences

Market performance

Market failure

Externalities

Public goods

Monopoly

Public choice theory

Economic rent

Political rent seeking
   (rent seeking)

Government failure

PROBLEMS AND TOPICS FOR DISCUSSION

1. **Alternative path theories.** The chapter proposes a simple theory to explain the existence of a path

across a grassy area on a certain college campus. Here is another theory that might also explain the path: "Economics lectures are so boring that students prefer to be late to them. However, near the sidewalk on one side of the quad there is a beehive, and many students have suffered stings; and on the other side of the quad is the chemistry building, which smells bad when the wind blows a certain way. Sometimes if you cut across the middle of the quad, you find four-leaf clovers that give you good luck on your exams. Those are the reasons that there is a path across the quad." Applying the principle of Ockham's razor, which theory do you think is better? Why? Would you reject the more complex theory out of hand, or would you first want to make some observations? What observations would you make?

2. **Italians in America.** According to a theory suggested in the chapter, people drive smaller cars in Italy than in the United States not because of different preferences but because they face different constraints on their opportunities—higher gasoline prices, narrower streets, and so on. On the basis of that theory, what prediction would you make about the cars driven by Italians who move to the United States? What kind of observations would you suggest to test whether preferences or constraints are the key factor in the choice of car size?

3. **An alternate definition of economics.** David Friedman has said that economics can be defined as "that way of understanding behavior that assumes that people are rational." Compare Friedman's definition with the one presented in Chapter 1 of this book. What similarities or differences do you see?

4. **The economics of voting.** Did you vote in the most recent state or national election? If so, how was your choice of a candidate influenced by your objectives and constraints? If you did not

vote, was your decision not to vote influenced by objectives and constraints? Do you think your choice of a candidate (or your choice not to vote) was a rational one? Discuss.

5. **Government failure versus market failure.** When the possibilities of both government failure and market failure are taken into account, does the fact that a government policy causes inefficiency necessarily mean that abolishing the policy would result in greater efficiency? Does the fact that a certain market fails to work efficiently necessarily mean that intervention by government would improve the situation? Discuss.

CASE FOR DISCUSSION

A Price That's Too Good to Be Bad

Almost any aisle of any supermarket is a battleground in the never-ending war between house brands and national brands. The weapons of the national brands are advertising, reputation, and brand recognition. The big gun on the side of the house brands is price. One day recently, for example, shoppers at a Virginia Safeway store could take their choice of Johnson & Johnson baby powder for $3.29 or a can of Safeway brand at $2.59; of Kellogg's cornflakes at $1.97 per box or the house brand at $1.59; of Wesson vegetable oil at $4.59 per bottle or Safeway's product at $3.39 per bottle; or of Heinz distilled vinegar at $1.93 per quart or Safeway's Townhouse brand at $1.23.

What logic lies behind this competition? One's first thought might be that it all depends on the law of demand. If so, one would think, the lower the price of the house brand, the higher its sales relative to the national brand. But marketers of consumer products have found that the law of demand applies only up to a point in the competition between house brands and national brands. Paradoxically, a price that is *too* low can actually hurt the sales of the house brand.

Consider the case of Pathmark supermarkets' Premium All Purpose cleaner. This house brand product was designed to compete head-to-head with Fantastik, the leading national brand. The two products were chemically identical. The house brand's packaging mimicked that of the national brand. And Pathmark's product was priced at just $.89, versus $1.79 for Fantastik.

Yet, from its first introduction, Premium All Purpose cleaner was a slow seller. Frustrated Pathmark marketers even added a sticker to the label that said, "If you like Fantastik, try me!" But the sticker did not help. Finally Pathmark decided to drop the product.

What went wrong? Interviewed by *The Wall Street Journal,* Robert Wunderle, a spokesman for Supermarket General Corporation, Pathmark's corporate parent, blamed the failure on a price "so low that it discredited the intrinsic value of the product."

Many retailers consider it risky to price their house brands more than 20 to 25 percent below the national brand. But there are exceptions. If the product is so simple and familiar that consumers believe there can be no quality difference, it is safe to establish a bigger discount. Thus, for example, Safeway puts a bigger discount on its house brand vinegar and vegetable oil than on its house brand baby powder or cornflakes.

Peter Schwartz, president of Daymon Associates, Inc., a private-label research and marketing firm, explains the problem this way: "The further the distance from the national brand, the higher the credibility problem for consumers. Once you get outside the customer's comfort zone, the consumer psychology becomes, 'Gee, they must have taken it out in quality.' "

Source: Based in part on Alix M. Freedman, "A Price That's Too Good May Be Bad," *The Wall Street Journal,* November 15, 1988, B1.

QUESTIONS

1. Would you characterize the behavior of consumers who buy Fantastik brand cleaner instead of Pathmark's Premium All-Purpose cleaner as full rationality, irrationality, or bounded rationality? Explain.

2. The case suggests that in choosing among alternative brands of goods, consumers sometimes rely on the rule of thumb that higher prices tend to be associated with higher quality. From your own experience as a shopper, do you think that this rule of thumb is valid on the average? Valid always? Rarely valid? Give examples.

3. A consumer who followed the assumptions of bounded rationality would be most likely to apply the preceding rule of thumb, rather than seeking independent information on product quality, in purchasing which kinds of goods?

   a. Major purchases such as automobiles.

   b. Goods that are purchased frequently and can easily be inspected, such as clothing.

   c. Goods like household cleaners that are purchased infrequently constitute a small part of the consumer's budget and cannot easily be inspected or tested before purchase. Discuss why the rule of thumb is more reasonable in some cases than others, and give additional examples of each case.

END NOTES

1. Thorstein Veblen, "In Dispraise of Economists," in *The Portable Veblen*, ed. Max Lerner (New York: Viking Press, 1958), 232–233.

2. See Richard H. Thaler, "From Homo Economicus to Homo Sapiens," *Journal of Economic Perspectives*, Volume 14, No. 1 (Winter 2000): 133–141.

3. For a representative collection of papers on the theory of rent seeking, see James M. Buchanan, Robert D. Tollison, and Gordon Tullock, eds., *Toward a Theory of the Rent-Seeking Society* (College Station: Texas A&M Press, 1980).

CHAPTER 5

Consumer Choice

After reading this chapter, you will understand:

1. The elements involved in consumers' rational choices
2. How consumers balance their choices of goods and services to achieve an equilibrium
3. What lies behind the effect of a price change on the quantity of a good demanded
4. Why demand curves have negative slopes
5. Why both consumers and producers gain from exchanges
6. Why the burden of a tax exceeds the revenue raised by government

Before reading this chapter, make sure you know the meaning of:

1. Substitutes and complements
2. Normal and inferior goods
3. Incidence of a tax

THIS CHAPTER EXPLORES the theory of rational choice as applied to choices made by consumers. No doubt the first image that comes to mind when you read the words "consumer choice" is one of people filling their shopping carts in a supermarket. The theory of consumer choice does apply in a supermarket, but it is broader than that. It extends to choices involving health and safety, like whether to smoke or whether to wear a seatbelt when driving. It extends to life choices like whether to marry and have children. As we will see in this chapter, it applies to any scenario in which people make choices so as to obtain the most satisfaction they can in a situation of scarcity, given the alternatives and opportunity costs that they face. This chapter begins by outlining a theory of rational choice by consumers. Later, it will explore a number of applications of the theory, some of them quite ordinary, others more surprising.

UTILITY AND THE RATIONAL CONSUMER

Economic theories have a typical structure that can be described in terms of statements about objectives, constraints, and choices. Theories of consumer choice fit this pattern. The study of consumer choice thus gives us a chance to fill in the general structure of economic theory with some specific content.

Utility

We begin with the question of consumer *objectives*—why is it that people consume goods and services at all? The answer that people usually give when they think about their own motivations is that consumption of goods and services is a source of pleasure and satisfaction. A loaf of bread to eat, a warm bed to sleep in, a book to read—each serves a particular consumer want or need.

Economists use the term **utility** to refer to the pleasure or satisfaction people get from the consumption of goods and services. The term goes back some 200 years to the work of the eccentric English social philosopher Jeremy Bentham (1748–1832). Bentham, who studied English law and came to hate it, was obsessed with reforming the law in a way consistent with the principle of the "greatest good for the greatest number." He thought ordinary words such as *pleasure, satisfaction,* or *happiness* were too weak to convey the power of his vision of maximum bliss, so he coined the new word *utility* and established a quasi-religious movement called utilitarianism to promote the idea. Over the centuries, the term *utility* has lost the mystical overtones that it had for Bentham and his followers, but economists still use it in preference to its more ordinary synonyms when they refer to the objective that consumers pursue when choosing among goods and services.

Utility

The pleasure, satisfaction, or need fulfillment that people obtain from the consumption of goods and services.

Constraints on Opportunities

Having established utility as the objective, the next step in constructing the theory of consumer choice is to find a way of describing the constraints on the set of opportunities available to consumers. Those constraints encompass all the circumstances that, in a world of scarcity, prevent people from consuming all they want of everything they want.

The most important constraints are limits on the types of goods available, the prices of those goods, and the size of the consumer's budget. A restaurant menu provides a classic example of a constrained opportunity set. You may want tofu salad for lunch, but it is not on the menu. Among the dishes that are on the menu, your favorite might be the filet mignon, but the filet is $18 a serving, and your budget constrains you to spend no more than $5 on lunch. In the end, you settle for a cheeseburger.

To be sure, there are situations in which constraints other than budgets and market prices may be the most important ones. In choosing how fast to drive your car, the "price" (opportunity cost) of greater safety may be taking more time to get where you are going. In choosing a spouse, one constraint is the law that says you can be married to only one person at a time. Later in the chapter, we will look at some examples of nonmarket choices, but choices made in markets remain the central focus of consumer theory.

In constructing a theory of the choices consumers make to maximize utility within their budget constraints, we will proceed in two steps. First, we look at a traditional version of the theory based directly on the notion of utility; then we look at a more modern version in which utility plays a less explicit role.

Diminishing Marginal Utility and Consumer Choice

Jeremy Bentham's notion of "the greatest good for the greatest number" was anything but scientific. In the late nineteenth century, William Stanley Jevons and other economists, working independently, took a major step forward in their understanding of rational choice by consumers when they developed the principle of diminishing marginal utility (see *Who Said It? Who Did It? 5.1*). That step was based on the insight that most of the choices consumers make are not all-or-nothing matters (such as whether to take up smoking or to swear off smoking forever); instead, they are incremental decisions (such as whether to eat chicken one more time a month). Whenever economists refer to the effects of doing a little more or a little less of something, they apply the adjective *marginal*. Thus, the **marginal utility** of a good is the amount of added utility that a consumer gains from consuming one more unit of that good, other things being equal.

The most important principle arrived at by Jevons and others is that of **diminishing marginal utility**. According to this principle, the greater the quantity of any good consumed, the less the marginal utility derived from consuming one more unit of that good.

Let us look at how the principle of diminishing marginal utility can be applied to an everyday situation. Assume that you are seated at a lunch counter where pizza is being sold at a price of $2 for a rather skimpy slice and lemonade is being sold at a price of $1 for a small glass. You have $10 to spend on lunch. What will you order?

Your objective is to choose a lunch that will give you the greatest possible utility. Will you spend all your money to buy five pieces of pizza? Probably not. However much you like pizza, you will not get as much satisfaction out of the fifth piece as the first—at least not according to the principle of diminishing marginal utility. Probably you will be willing to pass up the fifth piece of pizza to have a couple of glasses of lemonade with which to wash the first four down. Doing so will increase your total

Marginal utility

The amount of added utility gained from a one-unit increase in consumption of a good, other things being equal.

Principle of diminishing marginal utility

The principle that the greater the consumption of some good, the smaller the increase in utility from a one-unit increase in consumption of that good.

❧ **WHO SAID IT? WHO DID IT? 5.1**

WILLIAM STANLEY JEVONS AND MARGINAL UTILITY THEORY

The English economist William Stanley Jevons is credited with the first systematic statement of the theory of marginal utility. Jevons was trained in mathematics and chemistry. With this background, it is not surprising that when his interest turned to economics he tried to restate economic theories in mathematical terms. It was this effort that led him to the theory of marginal utility.

In his *Theory of Political Economy*, published in 1871, Jevons set forth the principle of diminishing marginal utility:

Let us imagine the whole quantity of food which a person consumes on an average during twenty-four hours to be divided into ten equal parts. If his food be reduced by the last part, he will suffer but little; if a second tenth part be deficient, he will feel the want distinctly; the subtraction of the third part will be decidedly injurious; with every subsequent subtraction of a tenth part his sufferings will be

more and more serious until at length he will be upon the verge of starvation. Now, if we call each of the tenth parts an increment, the meaning of these facts is, that each increment of food is less necessary, or possesses less utility, than the previous one.

Jevons was the first economist to put the new theory into print, but he shares credit for the "marginal revolution" with at least three others who were working along the same lines simultaneously. The Austrian economist Carl Menger also published his version of marginal utility theory in 1871. Three years later, the Swiss economist Leon Walras, who was not aware of Jevons's or Menger's work, came out with still another version. Finally, Alfred Marshall worked out the basics of marginal utility theory at about the same time in his lectures at Cambridge, although he did not publish his version until 1890.

---

utility, because the first two lemonades will give you a lot of satisfaction and the last piece of pizza only a little. How about the fourth piece of pizza? Maybe you will be willing to give up half of it for one more glass of lemonade. As you cut back on pizza and increase your consumption of lemonade, the marginal utility of pizza rises and that of lemonade falls. Finally you get to the point at which you cannot increase your utility by spending less on one good and more on the other within a given budget. You have reached a point of **consumer equilibrium**.

You reach consumer equilibrium when the marginal utility you get from a dollar's worth of one good equals the marginal utility you get from a dollar's worth of the other. Another way to state this is that the ratio of the marginal utility of a good to its price must be the same for all goods. Thus:

Consumer equilibrium

A state of affairs in which a consumer cannot increase the total utility gained from a given budget by spending less on one good and more on another.

$$\frac{\text{Marginal utility of good A}}{\text{Price of good A}} = \frac{\text{Marginal utility of good B}}{\text{Price of good B}}$$

This formula can be applied using an imaginary unit of utility, the "util." Suppose, for example, that you have adjusted the quantities of pizza and lemonade you buy so that you get 10 utils from another slice of pizza at a price of $2 per slice and 5 utils from another glass of lemonade at a price of $1 per glass. At these ratios, you get no more added satisfaction from an extra dollar's worth (one half-slice) of pizza than from an extra dollar's worth (one glass) of lemonade. It is not worthwhile to trade off some of either good for some of the other. You are in consumer equilibrium.

On the other hand, suppose you get 18 utils from another slice of pizza (9 utils per half-slice) and 4 from another glass of lemonade, still given the same prices. Now you are not in consumer equilibrium. Cutting back by one lemonade would lose you just 4 utils. You could then use the dollar you saved to buy another half-slice of pizza, thereby gaining 9 utils. By making this adjustment in your consumption pattern, you would not only gain total utility, but also move closer to consumer equilibrium, because the marginal utility you would get from pizza would fall slightly as you consumed more and the marginal utility you would get from lemonade would rise a little as you consumed less.

Attaching numbers to things in this way helps explain the principle involved. Remember, though, that in practice consumer choice is a much more subjective process. Some people count calories when they sit down to lunch; some count the pennies in their pockets; but no one counts "utils"—they cannot really be counted. Utility is something we feel, not something we think about. Because some people feel differently about what they eat than others do, they make different choices. Perhaps you would rather have a cold squid salad and a glass of iced coffee than either pizza or lemonade. Although your choice might differ from someone else's, the logic of the decision—the calculation of utility, the concept of equilibrium—is the same.

From Consumer Equilibrium to the Law of Demand

The concepts of consumer equilibrium and diminishing marginal utility can be combined to give an explanation of the law of demand. The explanation, which is useful even though it is not entirely precise, goes as follows: Suppose you have adjusted your pattern of consumption until you have reached an equilibrium in which, among other things,

$$\frac{\text{MU of pizza}}{\$2} = \frac{\text{MU of lemonade}}{\$1}$$

As long as this equality holds, you will not benefit from increasing your consumption of pizza; doing so would soon push down the marginal utility of pizza. The marginal utility per dollar's worth of pizza would drop below the marginal utility per dollar's worth of lemonade, making you better off if you switched back to more lemonade.

But what if the price of pizza were to drop to, say, $1.50 per slice, upsetting the equality just given? To make the two ratios equal again, given the new price of pizza, either the marginal utility of lemonade would have to rise or that of pizza would have to fall. According to the principle of diminishing marginal utility, one way to get the marginal utility of pizza to fall is to consume more pizza, and one way to get the marginal utility of lemonade to rise is to consume less lemonade. Perhaps you would do a little of both—that is, cut back a little on lemonade and consume a little more pizza. In so doing, you would be acting just as the law of demand would predict: A decrease in the price of pizza would have caused you to buy more pizza.

This line of reasoning connects the law of demand with the principle of diminishing marginal utility in a way that appeals to common sense. However, that is not good enough for all economists. In the next section, we will look at an alternative line of reasoning.

SUBSTITUTION AND INCOME EFFECTS

In the view of some economists, the whole concept of utility is suspect because of its subjective, unmeasurable nature. Instead, they favor an explanation of the law of demand based on the concepts of substitution and income effects of a change in price. The two approaches to demand are, in a broad sense, consistent, but the explanation based on income and substitution effects avoids direct dependence on marginal utility and the measurement of utility.

The Substitution Effect

One reason people buy more of a good whose price falls is that they tend to substitute a good with a lower price for other goods that are relatively expensive. In our earlier example, we looked at the effects of a drop in the price of pizza. The change in price will cause people to substitute pizza for other foods that they might otherwise have eaten—hamburgers, nachos, whatever. Broader substitutions are also possible. With the price of pizza lower than before, people may substitute eating out for eating at home or a pizza party for an evening at the movies. The portion of the increase in the quantity demanded of a good whose price has fallen that is caused by the substitution of that good for other goods, which are now relatively more costly, is known as the **substitution effect** of a change in price.

Substitution effect

The part of the increase in quantity demanded of a good whose price has fallen that is caused by substitution of that good for others that are now relatively more costly.

The Income Effect

A second reason that the change in a good's price will cause a change in the quantity demanded has to do with the effect of price changes on real income.

In economics, the term *nominal* is used to refer to quantities measured in the ordinary way, in terms of the dollar prices at which transactions actually take place. The term *real* is used to indicate quantities that have been adjusted to take into account the effects of price changes. The distinction between real and nominal income is a typical application of these terms: If your monthly paycheck is $1,000, that is your nominal income—the number of dollars you earn. If your nominal income stays at $1,000 while inflation doubles the average prices of all goods and services, your *real* income—your ability to buy things taking price changes into account—will fall by half. If your nominal income stays at $1,000 while the average prices of goods and services drop by half, your real income will double.

In macroeconomics the distinction between real and nominal income is widely used in connection with inflation, which involves changes in the prices of many goods at once. But the distinction can also be applied in microeconomics, which tends to emphasize the effects of price changes for one good at a time. The reason is that if the price of even one good changes while the prices of other goods remain constant, there will be some effect on the average price level and, hence, on real income.

With this in mind, let us return to our example. Again suppose that the price of pizza falls while your nominal income and the prices of all other goods and services remain the same. Although pizza occupies only a small place in your budget, a fall in its price means a slight fall in the average level of all prices and, hence, a slight increase in your real income. If you continued to buy the same quantity of pizza and other goods and services as before, you would have a little money left over. For example, if the price of pizza goes down by $.50 a slice and you usually buy ten slices a month, you would have $5 left over after making your usual purchases. That is as much of an increase in your real income as you would get if your paycheck were increased by $5 and all prices remained constant.

The question now is: What will you spend the $5 on? The answer: You will use it to buy more of things that are normal goods. If pizza is a normal good, one of the things you will buy with your increased real income is more pizza. The portion of the change in quantity demanded of a good whose price has fallen that is caused by the increase in real income resulting from the drop in price is known as the **income effect** of the price change.

Income effect

The part of the change in quantity demanded of a good whose price has fallen that is caused by the increase in real income resulting from the price change.

Income and Substitution Effects and the Demand Curve

In the case of a normal good, the income effect is an additional reason for buying more of a good when its price falls. With both the income and substitution effects causing the quantity demanded to increase when the price falls, the demand curve for a normal good will have a negative slope. We can reach this conclusion with no reference to the awkward concept of utility. So far, so good.

If we are dealing with an inferior good, however, the situation is a little different. Let us say that hot dogs are an inferior good for you. You eat them if you are hungry and they are all you can afford, but if your income goes up enough to buy pizza, you phase out hot dogs. Now what will happen if the price of hot dogs goes down while the prices of all other goods and services remain constant?

First, there will be a substitution effect. Hot dogs now are relatively cheaper compared with lemonade, pizza, pretzels, haircuts, or whatever. Taken by itself, the substitution effect will cause you to buy more hot dogs. Other things (including real income) being equal, the rational consumer will always buy more rather than less of something when its opportunity cost (in this case, its price relative to other goods) goes down. But here other things are not equal. At the same time that the fall in the price of hot dogs tempts you to substitute hot dogs for other things, it also raises your real income slightly. Taken by itself, the increase in your real income would cause you to buy fewer hot dogs because hot dogs are an inferior good for you. Thus, in the case of an inferior good, the substitution and income effects work at cross-purposes when the price changes.

What, then, is the net effect of a decrease in the price of hot dogs? Will you buy more or fewer of them than before? In the case of a good that makes up only a small part of your budget, such as hot dogs, it is safe to assume that a fall in price will cause you to buy more and a rise in price to buy less. The reason is that a change in the price of something of which you buy only a little anyway will have only a miniscule income effect, which will be outweighed by the substitution effect. Thus, when the substitution effect is larger than the income effect, the demand curve for an inferior good will still have a negative slope.

However, there is a theoretical possibility that the demand curve for an inferior good might have a positive slope. For this to be the case, the good would have to make up a large part of a person's budget so that the income effect would be large. Imagine, for example, a family that is so poor that they spend almost all of their income on food, and almost the only foods they can afford to buy are bread and oatmeal. They eat bread as a special treat on Sunday, but the rest of the week they must make do with inferior-tasting but cheaper oatmeal. One day the price of oatmeal goes up, although not by enough to make it more expensive than bread. The rise in the price of oatmeal is devastating to the family's budget. They are forced to cut out their one remaining luxury: The Sunday loaf of bread disappears and is replaced by oatmeal. The paradoxical conclusion, then, is that a rise in the price of oatmeal causes this family to buy more, not less, oatmeal. The family's demand curve for oatmeal has a positive slope. A good that has a positively sloped demand curve for such reasons is called a **Giffen good** after a nineteenth-century English writer, Robert Giffen, who supposedly mentioned the possibility.[1]

The conditions required for a positively sloped demand curve—an inferior good that makes up a large portion of the consumer's budget—are very special. Such conditions are unlikely to be encountered in the markets in which people usually conduct transactions. If you are in the pizza business—or even in the oatmeal business—you can be virtually certain that, taking the world as it really is, raising the price of any good or service will cause people to buy less of it and cutting the price will cause them to buy more of it. The Giffen-good phenomenon has been demonstrated under carefully controlled experimental circumstances, however, as reported in *Applying Economic Ideas 5.1*. And nothing in the pure logic of rational choice disproves the possibility of such a situation occurring in an actual market situation.

Giffen good

An inferior good accounting for a large share of a consumer's budget that has a positively sloped demand curve because the income effect of a price change outweighs the substitution effect.

Applications of Income and Substitution Effects

The law of demand and the concepts of income and substitution effects can be applied to any situation in which a consumer seeks to maximize utility in the face of established alternatives and constraints, even when the "goods" in question are not "for sale," and even when constraints and the opportunity costs of the available alternatives are not stated in money. This section will look at some of the wider applications of the theory of consumer choice.

⌐ APPLYING ECONOMIC IDEAS 5.1

TESTING CONSUMER DEMAND THEORY WITH WHITE RATS

Traditionally, most empirical work in economics uses observation of actual market behavior as its data source. In recent years, however, a growing number of economists have engaged in laboratory experimentation. Many of the experiments involve students as their subjects. For example, a group of students might simulate the operation of a stock exchange, with shares of stocks exchanged for tokens or pennies.

The use of human subjects in economic experiments has its limitations, however. For one thing, it is hard to get subjects to agree to participate in long-term experiments that might change their whole way of life. Moreover, human subjects inevitably are aware that they are participating in an experiment. This awareness might affect their behavior. To get around these drawbacks, economists John Kagel of the University of Houston and Ray Battalio of Texas A&M have used animal subjects in economic experiments for several years. These experiments have borne out many of the predictions of consumer choice theory in the laboratory.

For example, in one experiment, two white male rats were placed in standard laboratory cages, with food and water freely available. At one end of each cage were two levers that activated dipper cups. One dipper cup provided a measured quantity of root beer when its lever was depressed; the other provided a measured quantity of nonalcoholic Collins mix. Previous experimentation had shown that rats prefer these beverages to water.

Within this setup, each rat could be given a fixed "income" of so many pushes on the levers per day. The pushes could be distributed in any way between the two levers. Experimenters could also control the "price" of root beet and Collins mix by determining the number of pushes the rat had to "spend" to obtain one milliliter of liquid.

In an initial experimental run lasting two weeks, the rats were given an income of 300 pushes per day, and both beverages were priced at 20 pushes per milliliter. Under those conditions, rat 1 settled down to a pattern of drinking about 11 milliliters of root beer per day and about 4 milliliters of Collins mix. Rat 2 preferred a diet of almost all root beer, averaging less than one milliliter of Collins mix per day.

Once the initial conditions were established, the experimenters were ready to see how the rats would respond to changes in prices and incomes. First, the price (in pushes per milliliter) of root beer was doubled and the price of Collins mix was cut in half. At the same time, each subject's total income of pushes was adjusted to make it possible for each to afford to continue the previous consumption pattern if it were chosen. (That adjustment in total income was made in order to

eliminate any possible income effect of the price change and to concentrate solely on the substitution effect.) Economic theory predicts that under the new conditions the rats would choose to consume more Collins mix and less root beer than before, even though their income would be sufficient to maintain the original pattern of consumption if they chose to do so.

The rats' behavior exactly fitted these predictions. In two weeks of living under the new conditions, rat 1 settled down to a new consumption pattern of about 8 milliliters of root beet and 17 milliliters of Collins mix per day. Rat 2, which had chosen root beer almost exclusively before, switched over to about 9 milliliters of root beer and 25 milliliters of Collins mix.

Another experiment focused on income effects. In this case, the two liquids chosen were root beer, which rats love, and quinine water, which they are more reluctant to drink. At the beginning of the experiment, the price of root beer was set at twice the price of quinine water. If the rats' income of pushes per day was kept low, they would drink some of the relatively cheap quinine water along with some of the more expensive root beer. As their income was raised, they would switch away from quinine water toward more root beer. The conclusion: For rats, root beer is a normal good and quinine water an inferior good.

Having established that quinine water was an inferior good, Kagel and Battalio set out to see if they could demonstrate the Giffen-good effect. That effect requires an inferior good that also accounts for a large part of the subject's total expenditures. To produce these conditions, the rats were kept in "poverty." Their budget was kept so low that without drinking a fair amount of quinine, they would become dehydrated.

Without changing the total budget of pushes, the price of quinine water was then reduced. If they maintained their previous consumption pattern, the rats would have pushes left over. What would they spend the extra pushes on? Root beer, of course. Being able to afford more root beer, the rats could now cut back on their consumption of quinine without risking dehydration. The net result: Cutting the price of quinine with no change in nominal income (pushes per day) caused the rats to drink less quinine. For impoverished rats, quinine water is a true Giffen good.

Sources: The root beer–Collins mix experiment is reported in John H. Kagel and Raymond C. Battalio, "Experimental Studies of Consumer Demand Behavior," *Economic Inquiry* 8 (March 1975): 22–38, Journal of the Western Economic Association. Reprinted with permission. Kagel and Battalio's root beer–quinine experiment is summarized in Timothy Tregarthen, "Found! A Giffen Good," *The Margin* (October 1987): 8–10.

The Demand for Safety

Let's begin with an example from the field of automobile safety. When you get into a car to go somewhere, you face a trade-off between travel time and safety. A quick trip is good, but so is a safe one. Making the trip safer by driving more slowly, stopping for yellow lights, and so on has an opportunity cost in terms of time. Cutting travel time by driving faster and going through yellow lights has an opportunity cost in terms of safety.

If the opportunity costs change, the choices drivers make also tend to change. For example, suppose there is snow on the road; that makes the road less safe and raises the opportunity cost of speed. When it snows, then, drivers slow down and shift their choices away from speed in the interest of safety, just as the substitution effect would predict.

A change in the design of cars to make them safer, for example by adding seat belts as was done starting in the 1960s and air bags as in the 1990s, also changes the opportunity cost of speed relative to that of safety. Cutting travel time by speeding up and running yellow lights entails giving up less safety in a car with seat belts or air bags than in one without those devices. Because the opportunity cost of speed is lower in a safer car, logically the substitution effect would cause people to drive faster and less carefully. Does this really happen? In a classic 1975 study, economist Sam Peltzman reported evidence that it does. In a stunning example of the law of unintended consequences, he reported that while drivers who wore seat belts increased their own safety, they drove faster and less carefully, with the result being that they killed more pedestrians and bicyclists.[2]

Some studies have found an income effect as well as a substitution effect on driving behavior. Robert W. Crandall and John D. Graham suggest that safety is an inferior good. It seems that as people's incomes go up, they begin to feel that their time is too valuable to spend in a car. Perhaps they speed up so they can get to their high-paying jobs or fashionable parties more quickly. If they decide to run a greater risk of killing themselves and others along the way—well, that is part of the logic of consumer choice. Maybe people with less exciting destinations have less reason to be in a hurry.

Children as Durable Consumer Goods

University of Chicago economist Gary Becker, winner of the 1992 Nobel Memorial Prize for economics, has made his reputation by applying economic reasoning to areas of choice that many people think of as noneconomic. Some of his best-known research concerns choices made within the family. As an example, consider Becker's analysis of the number of children a family chooses to have.

Children, in Becker's view, are durable consumer goods. They return benefits to parents over many years in such forms as love, family pride, and mowing the lawn. But there are opportunity costs associated with having children. Those costs include the goods and services forgone to pay the extra grocery bills, clothing bills, and doctors' bills for the children. But in Becker's view, the biggest opportunity cost of having children is the time parents spend caring for them. That time, too, has an opportunity cost. Time not spent caring for children could be spent working to earn income. Thus the higher the parents' earning power, the greater the opportunity cost of having children.

What does this imply about the number of children a family chooses to have? It has been widely observed in many societies that as family income rises, the number of children per family tends to fall. Does this mean that children are inferior goods? Not at all, says Becker. Children are normal goods; other things being equal, the income effect would cause a family to want more children as its income increases. But other things are not equal. As Becker notes, there is also a substitution effect because, if the higher income reflects a higher hourly wage, it increases the opportunity cost of each hour spent caring for children. On the average, the substitution effect outweighs the income effect, so higher-income families end up having fewer children.

As confirmation of his analysis, Becker notes that the income and substitution effects can be partially distinguished by looking separately at the effects of changes in men's and women's incomes. Traditionally, women perform a greater proportion of child care than men. In a family where this is the case, an increase in a woman's income would have a stronger substitution effect than an increase in a man's income. The reason is that, in such a family, a woman with a high income would encounter a high opportunity cost for each hour taken off from work to devote to child care, whereas, by assumption, the man would take few hours off for child care regardless of his income. Empirical data in fact reveal such a pattern to be prevalent: Birth rates tend to vary directly with incomes earned by men because the income effect outweighs the relatively weak substitution effect. But birth rates vary inversely with incomes earned by women, who experience a relatively stronger substitution effect.

And what is it that parents substitute for a greater quantity of children when their incomes rise? Some, no doubt, substitute ski vacations in Austria, BMWs, and other luxuries. But, Becker notes, they have another reaction as well, one that is consistent with the theory of consumer choice. In place of a greater number of children, he says, upper-income families substitute investment in higher-quality children: piano lessons from the age of five; tutors to help cram for SAT exams; tuition payments to Yale Law School. It's all so *rational,* says Becker.

CONSUMER SURPLUS

This chapter has related consumer choice to the demand curve from two perspectives—that of utility theory and that of income and substitution effects. In both cases, the demand curve was viewed as answering the question, How much of a good will consumers wish to purchase at any given price? In this section, we turn to a different question to which the demand curve also can provide an answer: How much will consumers be willing to pay for an additional unit of a good given the quantity they already have?

The Demand Curve as Willingness to Pay

Figure 5.1 shows a demand curve for apples for a college student, Hannah Lee. Lee stocks up on snack foods at a local supermarket and often includes apples in her purchases. The demand curve given in the figure shows that the number of apples she eats each month depends on their price. Currently the price of an apple is $.40. At this price, she buys ten per month. On other days she substitutes an orange or a banana.

The demand curve indicates that $.40 is the maximum that Lee would be willing to pay for the tenth apple. If the price rose to $.45, she would substitute some other fruit for the tenth apple. However, she would not cut out apples altogether. Although $.40 is the maximum she is willing to pay for the tenth apple, she would not give up the ninth apple unless the price rose above $.45. Similarly, she would be willing to pay up to $.50 before giving up the eighth apple, up to $.55 before giving up the seventh, and so on. The height of the demand curve at each point (emphasized here by a vertical bar) shows the maximum that she would willingly pay for each unit consumed. That maximum decreases as the quantity consumed increases, in accordance with the principle of diminishing marginal utility.

Measuring the Surplus

Figure 5.1 shows the maximum that Lee is willing to pay for various quantities of apples, but it also shows that she need not actually pay this amount. At the going price of $.40, she pays only a total of $4 for the ten apples she buys each month. Except in the case of the last unit purchased, she gets each unit for less than what she would willingly have paid for it. The difference between what she would willingly have paid for each unit and the amount actually paid at the market is called the **consumer surplus** for that unit. The consumer surplus on each unit is shown by the shaded portion of the corresponding vertical bar. For example, the surplus on the first apple, for which Lee would have willingly paid $.85 if necessary, is $.45, because she actually paid only $.40. The total consumer surplus on all units purchased is shown by the sum of the shaded portions of the bars. The area of the triangle between the demand curve and the market price is an approximate measure of consumer surplus.[3]

Consumer surplus

The difference between the maximum that a consumer would be willing to pay for a unit of a good and the amount that he or she actually pays.

Consumer Surplus, Producer Surplus, and Gains from Exchange

The reasoning behind the notion of consumer surplus can be extended to the producers' side of the market as well. Consider Figure 5.2, which shows a typical market operating according to principles of supply and demand. The equilibrium market price is established at the point where the supply and demand curves cross. The demand curve, as we have seen, measures the maximum amount that consumers would be willing to pay for each unit sold; for example, they will pay no more than

FIGURE 5.1   CONSUMER SURPLUS

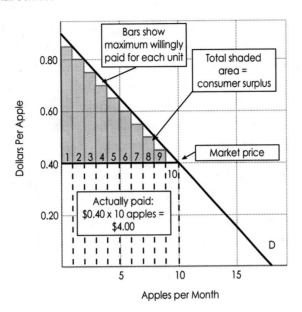

The height of a demand curve shows the maximum that this consumer would be willing to pay for an additional unit of a good. For example, she would be willing to pay up to $.85 for the first apple bought each month but only $.55 for the seventh. The maximum she would willingly pay for each unit is shown by a vertical bar. In this case, the market price is $.40; thus, she buys 10 apples a month, paying a total of $4.00. The difference between what she actually pays at the market price and the maximum she would have been willing to pay, shown by the shaded area, is called consumer surplus.

$1.50 for the one thousandth unit. Consumer surplus is a measure of the difference between the maximum that consumers would have been willing to pay and what they actually pay at the market price.

Now turn to the supply curve. The height of the supply curve at any point represents the minimum that producers would willingly accept for the unit. For example, producers would be unwilling to accept less than $.75 for the one thousandth unit sold. If they could not get at least that much, the producers would divert their resources to an alternative use rather than produce the one thousandth unit of this product.

However, as the figure is drawn, producers receive the market price of $1 per unit for all units sold, including the one thousandth. On that unit, they earn a producer surplus of $.25. The **producer surplus** earned on each unit is the difference between the market price and the minimum that the producers would have been willing to accept in exchange for that unit—the difference between $1 and $.75 for the one thousandth unit in our example. The total producer surplus earned on all units is shown by the area between the supply curve and the market price.

We see, then, that the concept of surplus in the market is symmetrical. Consumers buy the goods, except for the very last unit, for less than the maximum

Producer surplus

The difference between what producers receive for a unit of a good and the minimum they would be willing to accept.

amount they would have been willing to pay, and producers sell the goods, except for the very last unit, for more than the minimum amount they would have been willing to accept. Thus, *both buyers and sellers gain from exchange.* That is why markets exist. As long as participation is voluntary, they make everyone who buys and sells in them better off than they would be if they did not participate. Assuming an equilibrium at the intersection of the supply and demand curves, as in Figure 5.2, the total of the mutual gains from exchange—consumer surplus plus producer surplus—is equal to the entire shaded triangle between the supply and demand curves to the left of their intersection point.

Application: The Excess Burden of a Tax

Figure 5.3 provides an application of the concepts of consumer and producer surplus to the effects of a price of a tax on gasoline. Imposing a $.50-per-gallon tax on gasoline shifts the supply curve upward by that amount and raises the equilibrium price,

FIGURE 5.2   GAINS FROM EXCHANGE

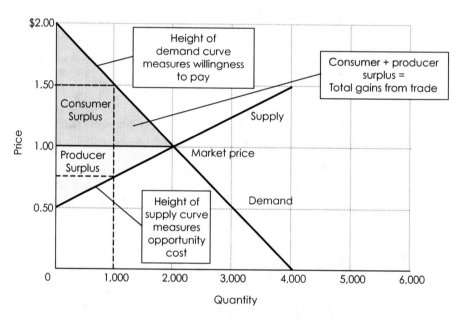

This figure shows that both consumers and producers gain from exchange. Here the equilibrium market price is $1 per unit. The demand curve shows the maximum that consumers would willingly pay for each unit. Consumers' gain from exchange takes the form of consumer surplus, shown by the area between the demand curve and the market price. The supply curve shows the minimum that producers would willingly accept rather than put their resources to work elsewhere. Producers earn a surplus equal to the difference between what they actually receive at the market price and the minimum they would have been willing to accept. The producer surplus is shown by the area between the supply curve and the market price. Assuming an equilibrium is reached at the point of intersection of the two curves, total gains from exchange are thus the entire area between them up to the intersection.

including tax, from $1 to $1.40 per gallon. The price received by sellers, after tax, falls from $1 to $.90 per gallon.

The concepts of consumer and producer surplus offer additional insight into the issue of tax incidence beyond those we gain by looking at price changes alone. Figure 5.3 shows that the tax brings in $4 million per day in revenue to the government. This equals the after-tax quantity Q_2, which is 8 million gallons, times the amount of the tax, which is $.50 per gallon. Part of that revenue is paid by consumers at the expense of the consumer surplus they otherwise would have earned by being able to buy 8 million gallons at $1 rather than at $1.40. Part is paid by suppliers at the expense of the producer surplus they would have earned by being able to sell 8 million gallons at $1 rather than at $.90. The sum of that part of the consumers' burden and that part of the producers' burden is equal to the tax revenue collected by the government.

However, there is an additional burden on consumers and producers that is not reflected in the government's revenue from the tax. That burden is associated with the reduction in quantity purchased from 10 million to 8 million gallons per day because of the tax. Consumers would have enjoyed a surplus on the extra 2 million gallons

FIGURE 5.3 EXCESS BURDEN OF A TAX

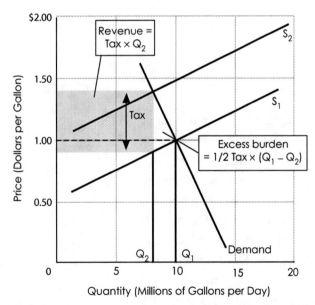

Imposition of a tax of $.50 per gallon on gasoline raises the equilibrium price from $1 to $1.40 per gallon. The price that sellers receive after the tax is paid falls to $.90. Revenue collected by the government equals the tax times Q_2, the equilibrium quantity after tax. The economic burden of the revenue is divided between consumers and sellers. There is also an *excess burden*, which takes the form of the consumer and producer surpluses that would be realized from the sale of the additional quantity that would have been sold without the tax. This is shown by the area of the triangle between the supply and demand curves and between the pretax quantity, Q_1, and the after-tax quantity, Q_2.

equal to the triangle above the pretax price of $1 between Q_1 and Q_2; producers would have enjoyed a surplus equal to the triangle below the pretax price between Q_1 and Q_2. The lost consumer-plus-producer surplus is called the **excess burden of the tax**.

Excess burden of the tax

The part of the economic burden of a tax that takes the form of consumer and producer surplus that is lost because the tax reduces the equilibrium quantity sold.

The common sense behind this is that the tax imposes a burden on consumers and producers that is larger than the amount the government takes in as revenue. It does so because the tax discourages buyers and sellers from doing as much business as they would have done without the tax. The potential mutual gain from pushing exchange in the gasoline market all the way out to 10 million gallons per day is lost. In geometric terms, the size of the excess burden can be calculated by applying the rule that the area of a triangle equals one-half of its height times its base. The height is the tax ($.50), and the base is $Q_1 - Q_2$ (2 million gallons). Thus, the excess burden is $500,000 per day. The total burden on consumers plus producers equals the $4 million collected by the government plus this $500,000 excess burden, or $4.5 million.

The example can be generalized to all taxes because virtually any tax causes firms or individuals to change their behavior by engaging in less of the taxed activity. For instance, income taxes have an excess burden related to their reduction of incentives to work and save. Similarly, tariffs (taxes on imports) have an excess burden related to the fact that they discourage international trade. The excess burden of taxes is just as much a part of the opportunity cost of the services that the government supplies as are the taxes actually collected by the government.

SUMMARY

1. **What elements are involved in consumers' rational choices?** Objectives and constraints on opportunities provide the setting for rational choice by consumers. Consumers choose rationally when they set goals and make systematic efforts to achieve them. The objective of consumer choice is *utility*—the pleasure and satisfaction that people get from goods and services. The added utility obtained from a one-unit increase in consumption of a good or service is its *marginal utility*. The greater the rate of consumption of a good, the smaller the increase in utility from an additional unit consumed.

2. **How do consumers balance their choices of goods and services to achieve an equilibrium?**

Consumer equilibrium is said to occur when the total utility obtained from a given budget cannot be increased by shifting spending from one good to another. In equilibrium, the marginal utility of a dollar's worth of one good must equal the marginal utility of a dollar's worth of any other good.

3. **What lies behind the effect of a price change on the quantity of a good demanded?** The change in quantity demanded that results from a change in a good's price, other things being equal, can be separated into two parts. The part that comes from the tendency to substitute cheaper goods for more costly ones is the *substitution effect*. The part that comes from the increase in real income that results from a decrease in the price of the good, other things being equal, is the *income effect*.

4. **Why do demand curves have negative slopes?** For a normal good, the substitution and income effects work in the same direction. The demand curves for normal goods therefore have negative slopes. For inferior goods, the income effect and the substitution effect work in opposite directions. For inferior goods, therefore, the demand curve will have a negative slope only if the substitution effect outweighs the income effect. In practice, this is virtually always the case, although *Giffen goods* with positively sloped demand curves are a theoretical possibility.

5. **Why do both consumers and producers gain from exchange?** When consumers buy a product at a given market price, they pay the same amount for each unit purchased. However, because of the *principle of diminishing marginal utility,* the first units purchased are worth more to them than the last ones purchased. The difference between what consumers actually pay for a unit of a good and the maximum they would be willing to pay is the *consumer surplus* gained on that unit of the good. Similarly, the difference between what sellers actually receive for a good and the minimum they would have accepted is known as *producer surplus.*

6. **Why does the burden of a tax exceed the revenue raised by government?** When a tax is imposed on a good or service, the equilibrium price including the tax rises while the equilibrium price net of the tax falls. As a result, the equilibrium quantity falls, making both consumers and producers forgo some surplus. The forgone surplus is not captured in the form of tax revenue and is called the *excess burden of the tax.* It is a burden on consumers and producers over and above the sum that the government collects as tax revenue.

KEY TERMS

Utility	Income effect
Marginal utility	Giffen good
Principle of diminishing utility	Consumer surplus
	Producer surplus
Consumer equilibrium	Excess burden of the tax
Substitution effect	

PROBLEMS AND TOPICS FOR DISCUSSION

1. **Externalities of automobile safety.** The increase in deaths of pedestrians and bicyclists resulting from drivers' use of seat belts or air bags is an example of an *externality,* a concept introduced in Chapter 4. What could the government do to prevent this externality while still achieving the goal of increased driver safety?

2. **Can there be increasing marginal utility?** Can there be increasing marginal utility in some cases? For example, suppose it would take eight rolls of wallpaper to decorate your kitchen. If someone gave you seven rolls of wallpaper, you would get only limited utility from them. An eighth roll, however, would give you great utility. Do you think this is a valid exception to the principle of diminishing marginal utility?

3. **Consumer equilibrium, marginal utility, and prices.** Martha Smith consumes two pounds of pork and five pounds of beef per month. She pays $1.50 a pound for the pork and $2 per pound for the beef. What can you say about the ratio of the marginal utility of pork to the marginal utility of beef, assuming that this pattern represents a state of consumer equilibrium for Smith? Is the ratio 3/4, 4/3, 5/2, 2/5, or none of these?

4. **A Giffen good.** A family living in Minnesota vacations in Florida each January. One year the price of home heating fuel goes up sharply. The family turns the thermostat down a little, but even so the heating bills go up so much that the family cannot afford to go to Florida that year. Staying home in January means that the house must be kept heated during that month. The extra fuel burned during January is more than what the family has been able to save by lowering the thermostat setting in other months. Thus, the total quantity of fuel burned in the winter rises as a result of the increase in the price of heating fuel. Analyze this case in terms of the income and substitution effects. Is home heating fuel a Giffen good for this family? (Hint: Winter vacations in Minnesota are an inferior good for this family. Heating fuel is a complement to winter vacations in Minnesota and hence is also an inferior good.)

5. **Excess burden of a tax.** Figure 3.5 in Chapter 3 demonstrates the incidence of a tax on apartment rents. Using the approach outlined in this chapter, calculate the revenue raised by this tax and the excess burden of the tax. How much of the excess burden is borne by landlords? How much by tenants?

CASE FOR DISCUSSION

Retailing Revolution on the Banks of the Danube

Riding the Metro to the Budapest's sleek new West End shopping mall produces a strange sense of time warp. The Metro, Budapest's fast, reliable underground transit system, is an exact copy of its big brother in Moscow, which first went into service in the 1930s. It has all the features of the Communist-era planned economy: carbon-copy sameness from one country to another, no-frills functionality, and barely adequate spending on maintenance. The West End mall, on the other hand, highlights the characteristics of the modern, consumer-oriented market system. It has spacious, well-lighted public areas, one featuring a three-story indoor waterfall. It has brightly decorated, well-stocked shops selling Italian shoes, Korean electronics, and, of course, local Hungarian brands as well. Yet the West End mall is not a carbon copy of its cousins in Chicago or Seattle. It has many adaptations to suit local shopping habits. For example, its single largest store is a supermarket. Most mall developers in the United States have found that supermarkets don't mix well in shopping malls. American consumers want to be able to load groceries directly into their cars. Central European shoppers shop more often and buy smaller quantities. They seem to find it no great inconvenience to leave the mall with a bag of groceries in one hand and a purchase of new clothing in the other.

But despite a degree of success that is obvious from the crowds, the mall has not completely conquered the Budapest shopping world. Right across the street from the West End mall is a district full of smaller, more traditional shops. Located right on the street level of the four- and five-story apartment buildings where most Budapest residents live, these shops carry much smaller selections, but they offer other things of great value: convenience and service. Did you forget to buy a loaf of bread, a carton of milk, a can of pet food? No need to take the time to head for the mall. Your nearest shop is never more than a block away. Also, many Hungarians prefer to talk over the cut of a piece of meat with a trusted neighborhood butcher rather than buy a pre-wrapped cut in a supermarket. And by keeping overhead low—no waterfalls!—the local merchants manage to compete on price, despite a scale of operation that seems inefficiently small.

One thing is certain: As Hungary has made its transition from a planned economy to membership in the European Union, the consumer has become the driving force of change. Whether catering to teens in the mall's Diesel shop or to pensioners at the local butcher shop, the new Budapest retail world strives to give people what they want. And this strong consumer orientation means that there will be more changes in the years ahead. In a market economy, change is the only constant.

QUESTIONS

1. What opportunity costs must a consumer consider in deciding whether to shop in the West End mall or a traditional small shop?

2. Why would someone prefer to wait in line at a traditional butcher shop to buy custom-cut meat rather than buy a pre-cut roast in a supermarket? Could you use the theory of consumer equilibrium to describe the tradeoff between convenience and quality that is involved in such a decision?

3. The planned economy delivered a limited selection of goods to consumers, but basic goods carried very low prices. Do you think all consumers gain from the transition to a market economy where there is a larger selection of goods but basic goods cost more? Why or why not? Discuss.

END NOTES

1. The positive slope of the demand curve for a Giffen good does not depend on an assumption of bounded rationality. A fully rational consumer would have a negatively sloped demand curve for house-brand cleaner.

2. Sam Peltzman, "The Effects of Automobile Safety Regulation," *Journal of Political Economy* 83 (August 1975): 677–725. In a follow-up study, Robert W. Crandall and John D. Graham ("Automobile Safety Regulation and Offsetting Behavior: Some New Empirical Estimates," *American Economic Review* 74 (May 1984): 328–331) also found that safety regulation had unintended consequences on driving behavior. In distinction to the original Pelzman study, some researchers claim that the effects are small, and that safety regulation has a net beneficial effect.

3. An intermediate-level microeconomics course would explain that for reasons associated with the income effect, the triangle does not provide a precise measure of consumer surplus. However, the approximation is close for goods that make up only a small part of consumers' total expenditures.

CHAPTER 6

Externalities and Environmental Policy

After reading this chapter, you will understand:

1. How the problem of pollution can be understood in terms of the economics of resource markets
2. How externalities can be controlled through voluntary exchange
3. The policies used by the government to control pollution
4. Alternatives to governmental regulation of pollution
5. How public choice theory can be applied to environmental issues
6. What problems are posed by pollution control on a global scale

Before reading this chapter, make sure you know the meaning of:

1. Externalities
2. Property rights
3. Market failure and government failure
4. Supply and demand in resource markets
5. Transaction costs
6. Public choice theory

I N CHAPTER 4 we introduced the term *externality* to refer to effects of production or consumption that have an impact on third parties. Pollution is a leading example. In addition, as noted in our earlier discussion, externalities are a potential source of market failure. They hinder the efficient operation of the price system inasmuch as uncompensated costs imposed on pollution victims are not reflected in market prices. As a result, users of the product that causes the pollution receive a false signal that tells them to use more of the product than they should, given its true opportunity costs. This chapter takes a closer look at this problem and at potential solutions that attempt to restore market signals where they would otherwise be missing.

POLLUTION ABATEMENT AS A PROBLEM IN RESOURCE ECONOMICS

Pollution, says the *American Heritage Dictionary,* is "the contamination of soil, water, or the atmosphere by noxious substances." That is a fine definition—from the victim's point of view. But an understanding of pollution as an economic problem must take into account the polluter's point of view as well. Seen from its source, pollution could better be defined as "the use of soil, water, or the atmosphere to provide valuable waste-disposal services." When both perspectives are taken into account, pollution can be understood as a problem of resource economics and analyzed in terms of pricing in resource markets.

The Benefits of Waste Discharge and the Costs of Pollution Abatement

Most of the types of pollution that dominate the news have their origins in the productive activities of business firms. They arise because noxious gases, toxic chemicals, and bulky solids are side effects of many production activities. Wastes must be disposed of so that workers will not be smothered and production equipment will not disappear under heaps of ashes, scraps, and wastepaper.

There are many methods of waste disposal. One is the discharge of unprocessed wastes into the environment. This method uses up natural resources in quantity but typically requires little labor and a minimum of capital—just a smokestack, a pipe to the nearest river, or a dump truck. Other methods—incineration, composting, compacting, reprocessing, recycling—reduce inputs of natural resources but require greater inputs of labor and capital. As far as the firm is concerned, determining the mix of productive inputs used in waste disposal is subject to the same economic principles as the use of other productive inputs: The value to the firm of a marginal unit of the input decreases as the quantity of the input used increases.

The marginal value of a one-unit increase in waste discharge is the avoided cost of disposing of the same unit of waste in a nonpolluting manner, that is, the marginal cost of **pollution abatement**. The marginal value of waste discharge decreases as the quantity discharged increases because the marginal cost of pollution abatement decreases as the amount of discharge increases.

Figure 6.1 illustrates this principle with the example of sulfur dioxide emissions from a coal-burning power plant. If the plant discharges all of its waste into the atmosphere through a simple smokestack, it will emit 75,000 tons of sulfur dioxide (SO_2) per year. The cheapest method of pollution abatement is to switch to

Pollution abatement

Reduction of the quantity of waste discharged into the environment.

FIGURE 6.1   VALUE OF WASTE DISCHARGE AND COST OF POLLUTION ABATEMENT

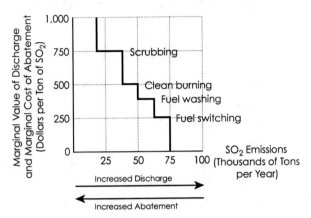

This graph shows the marginal value of waste discharge and marginal cost of pollution abatement for the case of sulfur dioxide emitted by a coal-fired electric power plant. With no pollution control, the plant would emit 75,000 tons of SO_2 per year. The cheapest method of pollution abatement, switching to low-sulfur coal, costs $250 per ton of SO_2 eliminated. The marginal value of waste discharge over the range of 60,000 to 75,000 tons is equal to this avoided cost of pollution abatement. As pollution is progressively reduced, more and more expensive abatement technologies must be introduced. For that reason, as the amount of discharge decreases, the marginal value of waste discharge and the marginal cost of abatement increase.

cleaner coal from a slightly more distant mine. That would cut total discharge to 60,000 tons per year at a cost of $250 per ton of SO_2. In the range of 60,000 to 75,000 tons, then, we can say that the marginal cost of pollution abatement is $250 per ton of SO_2. Or we can say that within that range the marginal value of waste discharge is $250 per ton, because that is how much the firm would avoid in abatement costs by burning the cheaper, dirty coal and discharging the waste into the atmosphere.

To reduce SO_2 emissions still more, the firm must invest in increasingly complex pollution abatement equipment and hire the labor to operate it. Equipment to remove part of the sulfur content of the fuel by "washing" it before it is burned would permit another 10,000 tons of abatement at $400 per ton. Buying an improved furnace to burn the coal more cleanly would cut another 10,000 tons of SO_2 at a cost of $500 per ton. Adding stack scrubbers to remove half the remaining SO_2 from combustion gases as they leave the plant would make possible a further 20,000 tons of abatement at a cost of $750 per ton. No further reduction of emissions would be possible without closing down the plant.

When read from right to left, the stair-step curve in Figure 6.1 represents the increasing marginal cost of pollution abatement. When read from left to right, it represents the diminishing marginal value of waste discharge. Each ton of waste discharge has a marginal value to the firm of $750 in the range of 20,000 to 40,000 tons; $500 in the range of 40,000 to 50,000 tons; and so on. Of course, it is not necessary for the curve to have a stair-step shape as in this example. In many cases marginal abatement costs would vary continuously, so that the curve would have a smooth slope.

The Marginal Social Cost of Pollution

We turn now from the benefits polluters receive from the discharge of wastes to the costs they impose on others. The total of the additional costs borne by all members of society as a result of an added unit of pollution can be termed the *marginal social cost of pollution*.

Each type of pollution has its own particular characteristics. In some cases pollution up to a certain threshold may do no harm at all, after which further increases become harmful. For example, in some locations naturally alkaline soils "buffer" the effects of acid rain. Lakes and streams are not damaged until a threshold of acidity is reached that exhausts the soil's buffering capacity. On the other hand, some pristine ecosystems are sensitive to very small amounts of pollution. In Siberia, the unique wildlife of Lake Baikal is threatened by the pollution from a single paper mill. If that one mill is enough to kill off the lake's native species, it could be argued that once they were gone a second or third mill would do comparatively little additional harm.

Extreme examples aside, the marginal social cost of pollution likely increases as the level of pollution increases. If it were measured accurately, however, the marginal social cost curves for particular types of pollution might well be full of flat spots, steps, dips, and discontinuities.

The Optimal Quantity of Pollution

Figure 6.2 shows a positively sloped curve representing the marginal social cost of pollution together with a negatively sloped curve representing the marginal value of waste discharge. The resulting figure makes it possible to identify the point—the intersection of the two curves—at which the marginal value of discharge (which is also the marginal cost of abatement) equals the marginal social cost of pollution. This is the economically optimal quantity of pollution.

If pollution is allowed to exceed this amount, the harm done by additional pollution will exceed the benefits of additional waste discharge. To the right of the intersection in Figure 6.2, then, a reduction in pollution would be worthwhile. The marginal cost of abatement practices (cleaner fuel, recycling, or whatever) would be more than justified by reduced social costs (better health, cleaner recreation facilities, and so on).

To the left of the intersection, however, the marginal value of waste discharge exceeds the marginal social cost of pollution. In that region further pollution abatement is not economically justified. The relatively small harm done by pollution is not enough to make it worth diverting scarce resources from other uses. Direct discharge

FIGURE 6.2 THE OPTIMAL QUANTITY OF POLLUTION

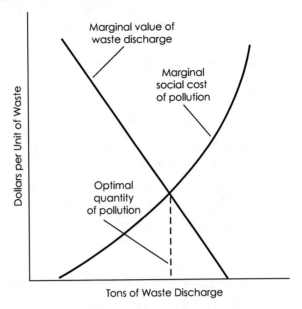

This figure shows a positively sloped curve representing the marginal social cost of pollution together with a negatively sloped curve representing the marginal value of waste discharge. (The marginal value of discharge is equal to the avoided marginal cost of pollution abatement.) The point where the two curves intersect is the optimal quantity of pollution. To the right of that point, the harm done by pollution exceeds the value to the firm of waste discharge. To the left of that point, the value of waste discharge exceeds the harm done by pollution.

of wastes into the environment is the most cost-effective means of waste disposal, even when all harm done to everyone is taken into account.

Criticisms of the Optimal-Pollution Concept

To economists, the logic of the optimal quantity of pollution is no different from that underlying the choice of the least-cost method of producing running shoes or the choice of the optimal balance of oil and vinegar in making a salad dressing. No one denies that cleaning up the environment entails costs and trade-offs. Few people would advocate choosing either of the extremes—the whole world as an uninhabitable sewer or the whole world as a pristine wilderness from which all humans have been eliminated. Therefore, say the economists, there must be an optimal point between the two extremes.

Yet some observers reject the optimal-pollution concept as a guide to public policy. The criticisms are of two types, some focusing on problems of measurement and some on problems of rights.

PROBLEMS OF MEASUREMENT   Attempts to measure the social cost of pollution usually focus on such factors as damage to property, health costs (measured in terms of medical expenses and time lost from work), and the value of wildlife and crops killed. These attempts encounter a number of problems. First, data on the costs of pollution are limited at best, and the many gaps must be filled by guesswork. Second, it is difficult to account for purely subjective costs, such as damage to natural beauty and discomforts that do not result in actual damage to health. Finally, estimates of the social costs of pollution rarely give more than the average cost figures, even though marginal cost data, which are much more difficult to obtain, are more important in making pollution policy decisions.

Data on abatement costs tend to be easier to come by. The processes are localized and the engineering is often well understood. The result, say critics, is that studies of the costs and benefits of pollution control tend to list dollars-and-cents data on the cost side against vague, subjective claims on the benefit side. This tends to stack the deck against pollution control. Economists often warn policy makers that the problems of measuring the social costs of pollution do not mean that those costs are small. Even so, the fear that benefit-cost studies tend to be biased in favor of pollution has given the whole idea of an optimal quantity of pollution a bad name among many environmentalists.

PROBLEMS OF RIGHTS   The optimal-pollution concept also encounters a quite different criticism. Environmental policy, it is said, must respect certain basic rights and should not be guided by economic trade-offs alone.

The idea here is that pollution should be viewed as a form of "invasive coercion" similar to the crimes of theft, vandalism, or rape. Suppose that a vandal breaks into a person's home and smashes a valuable statue. How should a court decide the case? Should it listen to testimony from the owner about the statue's value, then hear testimony from the vandal about the thrills of smashing it, and make its decision by weighing the vandal's marginal utility against the owner's? Most people would be outraged by such an approach. They would say that the vandal violated the owner's right to enjoy the statue and that the vandal's thrills from the smashing should count for nothing in deciding the case.

The discussion that follows employs the optimal pollution concept, but at the same time, we will keep in mind objections to the concept and refer to them as appropriate.

CONTROLLING EXTERNALITIES THROUGH VOLUNTARY EXCHANGE

At several points we have characterized markets as mechanisms for achieving coordination of plans among producers and consumers. We have seen that under proper conditions markets can be counted on to provide us with such things as shoes, cars, Wheaties, and manicure services in something close to the optimal quantities, and to use scarce labor, capital, and natural resources efficiently in the process. The question we take up here is under what conditions, if any, voluntary exchange in a market context will result in efficient waste disposal and an optimal quantity of pollution.

Markets Without Transaction Costs

We can begin by seeing how voluntary exchange would handle the problem of pollution in a world without transaction costs. In that world, technical information about the causes and effects of pollution is available to everyone at no cost. Also, people do not behave opportunistically. They honestly share information about how much they suffer from pollution or how much it would be worth to them to escape its effects, and they voluntarily abide by any agreements they reach.

Suppose that in our hypothetical world there is a forest owned by Joan Forester and, upwind from it, a steel mill owned by John Miller. Noxious fumes from the steel mill are killing the trees in the forest. (For simplicity, we assume that no one else is harmed by the pollution. If we change the example to include subjective harms such as damage to the natural beauty of the forest as well as objective ones such as the economic value of its trees, we introduce additional measurement problems, but we do not change the basic structure of the situation.) What will be done?

PROPERTY RIGHTS   To know how the situation will be handled, we first need to know Miller's and Forester's property rights. There are two possibilities. One is that ownership of the forest includes a right to exclude pollution from the air above it. The other is that ownership of the mill includes a right to emit wastes into the air regardless of where they end up. Let us consider each of these possibilities in turn.

First suppose that the air rights belong to Forester. Acting on the basis of these rights, she approaches Miller to inform him of the damage being done to her trees by pollution from his mill. He recognizes an obligation to do something. After an open and honest discussion, they reach one of several possible agreements:

1. Miller agrees to stop the pollution. He accomplishes this either by installing pollution-control equipment or by shutting down the mill, whichever is less costly to him.
2. Miller agrees to compensate Forester for the value of the trees killed by pollution. This alternative will be better for both parties than a reduction of pollution if the value of the trees killed by the pollution is less than the cost of pollution abatement.
3. Miller agrees to buy the forest at a price acceptable to Forester. He then manages the combined steel and forestry enterprise in a profit-maximizing man-

ner, installing whatever pollution control equipment, if any, is deemed cost-effective.

Suppose instead that the air rights belong to Miller. In that case, when Forester approaches him to discuss the pollution damage, he is under no obligation to do anything. In this case there is a different set of possible outcomes for their negotiations:

1. Forester pays Miller an agreed-upon amount to stop the pollution either by installing control equipment or shutting down the mill, whichever is less costly.
2. Forester buys the mill at a price acceptable to Miller and then manages the combined enterprise in a profit-maximizing manner.
3. The parties agree that the value of the trees killed by the pollution is less than the cost of pollution abatement, in which case no action is taken.

THE COASE THEOREM   Several aspects of the example of the forest and the steel mill are worth noting. First, negotiations between the parties will always result in an optimal quantity of pollution; pollution will be reduced if and only if the cost of abatement is less than the damage it does to the trees. Second, if pollution is to be reduced, the most efficient means of abatement—installing control equipment, shutting the mill, or whatever—will be used. Finally, these results will be achieved regardless of the initial assignment of property rights. Whether the air rights initially belong to the owner of the forest or to the owner of the steel mill will determine who must compensate whom, but will not affect the degree of pollution abatement or the means used to achieve it. Thus, for example, if it is cost-effective to install control equipment on the mill, the initial determination of property rights will determine whether Forester or Miller bears the cost of the equipment, but in either case it will be installed.

The proposition that, in the absence of transaction costs, problems of externalities will be efficiently resolved by private agreement regardless of the initial assignment of property rights is known as the **Coase theorem** after Ronald A. Coase, who first stated it in 1960.[1]

Coase theorem

The proposition that problems of externalities will be resolved efficiently through private exchange, regardless of the initial assignment of property rights, provided that there are no transaction costs.

Market Resolution of Externalities in Practice

Transaction costs are never zero in the real world. They are sometimes low enough, however, to permit externality issues to be resolved through voluntary exchange. *Economics in the News 6.1* provides one example. Other examples may be closer to home.

One common example is the use of restrictive covenants in real estate development—legally binding agreements that limit what owners can do on their property. Left to their own devices, people do many things that annoy their neighbors. They hold loud parties, leave bright outdoor lights on all night, park boats or junked cars in their front yards, and leave garbage uncollected. Real estate developers have found that many people will pay a premium price for a home in a neighborhood where they know their neighbors will not do those things. Accordingly, when they subdivide a

⇆ **ECONOMICS IN THE NEWS 6.1**

USING PROPERTY RIGHTS TO PROTECT THE LAND

Flagstaff, Arizona—The Grand Canyon Trust (GCT) and The Conservation Fund announced today that they have purchased an exclusive option from the Kane Ranch Land Stewardship & Cattle Company, LLC to buy the Kane and Two Mile Ranches, which own or control grazing permits on nearly 900,000 acres north of the Grand Canyon. The grazing allotments of the ranches share a boundary of approximately 80 miles with Grand Canyon National Park including some of the most varied wildlife habitat in the West. The ranches include 1,000 acres of private land in House Rock Valley, along the Vermilion Cliffs and on the Paria Plateau. Tied to this base property are federal and state grazing permits for nearly 900,000 acres.

"This project is creating a model for working ranchland conservation across the West," said The Conservation Fund's president, Larry Selzer. "The Fund is committed to forging partnerships with private landowners to find balanced solutions for increasingly complex conservation challenges. By integrating economic and environmental objectives, we are pioneering a unique brand of conservation that protects one of the most spectacular landscapes in the nation, safeguards important wildlife habitat, and preserves the ranching heritage that defines a way of life."

In addition to protecting important wildlife habitat, the acquisition of the Kane and the Two Mile ranches provides the Trust and the Fund with an opportunity to establish a model for large-scale sustainable ranching. As a demonstration project, the partners will develop a process to identify the lands most suitable for grazing, reduce grazing pressures on sensitive lands, restore and revitalize important wildlife habitat, and develop new tools for sustainable grazing practices.

As stewards of the last vast tracts of remaining old growth forest on the Kane Ranch, the partners are committed to reducing old-growth logging and promoting the reestablishment of healthy fire regimes.

"Stepping into these big shoes as a major public lands stakeholder in the region, we look forward to continuing our cooperative, collaborative relationships with the federal and state agencies, the public and our conservation partners to achieve our goal of preserving these important lands. Without such protection our children and grandchildren may not have the opportunity to experience the beauty this area has afforded previous generations," Hedden concluded.

Source: Grand Canyon Trust, Press Release, August 15, 2004 (http://www.grandcanyontrust.org/press/press_releases/pr04_0715.php).

---

tract of land for a new neighborhood, they add restrictive covenants to the deeds. When home buyers sign the deeds, they agree to a list of restrictions on loud parties, lights, boats, garbage, and so on. In most cases neighbors comply with the covenants voluntarily because they find it mutually beneficial to do so, but the covenants can be enforced in court if necessary.

Another example of the use of markets to handle externalities concerns the pollination of crops by honey bees. Although most of the examples discussed in this chapter concern harmful externalities, this one concerns a beneficial externality. In this case, farmers pay fees to beekeepers to bring their hives by truck to locations near their apple orchards, blueberry farms, or whatever. Such fees total more than $40 million a year in the United States. The fees the farmers pay are more than compensated by the increase in crop yield. Beekeepers, in turn, gain a second source of revenue.

Without such a market, beekeepers would limit the number of hives to the quantity at which the marginal cost just equals the marginal revenue derived from the sale of honey. The external benefit to fruit growers would not enter into their calculations. When they can earn extra revenue by selling pollination services, they expand the number of hives. Doing so benefits not only beekeepers and fruit growers but also consumers, who get more of both honey and fruit.

Transaction Costs as Barriers to Voluntary Resolution of Externalities

Unfortunately, there are many cases in which private negotiations are unable to resolve problems of externalities. The reason: high transaction costs. Three sources of high transaction costs are particularly troublesome. The case of acid rain, one of the most publicized pollution problems, will serve to illustrate all three.

SCIENTIFIC AND TECHNICAL UNCERTAINTIES   To resolve a pollution dispute through private negotiations, one must know the source of the pollution and the nature of the damage. Acquiring such knowledge is often expensive and sometimes impossible.

In the case of acid rain, intensive study has led to agreement that the phenomenon results from chemical reactions in the atmosphere involving sulfur dioxide and oxides of nitrogen, and that acid soils and water can sometimes be harmful to trees and aquatic wildlife, and possibly to cause other forms of damage as well. Beyond these general facts, however, major uncertainties remain.

First, patterns of atmospheric transportation of pollutants are poorly understood. As a result, it is not currently possible to trace the acid rain falling on any one area to any particular source. Victims of acid rain therefore do not know whom to negotiate with.

Second, the mechanisms of environmental damage are not known in detail. Reducing sulfur and nitrogen oxide emissions might or might not result in a proportional reduction in the acidity of rain in downwind areas. Thus, the environmental damage that would be avoided by any given reduction in emissions is not clear.

LEGAL UNCERTAINTIES   The Coase theorem suggests that voluntary agreements can resolve externalities regardless of the initial assignment of property rights. However, this assumes that all parties to the dispute agree on the initial property rights. In practice, environmental property rights are often open to dispute.

The acid-rain controversy again provides an illustration. Environmentalists typically assume that inhabitants of eastern states have a right to clean air. If so, they are in a position to demand action from midwestern pollution sources.

However, owners of midwestern pollution sources, such as electric utilities, assert certain legal rights of their own. They argue, for example, that their factories and power plants were built in accordance with all state and federal pollution standards that were applicable at the time. They claim that those regulations, in establishing certain limits, amounted to the grant of a right to discharge wastes up to those limits. If the limits are lowered, they ought to be compensated for the resulting loss of profits.

INHERENT COSTS OF NEGOTIATION   Even if all scientific and legal uncertainties were resolved, the process of negotiating and enforcing an agreement to resolve an externality might be prohibitively expensive. One problem is the sheer number of parties involved in many important environmental disputes. In the case of acid rain, the parties include tens of millions of inhabitants of the eastern states, on the one hand, and thousands of midwestern pollution sources, on the other. It is hard to imagine private negotiations taking place on such a scale.

In sum, private negotiations within a market framework cannot always resolve large-scale environmental problems, however useful they may be on a local scale. Externalities plus high transaction costs lead to market failure. The next question, then, is whether public policies can overcome these market failures without falling victim to the alternative problem of government failure.

GOVERNMENT POLICIES FOR CONTROLLING EXTERNALITIES

Awareness of environmental problems in the United States has increased greatly over the past few decades. Many of the problems that have been identified appear to be beyond resolution through voluntary exchange. As a result, pressures for governmental action have increased. This section examines both what the government has done to bring environmental externalities under control and what it might do to make its efforts more efficient and effective. Four approaches to pollution control are examined: command and control, tort law, pollution charges, and marketable pollution permits.

Command and Control

To date, most pollution-control efforts have taken the command-and-control approach. This strategy, as embodied in the original Clean Air Act, the Clean Water Act, the National Environmental Policy Act, the Noise Control Act, and several other laws enacted during the 1970s, relies on engineering controls and pollution ceilings. Such laws often state that a specific pollution control method must be used, without considering its cost compared with alternative methods. In other cases a quantitative goal, such as 90 percent cleanup, is set. Sometimes, in areas in which pollution is especially bad, new pollution sources are banned entirely.

The command-and-control strategy has scored some successes. However, in many cases this approach pays too little attention to efficiency. In the past, it was thought that regulators could find a safe threshold level for each type of pollutant, a level below which pollution would be harmless and above which it would be extremely dangerous. The prevailing view today, however, is that there are few identifiable thresholds. At least for many pollutants, cleaner is always safer. The scientific or engineering question of finding a threshold thus has been replaced by the economic question of how much safety people want to pay for. At the same time, requirements to use specific cleanup methods reduce the incentive to discover new, lower-cost techniques. If no attempt is made to balance the marginal social costs of various kinds of pollutants, the result is that the most serious problems are not always attacked first. Moreover, different plants are subject to quite different cleanup standards, depending on their age and location.

The high costs and uneven achievements of past policies have created pressure to cut back on pollution-control efforts. Economists see this as the wrong response to the problem. Instead, for years they have argued that the cost-effectiveness of pollution control can be greatly increased by using approaches other than command and control to achieve environmental quality. Three frequently discussed possibilities are making increased use of tort law, imposing emission charges, and emissions trading.

Private Litigation and Tort Law

Tort law is a long-established area of civil law that is concerned with harms ("torts") done by one person to another. Lawsuits involving accidental personal injury, product defects, and damage to property through negligence are familiar examples of tort litigation.

The areas of tort law that touch most directly on pollution are *nuisance* and *trespass*. The law of nuisance can be used for protection against externalities such as a neighbor's noisy parties or a firm's malodorous manufacturing processes. Trespass traditionally covers one person's entry onto another person's land, but it has been extended to include harmful invasions by smoke, chemical leakage, and so on. Pollution often raises issues of both nuisance and trespass.

Advocates of a rights-based approach to pollution, including many economists of the modern Austrian school, believe that tort law should play an important role in pollution control.[2] They see several advantages to this approach. First, it fits well with the philosophical view that people have a right to enjoy their property free of pollution and the right to self-defense if their property is invaded. Second, the threat of nuisance or trespass suits by a victim of pollution can encourage negotiated agreements leading to efficient resolution of the problem. And third, the tort law approach gives victims of pollution a right to do something on their own initiative, without depending on bureaucrats or legislators to take action on their behalf.

Unfortunately, wider use of tort law for the defense of pollution victims stumbles over many of the same problems of information asymmetries and transaction costs that impede the private resolution of externalities in general. One problem is scientific uncertainty, which may prevent a victim from proving his or her case in court: Was a plaintiff's cancer caused by hazardous wastes from a nearby chemical plant or by something else? Another problem is the difficulty of establishing legal liability when a person is victimized by pollution from more than one source. Still another is inability to collect damages for past pollution from a company that has gone out of business. Finally, lawsuits are a notoriously costly means of resolving disputes.

For the immediate future, tort law will probably continue to play a peripheral role in resolving environmental problems. This does not mean that it should be neglected altogether, however. Specific legal reforms have been suggested that, if enacted, would strengthen pollution victims' chances of winning lawsuits. For example, states might require companies handling hazardous wastes to post bonds so that funds would be available to pay victims in the event of an accident. Tagging pollutants at their source with radioisotopes so that they can be identified downwind or downstream would also help. And technical changes regarding such factors as the statute of limitations and admissibility of evidence might also help.[3]

Finally, lawsuits can be brought against polluters on other legal grounds than that of tort law. As an example, not long ago the Natural Resources Defense Council, acting on behalf of local homeowners, brought suit against China Shipping Company to block a planned expansion of its Long Beach, California, shipping terminal. The suit was brought under a federal law that required detailed study of the environmental impact of the expansion. To settle the suit and proceed with the terminal expansion, China Shipping agreed to use electric rather than diesel equipment in some cases and to contribute $55 million toward other mitigation measures.[4] In this case, it appears that the outcome was not much different than would have resulted from a tort action. However, lawsuits of this kind can be subject to abuse if their only purpose is to cause delay of an action that causes little or no measurable or demonstrable damage.

Emission Charges

When it works, control of pollution through tort law brings external social costs to bear on the party causing the discharge. If the legal system operated without transaction costs, pollution sources would be led to compare marginal abatement costs with the marginal social costs of pollution in an optimal manner. As we have seen, however, imperfections in the legal system often allow polluters to avoid paying the social costs of waste discharge. Recognizing this, economists have suggested other ways of bringing the costs of pollution to bear on the parties that cause the pollution. One proposal is to have the government impose a charge of a fixed amount per unit of waste on all emissions of a given kind of waste. Such charges would be, in effect, a tax on pollution. For example, all sources of sewage might be required to pay a charge of $40 per ton of sewage discharged into lakes and rivers.

Figure 6.3 interprets such a policy in terms of supply and demand. This graph shows a demand curve for waste-discharge opportunities based on the marginal benefits to pollution sources (that is, avoided abatement costs). The supply curve for waste-discharge opportunities is a horizontal line at a height equal to the per-unit emission charge, or $40 per ton in this example. Equilibrium occurs at the point where the supply and demand curves intersect.

FIGURE 6.3   EFFECT OF AN EMISSION CHARGE

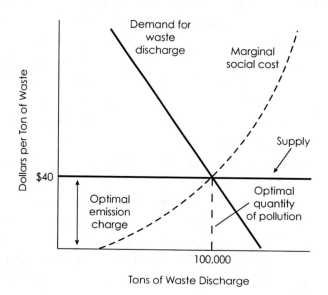

This figure shows the effect of an emission charge of $40 per ton of sewage discharged into lakes and rivers. The demand curve for waste-discharge opportunities is based on the marginal value of waste discharge to the sources of wastes. The supply curve of waste-discharge opportunities is a horizontal line with a height equal to the per-unit emission charge. The equilibrium quantity of waste discharge is established where the supply and demand curves intersect. If the emission charge is set at a level corresponding to the intersection of the demand curve with the curve representing the marginal social cost of pollution, as shown here, the equilibrium quantity of wastes discharged will also be the optimal quantity.

By raising or lowering the amount of the charge, any desired degree of pollution control can be achieved. Ideally, the charge is set so that the supply curve passes through the intersection of the demand curve and the marginal social cost of pollution curve. The optimal amount of pollution would then be achieved.

Of course, it is possible that the charge would be set too low or too high. There is no easy way to tell just where the curves intersect and, hence, how high the residual charge should be. Also, the damage done by a given amount of pollution is likely to vary from time to time and from place to place. However, advocates point out that emission charges encourage the use of efficient techniques to achieve a given level of pollution control even if the chosen level is not the optimal one. This is so because a charge applied uniformly to all pollution sources would exert equal pressure on all polluters to cut back at least a few units on their output of wastes. It would encourage them to eliminate pollution first from the sources that can be controlled most cheaply. Thus, it would avoid the present situation, in which some sources (for example, industrial plants and municipal sewage systems) pay high costs to reduce just a few marginal units of pollution, while other sources (for example, agricultural runoff and urban storm runoff) are almost entirely free from control.

Emission charges have been used successfully as one element in the control strategy for chlorofluorocarbons under the 1987 Montreal Protocol. These are chemicals used for items ranging from spray cans to refrigerators that have the potential for damaging the earth's protective ozone layer. Emission charges have also been used to control water pollution in several European countries.[5]

Emissions Trading

Emission charges represent a way of using market-like incentives to encourage efficiency in attaining environmental goals. Another approach to the same goal is the use of marketable waste-discharge permits, a technique commonly known as emissions trading or "cap and trade." These permits allow their holders to discharge a specified level of waste and can be bought and sold by firms that produce wastes. For various practical reasons, emissions trading become much more widespread than emissions charges.

Figure 6.4 interprets the marketable-permit system in terms of supply and demand. The system results in a vertical supply curve for waste-discharge opportunities rather than the horizontal supply curve resulting from an emission charge policy. The

FIGURE 6.4   EFFECT OF EMISSIONS TRADING

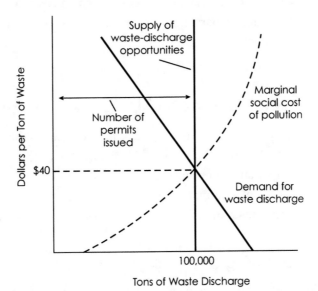

Tons of Waste Discharge

This figure shows the effect of a policy of emissions trading based on marketable waste-discharge permits. The total amount of waste that may be discharged is limited by the number of permits issued, corresponding, in this case, to 100,000 tons of sewage. Permits will be traded among pollution sources as those with higher marginal abatement costs buy permits from those with lower marginal abatement costs. An equilibrium will be established when the marginal cost of abatements equalize among all pollution sources. The equilibrium price of a permit will correspond to the intersection of the supply and demand curves, or $40 per ton in this case. If the number of permits issued corresponds to the intersection of the demand curve with the marginal social cost of pollution curve, as shown here, the optimum quantity of pollution will be achieved.

vertical supply curve corresponds to the "cap," that is, the overall limit on the amount of pollution allowed from all sources. Ideally, as shown in the figure, the limit corresponds to the optimal quantity of pollution.

Once the overall limit has been determined, it is divided into a fixed number of permits that are distributed among pollution sources that can be freely bought and sold. Presumably, the highest bidders will be the plants with the highest marginal costs of pollution abatement. As the market for permits approaches equilibrium at a price representing the intersection of the supply and demand curves, the marginal cost of abatement will be equalized for all firms. Thus, as in the case of emission charges, there is an incentive to use efficient means to achieve the target level of pollution abatement.

Emission trading has become widely used as a method to control air pollution from electric power plants under 1990 amendments to the Clean Air Act.

At first environmentalists were skeptical of the method, but they have come to view it as a valuable tool as its effectiveness has been demonstrated. Use of cap-and-trade techniques brought about a 41 percent reduction in sulfur dioxide emissions, a major source of acid rain, between 1980 and 2002. At the same time, industry concerns that the price of permits would soar to catastrophic levels have proved unfounded. Instead, trading prices of permits have been below forecast levels.

However, as discussed in *Economics in the News 6.2*, emissions remain a source of controversy in some cases. On balance, it is felt that emissions trading works best for types of pollution whose effects are spread over a wide geographical area, which come from many separate points, and which have widely varying costs of abatement at different points.

ENVIRONMENTAL POLICY AND PUBLIC CHOICE

The preceding section was devoted to policies that could be used to achieve environmental goals efficiently. This section turns to another set of issues regarding environmental policy, applying tools of public choice theory to explain why relatively inefficient command-and-control policies have often dominated, and under what conditions more efficient approaches become politically feasible.

Logrolling and Regional Interests

Legislation in a representative democracy is often shaped by the process of vote trading required to build a majority coalition. Often this process brings together diverse groups, each with its own particular interests. The resulting legislation provides something for each of them.

In the area of environmental policy, the control of sulfur dioxide emissions from coal-fired electric power plants provides a case in point. As pointed out in Figure 6.1, there are a variety of technologies for reducing sulfur dioxide emissions. Typically, switching to a low-sulfur coal is the cheapest alternative and scrubbing the sulfur

∽ ECONOMICS IN THE NEWS 6.2

CAP AND TRADE FOR MERCURY?

Mercury is a highly poisonous neurotoxin that can enter the human body through contaminated air, water, and food. In the United States, coal-fired power plants are the single largest source of mercury pollution. In an attempt to deal with the problem, in March 2005, the Environmental Protection Agency issued a set of regulations designed for the first time to control mercury emissions from power plants.

The regulations are based on the now-familiar cap-and-trade principle. The objective of the regulations is to bring about a 70 percent reduction in emissions by 2018 while giving industry the flexibility to explore the cost effectiveness of new control technologies. At the time the regulations were issued, there were no commercially proven methods to remove mercury from power-plant emissions, although several promising lines of research were underway. Until these technologies come on line, the main way to reduce power plant emissions is through switching to cleaner but more expensive fuels like natural gas.

Industry sources generally supported the EPA guidelines, but the guidelines found less favor with environmental groups. According to the environmentalists, the new regulations fell short in two respects.

First, the cost-benefit studies on which they were based were said to understate the impact of mercury on human health. Consequently, the overall cap, especially in early years of the program, were set too low.

Second, the EPA plan imposes national limits on emissions, but the effects of mercury pollution are seen as local or regional in their nature. That means that there is no guarantee that "hot spots" like Texas or the Chesapeake Bay region would experience adequate reductions even if national goals were met. In fact, since these areas may in some cases have higher control costs than other parts of the country, they could become net purchasers of permits so that pollution could locally become worse even while national goals were met.

Rather than tradeable permits, environmentalists favored stricter quantitative limits on each source to achieve a faster rate of pollution reduction and avoid hot spots.

from combustion gases is the most expensive. Nonetheless, in its 1977 amendments to Section 111 of the Clean Air Act, Congress required that any newly constructed electric power plant meet the emissions limit by scrubbing. This requirement applied regardless of how clean or dirty the plant's fuel or combustion technology was. Many old plants, including some of the dirtiest ones that burn the most sulfurous midwestern coal, were not forced to scrub. Instead, they were allowed to meet standards for local pollution by building tall smokestacks—up to 1,000 feet high—that keep the air in surrounding communities fairly clean. However, pollution injected into the upper atmosphere by the tall stacks is widely thought to contribute to the problem of acid rain hundreds of miles downwind. Why did Congress choose this approach to controlling sulfur dioxide emissions? The answer appears to lie in the coalition that passed the Clean Air Act, which included the following:

- Coal-mining interests in the high-sulfur areas of Ohio, Illinois, and elsewhere that wanted to strengthen demand for their product. These factions, including both mine owners and unions, were afraid that changing fuels would result in the loss of coal production jobs.
- Industrial and political interests from eastern and midwestern states that wanted to protect profits by stopping the flight of industry to western and southern states. By focusing control efforts on newly built plants, the Clean

Air Act gives old, dirty plants a few more years of life. Moreover, by focusing on scrubbing rather than changing fuels, the act ensures that coal-burning plants in the South and West are unable to exploit the cost advantage of a location close to sources of low-sulfur coal.

- Environmentalists, who were unable to obtain a majority in Congress by themselves and were willing to enter an unholy alliance on the theory that any pollution control measures were better than none.

After the passage of the 1977 Clean Air amendments, environmentalists became dissatisfied with the deal that had been made. The degree of pollution reduction was less than had been hoped, partly because scrubbers are not always reliable and partly because the regulations slowed the replacement of old, dirty facilities with new, cleaner ones. Thus, important elements of the coalition changed by the time the 1990 amendments were under consideration. This time, environmentalists broke with the midwestern coal and industrial interests, and supported wider experimentation with marketable permits.

The Influence of Special Interests

Small, well-organized interest groups tend to have proportionately more influence than larger, less well-organized groups, in part because of their superior ability to make use of information and communication resources. The power of high-sulfur coal interests to influence clean-air legislation could be considered an example of this tendency. In other cases special-interest groups have done more than just weaken measures intended to preserve the environment. They have won the implementation of policies that are actively destructive to the environment.

Western water policy provides an example. According to Marc Riesner, a historian of water use in the West, agriculture causes more environmental damage than any other single activity in that area.[6] Riesner blames much of the problem on the Bureau of Reclamation, which sells water to ranchers and farmers at "astoundingly subsidized rates, often as little as a quarter of a cent per ton." The Bureau began its life as an organization that would aid farmers through sales of water at rates that would recoup all costs for dams and irrigation systems, but the concept of self-financing has long since been abandoned. Most of the water goes for such crops as cattle feed that could be produced more economically elsewhere in the country.

Logging in national forests provides another example of a policy that is destructive to the environment. In Alaska's rain forests and other areas of the West, the U.S. Forest Service subsidizes logging by constructing access roads and making other investments for which loggers are not charged. Often the value of the timber is below what the government spends building roads to get it out. Well-organized logging interests benefit while the environment is destroyed and taxpayers are burdened.

GLOBAL ASPECTS OF POLLUTION CONTROL

Up to this point, we have looked primarily at examples of pollution control on a local and national scale. Some kinds of pollution operate on a global scale, however. The leading example is emissions of carbon dioxide (CO_2) and other "greenhouse gasses" that are believed to be a major source of global warming.

The 1997 Kyoto Protocol is, at this time, the major international effort to deal with global warming by reducing CO_2 emissions. Its approach is based on a global version of emissions trading. The problems it faces illustrate the application of a number of issues in pollution control applied on a global scale.

SCIENTIFIC UNCERTAINTY   We have already noted that scientific uncertainties pose a significant barrier to pollution control. If there is no agreement on the cause of an environmental problem, the nature of the harm, or the effectiveness of proposed control efforts, agreement on a plan of action is unlikely. The issue of global warming illustrates this problem on a large scale.

Although there continue to be scientists who question whether the planet is in fact getting warmer at all and if so, whether human activity has anything to do with it, as time has gone by, these have become a smaller and smaller minority. In many forums, the administration of U.S. President George W. Bush has emphasized scientific uncertainty in arguing for a go-slow approach. In a change, at the 2005 G-8 summit in Scotland, the president appeared to back away from this position by accepting that the world was getting warmer and that human activities contributed to the process. That does not put the scientific debate to rest, however. Various global climate models produce very different quantitative results, so that much uncertainty remains as to the specific effects on climate of changes in the rate of CO_2 emissions. Without a greater agreement among climate models, estimates of economic costs and benefits of emissions reduction also remain highly uncertain. As mentioned earlier, to say that the benefits of emissions reduction are uncertain is not the same as to say that they are small. However, the uncertainty makes it far harder to design an efficient cleanup policy.[7]

LEGAL ISSUES   We have seen that the law of property rights can, under the right circumstances, be a powerful tool to control externalities. Also, a strong legal system is needed to monitor and enforce policies of emissions taxes or permit trading. Unfortunately, there is no established system of international property rights to the atmosphere. International treaties, like the Kyoto Protocol, are the only instrument for restraining countries from dumping as great a quantity of greenhouse gasses into the atmosphere as they want, gaining all the benefits of cheap waste disposal for themselves and imposing most of the cost of climate change on others. This is reflected in the fact that countries accounting for a large share of CO_2 emissions are not participants. Furthermore, one can only imagine the difficulties that would arise if a country like Russia, which has ratified the Protocol, were to be suspected by other signatories of not complying with its obligations.

REGIONAL INTERESTS AND LOGROLLING   We have seen that within a country like the United States, regional interests and logrolling can have a major impact on policy. The same is true on a global scale. For example, in negotiating the Kyoto Protocol, the issue arose as to the relative responsibilities for global warming of established industrial countries compared with emerging market counties. The emerging market countries argued that the industrialized countries should bear the burden of cleanup since the CO_2 now in the atmosphere includes that emitted by decades of coal and oil use in the past. The industrialized countries, in turn, pointed out that emerging market countries are not only growing more rapidly but emit more CO_2 per dollar of GDP than advanced economies. (Already China and India together emit more CO_2 than the United States, the world's largest source. Soon China alone will be the largest CO_2 source.)

With no mechanism to bring all countries on board, the Kyoto Protocol achieved only an unsatisfactory compromise on this issue. Only industrialized countries are subject to mandatory emissions reductions. Emerging market countries are free to continue to increase their emissions, although they have incentive to sell some rights to do so within the proposed emission trading systems. Also, because of long and difficult political negotiations, the initial ceilings imposed by the Kyoto Protocol are far from stringent. Even if fully implemented, they would do little to reduce CO_2 emissions over the coming decade.

ECONOMIC POLICY DESIGN   n combination, the above considerations have left the Kyoto Protocol open to criticism in terms of economic policy design. An ideal policy, as we have seen, should achieve an overall equilibrium close to the point where the marginal costs and marginal benefits of abatements balance, and at the same time, should equate the marginal costs of cleanup from all sources. The Kyoto Protocol does neither of these. In terms of overall balance, some critics see it as actually achieving little or no CO_2 reduction even if fully implemented, while others believe full implementation would involve costs that exceed benefits by ten times or more. Furthermore, there is no likelihood that marginal costs of abatement would be equalized among the three classes of countries under the Protocol—industrialized signatory countries with mandatory limits, emerging market signatories with no mandatory limits, and industrialized nonsignatory countries.

In short, despite progress in recent decades in controlling many local pollution problems (London and Los Angeles smog) and some national ones (acid rain in the United States), the likelihood of much progress against global pollutants like greenhouse gasses seems small for the foreseeable future.

⬱

SUMMARY

1. **How can the problem of pollution be understood in terms of the economics of resource markets?** Pollution occurs when firms (or sometimes consumers) discharge wastes into soil, water, or the atmosphere. The marginal value to a firm of resources used for waste discharge is equal to the avoided cost of disposing of the wastes in a nonpolluting manner; that is, it is equal to the marginal cost of *pollution abatement*. The optimal quantity of pollution is the quantity beyond which the marginal social cost of pollution exceeds the marginal value of waste disposal.

2. **How can externalities be controlled through voluntary exchange?** In a world without transaction costs, problems of externalities would be resolved through voluntary exchange. For this to happen, all parties would need complete information and there would have to be no opportunistic behavior. According to the *Coase theorem*, voluntary exchange would result in efficient resource allocation regardless of the initial assignment of property rights, provided that the rights were clearly defined.

3. **What policies has the government used to control pollution?** To date, most pollution control policy in the United States has followed the command-and-control approach. This approach has been successful in reducing the levels of some, but not all, pollutants. Economists have criticized the command-and-control approach for poor performance in terms of efficiency. Current regulations often do not take marginal abatement costs into account and do not provide incentives to employ the least-cost control technology.

4. **What alternatives to governmental regulation of pollution are available?** One alternative to the command-and-control approach is the use of tort law, under which pollution is equated with nuisance or trespass. A second is the imposition of emission charges, which would require pollution sources to pay a per-unit fee for the discharge of wastes into the environment. A third is a system of emissions trading based on marketable waste-discharge permits. Economists favor these approaches because they include incentives to meet a given pollution control target in an efficient manner.

5. **How can public choice theory be applied to environmental issues?** Public choice economics can help explain why the pollution control policies adopted by government are not always the most efficient ones. Often those policies reflect the use of logrolling to build majority coalitions. In addition, small, well-organized interest groups, such as loggers and ranchers, sometimes persuade the government to undertake policies that are destructive to the environment. Environmental policy thus provides many examples of government failure as well as market failure.

6. **What problems are posed by pollution control on a global scale?** Control of global pollution, such as the greenhouse gas emissions believed to be causing global warming, pose great challenges. Scientific uncertainties tend to be greater the greater the scale of the problem, with global warming being a case in point. The international legal framework, based on voluntary adherence to negotiated treaties, is much weaker than within countries. As a result, existing control mechanisms, such as the Kyoto Protocol on greenhouse gasses, are open to considerable criticism in terms of economic program design.

KEY TERMS

Pollution abatement   Coase theorem

PROBLEMS AND TOPICS FOR DISCUSSION

1. **Environmental rights.** Where do you stand on the issue of environmental rights? Do you think people (or other species) have some environmental rights that ought to be upheld regardless of the economic cost of doing so? Discuss.

2. **Beneficial externalities and property rights.** Beekeepers need flowers to produce honey, and farmers need bees to pollinate crops. At present, beekeepers have the right to place hives where their bees will fly onto neighbors' property, and the neighbors do not have the right to exclude the bees. Suppose instead that invasion by bees was considered a form of trespass, so that property owners could sue beekeepers who allowed the insects to fly onto their land without permission. How would this alter the economic relations between farmers and beekeepers? Do you think that it might lead to a situation in which beekeepers have to pay farmers for access to the blossoms of their crops? Discuss in terms of the Coase theorem and the Miller-Forester example.

3. **Smoking in restaurants.** Smoking results in externalities that are unpleasant for nonsmokers. Given this fact, why would a restaurant find it profitable to establish smoking and nonsmoking areas? Do you think that the problem of smoking in restaurants is adequately resolved by voluntary market incentives, or should there be a government policy mandating (or preventing) designated smoking areas in restaurants? Do you think that the same conclusions apply to smoking on airplanes? In a government office? Discuss.

4. **Automobile pollution.** At present, automobile pollution is controlled by the addition of catalytic converters and other devices to cars so that they do not exceed a certain quantity of pollution per mile driven. For comparison, imagine a system in which drivers had to pay an annual tax based on the total pollution emitted by their cars. The tax would be calculated by measuring the quantity of pollution per mile, using a testing device such as those now used for vehicle inspections, and multiplying that figure by the number of miles per year shown on the car's odometer. People could choose to buy catalytic converters, more expensive and effective devices, or no control devices at all. What considerations would determine the type of pollution control device purchased? Do you think that the tax system would be more efficient than the current command-and-control system? Would it be as effective in reducing pollution? Would it be as fair? Discuss.

CASE FOR DISCUSSION

Electric Tractors

California's San Joaquin Valley is known for yielding large quantities of high-quality agricultural products. In addition to crops, the land of milk and honey produces something else: heavy air pollution. The summer harvest season is when it's most noticeable. Diesel farming equipment, dust, and organic matter combined with the region's growing number of automobiles have resulted in poor air quality for California's central valley.

According to the American Lung Association's "State of the Air, 2003" report, three major metropolitan areas located in the San Joaquin Valley—Fresno, Bakersfield, and Visalia-Tulare-Porterville—were behind only the Los Angeles-Riverside-Orange County area in worst air quality. The ALA's annual report looks at ozone levels across the country. Ozone, one of the toxic components of smog, is a form of oxygen that even at low levels can cause health problems such as shortness of breath, coughing, and wheezing.

To help cure air pollution, state Senator Dean Florez wants to lower growers' electricity bills, enticing them to make the voluntary switch and spare the sky a hefty dose of pollution. Farmers say [standby charges for the pumps] can total as much as 40 percent of their electricity bills, even when the pumps are rarely used, leading many to choose cheaper, but dirtier, diesel fuel.

According to the California Air Resources Board, eliminating approximately 8,200 agricultural diesel pump engines in use statewide (about 4,500 of which are in the San Joaquin Valley) would prevent 1,000 tons of small bits of dust and chemicals from entering the air each year. It also would cut about 13,200 tons of smog-forming nitrogen oxide and volatile organic compounds.

"We'd like to see more and more of these be electric," said Dave Jones, planning director for the San Joaquin Valley Air Pollution Control District.

Keith Nilmeier, a central valley farmer, said that most farmers prefer diesel power because it's less expensive than electricity. He started converting his irrigation pumps to diesel from electricity about fifteen years ago to save money. "Diesel fuel was very cheap at the time," Nilmeier said. "We sat down and put a pencil to it and saw what we could save in our own operation." Nilmeier estimates that he saves about 35 percent by moving water with a diesel-powered pump instead of one powered by electricity.

Florez proposes to raise or use a chunk of a surcharge already built into utility bills to pay farmers' standby charges. The surcharge—called the public goods charge—accounts for about 1 percent of each customer's electricity bill for a total of about $540 million statewide. Opponents of Florez's bill have argued it is unfair for all electricity users to pay for an agriculture subsidy.

"Energy costs are already high," said state Assembly Member Sarah Reyes. "I don't know of any ratepayer who is willing to pay for one industry's problem, because that will just increase their energy bills."

Source: Jennifer M. Fitzenberger, "Taking diesel out of farm air," *Sacramento Bee*, January 25, 2004. American Lung Association, State of the Air: 2003, May 2003.

QUESTIONS

1. Draw a supply and demand diagram for farm goods. Include two supply curves, one based on costs excluding pollution externalities and one including pollution externalities. How are the price and quantity of farm goods affected?
2. One aim of pollution control is to equalize the marginal cost of abatement across various pollution sources. Does the idea of subsidizing electric rates for farming, while leaving rates unchanged for other industries, further this aim? Discuss.
3. Another aim of pollution control is to provide incentives to use the least-cost method of abatement. Do you think a subsidy to electric rates is consistent with this aim? Why or why not? What other methods might be used instead?
4. Generating electricity also causes some pollution, but it may occur far away from the San Joaquin Valley. Do you think State Senator Florez's plan might be influenced by regional considerations, that is, by where the costs and benefits of the electric subsidy occur rather than the overall size of those costs and benefits?
5. Good pollution policy should reflect the *marginal* cost of abatement methods, not their fixed costs. Although it is not completely clear from the text of the article, it appears that a rebate for the "standby charge" may affect only the fixed costs of hooking up an electric pump, not the marginal

cost of operating it. If that is the case, how would your evaluation of the policy change, especially in terms of the issues raised in questions 3 and 4 of "Problem and Topics for Discussion"?

END NOTES

1. Ronald Coase, "The Problem of Social Cost," *Journal of Law and Economics* (October 1960): 1–44. This is the same Ronald Coase who is known for work on the theory of the firm.
2. See Murray Rothbard, "Law, Property Rights, and Air Pollution," *Cato Journal* (Spring 1982): 55–100. Several other papers in a symposium on pollution in the same volume also discuss pollution-engendered torts.
3. This list of suggestions is taken from Richard L. Stroup, "Environmental Policy," *Regulation* (1988) no. 3, 48.
4. Felicity Barringer, "California Air is Cleaner, but Troubles Remain," *New York Times*, Aug 3, 2005, p. 1.
5. These programs are discussed in Robert W. Hahn, "Economic Prescriptions for Environmental Problems: How the Patient Followed the Doctor's Orders," *Journal of Economic Perspectives* (Spring 1989): 104–107.
6. Marc Riesner, "No Country on Earth Has Misused Water as Extravagantly as We Have," *The New York Times*, October 30, 1988, 4E, cited in "Using Private Property Rights to Conserve Water Resources and End Pork-Barrel Projects," *FREE Perspectives on Economics and the Environment* (February 22, 1989): 6–13.
7. A good summary of the scientific uncertainties and their impact on design of an efficient cleanup strategy can be found in Warwick J. McKibbon and Peter J. Wilcoxen, "The Role of Economics in Climate Change Policy," *Journal of Economic Perspectives,* Vol 16 No.2 (Spring 2002): 107–129.

CHAPTER 7

Global Trade and Trade Policy

After reading this chapter, you will understand:

1. How the principle of comparative advantage can be applied to international trade
2. How the notion of competitiveness is related to that of comparative advantage
3. The trend of international trade policy in recent years
4. How international trade affects income distribution within each country
5. How protectionist policies can be understood in terms of public choice theory and rent seeking

Before reading this chapter, make sure you know the meaning of:

1. Comparative advantage
2. Political rent seeking
3. Human capital
4. Public choice theory

GLOBAL TRADE IS changing the world economy. Over the half-century from 1948 to 1997, the volume of world trade increased by a factor of 17, compared with a six-fold growth of output. Figure 7.1 shows shares of the biggest players in terms of imports and exports. Not surprisingly, the United States is the world's largest importer of goods and services. In light of the constant hand-wringing about its competitiveness, some readers may be surprised to see that it is also the world's largest exporter, having taken over that honor from Germany in the 1980s. Two other trends are notable in the figure: One is that U.S. imports have grown much more rapidly than exports in recent years, a topic to which we will return later in the chapter. The other is the rapid rise of China as a major player in world trade. China is now the world's fifth largest exporter and sixth largest importer.

But Figure 7.1 shows only the raw data of trade. The most interesting questions will require digging beneath the surface. What determines who exports to whom and who imports from whom? Does the growth of imports and exports make people bet-

FIGURE 7.1 **WORLD TRADE SHARES OF LEADING EXPORTERS AND IMPORTERS**

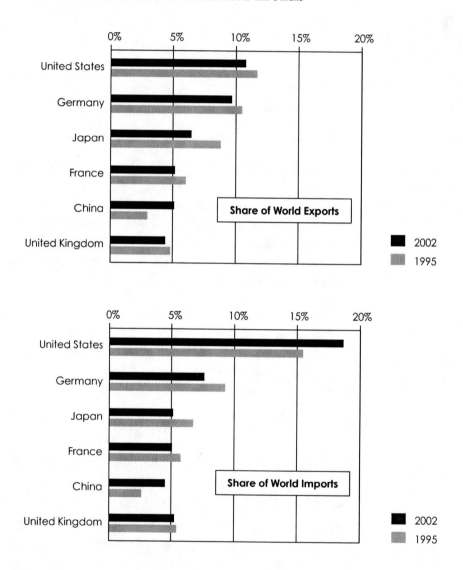

The United States is both the world's largest exporter and its largest importer. In recent years, U.S. imports have grown more rapidly than its exports. Over the same period, China's importance as an exporter has grown substantially, while that of Japan has declined.

Source: World Trade Organization

ter off or worse off? And how are trade patterns affected by national and international trade policy? The rest of the chapter will explore these questions.

THE THEORY OF COMPARATIVE ADVANTAGE: REVIEW AND EXTENSIONS

The answer to the first question—who trades with whom?—begins with the concept of *comparative advantage,* which we introduced in Chapter 1. Although it can be applied to the division of labor within an economy of a single country, the concept was originally developed by David Ricardo as an explanation of trade between countries. We will begin our discussion of international trade by reviewing this theory, first using a numerical example and then applying a graphical approach.

Numerical Approach

For illustrative purposes, imagine a world with just two countries—Norway and Spain. Both have farms and offshore fishing grounds, but Spain's moderate climate makes both the farms and the fishing grounds there more productive. A ton of fish can be produced in Spain with 4 hours of labor and a ton of grain with 2 hours of labor. In Norway, 5 labor hours are required to produce a ton of fish and 5 labor hours to produce a ton of grain. We will consider only labor costs in this example; other costs can be assumed to be proportional to labor costs. Also, we will assume constant per-unit labor costs for all output levels.

Absolute advantage

The ability of a country to produce a good at a lower cost, in terms of quantity of factor inputs, than the cost at which the good can be produced by its trading partners.

Because it takes fewer labor hours to produce both fish and grain in Spain, Spain can be said to have an **absolute advantage** in the production of both goods. However, absolute cost differences do not matter for international trade; it is the difference in opportunity costs between the two countries that matters. In Norway, producing a ton of fish means forgoing the opportunity to use 5 labor hours in the fields. A ton of fish thus has an opportunity cost of 1 ton of grain there. In Spain, producing a ton of fish means giving up the opportunity to produce 2 tons of grain. In terms of opportunity costs, then, fish is cheaper in Norway than in Spain and grain is cheaper in Spain than in Norway. The country in which the opportunity cost of a good is lower is said to have a *comparative advantage* in producing that good.

Considering only labor costs, mutually beneficial trade between Spain and Norway might not seem possible. Norwegians might like to get their hands on some of those cheap Spanish goods, but why would the Spanish be interested? After all, couldn't they produce everything at home more cheaply than it could be produced abroad? If that is the case, how could they gain from trade? A closer analysis shows that this view is incorrect and that absolute advantage is unimportant in determining patterns of trade; only comparative advantage matters.

To see the possibilities for trade between the two countries, imagine that a Norwegian fishing boat decides to sail into a Spanish port with a ton of fish. Before the Norwegians' arrival, Spanish merchants in the port will be used to exchanging 2 tons of locally produced grain for a ton of fish, while the Norwegians will be accustomed to getting only 1 ton of Norwegian grain for each ton of Norwegian fish. Thus, any exchange ratio between 1 and 2 tons of grain per ton of fish will seem attractive to both parties. For instance, a trade of 1.5 tons of grain for a ton of fish will make both the Spanish merchants and the Norwegian fishers better off than they would be if they traded only with others from their own country.

The profits made by the first boatload of traders are only the beginning of the story. The more significant benefits come as each country begins to specialize in producing the good in which it has a comparative advantage. In Norway, farmers will discover that instead of working 5 hours to raise a ton of grain from their own rocky soil, they can fish for 5 hours and trade their catch to the Spaniards for 1.5 tons of grain. In Spain, people will find that it is no longer worth their while to spend 4 hours catching a ton of fish. Instead, they can work just 3 hours in the fields, and the 1.5 tons of grain that they grow will get them a ton of fish from the Norwegians. In short, the Norwegians will find it worthwhile to specialize in fish, and the Spaniards will find it advantageous to specialize in grain.

Now suppose that trade continues at the rate of 1.5 tons of grain per ton of fish until both countries have become completely specialized. Spain no longer produces any fish, and Norway no longer produces any grain. Norwegians catch 200 tons of fish, half of which are exported to Spain. The Spanish grow 500 tons of grain, 150 tons of which are exported to Norway. Table 7.1 compares this situation with a nonspecialized, pretrade situation in which each country produces some of both products. The comparison reveals three things. First, the Norwegians are better off than before; they have just as much fish to eat and 50 tons more grain than in the pretrade equilibrium. Second, the Spaniards are also better off; they have just as much grain to consume as ever-and more fish. Finally, total world output of both grain and fish has risen as a result of trade. Everyone is better off, and no one is worse off.

Graphical Presentation

Comparative advantage can be illustrated graphically using a set of production possibility frontiers based on the example just given. This is done in Figure 7.2, which shows three production possibility frontiers.

Part (a) is the production possibility frontier for Spain. Given 1,000 available labor hours and a cost of 2 labor hours per ton of grain, Spain can produce up to 500 tons of grain per year if it produces no fish (point B). If it produces no grain, up to 250 tons of fish per year can be caught at a cost of 4 hours per ton of fish (point D). The combinations of grain and fish that Spain can produce are represented by the line running from B to D.

TABLE 7.1   EFFECTS OF TRADE ON PRODUCTION AND CONSUMPTION

	Spain	Norway	World Total
Before Trade			
Fish			
Production	75	100	175
Consumption	75	100	175
Grain			
Production	350	100	450
Consumption	350	100	450
After Trade			
Fish			
Production	0	200	200
Consumption	100	100	200
Grain			
Production	500	0	500
Consumption	350	150	500

All figures represent tons produced or consumed

This table shows production and consumption of fish and grain in Spain, Norway, and the world as a whole before and after trade. It is assumed that each country specializes in the product in which it has a comparative advantage and that fish are traded for grain at the rate of 1.5 tons of grain per ton of fish.

Part (b) shows the production possibility frontier for Norway. In Norway, fish and grain both take 5 labor hours per ton to produce. If Norwegians devote all their time to fishing, they can catch up to 200 tons of fish per year (point B_1). If they devote all their time to farming, they can grow up to 200 tons of grain (point D_1). The line between B_1 and D_1 represents Norway's production possibility frontier.

According to the example summarized in Figure 7.2, before trade begins, Spain produces and consumes 350 tons of grain and 75 tons of fish. This is shown as point A on Spain's production possibility frontier. Norway is assumed to produce and consume 100 tons each of fish and grain. This is shown by point A_1 on Norway's frontier.

The World Production Possibility Frontier

A production possibility frontier for the world as a whole (consisting of just these two countries in our example) can be constructed as shown in part (c) of Figure 7.2. First, assume that both countries devote all their labor to grain. That results in 500 tons of grain from Spain plus 200 from Norway, or 700 tons of grain in all (point R in part (c)

FIGURE 7.2 A GRAPHIC ILLUSTRATION OF COMPARATIVE ADVANTAGE

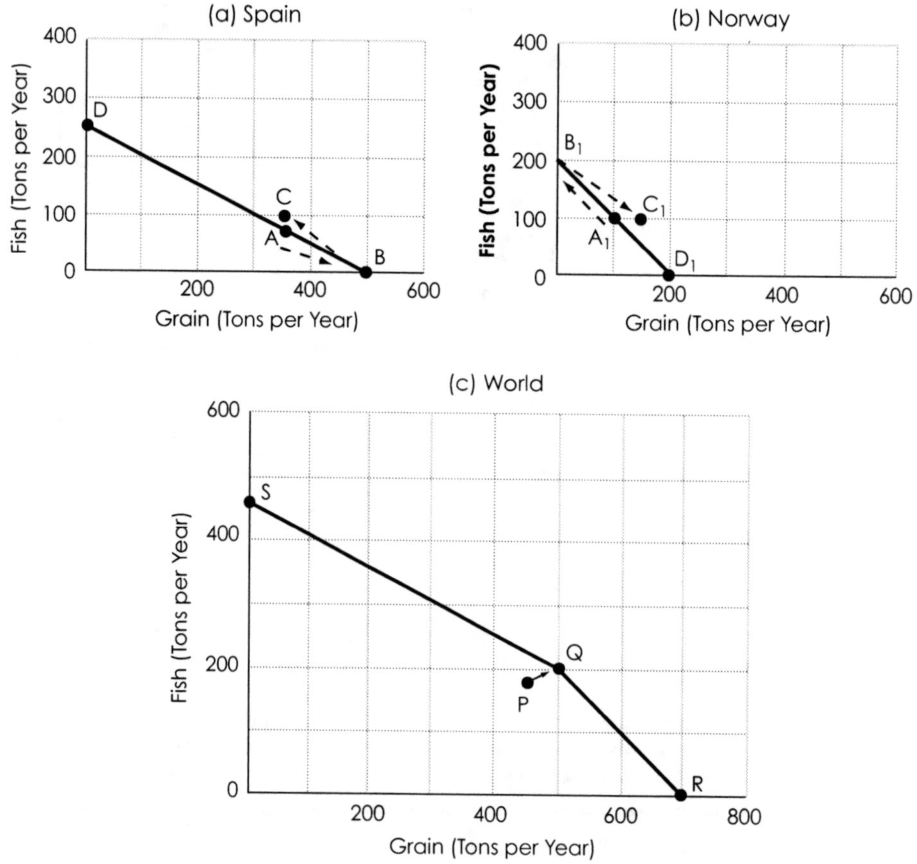

This figure shows production possibility frontiers for Spain, Norway, and the two countries combined. Before trade, Spain produces and consumes at point A and Norway at point A. Together these correspond to world consumption point P, which is inside the world production possibility frontier. After trade begins, Spain specializes in producing grain (point B) and trades part of the grain for fish, moving to consumption point C. Norway specializes in producing fish (point B_1) and reaches consumption point C_1 through trade. As a result, world efficiency is improved and point Q on the world production possibility frontier is reached.

of Figure 7.2). Starting from there, assume that the world output of fish is to be increased. For the sake of efficiency, Norwegian farmers should be the first to switch to fishing, because the opportunity cost of fish is lower in Norway (1 ton of grain per ton of fish) than in Spain (2 tons of grain per ton of fish). As Norwegians switch to fishing, then, world production moves upward and to the left along the line segment RQ.

When all Norwegians have abandoned farming for fishing, the world will have arrived at point Q–500 tons of grain (all Spanish) and 200 tons of fish (all Norwegian). From that point on, the only way to get more fish is to have Spanish farmers switch to fishing. At the opportunity cost of 2 tons of grain per ton of fish, this moves the economy along the line segment QS. When all Spanish farmers are fishing, the world arrives at point S, where 450 tons of fish and no grain are produced. The production possibility frontier for the world as a whole, then, is the kinked line RQS.

Effects of Trade

The pretrade production point for the world as a whole lies inside the world production possibility frontier. Adding together the quantities of fish and grain from A and A_1, we arrive at point P in part (c) of Figure 7.2–450 tons of grain and 175 tons of fish. This is inefficient; the world economy as a whole could produce more of both goods. To increase efficiency, both countries must specialize.

Suppose that Spain shifts its production from 350 tons of grain and 75 tons of fish (point A) to 500 tons of grain and no fish (point B). It then trades the extra 150 tons of grain for 100 tons of Norwegian fish. Spain's consumption thus ends up at point C, while its production remains at B. At the same time, Norway shifts its production from A_1 to B_1, that is, it specializes entirely in fish. The extra 100 tons of fish are traded for the 150 tons of Spanish grain, moving Norwegian consumption to point C_1.

As a result of specialization plus trade, then, both Spain and Norway have moved to points that lie outside their own production possibility frontiers. As they do so, the world as a whole moves from point P inside its production possibility frontier to point Q on the frontier. Thus, specialization improves the efficiency of the world economy as a whole, increases production of both goods, and leaves both countries better off than they would be if they did not trade.

Empirical Evidence on Comparative Advantage

Ricardo's theory of comparative advantage suggests that each country will export goods for which its labor is relatively productive compared with that of its trading partners. A number of economists have put this simple version of the theory to empirical tests.

One of the first to do so was G.D.A. MacDougal. In 1951 MacDougal published a study of U.S.-British trade, using data from 1937.[1] He compared a number of industries in terms of relative labor productivity in the two countries with the ratio of their exports of the products of those industries. The results strongly supported the Ricardian theory. Labor productivity was higher in the United States than in the United Kingdom for all of the industries studied, indicating that the United States had a Ricardian absolute advantage in all of the products. As predicted by the theory, however, the United Kingdom was relatively successful in exporting the goods in which its labor productivity disadvantage was lowest. British exports were greater than U.S. exports for all the industries studied in which British labor was more than half as productive as U.S. labor (for example, woolen cloth, footwear, hosiery). U.S. exports exceeded British exports for all the industries in which U.S. labor was more than twice as productive as British labor. Later studies using different sets of data have tended to confirm this result.

Comparative Advantage with Multiple Factors of Production

The Ricardian model of comparative advantage focused on a single factor of production: labor. Studies such as MacDougal's indicate that the single-factor version of the theory has considerable explanatory power. However, it can also be extended to take multiple factors of production into account.

THE HECKSCHER-OHLIN THEOREM   Early in the twentieth century two Swedish economists, Eli Heckscher and Bertil Ohlin, developed a model that took into account two factors of production: capital and labor. They reasoned that countries with abundant supplies of labor and little capital would have a comparative advantage in labor-intensive goods, whereas countries with abundant capital and relatively less labor would have a comparative advantage in capital-intensive goods. The proposition that countries would tend to export products that use their relatively more abundant factor more intensively has come to be known as the **Heckscher-Ohlin theorem**. An illustration of this theorem is the pattern in which the United States exports capital-intensive aircraft and computers to China in exchange for labor-intensive clothing and handicrafts.

Heckscher-Ohlin theorem

The proposition that countries tend to export goods that make intensive use of the factors of production that the country possesses in relative abundance.

The Importance of Demand

Both single-factor and multiple-factor versions of the theory of comparative advantage focus on supply conditions as the explanation of trade patterns. They implicitly assume that the consumer tastes that underlie the demand for goods and services are identical in all countries. In practice, however, patterns of trade contain some features that can be explained only by taking demand into account.

One such feature is the tendency of countries to trade most heavily with others at a similar level of economic development. This is not predicted by the simple Ricardian theory, which suggests that trade would be most profitable between countries that differ from each other as much as possible. For example, simple comparative advantage would suggest that the United States would have more trade with Mexico, structurally a very different economy, than with Canada, which not only has a much smaller population than Mexico, but also is more similar in many ways to the United States. However, Canada turns out to be the largest U.S. trading partner, and several distant countries, including Germany and Japan, rank close to nearby Mexico.

A closely related puzzle is the fact that countries both import and export the products of many industries. The United States is both a major importer and exporter of motor vehicles, textiles, computers, foodstuffs, and footwear, to name just a few examples.

Comparative advantage can explain these trade patterns only at the expense of trivializing the concept—by saying, for example, that Germany has a comparative advantage in producing Audis and the United States has a comparative advantage in producing Cadillacs. A better explanation is that such trade patterns reflect the influence of demand and tastes. Firms in developed countries sell where the demand for their products is greatest—in other developed countries. Cross-trade within product categories reflects patterns of tastes: Although U.S. automakers pattern their cars to fit the tastes of a majority of domestic consumers, some domestic buyers share European tastes for Audis and BMWs. These demand-side influences are not taken into account by the Ricardian theory and its modern variants, which look only at production costs.

Comparative Advantage and "Competitiveness"

As noted at the beginning of the chapter, U.S. involvement in world trade has grown greatly in recent decades. However, as U.S. exports have set records, imports have grown even more rapidly. In the first decade of the twenty-first century, the *trade deficit*—the amount by which imports exceed exports—reached an all-time high. This became a major cause of national concern. News reporters, editorialists, and politicians feared that the United States was no longer "competitive" in the world economy. Competitiveness means different things to different people, but at the heart of it is a concern that foreign workers work harder and foreign business managers have become smarter than their U.S. counterparts. "Soon the Japanese, the Koreans, and the Europeans will be better at everything than we are," people have said. "Eventually we won't be able to export anything at all!"

Some aspects of U.S. trade trends are a legitimate cause for concern. However, the theory of comparative advantage casts doubt on the notion that a country can reach a point at which it imports everything and exports nothing. In fact, classical trade theory, as embodied in the Spain-Norway example presented earlier, maintains that a country always has a comparative advantage in producing something even when it has an absolute disadvantage (in terms of labor hours or other factor inputs) for all goods. In terms of comparative advantage, then, a country must always be "competitive" in producing something.

Nevertheless, comparative advantage does not guarantee an exact match between the value of a country's exports and the value of its imports. The numerical examples given earlier, which suggest that this must be the case, omit two important details. First, they leave out international financial transactions, including purchases and sales of corporate stocks, government bonds, and other securities, as well as several kinds of international banking transactions. Second, they assume that trade takes the form of barter, whereas in practice most international trade uses money as a means of payment. Let us look briefly at the implications of each of these considerations for comparative advantage and competitiveness.

FINANCIAL TRANSACTIONS AND THE BALANCE OF TRADE   International financial transactions are important because they allow a country to import more goods and services than it exports, or to export more than it imports, in a given year. To take a very simple case, suppose that U.S. consumers decide to buy $100 million worth of television sets from Korean firms. What will the Korean firms do with the $100 million they receive? They can use it to buy airliners built in the United States, in which case trade in goods between the United States and Korea will balance. However, they can instead use it to buy U.S. government bonds or make deposits in U.S. banks. In that case, no U.S. goods will be exported in the current year to balance the imports. The Korean owners of the bonds or bank deposits have a claim on future exports from the United States; they can cash in their financial assets and spend them any time they like. But meanwhile, despite the U.S. comparative advantage in producing airliners, the U.S. trade accounts will not be balanced.

Could we say, then, that recent U.S. balance-of-trade deficits reflect a comparative advantage for the United States in the production of financial assets? That would certainly be one way to look at it. We could also say that Korean buyers simply prefer future U.S. airliners over current ones. That would be closer to the truth. A large part of the current U.S. trade deficit can be explained by the fact that many other countries, especially in Asia, have much high savings rates than the United States, which does indicate a preference for future consumption over current consumption. Looked at in this light, we should be cautious about assuming that the imbalance in merchandise trade reflects a loss of "competitiveness" in the sense of lost comparative advantage.

EXCHANGE RATES AND COMPETITIVENESS   To understand international trade fully, we must also take into account the fact that it is conducted in terms of money. However, there is no "world money"; each country has its own currency. Thus, before one can buy goods, services, or financial instruments from abroad, one must first visit the *foreign-exchange markets*, in which one currency can be traded for another. The windows at international airports where tourists can use dollars to buy European euros or British pounds are a tiny part of these markets. Larger exchanges of currency are carried out through major banks in New York, London, Tokyo, and other world financial centers.

The rates at which two currencies are exchanged are determined by the forces of supply and demand. These vary greatly from day to day and from year to year. For example, in early 2000 a U.S. dollar was worth 1.10 euros; by 2005 it was worth only 0.80 euros. As exchange rates vary, so do the prices of countries' imports and exports. At 1.10 euros to a dollar, an American firm need spend only $50 to import a 55-euro bottle of French wine. At 0.80 euros to the dollar, it takes $62.50 to buy the same 55-euro bottle. Similarly, at 1.10 euros to the dollar, a French buyer would have to lay out 2,200 euros to buy a $2,000 Apple computer made in the United States. At 0.80 euros to the dollar, the price to the French buyer would be much less—only 1,600 euros.

We see, then, that the ability of U.S. exporters to compete in world markets—and the ability of U.S. firms to compete against imports in their home markets—depends not only on Ricardian considerations of factor productivity but also on exchange rates.

That is one reason why countries that do not allow their exchange rates to fluctuate freely in response to market forces are often subject to criticism. For example, for many years China held its exchange rate fixed at about 8 yuan per U.S. dollar, despite strong indications that supply and demand conditions would dictate a stronger yuan. U.S. politicians saw this as giving China an "unfair" advantage by making its exports cheaper for U.S. buyers, and making U.S. goods more expensive in China. When China, in mid-2005, began to move toward a more flexible exchange rate policy, U.S. exporters, and firms that competed with imports from China, breathed a sigh of relief. However, it often takes several years for changes in exchange rates to affect trade patterns, so the long-run effects of the change in Chinese policy cannot yet be seen.

TRADE POLICY AND PROTECTIONISM

Up to this point we have not mentioned governmental policy regarding international trade. We have pictured a world in which Norwegian fishers and Spanish farmers are free to trade as dictated by comparative advantage. In practice, however, governments are deeply involved in the regulation and promotion of trade. In this section we examine government's role in international trade.

Moves Toward Freer Trade Since World War II

The post–World War II period saw a broad movement toward freer trade aided by several new international organizations. The International Monetary Fund was created in 1944 to maintain a stable financial climate for trade. The General Agreement on Tariffs and Trade (GATT) was founded in an attempt to prevent a return of **protectionism**—policies designed to shield domestic industries from competition by imports—which was common in the 1930s. In 1995, GATT was replaced by the World Trade Organization (WTO), which is now the world's principal authority overseeing international trade.

Protectionism

Any policy that is intended to shield domestic industries from import competition.

Tariff

A tax on imported goods.

WTO rules permit taxes on imports, known as **tariffs**, but restrict their use. Under the so-called most-favored-nation principle, WTO member nations are supposed to charge the same tariff rates for imports from all WTO countries. A series of multinational negotiations sponsored by the WTO succeeded in lowering the average level of tariffs from 40 percent at the end of World War II to less than 10 percent today. Throughout this period, as noted earlier, the volume of world trade grew consistently faster than the volume of world output. Also, the WTO has tried,

Import quotas

A limit on the quantity of a good that can be imported over a given period.

with far from complete success, to discourage the use of **import quotas**—restrictions on the quantity of a good that can be imported during a given period.

REGIONAL TRADING BLOCS   In addition to the activities of the WTO, there have been efforts to set up regional trading blocs in several parts of the world. The best known of these is the European Union (EU). A key aim of the EU has been to eliminate all barriers to trade among the major European countries, eventually leading to a situation in which trade among these countries is nearly as free as trade among the states of the United States.

Not all goals of the EU have been achieved in full. Differences in levels of economic development among the countries of the EU, which are greater than those among the states of the United States, have been a recurring source of problems. Also, the goal of a single currency for Europe has proved more difficult to achieve than many had hoped. Nonetheless, after its expansion to 25 countries in 2004, the EU, with a population of 450 million, can fairly be considered the world's largest unified economic zone in most respects.

On the other side of the Atlantic, progress was under way toward the formation of an even larger trading bloc. Its foundations were laid when the United States reached an agreement with Canada, its largest trading partner, to eliminate almost all trade barriers over a ten-year period beginning in 1989. (The U.S.-Canada treaty does allow for continued use of quotas on some farm, forest, and fishery products, and in some other respects falls short of the free-trade ideal.) This was soon followed by the North American Free Trade Agreement (NAFTA), discussed in *Applying Economic Ideas 7.1*.

Still another regional trading bloc, formed in late 1992, unites six countries of the Association of Southeast Asian Nations in the ASEAN Free Trade Area (AFTA). The member countries—Thailand, Philippines, Malaysia, Brunei, Singapore, and Indonesia—have a total population of 320 million people.

There is a downside to regional free trade blocs, however. That is the tendency of such blocs to raise protectionist barriers against outsiders. Thus, NAFTA contains provisions protecting North American (mainly U.S.) firms against competition from Asian and European rivals. The EU is notorious for shielding its farmers from outside competition. Serious worries remain about the possibility of open trade war between the blocs. The AFTA, on the other hand, is composed of relatively poor nations that cannot afford to cut themselves off from world trade. Their bloc is based on the principle of "open regionalism" that will lower barriers within the group without raising them against outsiders.

Countertrends: The New Protectionism

Spurred by the strengthening of free-trade institutions, the volume of world trade has increased greatly in the past four decades. However, protectionism is far from dead. In addition to the continued use of traditional tariffs and quotas, especially in agricul-

⮞ APPLYING ECONOMIC IDEAS 7.1

NAFTA AT TEN YEARS

In 1994, Mexico, Canada, and the United States entered into the North American Free Trade Agreement (NAFTA). Ten years later, in the 2004 presidential election, NAFTA remained a hot-button issue.

NAFTA has brought some obvious positive results. Between 1993 and 2003, trade within NAFTA countries doubled. Mexico replaced Japan as America's second largest trading partner behind Canada. Early winners included U.S. export powerhouses like Caterpillar, Inc. The construction equipment giant saw its exports to Mexico triple in the five years after NAFTA was initiated, and captured the lion's share of future growth in this market. A key reason: NAFTA resulted in elimination of Mexico's 20 percent import tariff on U.S. construction equipment, while leaving the tariff in place on equipment made by Japanese rivals.

For U.S. firms, the opening of the Mexican market meant building new plants south of the border. Hoover Company, for example, started building handheld vacuum cleaners in Ciudad Juarez, just across the border from El Paso, Texas. Hoover previously manufactured these machines in Asia, but believed it would be more economical to move the work to Mexico.

The free trade agreement is not limited to manufacturing. It has created significant opportunities for U.S. service industries, as well. Southwestern Bell Corporation helped to rebuild Mexico's creaky telephone system. Bank of America, which already has branches in every U.S. state along the Mexican border, expanded into Mexico itself as barriers to international banking were relaxed.

Not all results of NAFTA have been as positive as had been hoped by those who conceived and negotiated the pact in the 1990s. In particular, effects on Mexican labor markets have been mixed. More than half a million new manufacturing jobs have been created, but NAFTA has opened Mexico's farm sector to competition from efficient and often subsidized U.S. producers. The result: more farm jobs have been lost than were gained in the factory sector. Also, although there have been huge gains in productivity growth due to foreign investment in Mexico, this has not fed through to the labor force in the form of higher real wages.

"NAFTA has had positive effects in Mexico but they could have been better," said David de Ferranti, World Bank Vice President for Latin America and the Caribbean, summarizing his organization's report on the first ten years of NAFTA. "Free trade definitely brings new economic opportunities, but the lessons from NAFTA for other countries negotiating with the United States are that free trade alone is not enough without significant policy and institutional reforms."

Source: Daniel Lederman, Louis Maloney, and Louis Serven, *Lessons from NAFTA*, World Bank, 2003; John J. Audley and Demetrios Papademetriou, Sandra Polaski, and Scott Vaugh, *NAFTA's Promise and Reality*, Carnegie Endowment for World Peace, 2003.

ture, new types of protectionism have sprung up, resulting in the imposition of additional restrictions on international trade. The new protectionism consists in part of devices such as "orderly marketing agreements" and "voluntary export restraints." These involve the use of political pressure—usually backed by the threat of a tariff or quota—to restrain trade in a particular good.

A leading example of the new protectionism was the so-called Multifiber Agreement (MFA), formally adopted in 1974.[2] This agreement, which began as a temporary restriction on imports of Japanese cotton textiles into the United States, grew into a vast web of quotas that all major trading countries used to manage trade in all types of textiles and apparel. The agreement was a major violation of WTO principles, not only in its emphasis on quotas, but also in its open discrimination among exporting nations. By imposing much more stringent limits on imports from developing countries than from industrialized exporters in the EU and elsewhere, the

MFA undermined not only the principles of the WTO, but also the stated U.S. policy of promoting economic development in low-income countries. Several developing countries complained about unfair treatment because of the MFA restrictions, which cost them as much as 20 million jobs each year. These complaints led to the termination of the MFA at the end of 2004. Termination of the MFA will potentially rationalize patterns of international textile trade; however, it has had some painful effects in the short run. Under the MFA, some countries were subject to tighter restrictions than others, with the result of a shift in textile production patterns among developing countries. Since the end of the MFA, countries like Bangladesh, which had large quotas under the MFA, have lost market share to more efficient producers in China.

The new protectionism not only applies to preventing the import of foreign goods, but to preventing the export of jobs. Many companies in the United States and other countries have shifted their operations away from the high-wage environment at home to one with cheaper labor to lower their costs of production. This practice of shifting jobs from one country to another is known as outsourcing. As discussed in *Economics in the News 7.1*, countries such as China and India are the most common locales for outsourcing everything from customer service centers to city government administrative services. In 2004, the backlash against the foreign outsourcing of U.S. jobs grew in state legislatures around the country. Bills aimed at curbing the outflow of jobs were introduced in several states. Most required that state contracts go only to companies that certify the work will be done inside the United States.

Although these new protectionist agreements are referred to as voluntary, their effects on consumers scarcely differ from those of a compulsory tariff or quota. Prices go up and reductions in efficiency occur as production moves against the direction of comparative advantage. For example, the cost of the Multifiber Agreement to U.S. consumers was estimated at more than $20 billion per year, or about $238 per U.S. household as of 1986.

Antidumping rules are another aspect of the new protectionism. A country is said to be "dumping" its goods when it sells them in a foreign market for less than the price at which it sells them at home or for less than the cost of producing them. Under certain provisions of U.S. law, domestic producers facing competition from imports that have been "dumped" on the U.S. market can seek tariffs. Steel is one of the industries that have sought this type of protection. Application of antidumping rules has been a constant source of friction between the United States and the EU. The WTO has ruled against the United States in several recent antidumping cases, including an attempt by President George W. Bush to impose antidumping tariffs on steel imports.

Advocates of free trade object to antidumping laws on two grounds. First, they point out that in times of slack world demand for a product, efficiency requires that firms temporarily sell that product at prices below average total costs. Second, they claim that "dumped" imports, like all other imports, produce benefits for consumers that must be weighed against the harm done to producers.

ECONOMICS IN THE NEWS 7.1

OUTSOURCING

Shifting U.S. jobs overseas has become a hot-button political issue. But the bottom line for companies is that outsourcing saves them a lot of money.

Early in 2004, Gregory Mankiw, chairman President Bush's Council of Economic Advisers, took a lot of heat from both sides of the political aisle for suggesting that outsourcing to India and other countries is a win-win for both sides. Democratic presidential candidate John Kerry and Republican House Speaker Dennis Hastert sharply criticized the senior Bush aide, saying jobs should stay in the United States. Kerry said offshoring is done by "Benedict Arnold CEOs."

Just as China is the top low-cost manufacturer, India is the equivalent in business services. India exported nearly $10 billion in tech services in 2003, mostly to the United States. The volume is said to be growing more than 30 percent a year. Some big changes in the past decade are driving this growth. India has opened itself to trade and eased business restrictions. Plus, communications advances have made it far easier to have operations around the world. That $10 billion makes up less than 3 percent of global spending on IT services, says Ashish Thadhani, senior vice president of Brean Murray & Co. "So there's lots of room to grow," he said.

Putting a stop to such growth now won't be easy. Savings are a big draw, with quality of work a close second. "The rule of thumb is that each employee in India translates into annual savings of $20,000 to $30,000," said Thadhani. "General Electric is saving well over $300 million doing captive in-house business process outsourcing in India. Recently IBM indicated its savings (in information technology services) could be more than $150 million a year," he said.

GE spokesman Peter Stack, echoing Mankiw's win-win sentiment, says savings are only part of the allure. "The abilities of (developing) countries to rapidly grow middle classes and well-compensated work forces benefits us tremendously. They create markets for us to sell into," he said. "It's about global competitiveness."

Since entering India in 1997, GE's work force there has swelled to over 20,000. Stack says jobs done in India are increasingly sophisticated and include pure science research and development.

China and India have a seemingly endless supply of lower cost workers. India's 1.1 billion population is second only to China's 1.3 billion. But India has a steady stream of high-caliber professionals. They are English-speaking engineers, software technicians, and other high-tech specialists. They're also call-center personnel trained to modify their Raj-rooted Anglo-Indian accents and speak like Americans. "The Indian education system places strong emphasis on technical and quantitative skills, English proficiency and a diligent work ethic," Thadhani said.

Source: Marilyn Alva, "U.S. Firms' Outsourcing To India Reaps Big Savings, Political Heat," *Investor's Business Daily*, February 20, 2004. Portions reprinted with permission.

In recent years, some economists have argued that the traditional case for free trade relies too much on the model of perfect competition. They say that in an era of global oligopolies, such as electronics and airline industries, countries can sometimes gain, at the expense of their trading partners, from "strategic" use of new protectionist policies. However, the case for the new strategic protectionism has many of the weaknesses of the case for the old protectionism: Retaliation by trading partners pursuing their own strategies may lead to a situation in which everyone is left worse off than under free trade. And rent seeking by special interest groups is likely to steer trade policies toward strategies that make one group better off at the expense of others within the country, rather than at the expense of foreign competitors.[3] For example, U.S. manufacturers of flat display screens for laptop computers have recently sought protection against competing screens made in Asia. But among the biggest losers from such a trade restriction would be U.S. firms manufacturing laptop computers (many for export) using screens made in Asia.

Understanding Protectionism: Impacts of Trade on Income Distribution

Why is it that protectionist measures are so widely used, despite the potential economic efficiency to be gained from free trade? To understand the sources of protectionism, we can begin by considering the effects of trade on the distribution of income within each country. A modification of the Spain-Norway example to take into account more than one factor of production will illustrate some basic principles.

Suppose that fishing requires a relatively large capital investment per worker, in the form of expensive boats, nets, and navigation equipment, while farming requires a relatively small investment in tractors and plows. Fishing can then be said to be capital intensive and farming to be labor intensive. Also assume, as before, that in the absence of trade the opportunity cost of fish will be higher in Spain than in Norway, so that Spain has a comparative advantage in grain and Norway has a comparative advantage in fish. As in the single-factor example, international trade will still make it possible for total world production of both fish and grain to increase. It will still enable the quantities of both goods available in both countries to rise. Now, however, a new question arises:

How will the gains from trade be distributed within each country?

To answer this question, we must look at what happens in factor markets as trade brings about increasing specialization in each country. In Norway, production shifts from farming to fishing. As grain production is phased out, large quantities of labor and relatively small quantities of capital are released. The shift in production thus creates a surplus of labor and a shortage of capital. Factor markets can return to equilibrium only when wages fall relative to the rate of return on capital. Only then will fisheries adopt more labor-intensive production methods. Meanwhile the opposite process occurs in Spain: The shift from fishing to farming depresses the rate of return on capital and increases the wage rate.

These changes in relative factor prices determine how the gains from trade are distributed among the people of each country. Spanish workers and Norwegian boat owners will gain doubly from trade: first because trade increases the size of the pie (the total quantity of goods) and second because the shifts in factor prices give them a larger slice of that pie. For Norwegian workers and Spanish owners of agricultural capital, in contrast, one of these effects works against the other. These groups still benefit from the growth of the pie, but they get a smaller piece of it than before. They may or may not end up better off as a result of the trade.

Suppose that the comparative advantage in the pretrade situation is large and the difference in factor intensity between the two countries is small. Norwegian workers and owners of Spanish farms will still gain from trade in an absolute sense, even though they will lose ground relative to others in their own country. If conditions are less favorable, however, they can end up worse off than they were before trade began. Who gains and who loses depends partly on the degree of specialization of factors of production.

So far we have looked at matters only in terms of broadly defined labor, as if workers could move from job to job without cost. However, suppose instead that we think not in terms of labor in general but in terms of people with farming skills and people with fishing skills, or auto workers and textile workers. When specialized skills and locational factors are taken into account, the effects of trade include not only changes in relative wages, but also periods of unemployment, costs of retraining, and moving expenses.[4] The uneven impact of changes in trade patterns on the lives and jobs of specific categories of workers turns out to be one of the main sources of political support for protectionism, as we will see in the next section.

Protectionism and Public Choice

International competition, like other forms of competition, tends to drive wages and returns to other factors of production toward the level of opportunity costs. Protection against foreign competition relieves the pressure and permits the protected firms and workers to earn rents, that is, profits and wages in excess of opportunity costs. Thus, the political process that results in trade restrictions can be analyzed in terms of public choice theory and rent seeking.

As a specific example, consider the costs and benefits of U.S. trade restrictions on sugar imports. Historically, the United States produced about half of the sugar it consumed and imported the rest.[5] By the early 2000s, as a result of trade restrictions, it was importing only about 12 percent of its sugar. As a result, sugar prices in the United States have ranged from two to three times the world price, at a cost to U.S. consumers of some $1.9 billion per year. The European Union has a similar program of restrictions on sugar imports.

What explains the willingness of U.S. consumers to pay high prices for sugar? It is, apparently, a classic case of concentrated benefits and thinly spread costs. The benefits are concentrated on producers, who are few in number. Large companies like Flo-Sun and U.S. Sugar contributed hundreds of thousands of dollars to candidates of both major parties during the 2000 election cycle. On the other hand, the $1.9 billion cost of sugar quotas to consumers comes to just $6 per individual. For them, sugar policy is an insignificant consideration in making political choices.

Sugar policy can also be viewed in terms of its impact on jobs. Only about 16,000 U.S. workers are employed in sugar production and refining in the United States, and the jobs of only about 3,000 of those would be threatened by an end to quotas. Production of corn sweetener, which benefits indirectly from high sugar production, employs more workers, perhaps as many as 250,000, but the threat to those jobs is also less direct. If sugar quotas were removed, the chief employment benefit would be creation of new jobs in the food processing industry, which already employs far more workers, more than 500,000. The political impact of changes in the job market, however, is not proportional to the number of jobs affected. The key consideration is that workers in sugar production know who they are and understand that their jobs might be threatened by a policy change. Potential new workers in food processing, currently employed elsewhere or unemployed, do not specifically identify sugar policy as a factor affecting their welfare. As a result, sugar workers are politically active on the issue and potential new food processing workers are not.

This analysis could be repeated for any protected market. For example, the cost to consumers of each job saved in the apparel industry by the MFA was estimated at $46,000 per year, compared with average earnings of just $11,000 per year for textile workers.[6] Studies of tariffs and quotas on peanuts, books, ceramic tile, and other products give similar results. In each case economic investigators have found that total gains to producers fall short of total costs to consumers; however, the benefits are concentrated on compact, politically active groups while the costs are spread among millions of households.

A Race to the Bottom?

Often opponents of free trade speak a simple language of self-interest, using money and political power to advance their position regardless of effects on others. However, some opponents of globalization in high-income countries have a genuine concern for possible adverse effects of trade on people in their low-income trade partners.

One such concern is that free trade leads to a "race to the bottom" in global labor standards. Trade based on comparative advantage is all well and good, they would say, if a country does have a genuine advantage in producing something at a low cost. They would hardly want Iceland to be self-sufficient in coffee or the city-state of Singapore to have to produce all its own rice. Still, they say, some kinds of cost advantage should not be recognized as a legitimate basis for trade.

In an evaluating such concerns, it may be helpful to distinguish between "cash standards" and "core standards." Cash standards mean wages and nonwage labor benefits like employer-paid health care or paid vacation. To insist that workers in poor countries be paid the same as those in rich ones would be to deprive them of the benefits of economic growth based on their countries' one abundant resource—labor power. It would also fly in the face of evidence that countries like Korea or Taiwan, where living standards have grown most rapidly in past decades, began as low-wage countries and have been among the most open to trade.

Core labor standards, on the other hand, are seen more as a matter of universal human rights than simply of labor costs. They include such things as abolition of forced labor and abusive child labor, the right for workers to associate freely and bargain collectively, and the absence of discrimination in employment. A true "race to the bottom" would occur if policies encouraged production to move to the countries that most flagrantly ignored core labor standards.

A similar concern is that trade policy could promote a "race to the bottom" in terms of environmental standards. Sustainable waste disposal practices are typically more costly for producers than dumping untreated wastes into the environment. Again, a distinction could be made between environmental standards that reflect economic choices and those that could be regarded as core standards. With regard to economic choice, it can be argued that people in low-income countries might not be willing to sacrifice as much material consumption for a given marginal improvement in local air or water quality as those in high-income countries. Environmental quality is a "normal good" as we defined it in Chapter 5. As incomes rise, people are willing to "buy" more environmental quality, and trends over time show that they do so. (Compare urban air quality in London today with that in Charles Dickens' time, for example.)

On the other hand, companies and sometimes countries may be tempted to cut costs by ignoring more fundamental environmental standards. Suppose, for example, that two countries both have well-designed environmental laws, but in one, the laws are enforced, whereas in the other, corrupt inspectors take bribes and turn their backs on violations. Would it be right to say that the latter country had a comparative advantage based on lower costs? Economic analysis says that it would not. Total costs of production, including both internal and external costs, are likely to be higher, not lower, in the country where externalities go uncontrolled. Costs only appear lower because lax enforcement allows producers to impose the costs on their neighbors. If the pollution in question has a cross-border nature, like emissions of greenhouse gasses or the chemicals that destroy the earth's protective ozone layer, it is even harder to argue that world efficiency gains when trade moves production to high-pollution countries.

The debate over the Central American Free Trade Agreement (CAFTA), ratified by the U.S. Senate in mid-2005, was a showcase for debate over labor and environmental standards. The administration of President George Bush, which strongly backed CAFTA, pointed to clauses in the agreement that promised enforcement of core standards. Opponents argued that those provisions were a sham, that during negotiations, log-rolling by special interests had watered them down to the point where they would be completely ineffective. The debate often generated more heat than light even though real issues were at stake.

There is no reason to expect the war of words over globalization and trade policy to end soon. There is also no indication that firms and workers will stop using the machinery of representative democracy to pursue their own economic interests, sometimes at the expense of their neighbors. We can only hope that an understanding of the economics of international trade can help in evaluating the claims made by the various participants in this ongoing debate.

SUMMARY

1. **How can the principle of comparative advantage be applied to international trade?** A country is said to have a comparative advantage in the production of a good if it can produce it at a lower opportunity cost than its trading partner can. Trade is based on the principle that if each country exports goods in which it has a comparative advantage, total world production of all goods and services can increase and boost total consumption in each trading country. The *Heckscher-Ohlin theorem* proposes that countries will tend to have a comparative advantage in goods that make intensive use of the factors of production that are relatively abundant in that country.

2. **How is the notion of competitiveness related to that of comparative advantage?** In recent years, U.S. imports have expanded more rapidly than exports, leaving the country with a record trade deficit. Some observers interpreted this situation as indicating a loss of competitiveness, implying that U.S. firms were no longer capable of producing goods that other countries wanted. However, trends in imports and exports cannot be evaluated without consideration of international financial transactions and exchange rates. When these are taken into account, a country that is "competitive" in the sense that it produces high quality goods using state-of-the-art management and technology can still import more than it exports.

3. **What has been the trend of international trade policy in recent years?** The general trend in international trade policy has been toward a reduction of traditional *tariff* and *quota* barriers to trade. Another important trend has been the formation of regional trade groups like the European Union and NAFTA. However, recent years have also seen increased use of protectionist devices such as orderly marketing agreements, voluntary quotas, antidumping laws, and restrictive product standards.

4. **How does international trade affect income distribution within each country?** In a world with two or more factors of production, trade tends to increase the demand for factors that are used relatively intensively in producing goods for export and to decrease the demand for factors that are used relatively intensively in producing goods that compete with imported goods. Thus, although trade benefits a country as a whole, it may not benefit owners of factors that are specialized for producing goods that compete with imports.

5. **How can protectionist policies be understood in terms of public choice theory and rent seeking?** Because protectionist policies shield firms and factor owners from international competition, they allow rents—that is, payments in excess of opportunity costs—to be earned. Often those who benefit from these rents are small, well-organized groups that have political influence out of proportion to their numbers. Although the overall costs of protectionism tend to outweigh the benefits, the costs are spread widely among consumers, each of whom is affected less than producers by any given trade barrier.

KEY TERMS

Absolute advantage	Protectionism
Heckscher-Ohlin	Tariff
theorem	Import quotas

PROBLEMS AND TOPICS FOR DISCUSSION

1. **NAFTA and comparative advantage.** What does the example of NAFTA (*Applying Economic Ideas*

7.1) suggest about U.S. versus Mexican comparative advantage in the production of construction equipment? Of vacuum cleaners? Do these examples suggest a pattern of trade that would be consistent with the Heckscher-Ohlin theorem? What are the potential benefits and costs of NAFTA for U.S. and Mexican workers? Consumers? Owners of productive resources other than labor?

2. **A change in costs and comparative advantage.** Suppose that new, high-yield grains are introduced in Norway and that the number of labor hours needed to grow a ton of grain there is cut from 5 hours to 2.5 hours. What will happen to trade between Norway and Spain? If the number of labor hours needed to grow a ton of grain in Norway falls all the way to 2, what will happen to the pattern of trade?

3. **Competitiveness.** Consider the following statement: "The United States may still be number one, but I don't think we will be much longer. The European Union, Japan, all areas of the world are catching up. Soon it will no longer be economical for us to produce anything." On the basis of what you have learned about the principle of comparative advantage, do you think it is possible to reach a point at which it is no longer worthwhile to produce anything—that is, a point at which it becomes economical to import all goods? Discuss.

4. **Trade bargaining.** If you were a strong supporter of free trade and in charge of U.S. international trade policy, would you cut tariffs and quotas or would you negotiate with the nation's trading partners, maintaining trade barriers unless they lowered theirs too? Discuss.

5. **The globalization debate.** Do a Web search for "globalization + environment standards" or "globalization + labor standards." Reading pro- and anti-globalization sources, can you identify "economic" issues and "core" issues? Can you identify any cases in which it appears that parties to the debate are using altruistic rhetoric to defend simple self-interest?

CASE FOR DISCUSSION

WTO Ruling in Cotton Subsidy Case Makes U.S. Farmers Nervous

A ruling by the World Trade Organization condemning U.S. subsidies to cotton producers could open the door to similar cases, perhaps forcing advanced countries to agree to deeper cuts in their subsidies, say trade officials and agricultural experts.

The WTO ruled in a confidential decision that the U.S. had fallen foul of its WTO obligations by providing subsidies of $12.5 billion to U.S. cotton growers between 1999 and 2002, boosting U.S. exports and depressing prices at the expense of Brazilian cotton growers and other producers.

Under its left-leaning president, Luis Inacio Lula da Silva, Brazil has taken a lead among emerging countries in pushing for reductions of agricultural subsidies in the developed world.

The threat of further cases should help strengthen the bargaining position of agricultural exporting countries. Farm exporters are pressing for big cuts in domestic supports for rich-country producers, but the U.S. and European Union say developing countries must also make concessions, for instance, by cutting tariffs on agricultural and industrial goods.

U.S. farmers are nervous that the ruling could set a broad precedent. Payments similar to the cotton subsidies are made for other U.S. commodities such as soybeans, rice, and wheat.

Source: Jonathan Wheatley, Edward Alden, and Frances Williams, "Brazil Victory Could Prompt Subsidies Cases," *Financial Times,* April 28, 2004, p. 8..

QUESTIONS

1. A subsidy on exports is, in a sense, the opposite of a tariff on imports. If a tariff lowers efficiency, would you expect a subsidy to increase efficiency, or also lower it? How do tariffs and subsidies compare in the way they distort trade according to comparative advantage?

2. Who gains and who loses from U.S. cotton subsidies? Consider each of the following groups: U.S. producers, U.S. taxpayers, Brazilian producers, consumers in both countries? Do you think total gains exceed or fall short of total losses?

3. How could you explain the expenditure of billions of taxpayer dollars to subsidize a relatively few, highly prosperous U.S. cotton producers? Do the categories of public choice theory help here?

END NOTES

1. G. D. A. MacDougal, "British and American Exports: A Study Suggested by the Theory of Comparative Costs," *Economic Journal* (December 1951).

2. For a thorough discussion of the MFA, see Thomas Grennes, "The Multifiber Arrangement and the Management of International Textile Trade," *Cato Journal* (Spring/Summer 1989): 107–131.

3. For a good summary of the literature on strategic use of new protectionist devices, see Robert E. Baldwin, "Are Economists' Traditional Trade Policies Still Valid?" *Journal of Economic Literature* (June 1992): 804–829.

4. Data cited by Grennes give some idea of the size of these impacts. Between the 1950s and the 1980s, employment in the U.S. apparel industry decreased from more than 9 percent of manufacturing employment to less than 6 percent, and wages fell from 82 percent of average manufacturing earnings to 60 percent. These changes can be attributed at least in part to the increases in apparel imports that took place despite MFA quotas. The average apparel worker displaced from a job by imports was unemployed for 24 weeks before finding a job elsewhere. Without the MFA, the declines in the wages and jobs of apparel workers would have been even greater. Total employment in the U.S. apparel industry is estimated to be some 200,000 or more higher than it would be without the MFA.

5. Information on sugar policy and its effects based on Mark A. Groombridge, "American's Bittersweet Sugar Policy," Cato Institute Center for Trade Policy Studies, December 4, 2001.

6. See Grennes. The comparison of consumers' costs to workers' wages actually understates the true cost-benefit ratio because the MFA's cost to consumers continued year after year, whereas displaced apparel workers are out of work less than six months, on the average. Taking this fact into account, it has been estimated that consumers bear $31 in costs through higher apparel prices for each $1 benefit to apparel workers.

PART II

In Search of Prosperity and Stability

MANY ECONOMISTS DATE the beginning of their discipline from the publication, in 1776, of Adam Smith's book *The Wealth of Nations*. (See *Who Said it? Who Did It? 1.2*) Why is it, asked Smith, that some nations prosper while others lag behind? The issue remains a central focus of macroeconomic policy in our own time. In the U.S. presidential election of 2004, each party claimed that it would do best at creating jobs and raising living standards. In Germany in 2005, rising unemployment and slowing growth forced Chancellor Gerhard Schroeder to call early national elections. In Russia, President Vladimir Putin made doubling national product in ten years a major goal of his presidency. And in China, policy makers worried that a growth rate of nearly 10 percent per year was too fast to maintain economic and political stability. This chapter begins the exploration of macroeconomics by giving two broad perspectives on the search for prosperity and stability: A long-run perspective that emphasizes economic growth, and a short-term perspective that emphasizes the business cycle, employment, and inflation.

MACROECONOMICS IN THE LONG RUN: ECONOMIC GROWTH

No country becomes wealthy overnight. Nations that have become prosperous have done so as the result of steady growth over long periods of decades and even centuries. Countries that are poor rarely becomes so because of sudden catastrophe, but rather as the result of long periods of slow growth that lags behind the leaders.

Figure 8.1 shows how widely growth rates have differed among major areas of the world. During the second half of the 20th century, standards of living in much of Asia rose by a factor five. Countries like Korea and Japan caught up with European and North American levels of prosperity. At the same time, average incomes in Sub-

FIGURE 8.1

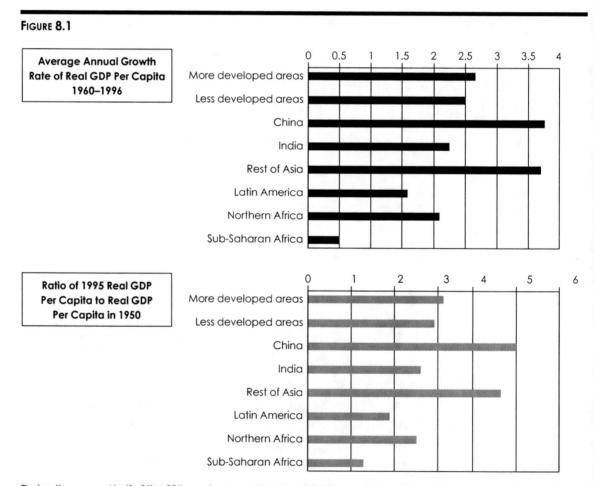

During the second half of the 20th century, growth rates of GDP per capita varied widely among regions of the world. Growth rates in China and other countries of Southeast Asia were rapid, allowing these countries to catch up with the world's most developed regions. Latin America and Africa lagged behind.

Source: Richard Easterlin, "The World Standard of Living Since 1800," *Journal of Economic Perspectives*, Vol 14 No 1 (Winter 2002), pp. 7-26. Data from Easterlin, Table 3; Chart by author.

Saharan Africa increased only 20 percent, and in some countries actually decreased. Economic growth theory seeks to explain the reasons for these differences in growth over time and among countries.

Measuring Economic Growth

Real

In economics, a term that refers to data that have been adjusted for the effects of inflation.

Economic growth is most often expressed in terms of *Gross Domestic Product (GDP)*, a measure of the value of total output of goods and services produced within a nation's borders during a period of time.[1] If GDP is to provide a meaningful measure of growth over time, it, like other economic quantities, must be expressed in **real** terms; that is, it must be adjusted for the effects of changes in the average price level. For example, from 1995 to 2005 U.S. **nominal** GDP (that is, GDP measured according to prices at which goods were actually sold in the given year) grew from $7,298 billion to $12,191 billion, or 68 percent. However, part of the increase in nominal GDP can be attributed to a 20 percent rise in the average price level during the period. Adjusted for inflation and expressed in constant 1995 dollars, real GDP increased over the decade by only about 40 percent. The term **real output** is frequently used as a synonym for real gross domestic product.

Nominal

In economics, a term that refers to data that have not been adjusted for the effects of inflation.

Sources of Economic Growth

Real output

A synonym for real gross domestic product.

The sources of economic growth can be divided into two main components: the growth of total labor inputs, on the one hand, and the growth of output per unit of labor, or labor productivity, on the other.

The growth of total labor inputs tends to be determined by social and demographic factors that differ from one country to another, but that do not change rapidly within any one country. One source of growth of labor inputs is, of course, population growth. Population in the United States is now growing at about 1 percent per year or less, largely thanks to immigration. Population in most other advanced countries is stable or slowly declining. Another possible source of increased labor input is increased labor force participation. In the United States, for example, from 1960 to 1989, labor force participation by women increased from 37 percent to 57 percent, more than offsetting a small decline in labor force participation among men. Since 1990, labor force participation trends of various groups have roughly balanced out, so that the total rate has not changed much. Over the same period, both population growth and increased labor force participation have been offset, in part, by a decrease in average weekly hours worked from about 39 in 1960 to about 34 today. Taking all these trends together, total hours worked in the U.S. economy have grown moderately.

In contrast to the relatively steady growth of hours worked, productivity in the United States has increased erratically over the past 50 years. From the end of World War II up to the early 1970s, productivity grew at an average rate of about 2.8 percent per year. From the mid-1970s to the early 1990s, productivity suffered a puzzling slowdown, falling to less than half its previous rate. Since the 1990s, productivity growth has recovered. In the early years of the 21st century, U.S. productivity has grown at the exceptionally rapid rate of about 4 percent per year.

Since hours worked per capita tend to fall as countries get richer, productivity growth holds the key to prosperity in the long run. What determines whether productivity grows rapidly or slowly?

According to one widely used economic model, output per labor hour can be attributed to changes in capital per worker and a catch-all category called **total factor productivity**.

Increasing capital per worker means giving workers better tools to do their jobs. These include industrial equipment like bulldozers and assembly robots, capital used in service jobs like hospital equipment and office computer systems, and infrastructure capital like roads and communications systems. Sources of total factor productivity growth include technological innovation, better education of the labor force

Total factor productivity

A measurement of improvements in technology and organization that allow increases in the output produced by given quantities of labor and capital.

 APPLYING ECONOMIC IDEAS 8.1

DECODING KOREA'S ECONOMIC MIRACLE

South Korea's record of economic growth from 1970 to 2000 is one of the most remarkable of any country in the world. At the beginning of the period, Korea was a poor country with per capita GDP about one-seventh that of the United States. By the end of the period, its GDP per capita was half that of the United States, about the same as middle-income European countries like Greece and Portugal. Where did this miraculous growth come from?

Economists divide the sources of economic growth into three components: Increases in labor inputs, increases in capital per worker, and improvements in technology and organization (total factor productivity). Each of these was important in Korea.

Hours worked increased largely because of an increase in the working-age population that averaged 1.9 percent per year. (Labor force participation in Korea is relatively low because only about half of Korean women work outside the home, compared with an average of more than 70 percent in other developed countries.) Adding to the effect of increases in the quantity of labor inputs were gains in education. In 1970s, only about a quarter of Korean workers had graduated from high school and less than 10 percent from college. By 2000, a quarter had graduated from college and about two-thirds from high school.

Growth in capital per worker was very rapid. At the peak of Korea's economic boom in the early and mid-1990s,

investment in new capital averaged 36 percent of GDP, higher even than in Japan during that country's period of fastest growth, and more than double the share of investment in GDP for the United States. Much of this investment was fueled by a high domestic saving rate and some also by foreign investment.

Finally, improvements in technology and organization, known to economists as total factor productivity, contributed about 1.9 percentage points to Korea's annual growth rate. This was respectable, but not exceptional, being only about the average for the world's more developed economies.

Measured over the period 1980-2002, the final scorecard looks like this:

Source of growth	Contribution to growth
Total Growth of real GDP	6.8%
Capital accumulation	2.0%
Growth of labor inputs	2.8%
Growth of labor force	1.9%
Improved education	0.9%
Total factor productivity	1.9%

Source: International Monetary Fund, "Republic of Korea: Selected Issues," IMF Country Report 03/80, March 2003.

(sometimes called "human capital,"), and improvements in political institutions that reduce productivity-sapping corruption and conflict. Meanwhile, *Applying Economic Ideas 8.1* illustrates the sources of economic growth with the case of South Korea.

The Benefits and Costs of Economic Growth

Economic growth has many benefits. First and foremost, growth provides consumers with a higher standard of living in the form of more goods and services. Growth also provides people with greater opportunities to choose between work and leisure. If more people choose to work, as has recently been the case in the United States, economic growth makes possible the capital investment needed to create jobs for them. Over a longer span of U.S. history, however, people have opted for more leisure. As the economy grew during the nineteenth and early twentieth centuries, it was possible to shorten the average workweek at the same time that material living standards were rising. Finally, economic growth is seen by many people as a necessary condition for reducing poverty and economic injustice. Whether a rising tide lifts all boats more or less automatically, as some people would have it, or whether, at least in some periods, the rich benefit more from growth than the poor remains a source of controversy. However, there is little dispute that issues of social equality are even harder to resolve in countries where the tide is going out.

 WHO SAID IT? WHO DID IT? 8.1

JOHN STUART MILL ON THE STATIONARY STATE

Economic growth was a major concern of the classical economists of the nineteenth century. Then, as now, most of the leading economists were inclined to view economic growth as a good thing. However, some of them feared that the pressure of growing populations on limited natural resources would sooner or later bring economic growth to a halt. Economists portrayed the "stationary state" toward which society was moving as one of poverty and overpopulation, causing one critic to dub economics the "dismal science."

John Stuart Mill thought otherwise. Mill was one of the most remarkable figures of the nineteenth century. Eldest son of the prominent economist James Mill, John Stuart Mill began studying Greek at age 3, was tutoring the younger members of his family in Latin at age 8, and first read Smith's Wealth of Nations at age 13. His Principles of Political Economy, published in 1848, was the standard text on the subject until Alfred Marshall transformed "political economy" into "economics" at the end of the century.

Mill agreed with earlier classical economists that the economy would sooner or later reach a stationary state, but he did not view the prospect as entirely gloomy:

I cannot . . . regard the stationary state of capital and wealth with the unaffected aversion so generally manifested towards it by political economists of the old school. I am inclined to believe that it would be, on the whole, a very considerable improvement on our present condition. I confess I am not charmed with the ideal of life held out by those who think that the normal state of human beings is that of struggling to get on; that the trampling, crushing, elbowing, and treading on each other's heels, which form the existing type of social life, are the most desirable lot of human kind, or anything but the disagreeable symptoms of one of the phases of our industrial progress. . . .

If the earth must lose that great portion of its pleasantries which it owes to things that the unlimited increase of wealth and population would extricate from it, for the mere purpose of enabling it to support a larger, but not a better or happier population, I sincerely hope, for the sake of posterity, that they will be content to be stationary long before necessity compels them to.

Today Mill's sentiments have been echoed by writers who are concerned about problems of population, pollution, and resource depletion.

Nevertheless, economic growth has had its critics. More than a century ago the English economist John Stuart Mill worried that growth might cause the loss of "a great portion of the earth's pleasantries" (see *Who Said It? Who Did It? 8.1*). This sentiment is shared in our own time by environmentalists, who worry that growth is accompanied by increased pollution, destruction of wilderness areas, and the possibility of a global climatic disaster.

Criticisms of economic growth have their merits. We have only to look around us to see that the economic growth we have experienced has brought costs as well as benefits. However, the critics can be faulted for often failing to distinguish between two issues: the *rate* of economic growth and its *direction*.

In Figure 8.2, a production possibility frontier is used to help separate the two issues. The diagram shows an economy in which resources can be devoted either to improving environmental quality or increasing per capita consumption of material goods. To put it even more simply, we could think of the tradeoff as one between clean air and cars. For an economy operating efficiently on its production possibility frontier, more cars will make the air dirtier; fewer cars will make possible cleaner air.

FIGURE 8.2 ENVIRONMENTAL QUALITY AND ECONOMIC GROWTH

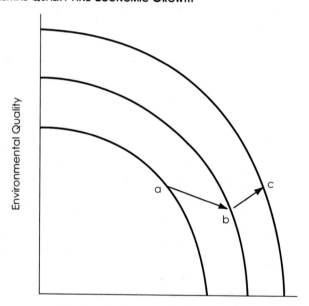

Per Capita Consumption of Material Goods

This figure shows a production possibility frontier for consumption of material goods, on the one hand, and environmental quality, on the other. At any given time there is a trade-off. For example, more cars of an unchanged kind mean dirtier air; investing more to make cars cleaner means that fewer cars can be produced. Over time, improvements in technology and the availability of additional productive resources shift the production possibility frontier outward. A choice can be made between two growth paths as the frontier expands. The path from A to B shows an increase in the output of goods and a decrease in environmental quality. The path from B to C shows growth accompanied by strong investment in pollution abatement and environmental improvements.

As technology is improved and more resources become available, the production possibility frontier shifts outward. If the economy follows a growth path from point A to point B, people will complain that growth has led to a deterioration of environmental quality. It is not the mere fact of growth that is to blame, however. Instead, the problem lies in the *direction* of growth, that is, the choice of the mix of outputs. An equivalent expansion of the production possibility frontier could have made possible a growth path from point B to point C. That growth path would be possible if more effort and expense were devoted to building cars that run more cleanly, cleaning up rivers, and restoring wildlife habitats. Comparing the arrow from A to B with that from B to C, we see that growth can bring both more material output and improved environmental quality *if people choose to go that way.* As is often the case, our problems turn out to arise not from inescapable economic laws but from the choices we make.

Of these two possibilities, in which direction is the world actually headed? Many economists believe that the early stages of economic development move a country in a direction like that from A to B, and later development moves it from B to C. Among other evidence, they point to the fact that standard measures show better air and water quality in the wealthiest countries than in middle-income countries. There are also indications that measured air quality has improved in most American cities in recent decades after deteriorating through much of the 19th and early 20th centuries. Not everyone agrees with this optimistic view, however. Many environmentalists worry that in the future, poor countries will cut corners on environmental standards to attract investment, and that as old types of pollution are cleaned up, previously unknown types of toxic waste will replace them.[2]

SHORT-RUN MACROECONOMICS AND: THE BUSINESS CYCLE

Natural level of real output

The trend of real GDP growth over time, also known as potential real output.

Business cycle

A pattern of irregular but repeated expansion and contraction of aggregate economic activity.

The first section of this chapter focused on prosperity—economic growth and its causes in the long run. In this section we turn to issues of stability, that is, to the unfortunate short-run tendency of the economy to veer off the path of steady growth.

Figure 8.3 shows growth of the U.S. economy since 1950. Because of increasing labor inputs, capital accumulation, and technological and organizational improvements, the material standard of living has risen substantially. The straight trend line drawn in the figure represents the growth over time of the economy's **natural level of real output**, sometimes also known as *potential real output.* As the chart shows, real GDP has moved sometimes above and sometimes below the long-term trend line. In some years real GDP has not just grown more slowly than the trend, but actually fallen. This pattern of irregular but repeated expansion and contraction of overall economic activity about its natural level is known as the **business cycle**.

FIGURE 8.3   ECONOMIC GROWTH IN THE UNITED STATES

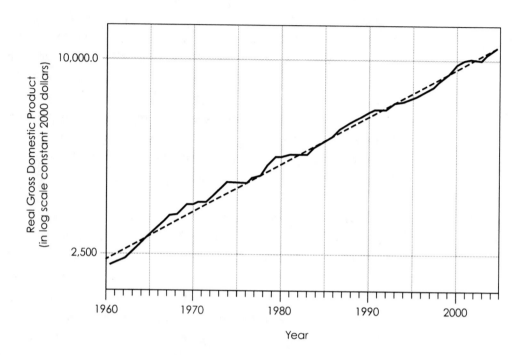

This chart shows the growth of the U.S. economy since 1960. Real Gross Domestic Product is shown for each year, along with a trend line showing average growth of about 2.5 percent per year. In some years real GDP rises above the trend and in some years it falls below it.

Source: Economic Report of the President, 2005, Table B-2.

Phases of the Business Cycle

An idealized business cycle is shown in Figure 8.4. The cycle can be divided into four. The peak of the cycle is the point at which real output reaches a maximum. The period during which real output falls is known as the contraction phase. At the end of the contraction, real output reaches a minimum known as the trough of the cycle. After the trough, real output begins to grow again and the economy enters an expansion that lasts until a new peak is reached.

According to a commonly used (although somewhat simplified) definition, a contraction lasting six months or more is a **recession**. Several recessions, of which the most recent began in March 2001 and ended in November of the same year, can be identified in Figure 8.3.

The nineteenth and early twentieth centuries saw a number of cyclical contractions that were much more severe than any since World War II. These were called *depressions*. The most spectacular of these was the Great Depression of the 1930s, which actually consisted of two contractionary periods separated by an incomplete

Recession

A cyclical economic contraction that lasts six months or more.

FIGURE 8.4   AN IDEALIZED BUSINESS CYCLE

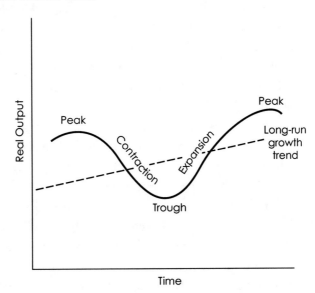

This figure shows an idealized business cycle. The cycle begins from a peak, then enters a contraction. A contraction lasting six months or more is called a recession. The low point of the cycle is known as its trough. Following the trough, the economy enters an expansion until a new peak is reached. Because real GDP varies about an upward trend, each cyclical peak tends to carry the economy to a higher level of real GDP than the previous one.

recovery. During this episode, real output fell by one-third, the price level fell by one-quarter, and the unemployment rate climbed to 24 percent of the labor force. Because no succeeding contraction has come close to it in severity, the term *depression* has passed out of use in all but historical contexts.

Employment and the Business Cycle

Figures 8.3 and 8.4 show the business cycle in terms of real domestic product, but real output is not the whole story. In the short run, changes in real output above or below the trend line are linked to changes in employment. These changes in employment tend to get more attention than changes in output, which is hardly surprising. Real GDP is a very abstract concept, whereas employment has a much more personal meaning. The security of your own job, and those of your relatives and close friends, have a far bigger impact on your life that a percentage-point wiggle one way or the other in real GDP.

Unemployment rate

The percentage of the labor force that is unemployed.

MEASURING UNEMPLOYMENT TRENDS   The most widely-used measure of the employment situation is the **unemployment rate**, which is the percentage of the labor force that is unemployed at a given time. Understanding this deceptively simple statistic requires some definitions of related terms and a discussion of measurement technique.

The U.S. Bureau of Labor Statistics, in conjunction with the Bureau of the Census, obtains the data used in calculating unemployment from a monthly sample of about 50,000 randomly selected households. Field agents go to those households and ask a series of questions about the job status of each member of the household. The questions include such things as: Did anyone work last week? Did anyone look for work? How long has the person been looking for work? How did the person go about looking?

On the basis of their answers to these questions, people are counted as employed or unemployed. A person is considered to be **employed** if he or she works at least 1 hour per week for pay or at least 15 hours per week as an unpaid worker in a family business. A person who is not currently employed but is actively looking for work is said to be **unemployed**. The employed plus the unemployed—that is, those who are either working or looking for work—constitute the **labor force**. The unemployment rate is simply the percentage of the labor force that is unemployed.

If people are neither employed nor actively looking for work, they are not counted as members of the labor force. People out of the labor force include many people who could work but choose not to for one reason or another. For example, they may be full-time students or retired, or they may work full time but without pay at home. Two groups are automatically considered to be outside the labor force: children under 16 years of age and people who are confined to prisons and certain other institutions. The most commonly reported data for the labor force and employment also exclude members of the armed forces.

Figure 8.5 presents unemployment data for the United States since 1950. The shaded band labeled "low to moderate unemployment" reflects a range of views about reasonable economic performance. During the 1950s and 1960s, the unemployment rate generally stayed within this range. In the 1970s and early 1980s, the unemployment rate took a turn for the worse. It jumped to 8.3 percent in 1975 and fell into the moderate range in only 2 of the next 12 years. Only in 1989, just before the onset of a new recession, did it again reach the levels achieved in the early 1970s.

GRAY AREAS IN THE MEASUREMENT OF UNEMPLOYMENT There are many gray areas in the measurement of unemployment. The official unemployment rate can be criticized for both understating and overstating the "true" number of unemployed adults. One way to understand these gray areas better is to compare the official definition of unemployment with two common-sense definitions, namely, "not working" and "can't find a job."

The official definitions of employment and unemployment differ greatly from the simple definitions of "working" and "not working." On the one hand, there are many people who work but are not officially employed. By far the largest such group consists of people who work full time at housekeeping and child care. These occupations are counted as employment if they are performed for pay, but the bulk of such work

---

Employed

A term used to refer to a person who is working at least 1 hour a week for pay or at least 15 hours per week as an unpaid worker in a family business.

Unemployed

A term used to refer to a person who is not employed but is actively looking for work.

Labor force

The sum of all individuals who are employed and all individuals who are unemployed.

FIGURE 8.5 UNEMPLOYMENT IN THE UNITED STATES SINCE 1960

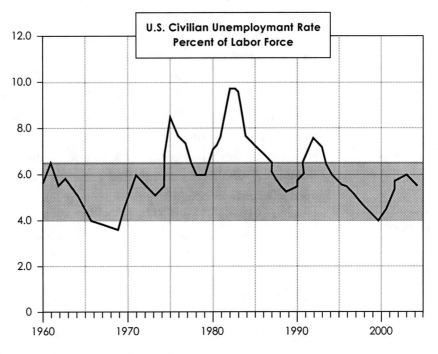

There is no one level of unemployment that is universally accepted as best for the economy. Some unemployment is always present as people change jobs and enter the labor force in a normally functioning economy. This figure highlights a range of 4 to 6.5 percent unemployment that can be considered "low to moderate." Until 1975, unemployment stayed within that range, for the most part. The mid-1970s and early 1980s saw much higher rates. During the 1990s, unemployment returned to the moderate range.

Source: Economic Report of the President, 2005, Table B-42

is done without pay. Also, children under 16 working without pay for a family farm or business also are not counted as employed.

On the other hand, not everyone who does not work is counted as unemployed. There are millions of people who are not looking for work and therefore are not counted in the labor force. There are also those who are absent from their jobs because of illness, bad weather, or labor disputes. All of these are counted as employed. Finally, there are those who work part time and are counted as employed but are actively seeking full-time employment. People in this last situation are sometimes referred to as *underemployed*.

The second common-sense definition of unemployment, "can't find a job," also only loosely fits the official definition. In some ways, the official definition overstates the number of people who cannot find jobs. Some people who are counted as unemployed are on layoffs from jobs to which they expect to be recalled, or have found jobs that they expect to start within 30 days. Other people who are counted as unemployed could easily find a job of some kind but prefer to take their time and find just the kind of job they want. (People who are not the sole income earners in their households, for example, may be in a position to look longer and be more selective than people in households with no other income.) Still other people register as unemployed to meet the requirements of income transfer programs even though they may not be qualified for any available work and only go through the motions of looking for a job. Finally, there is some doubt as to whether the description "can't find a job" fits people who could have stayed on at their last job but quit to look for a better one.

In other ways, however, the official definition of unemployment understates the number of people who cannot find jobs. For example, it does not include **discouraged workers**—people who are not looking for work because they believe no suitable jobs are available. The Bureau of Labor Statistics officially counts as a discouraged worker anyone who has looked for work within the last six months but is no longer actively looking. The description "can't find a job" could also be applied to the underemployed—those who have part-time jobs but would take full-time jobs if they could find them.

THE NATURAL RATE OF UNEMPLOYMENT   Figure 8.5 emphasized short-term swings in the unemployment rate associated with the business cycle. For a longer-term perspective, it is useful to look at trends in what economists call the **natural rate of unemployment**.[3] This is the level of unemployment reached by the economy when real GDP is at its natural level, that is, the unemployment rate associated with the trend line for GDP that was shown in Figure 8.3.

Figure 8.6 shows the trend of the natural rate of unemployment in the United States, with comparison to that in major economies of European Union. As the figure shows, the natural rate of unemployment has fallen gradually in the United States since the 1980s. It is now lower than that in the largest European economies. Similar data for the United Kingdom and Ireland, whose labor markets are structurally more similar to that of the United States than to those of Continental Europe, would show a healthier unemployment trend than the two largest Continental European economies, France or Germany.

This divergence of unemployment trends has been a huge source of controversy within the European Union. Some economists argue that the trends show a clear superiority of the so-called "Anglo-American" model of flexible labor markets, with relatively few restrictions on hiring and firing workers, and a relatively modest social safety net for the unemployed. By comparison, according to these thinkers, the "Franco-German" model is fundamentally flawed. Although it intends to protect jobs by making layoffs difficult and making life easy for the unemployed, it actually has the unintended effect of providing too few incentives for employers to hire and workers to seek jobs. In reply, thinkers aligned with Europe's tradition of social democracy see the Anglo-American model as harsh and uncaring. Many social democratic

Discouraged worker

A person who would work if a suitable job were available but has given up looking for such a job.

Natural rate of unemployment

The sum of frictional and structural unemployment; the rate of unemployment that persists when the economy is experiencing neither accelerating nor decelerating inflation.

FIGURE 8.6   UNEMPLOYMENT TRENDS IN THE UNITED STATES AND EUROPE

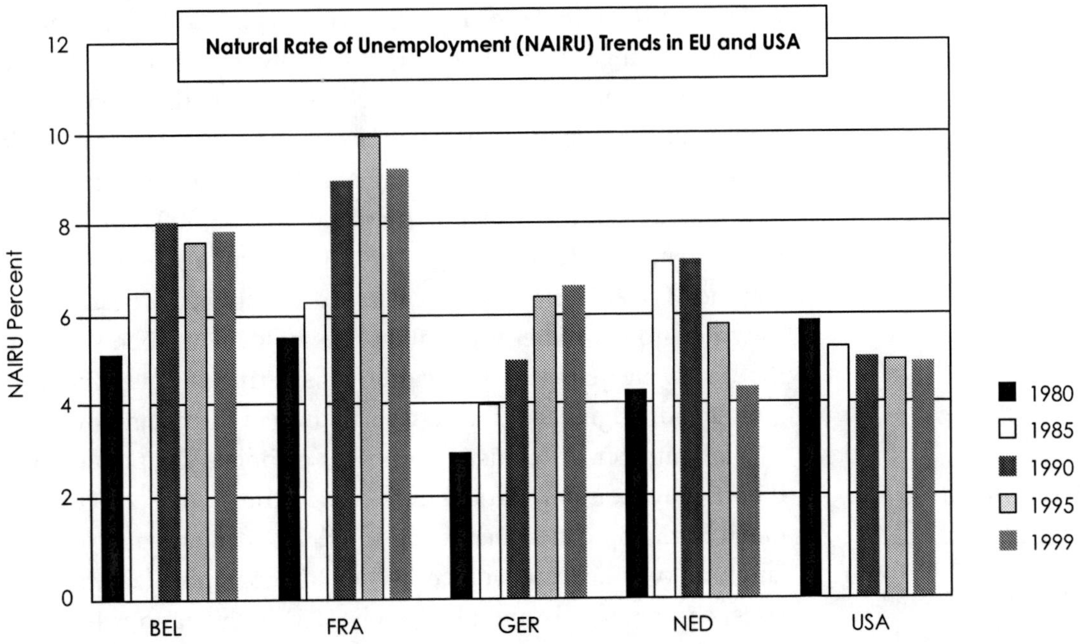

This figure shows trends in the natural rate of unemployment for the United States and several European economies. While the natural rate of unemployment has fallen gradually in the United States since 1980, it has risen in France and Germany, Europe's largest economies. Unemployment rates, which were once much lower in France and Germany than in the United States are now higher.

Source: Achim Kemmerling et. al, Regional Input: Labor Markets, Eurozoneplus Working Paper 6a, Jean Monnet Center of Excellence, Freie Univertaet Berlin, Sept. 2002, Chart 1

thinkers in France and Germany believe their labor markets can be reformed without sacrificing their countries' traditional emphasis on generous social protection of workers.

OTHER MEASURES OF UNEMPLOYMENT   The unemployment rate is not the only measure of the state of the labor market. Quite aside from the problems of definition just discussed, the unemployment rate may give a misleading picture of what is happening in the labor market because it is sensitive both to changes in its numerator (the number of unemployed) and its denominator (the size of the labor force). During the early stages of recovery from a recession, the labor force often grows at the same time that the number of employed people grows, and the unemployment rate remains unchanged. This happens because news of possible new jobs draws discouraged workers back into the labor force, but the new workers do not immediately find work. Once a recovery is underway, the size of the labor force stabilizes and the unemployment rate may fall even though just a few new jobs are created.

Because month-to-month changes in the unemployment rate may send misleading signals, news reports of short-term labor market developments often focus instead on the number of new payroll jobs created in a given month. The monthly figure for change in payroll jobs is based on a survey of employers that is entirely separate from the household survey used to calculate the unemployment rate. The sample size of the employer survey is larger, and some people consider it more reliable. For example, in May 2005, the Bureau of Labor Statistics reported that the number of new jobs created was a smaller-than-expected 78,000, but at the same time, that the unemployment rate fell from 5.2 to 5.1 percent, a six-year low. Press reports on the day the May 2005 figures were released mostly had a pessimistic tone, focusing on slow job growth rather than falling unemployment. The stock markets fell the day the data were released, apparently considering the negative signal from slow job growth more significant than the small drop in the unemployment rate.

Still another job statistic that helps complete the picture of the labor market is the **employment-population ratio**. This ratio is the percentage of the noninstitutional adult population that is employed. The denominator of the employment-population ratio, which is governed by such demographic factors as birthrates and death rates, changes slowly and predictably. Hence, this ratio is less likely than the unemployment rate to stand still while the economy moves ahead, or to give other misleading signals. In particular, during the early stages of an economic recovery when firms first start hiring new workers, the employment-population ratio will rise even though the unemployment rate may temporarily not change because of the return of discouraged workers to the labor force.[4]

FRICTIONAL, STRUCTURAL, AND CYCLICAL UNEMPLOYMENT Still another way to look at unemployment is to ask how long people remain unemployed. Figure 8.7 shows that as of May 2005, about a third of unemployed workers were out of a job for 5 weeks or less, and about a fifth for half a year or more. The term **frictional unemployment** is used to refer to short-term, largely voluntary unemployment spells needed to match jobs and workers. It represents people who quit old jobs to look for new ones, people who take a week or so to move or go on vacation before starting a newly found job, and people who enter occupations, such as construction work, in which temporary layoffs are frequent but year-round earnings are good. Economists view a certain level of frictional unemployment as necessary in a labor market in which information is incomplete and the costs of job search are often high.

The term **structural unemployment** refers to a situation in which people spend long periods out of work, often with little prospect of finding adequate jobs. This prolonged joblessness occurs partly because the shifting structure of the economy has made their skills obsolete. This category of workers also includes people with few skills and little work experience. Teenagers and some minority groups are particularly affected by this type of unemployment.

Employment-population ratio

The percentage of the noninstitutional adult population that is employed.

Frictional unemployment

The portion of unemployment that is accounted for by the short periods of unemployment needed for matching jobs with job seekers.

Structural unemployment

The portion of unemployment that is accounted for by people who are out of work for long periods because their skills do not match those required for available jobs.

FIGURE 8.7   U.S. UNEMPLOYMENT BY DURATION, MAY 2005

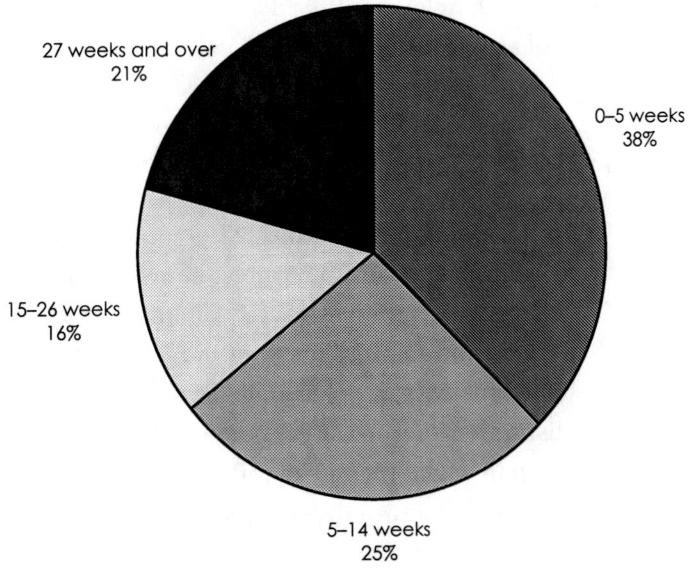

27 weeks and over
21%

0–5 weeks
38%

15–26 weeks
16%

5–14 weeks
25%

As this chart shows, there is considerable variation in the length of time people are unemployed. As of May 2005, about a third of workers spent less than five weeks out of work, while about a fifth were out of work for six months or more.

Source: Bureau of Labor Statistics, Current Employment Situation, May 2005.

For these people, structural unemployment is not merely a problem of lack of jobs. Certain types of jobs—hospital workers, fast-food work, and car washing, for example—are almost always available and require few specific skills. But structurally unemployed workers who do take such jobs often work at them only for short periods before quitting to look for something better. Working for brief periods at dead-end jobs tends to build up a pattern of poor work habits and absenteeism that makes many structurally unemployed workers unattractive to potential employers.

Frictional and structural unemployment are present in good years as well as bad ones. Together, they constitute the natural rate of unemployment. But unemployment is not always at its natural level. On the one hand, a vigorous economic expansion can make jobs so easy to find that the duration of unemployment falls below normal, reducing the number of unemployed below the number normally unemployed for frictional and structural reasons. Even many of the hard-core structurally unemployed find jobs. On the other hand, in periods of business contraction, the unemployment rate rises above its natural rate. At such times even workers who have worked a long time for their present employer and who have excellent skills may find themselves temporarily laid off. The average duration of unemployment rises above normal frictional plus structural levels.

Cyclical unemployment

The difference between the observed rate of unemployment at a given point in the business cycle and the natural rate of unemployment.

Inflation

A sustained increase in the average level of prices of all goods and services.

Price stability

A situation in which the rate of inflation is low enough so that it is not a significant factor in business and individual decision making.

Transfer payments

Payments to individuals that are not made in return for work they currently perform.

The difference between the actual unemployment rate at a given time and the natural rate is known as **cyclical unemployment**. When the economy slows down, cyclical unemployment is added to frictional and structural unemployment. At the peak of an expansionary period, cyclical unemployment is negative.

PRICE STABILITY

Up to this point, both the discussion of long-run growth and the short-run business cycle have focused on the real economy—real output and the level of employment. But changes in nominal macroeconomic variables, linked to changes in the prices that goods and services are sold out, are also important. **Inflation**, which means a sustained increase in the average level of prices of all goods and services, is a potential disruptive force in the economic life of nations and individuals. **Price stability**—a situation in which the rate of inflation is low enough so that it is not a significant factor in business and individual decision making—can be considered another of the major goals of macroeconomic policy.

Figure 8.8 shows inflation trends in the U.S. economy and around the world. Figure 8.8a shows that U.S.inflation was low throughout the 1950s and early 1960s. In fact, for the entire century from the Civil War to the mid-1960s, the U.S. peacetime inflation rate averaged only about 2 percent per year. Beginning in 1968, however, inflation rose and became highly variable. The struggle against inflation was a dominant theme in economic policy throughout the 1980s. By the late 1980s, inflation was again brought under control, and has remained low since.

Figure 8.8b shows that the rise of inflation in the 1970s and its decline since the 1990s was part of a world-wide phenomenon. It also shows that the U.S. inflation experience was moderate by comparison with the average for other countries

Short-Run Costs of Inflation

As Figure 8.8 shows, the rate of inflation varies to a considerable extent over the business cycle. As the cycle approaches its peak, inflation accelerates. During recessions, inflation shows again. As inflation rises and falls over the business cycle, its costs are distributed unevenly across the population.

Most people receive the bulk of their income in the form of wages and salaries. Wage and salary earners often feel that they are badly hurt by inflation. They compare what their paychecks can buy each month at ever-higher prices with what they would be able to buy with the same paychecks if prices remained stable. However, measured over a period of several years, nominal wages and salaries tend to adjust to inflation. Real wage and salary earnings in the United States rose during the inflationary 1970s and 1980s and also during the low-inflation 1960s and 1990s. The same is true of people who receive their income in the form of social security and other **transfer payments**. In most cases, these are adjusted automatically to reflect changes in consumer

FIGURE 8.8   INFLATION IN THE UNITED STATES AND AROUND THE WORLD

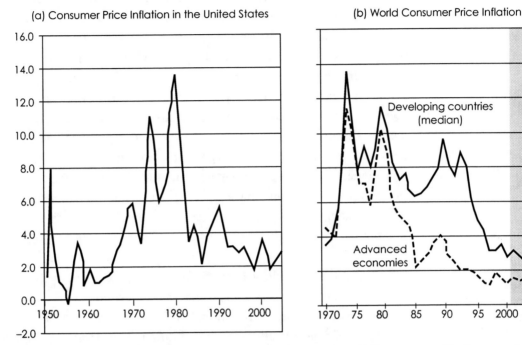

(a) Consumer Price Inflation in the United States

(b) World Consumer Price Inflation

Part a of this figure shows the trend of inflation in the United States since 1950, as measured by the annual percentage change in the Consumer Price Index. Inflation rose beginning in the late 1960s and was not brought under control again until the late 1980s. Part b shows that the U.S. experienced was shared by both developing and advanced economies around the world.

Source: Figure 4.8a, Economic Report of the President, 2005, Table B-64. Figure 4.8b, IMF, World Economic Outlook 2003, Figure 1.1

Indexation

A policy of automatically adjusting a value or payment in proportion to changes in the average price level.

prices, so that real living standards are protected. This process of adjustment for inflation is called **indexation**.

Inflation also affects the income of creditors, who receive interest from mortgage loans, corporate bonds, and the like, and that of debtors, who pay that interest. The effects of inflation in this case are somewhat more complex than is true for wage income and transfer payments.

The traditional view is that inflation injures creditors and aids debtors. Suppose, for example, that I borrow $100 from you today, promising to repay the $100 of principal plus $5 interest, or $105 in all, at the end of a year. If there is no inflation during the year, I get the use of the funds for the year and you get $5 of real income in the form of the interest on the loan. But suppose that during the year the price level goes up by 10 percent. In that case I get the use of the funds for the year, and what is more, I pay you back in depreciated dollars. The $105 I give you at the end of the year will buy only about as much then as $95 will buy today. Your real income is negative, because the real value of $105 a year from now is less than the real value today of the $100 that I borrow. I, the debtor, benefit from inflation, and you, the creditor, are hurt.

However, the traditional view of the effects of inflation is incomplete in that it does not distinguish between *unexpected* and *expected* inflation. The example just given implicitly assumes that neither I, the borrower, nor you, the lender, expected any inflation at the time the loan was made. Suppose instead that we both had expected a 10 percent increase in the price level between the time the loan was made and the time it was repaid. In that case, you would not have loaned me the $100 in return for a promise to repay just $105 at the end of the year. Instead, you would have insisted on a repayment of $115—the $100 principal, plus $10 to compensate you for the decline in purchasing power of the principal plus $5 of real interest income. I, in turn, would have agreed to those terms, knowing that the $115 payment under conditions of 10 percent inflation would be no more burdensome than the $105 payment I would have agreed to if no inflation had been expected.

This example shows that we need to distinguish between two interest concepts: the **nominal interest rate**, which is the interest rate expressed in the ordinary way, in current dollars, and the **real interest rate**, which is the nominal rate minus the rate of inflation. In the example, a 15 percent nominal interest rate, given a 10 percent rate of inflation, corresponds to a 5 percent real interest rate.

The distinction between nominal and real interest rates helps us to understand the impact of expected and unexpected inflation on debtors and creditors. Expected inflation, it turns out, is neutral between debtors and creditors, because the parties will adjust the nominal interest rate to take the expected inflation into account. If they would agree to a 5 percent nominal interest rate given no expected inflation, they would agree to a 15 percent nominal rate given 10 percent expected inflation, a 20 percent nominal rate given 15 percent expected inflation, and so on. All of these adjusted rates correspond to a 5 percent real rate. Unexpected inflation is not neutral, however. Unexpected inflation harms creditors and benefits debtors. If you lend me $100 at a 5 percent nominal rate of interest, and the price level unexpectedly rises by 10 percent over the year before I repay the loan, the real rate of interest that you receive is minus 5 percent.

Long-Run Costs of Inflation

The distributional costs of inflation cancel one another out, helping some people while they hurt others. In the long run, however, inflation has other costs that place a burden on the economy as a whole without producing offsetting benefits for anyone.

One set of costs has to do with the way inflation upsets economic calculations. In an inflationary environment, households and firms have a hard time distinguishing between changes in the relative prices of goods and services and changes in the general price level. Partly for this reason, in an economy in which the rate of inflation is high and variable, as it was in the United States in the 1970s and early 1980s, business planning becomes difficult. The outcomes of investment projects that require firms to incur costs now in the hope of making profits later come to depend less on manufac-

---

Nominal interest rate

The interest rate expressed in the usual way: in terms of current dollars without adjustment for inflation.

Real interest rate

The nominal interest rate minus the rate of inflation.

turing and marketing skills than on the ups and downs of wages, interest rates, and the prices of key raw materials. As the investment environment becomes riskier, firms may avoid projects with long-term payoffs and gamble instead on strategies that promise short-term financial gains. Similarly, households, facing more uncertainty about future price trends, may reduce their long-term saving in favor of increased current consumption. These effects are hard to measure, but many economists think that they are substantial.

Another set of costs arise from the effort to rid the economy of inflation once it has become established. The experiences of many countries in many periods suggest that bringing inflation under control often causes serious economic disruption during a transition period. The slowdown of inflation in the United States from 1980 to 1983 is a case in point. A careful comparison of Figures 8.3, 8.4, and 8.8 shows that the drop in inflation during those years coincided with a back-to-back recessions during which the unemployment rate which reached a peak of more than 10 percent, the worst in half a century.

Looking around the world, the adverse effect of inflation on the growth of real incomes is quite pronounced. Figure 8.9 shows data on the relationship between growth and inflation from a sample of 103 countries over a 30-year period. There is a clear tendency for inflation to undermine economic growth. Countries that experi-

FIGURE 8.9   INFLATION AND ECONOMIC GROWTH

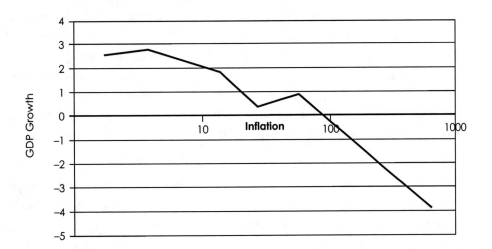

On average, inflation higher than a very moderate rate is harmful to economic growth. This chart, based on a sample of 103 countries over a period of 30 years, shows a clear inverse relationship between growth and inflation. Countries with inflation over 100 percent per year tend to have negative economic growth.

Source: Based on data from Atish Gosh and Steven Phillips, Inflation, Disinflation, and Growth, IMF Working Paper 98/68, May 1998

enced inflation of more than 100 percent per year (that is, a doubling or more of the price level each year) on average experienced decreases in real GDP.

However, Figure 8.9 also suggests that moderate inflation does not necessarily have negative effects on economic growth. The sample on which this figure was based did not include many very low-inflation counties, but other studies suggest that complete price stability is not necessarily the best of all possible worlds. Policy makers in most countries aim not for zero inflation but rather, for a steady, moderate increase of prices of something like 2 to 4 percent per year.

⬿

SUMMARY

1. **What trend has economic growth followed in the United States?** Economic growth is most commonly expressed in terms of the rate of growth of *Gross Domestic Product (GDP)*, a measure of the value of the economy's total output of goods and services during a given period of time. To avoid distortions caused by inflation, gross domestic product is expressed in real terms. Real gross domestic product has grown at an average rate of about 2–3 percent since 1950, although that growth has not been steady. Economic growth is widely seen as beneficial, in that it makes possible higher living standards, jobs for those who want them, and more leisure for those who want it. Some people criticize growth as damaging to the environment. In evaluating such damage, the composition of real domestic product as it grows must be considered as well as its rate of growth.

2. **What is the business cycle?** Over time, the economy undergoes a pattern of irregular but repeated expansion and contraction of aggregate economic activity that is known as the *business cycle*. The point at which output reaches a maximum is known as the peak of the cycle. This is followed by a contraction, a trough, an expansion, and a new peak. A contraction lasting six months or more is known as a recession. Over the course of the business cycle, the economy sometimes rises above and sometimes falls below its *natural level of real output*.

3. **What is unemployment and why is it important for economic policy?** A person who works at least 1 hour a week for pay or 15 hours per week as an unpaid worker in a family business is considered to be *employed*. A person who is not currently employed but is actively looking for work is *unemployed*. The *unemployment rate* is the percentage of the *labor force* that is not employed. Unemployment may be classified as *frictional*, *structural*, or *cyclical*, depending on its cause. Structural plus frictional unemployment is known as the *natural rate of unemployment*. The *employment-population ratio* is the percentage of the adult noninstitutional population that is employed.

4. **What is inflation and what impact does it have on the economy?** *Inflation* is a sustained increase in the average level of prices of all goods and services. *Price stability* is a situation in which the rate of inflation is low enough so that it is not a significant factor in business and individual decision making. Inflation is frequently measured in terms of the rate of change in the *consumer price index*. In measuring economic quantities, a distinction

must be made between *real* values, or values adjusted for inflation, and *nominal* values, or values expressed in the ordinary way, in current dollars. Applying these concepts to interest rates, we can say that the *real interest rate* is equal to the *nominal interest rate* minus the rate of inflation. Inflation disrupts the economy in two ways. First, it harms or benefits individuals according to their source of income; second, it disrupts economic calculation, thereby discouraging saving and investment. In addition, the effort to stop inflation once it has begun often entails substantial costs.

KEY TERMS

Real	Employment-population
Nominal	ratio
Real output	Frictional unemploy-
Total factor productivity	ment
Natural level of real	Structural unemploy-
output	ment
Business cycle	Cyclical unemploy-
Recession	ment
Unemployment rate	Inflation
Employed	Price stability
Unemployed	Transfer payments
Labor force	Indexation
Discouraged worker	Nominal interest rate
Natural rate of	Real interest rate
unemployment	

PROBLEMS AND TOPICS FOR DISCUSSION

1. **Your personal labor force status.** What is your current labor force status? Are you a member of the labor force? Are you employed? Unemployed? Explain the basis for your answers. When was the last time your labor force status changed? Do you expect it to change soon? Give details.

2. **Employment hardship.** It has been suggested that the unemployment rate should be replaced with an "employment hardship index" that tries to measure the percentage of people who suffer hardship because of their labor force status. What kinds of people who are not now counted as unemployed might fit into this category? What kinds of people who are now counted as unemployed would not suffer hardship? Discuss.

3. **Real and nominal interest rates.** Check with your local bank to find out what interest rates currently apply to (a) one-year savings certificates and (b) three-year automobile loans. Compare these nominal interest rates with the current rate of inflation as measured by the most recently announced rate of change in the consumer price index. (You can get this statistic from the web site of the Bureau of Labor Statistics, www.bls.gov.) If the current rate of inflation were to continue unchanged, what real rate of interest would you earn on the saving certificate? What real rate of interest would you pay on the loan?

4. **Economic growth and the environment.** The pace of economic growth varies from one area of the United States to another. Some regions are growing rapidly, with people moving in, much new construction, rising incomes, and so on. Other areas are stagnant or declining, with little new construction and people moving away. Which type of area do you live in? Can you identify any environmental problems in your area that seem to be caused by economic growth? Can you identify any environmental problems that seem to be caused by economic decline? What policies could you suggest that would permit growth in your area to take place with less environmental disruption?

5. **The current state of the business cycle.** Unemployment and inflation data are announced monthly, and data on economic growth are announced on a quarterly basis. Watch your local newspaper, The *Wall Street Journal*, or business magazines such as Business Week for discussions of the most recent data. What changes have there been? What is happening to the employment rate? Are the employment and unemployment rates moving in the same direction or in opposite directions? What is the current rate of inflation? Is it increasing, decreasing, or staying the same? Judging from available data, in which phase of the business cycle does the economy appear to be at the moment?

CASE FOR DISCUSSION
Unemployment and Politics

What did the elections of Presidents Truman, Johnson, Nixon, and Clinton have in common? Those of Presidents Kennedy and Reagan? The answer, for the first four, is that they all won as incumbent presidents in election years when the unemployment rate was falling. The other two were successful challengers in years when the unemployment rate was stagnant or rising.

Given these precedents, it is easy to imagine the dismay that ran through the first Bush administration in June 1992, when the unemployment rate hit an 8-year high, just as the election campaign was getting started in earnest. All during the spring, employers had been cautiously hiring. The National Bureau of Economic Research (NBER) had not yet officially announced the end of the recession, but almost all economists thought (correctly, it turned out) that the recovery had begun. But although the economy was growing, it was doing so at a rate of only about 2 percent per year. That was well below the average rate of growth of 4.6 percent per year for the six post-World War II elections in which the incumbent party retained power. In June, employers slashed 117,000 jobs from their payrolls. The new data made every news broadcast, and the news was bad.

Moreover, although the first President Bush could hope for good news between early summer and election time, history suggests that such news would be too little, too late. Economists like Ray Fair of Yale, who have studied the economics-politics link in detail, say that last-minute improvements are not enough. The economy's performance during the spring and summer is more important in an election year.

As it turns out, the economic numbers did improve later in the year. Unemployment fell again. An early estimate of the rate of economic growth in the third quarter, announced just before the election, turned out to be 2.7 percent, higher than forecasters had anticipated. Three weeks after the election, this was revised upward to 3.9 percent. But the third-quarter improvement was indeed too little, too late. Challenger Clinton sailed through the election by a wide margin. His job (and no easy one): Make good on campaign promises to get the economy moving well in advance of the 1996 election. This Clinton accomplished and was re-elected, despite the scandals in his personal life.

While NBER announced an official end to the November 2001 recession, the employment figures seemed to lag behind other economic indicators such as real GDP growth and real sales. This could play an important role in determining the outcome of the 2004 presidential election with the second President Bush as the incumbent.

QUESTIONS

1. If the economy was growing at a rate of 2 percent or better in mid-1992, how is it possible that the unemployment rate was rising?

2. The unemployment rate rose by only 2.7 percentage points from its low of 5.1 percent in March 1989, to its peak in June 1992. A loss of 2.7 percent of voters would not have been nearly enough to defeat the incumbent president, however. His actual vote total fell far more than that. This implies that a rise in unemployment affects the voting behavior not just of those who are actually unemployed, but of many more people as well. Why do you think this is the case?

3. Use your Internet research talents to compare the role of employment as an issue in the 1992 presidential election with that in the 2004 election. How long a period elapsed between the end of the previous recession and the presidential election? How strong were data on job growth and unemployment in the first half of 2004? On balance, do you think employment was an issue that helped George W. Bush win re-election that year, or did he win re-election despite a jobs situation that favored the Democrats?

END NOTES

1. Chapter 11 will give a formal definition of GDP and explain the methods used to measure it.
2. For a thorough discussion of these issues, see Susmita Dasgupta et al., "Confronting the Environmental Kuznets Curve," *Journal of Economic Literature*, Vol. 16 No. 1 (Winter 2002), pp. 147–168. Chapter 17 in the companion volume, *Introduction to Microeconomics*, explores this and related issues in detail.
3. The natural rate of unemployment tends to be associated with periods during which the rate of inflation is neither accelerating nor decelerating. For that reason, another name for it is the *nonaccelerating-inflation rate of unemployment*, or NAIRU.
4. All three measures of the U.S. labor market situation can be obtained from the Employment Situation Summary released monthly by the Bureau of Labor Statistics, available on line at www.bls.gov.

CHAPTER 9

The Circular
Flow of Income
and Expenditure

After reading this chapter, you will understand:	1. How households and firms are linked by incomes and expenditures
	2. How expenditure is divided into consumption, investment, government purchases, and net exports
	3. The relationships between injections and leakages in the circular flow
	4. Why some investment is planned and other is unplanned
	5. How the concept of equilibrium can be applied to the circular flow of income and expenditure
	6. What the multiplier effect is and how it is related to the business cycle
Before reading this chapter, make sure you know the meaning of:	1. GDP
	2. Opportunity cost
	3. Equilibrium
	4. Inventories
	5. Gross domestic product
	6. Real and nominal values
	7. The business cycle

THE PREVIOUS CHAPTER took a long-term perspective on growth of GDP. Sources of output growth were broken down into growth of labor inputs, increases in capital per worker, and improvements in technology and organization. Discussions of changes in GDP in the short run typically take a different perspective. For example, in May 2005 the government reported that U.S. GDP grew at a rather healthy annual rate of 3.5 percent. News reports said nothing about growth of population, capital, or total factor productivity. Instead, they focused on the behavior of individual components of GDP. First, they noted that although imports of goods and services produced abroad were greater than exports of goods and services produced in the United States, the gap between the two was less than expected. They also noted that spending on housing construction was strong. General consumer spending was somewhat slowed by higher energy prices, but the drag of energy prices was less than expected. All in all, it added up to a favorable GDP picture.

This chapter will follow the same short-term perspective of the news reports. It begins by introducing the **circular flow of income and product**, dividing the economy into five major sectors, and showing important linkages among them. In the second part of the chapter, the circular flow is used to develop the important concept of planned expenditure, which we can regard as a first step in building a general theory of macroeconomics.

Circular flow of income and product

The flow of goods and services between households and firms, balanced by the flow of payments made in exchange for goods and services.

THE CIRCULAR FLOW

Figure 9.1 divides the economy into five main sectors: firms, households, government, financial markets, and the rest of the world. Arrows indicate flows of payments

FIGURE 9.1   THE CIRCULAR FLOW OF INCOME AND EXPENDITURE

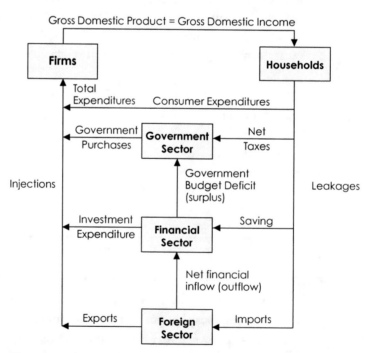

This figure shows flows of income and expenditure among five major sectors of the economy. Households receive income from firms in return for labor and other factor services used to produce gross domestic product. Most of the income goes to consumption expenditure. Some is paid to government as taxes, used to purchase imports, or saved. Government purchases, investment, and exports are additional categories of expenditure.

among the sectors. We can begin with the largest and most important set of flows, those representing the incomes that households receive from business firms and the expenditures they make in purchasing goods and services from those same firms.

Gross Domestic Product and Gross Domestic Income

At the very top of Figure 9.1 we encounter gross domestic product (GDP), defined in the previous chapter as a measure of a country's total output of goods and services. When these goods and services are produced, they generate income for the country's households.[1] The largest share of income is paid to households as wage and salary income in return for labor services. Some is also paid out as interest on funds that households have loaned to the firms that produce the goods and services or as rents and royalties on natural resources sold or leased to those firms. The difference between the value of goods produced by a firm and the wages, salaries, interest, rents, and other costs paid out to produce those goods is profit. Profit, which accrues to the firms' owners, is still another category of income received by households.

The sum of income received in the form of wages, rents, interest, and profit by all households is known as *gross domestic income,* or for short, simply *domestic income.* Conceptually, domestic income and domestic product are equal, since the act of producing any good or service necessarily creates income in one form or another (wages, profits, interest, or rents) for the people who produce it. The macroeconomic theories and models used in this book assume the equality of domestic income and domestic product. As will be explained briefly in the next chapter, however, because of various measurement problems and accounting conventions, official accounts show a value for domestic income that is not exactly equal to GDP.

Components of GDP

In building a model of the macroeconomy, it is useful to break GDP down into four components: consumption expenditures, investment expenditures, government purchases, and net exports. In equation form

$$Q = C + I + G + (Ex - Im)$$

Consumption includes all purchases of goods and services by households for the purpose of immediate use. In principle, purchases of long-lasting consumer goods can be counted as a form of investment rather than consumption expenditure, but for practical purposes, the national income accounts usually do not make this distinction. Purchases of newly built housing are the only important category of household purchase that is counted as investment rather than consumption.

Investment, as the term is understood in macroeconomics, is made up of two components. The first, **fixed investment,** means purchases of newly produced capital goods— machinery, office equipment, software, farm equipment, construction of buildings used

---

Consumption

All purchases of goods and services by households for the purpose of immediate use.

Investment

The sum of fixed investment and inventory investment.

Fixed investment

Purchases of newly produced capital goods.

Inventory investment

Changes in stocks of finished goods ready for sale, raw materials, and partially completed goods in process of production.

Government purchases of goods and services (government purchases)

Purchases of goods by all levels of government plus purchases of services from contractors and wages of government employees.

Government expenditures

Government purchases of goods and services plus transfer payments.

Transfer payments

Payments by government to individuals not made in return for services currently performed, for example, unemployment compensation and pensions.

Tax revenue

The total value of all taxes collected by government.

Net taxes

Tax revenue minus transfer payments.

Net exports

Exports minus imports of goods and services.

Injections

The government purchase, investment, and net export components of the circular flow.

Leakages

The saving, net tax, and import components of the circular flow.

for business purposes, and so on. The second component, inventory investment, means changes in stocks of finished goods ready for sale, stocks of raw materials, and stocks of partially completed goods in process of production. Inventory investment has a negative value if stocks are decreasing in a given period.

The term *investment* as used in macroeconomic models is sometimes called *economic investment* to emphasize that it means expenditures on real productive assets and inventories. Economic investment should not be confused with *financial investment*, which means purchases of corporate stocks, bonds, and other securities. The latter are not included in GDP because they do not represent new production, but rather, changes in ownership claims against assets that already exist. When the term *investment* is used without modifier, either in this book or in the daily economic news, it is usually clear from context whether economic or financial investment is meant.

The next element, **government purchases of goods and services (government purchases**, for short) includes all purchases of goods made by all levels of government (national, regional, and local) plus services purchased from contractors and the wages paid to all government employees. It is important to distinguish between government purchases and **government expenditures**. The latter include not only purchases of goods and services but also **transfer payments**. Transfer payments are payments by government to individuals that are not made in return for services currently performed for the government. Pensions, disability payments, and unemployment compensation are examples of transfers.

On the revenue side of the government's budget, we refer to the total value of taxes collected by government as **tax revenue**. The value of the government's tax revenues minus transfer payments is known as **net taxes**.

The final component of GDP is net exports, which means exports of goods and services minus imports. Often the term *net exports* is instead called the *trade surplus* (or the *trade deficit* if imports exceed exports).[2] Because some goods included in the consumption, investment, and government purchases components of GDP are not produced in the given country, the equation for GDP must use net exports rather than total exports. If not, there would be a problem of double counting, and the sum of GDP components would overstate the value of goods and services produced in the country.

Injections and Leakages

Government purchases, investment expenditures, and exports are known as **injections**. If the flows of income and consumption expenditures shown at the top of Figure 9.1 are thought of as the "basic" circular flow, then government purchases, investment expenditures, and export expenditures can be thought of as extra components "injected" into the basic circular flow. By the same reasoning, net taxes, saving, and imports are known as **leakages**. Total injections must be equal to total leakages:

$$S + T + Im = I + G + Ex$$

Saving

The part of household income that is not used to buy goods and services or to pay taxes.

The reason injections must equal leakages arises from the way economists define **saving**, by which they mean the part of domestic income that is not devoted to purchase of domestically produced consumer goods, payment of taxes, or purchase of imports. Note that this definition differs slightly from the everyday notion of savings as "money put in the bank." In particular, from the economic point of view, the part of one's income that is used to repay debts counts as saving, as does money used to purchase durable consumer assets, particularly housing.

Two other additional flows shown in Figure 9.1 connect financial markets to the rest of the circular flow of income and product.[3]

The first of these is the government deficit. If government purchases exceed net taxes, the government budget deficit can be financed by borrowing from financial markets, shown by the arrow in Figure 9.1. Using the definitions given earlier, we can express the government deficit in either of two equivalent ways:

Deficit = Government expenditures – tax revenues

Deficit = Government purchases – net taxes

If net taxes are greater than government purchases, the government budget is in surplus. In that case, the government becomes a net supplier of funds to financial markets through the repayment of previously issued government debt or loans to the private sector. The arrow shown in Figure 9.1 would then be reversed.

The final flow connects financial markets to the foreign sector. If a country's imports exceed its exports, the country must somehow obtain funds to pay for the extra imports. This is done either by borrowing from foreign sources or by selling financial assets to foreign purchasers. In that case, as shown in Figure 9.1, there is a flow of funds from the foreign sector into domestic financial markets. If exports exceed imports, then the situation is reversed. In order to buy all those exports, other countries must borrow from domestic financial markets. In that case, there is a financial outflow from the country's financial markets to the rest of the world and the arrow is reversed.

The two flows linking the financial sector to the government and foreign sectors allow the financial sector to serve a balancing function in the circular flow. Although total leakages must equal total injections, the individual leakage-injection pairs do not have to balance: government purchases need not equal net taxes, imports need not equal exports, and saving need not equal investment.

The elements of the leakages and injections equation can be grouped in various ways to highlight important macroeconomic principles. For example, we can write the following relationship:

$$(G - T) = (S - I) + (Im - Ex)$$

This equation focuses attention on the way a country can finance a government budget deficit. The excess of government purchases relative to net taxes can be financed by domestic saving, but only to the extent that private domestic saving exceeds domestic investment. If the country has insufficient saving to finance both its investment and its budget deficit, the additional financing has to come from abroad. The financial inflow is reflected in the leakages and injection equation by net imports, the term (Im – Ex). *Applying Economic Ideas 9.1* shows how the leakages-injections equation helps to understand the U.S. trade and budget deficits of the late twentieth and early twenty-first centuries.

THE DETERMINANTS OF PLANNED EXPENDITURE

Up to now, we have focused on definitions and relationships, but economic theory is concerned with more than that. To really understand the economy, we need to be able to explain why GDP or other variables have one value rather than another and why they change over time. In order to do that, we need to look at the choices made by consumers, business managers, and other decision makers. This section provides an overview of the choices that affect the various components of GDP.

Planned Versus Unplanned Expenditure

Planned inventory investment

Changes in the level of inventory made on purpose, as part of a firm's business plan.

Unplanned inventory investment

Changes in the level of inventory arising from a difference between planned and actual sales.

Planned investment

The sum of fixed investment and planned inventory investment.

Planned expenditure

The sum of consumption, government purchases, net exports, and planned investment.

Earlier in the chapter, we pointed out that investment can be broken down into *fixed investment* and *inventory investment*. Inventory investment, in turn, can be divided into planned and unplanned components. Inventory investment is considered **planned** if the level of inventories is increased (or reduced) on purpose as part of a firm's business plan. For example, a retail store might increase inventories in response to growth in the number of customers it serves. Inventory investment is considered **unplanned** if goods accumulate contrary to a firm's business plan because demand is less than expected so that some goods the firm wanted to sell remain unsold. If demand is greater than expected, so that inventories unexpectedly decrease (or increase at a rate less than scheduled in the business plan), there is negative unplanned inventory investment (disinvestment).

All fixed investment is treated as planned. Total **planned investment**, then, means fixed investment plus planned inventory investment. All other types of expenditure—consumption, government purchases, and net exports—are also considered to be planned. For that reason, we use the term **planned expenditure** to mean the sum of consumption, government purchases, net exports, and planned investment. In equation form:

$$Ep = C + Ip + G + (Ex - Im)$$

We can explain the level of planned expenditure as a whole by looking at the choices that lie behind each of its components.

⤳ APPLYING ECONOMIC IDEAS 9.1

UNDERSTANDING THE TWIN DEFICITS

Over the past fifteen years, the government budget and trade deficits of the United States have inspired a great amount of comment and controversy. To understand many of the issues raised by these "twin deficits," it is helpful to interpret them in terms of the concepts of leakages and injections. The needed data are shown in the chart.

The upper part of the chart is based on a classification of leakages and injections into three components corresponding to the equation (G – T) = (S – I) + (Im – Ex). G – T represents the budget deficit, or more precisely, *net government saving*, a broad measure that takes into account state and local as well as federal budget activity. Im – Ex is the trade deficit, or net imports. The S – I component is positive if there is more than enough domestic saving to finance domestic investment, and negative if saving falls short of investment. The lower part of the chart shows saving and investment separately.

Looking at the chart, we see that net government saving swung from deficit to surplus in the 1990s and back to deficit in the early 2000s. Over the same period, the trade deficit has grown steadily, from less than 1 percent of GDP in 1991 to a record level of over 5 percent of GDP by 2005. Are the twin deficits that the United States faced going into 2005 just coincidental, or is there a causal relationship?

The leakages-injections equation tells us that the budget deficit can be financed either by an excess of private domestic saving over private investment, or by a financial inflow, the mirror image of the trade deficit. The chart shows three distinct periods in the relationships among leakages and injections.

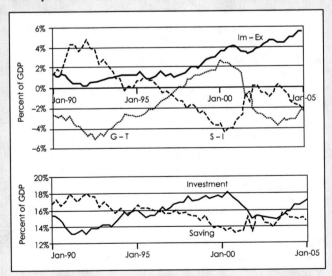

In the early 1990s, there was almost enough private saving to finance both private investment and the government deficit, so that the needed financial inflow from abroad, and the associated trade deficit, were small.

During the later 1990s, the government budget swung sharply to surplus, so that net government saving became positive. Other things being equal, this could have allowed the United States to finance all of its own investment from internal sources with some left over, and the trade balance could have moved into surplus, but this did not happen. Instead, as the lower part of the chart shows, just at this time the U.S. economy experienced a high-tech investment boom. Simultaneously, private saving fell. The government surplus helped to finance the investment boom, but was unable to do so in full, so financial inflows from abroad were still needed. In this period, it is best to think of good private investment opportunities in the United States as a magnet for foreign investment. Since inflows of foreign investment are the mirror image of the trade deficit, these inflows pushed the trade deficit higher. Some economists characterized this situation as a "healthy" trade deficit that reflects structural strength, not weakness, of the country receiving the financial inflows.

At the end of the 1990s, the high-tech investment boom collapsed. Investment being a major component of GDP, this dragged the whole economy down into recession. With incomes falling and transfer payments for unemployment compensation rising, the government budget swung into deficit. The administration of President George W. Bush, victor in the 2000 election, decided to use tax cuts to stimulate spending as a way of overcoming the recession. Perhaps in part because of the tax cuts, the recession did prove to be a short one, but economic recovery did not restore the government budget to surplus. Instead, the continued effects of tax cuts, spending to finance the war in Iraq, and other factors pushed the government budget to record levels. Where was the government to find the funds to finance its huge deficit? Not from domestic saving, which did not rise even by enough to finance the increase in domestic investment. That left just one source: the foreign sector. Once again, as in the late 1990s, financial inflows flooded into the country. This time, though, they were pulled in not by the magnet of private investment opportunities, but by the expanding sinkhole of the federal budget deficit. This gave rise to what many economists characterized as an "unhealthy" trade deficit that reflected not structural strength of the U.S. economy but structural weaknesses—an out-of-control budget deficit and weak domestic savings.

Consumption Expenditure

Choices made by consumers have a more powerful effect on the economy than those made by any other group. Consumer expenditure accounts for about two-thirds of GDP in the United States. In some other countries it is a little more, in some a little less, but everywhere consumption is the largest single component of expenditure. This being the case, we can begin by asking what determines the amount of consumer spending.

Among the first economists to pose this question was John Maynard Keynes (*Who Said It? Who Did It? 9.1*). In his path-breaking book *The General Theory of Employment, Interest, and Money*, he put it this way: "The fundamental psychological law, upon which we are entitled to depend with great confidence . . . is that men are disposed, as a rule and on the average, to increase their consumption as their income increases, but not by as much as the increase in their income."[4] He called the amount of additional consumption resulting from a one-dollar increase in income the **marginal propensity to consume**. For example, if the marginal propensity to consume is

Marginal propensity to consume

The proportion of each added dollar of real disposable income that households devote to consumption.

 WHO SAID IT? WHO DID IT? 9.1

JOHN MAYNARD KEYNES: THE GENERAL THEORY

John Maynard Keynes was born into economics. His father, John Neville Keynes, was a lecturer in economics and logic at Cambridge University. John Maynard Keynes began his own studies at Cambridge in mathematics and philosophy. However, his abilities so impressed Alfred Marshall that the distinguished teacher urged him to concentrate on economics. In 1908, after Keynes had finished his studies and done a brief stint in the civil service, Marshall offered him a lectureship in economics at Cambridge; Keynes accepted.

Keynes is best remembered for his 1936 work, *The General Theory of Employment, Interest, and Money*, a book that many still see as the foundation of what is today called macroeconomics. Although this was by no means Keynes's first major work, it was the basis for his reputation as the outstanding economist of his generation. Its major features are a bold theory based on broad macroeconomic aggregates and a strong argument for activist and interventionist policies.

Keynes was interested in more than economics. He was an honored member not only of Britain's academic upper class, but also of the nation's highest financial, political, diplomatic, administrative, and even artistic circles. He had close ties to the colorful "Bloomsbury set" of London's literary world. He was a friend of Virginia Woolf, E. M. Forster, and Lytton Strachey, and in 1925 he married ballerina Lydia Lopo-

kovia. He was a dazzling success at whatever he turned his hand to, from mountain climbing to financial speculation. As a speculator, he made a huge fortune for himself; as bursar of Kings College, he built an endowment of 30,000 pounds into one of over 380,000 pounds.

In *The General Theory*, Keynes wrote:

The idea of economists and political philosophers, both when they are right and when they are wrong, are more powerful than is commonly understood. Indeed the world is ruled by little else. Practical men, who believe themselves to be quite exempt from any intellectual influences, are usually the slaves of some defunct economist. Madmen in authority, who hear voices in the air, are distilling their frenzy from some academic scribbler of a few years back. . . . There are not many who are influenced by new theories after they are twenty-five or thirty years of age, so that the ideas which civil servants and politicians and even agitators apply to current events are not likely to be the newest.

Was Keynes issuing a warning here? Whether or not he had any such thing in mind, his words are ironic because he himself has become one of the historical economists whose ideas remain influential long after they were first articulated.

.75, a you will tend to increase your spending by $750 if your income goes up by $1,000.

This "psychological law" regarding consumption needs a few qualifications if it is to be stated exactly. First, in place of "income," we really should say **disposable income**. That means the amount of income left after taxes. If a person in one state earns $40,000 and pays $5,000 in taxes, while a person in another state earns $50,000 and pays taxes of $15,000, both would have the same disposable income of $35,000. Other things being equal, we would expect them to spend the same amount on consumption.

Second, the relationship between consumption and disposable income is properly stated in real terms. If both prices and nominal disposable income rise in exact proportion, there is no change in real income, so we would expect no change in real consumption expenditure, other things being equal.

Third, the marginal propensity to consume is not equal to the average obtained by dividing total consumption by total income. Instead, there is a minimum level of consumption that people would like to maintain even if their income were zero. Keynes called this "autonomous consumption." Intuitively, you can think of the case of a college student who has no income but maintains a minimum level of consumption by borrowing against future income, or a retired person who has no income but maintains a minimum level of consumption by drawing on past saving.

Although income is the principal factor that determines consumption spending, there are certain other factors that also can have an effect. Among them are:

- Changes in net taxes (either taxes paid or transfer payments received), which act by changing the amount of disposable income associated with a given total income.

- Changes in consumer wealth, that is, the accumulated value of assets a person owns, considered apart from current income. One very important example concerns the value of housing, since a home is the biggest asset for many households. In a period when housing prices rise more rapidly than income, as happened in the United States in the early 2000s, consumer spending rises more in proportion to income than it otherwise would.

- Interest rates. If interest rates fall, people can borrow more cheaply, and may buy more goods and services on credit. Also, the amount they have to pay in interest on credit cards, mortgages, and other debt decreases, leaving more to buy consumer goods.

- Consumer confidence. In periods when consumers feel secure about their jobs and expect their incomes to rise in line with general prosperity, they tend to spend more for any given level of income. In times of pessimism and insecurity, people tend to be cautious and increase their saving as protection against the expected rainy day.

Disposable income

Income minus taxes.

Planned Investment

The second component of planned expenditure is planned investment. It depends on two principal factors.

First, planned investment depends on interest rates (more specifically, on real interest rates, that is, interest rates adjusted for inflation). This is easiest to understand in the case of a business that needs to borrow in order to undertake an investment. Suppose you run a construction business, and you are thinking about improving the productivity of your workers by buying a new backhoe, which costs $50,000. Your banker is willing to lend you the money, but you will have to pay 6 percent per year interest, equivalent to $250 per month on the loan of $50,000. If the bank charged 12 percent interest, your monthly interest payments would rise to $500, and you would be less likely to buy the new machine. If the interest rate was just 3 percent, monthly interest payments would be only $125, and you would be more likely to make the investment.

Although it is not so obvious, interest rates also play a role in investment decisions for a company that plans to finance investment from accumulated profits. Suppose that as a result of good profits in the previous year, your construction company had put aside $100,000 in cash. You would not then have to borrow from the bank to buy the backhoe. However, using half of your cash reserves to buy the backhoe still has an opportunity cost that depends on interest rates. For example, if the rate of interest on government bonds is 6 percent, your company could earn $250 per month by using $50,000 of your cash reserves to buy bonds instead of buying the backhoe.[5] That is an opportunity cost. If the interest rate were 12 percent per year, your monthly income from the bonds would be $500—a greater opportunity cost—and you would be more tempted to buy the bonds instead of the backhoe.

Interest rates influence investment decisions by consumers as well as business. Residential construction accounts for about a third of all private fixed investment in the United States. When mortgage interest rates are low, as they have been in recent years, housing construction booms.

The importance of interest rates for investment spending is one of the reasons that we will spend several chapters in this book talking about banking, financial markets, and related topics.

Interest rates are not the only factor influencing investment decisions. The psychological factor of *business confidence* is also important. By this, we mean the whole complex of expectations and hopes on which firms make their plans for the future. If you expect a boom in the housing market in your area, your construction company is more likely than otherwise to buy that backhoe. If you expect doom and gloom ahead, you'll play it safe by buying the government bonds. Keynes referred to business confidence using the colorful term "animal spirits." In doing so, he wanted to emphasize the fact that business confidence can change quickly for reasons that are hard for economists to measure exactly.

On a global scale, the decision of how much to invest in a given country depends on the country's *investment climate*. This term is used to refer to an entire range of conditions that lead businesses to expect a reliable or questionable return on investments they make. Among the conditions that make up a country's investment climate are its tax laws, the amount of "red tape" imposed by the country's bureaucracy, the likelihood that profits will be drained away by criminal gangs or corrupt officials, and the stability of macroeconomic conditions. In countries where the investment climate is good, domestic firms are willing to put profits into expansion of their operations, and international firms are willing to bring in new capital and know-how. In countries where the investment climate is bad, domestic firms send their profits abroad for safekeeping rather than investing them at home, and global business stays away. Sometimes a change of government can make an improvement in investment climate that leads to a prolonged period of prosperity. The countries of Eastern and Central Europe that changed from Communist central planning to Western market economies in the 1990s are a good example.

Government Purchases

Exogenous

Term applied to any variable that is determined by noneconomic considerations, or by economic considerations that lie outside the scope of a given model.

Government purchases are considered to be **exogenous** in most simple macroeconomic models. This means that they treated as a "given" that is determined by political considerations that lie outside the model rather than other variables included in the model. Transfer payments and tax revenues, on the other hand, are **endogenous**, in that they depend on variables included in the model, especially the level of GDP. During the expansion phase of the business cycle, tax revenues rise and transfer payments, especially for unemployment benefits, fall. During a recession, tax collections fall and transfer payments rise.

Chapter 13 will take a closer look at the determination of government purchases and net taxes.

Endogenous

Term applied to any variable that is determined by other variables included in an economic model.

Net Exports

Net exports are an endogenous variable because they depend on other variables in the macroeconomic model. For example, as real GDP expands and national income increases, both consumers and businesses spend some of their increased income on imported goods. For this reason, net exports tend to fall, and a country's trade deficit tends to rise during the expansion phase of the business cycle.

The exchange rate of a country's currency relative to the currencies of its trading partners is another factor affecting net exports. For example, during the early 2000s, the U.S. dollar weakened relative to the euro, the currency used by the country's major European trading partners. As the dollar weakened, it became easier for U.S. firms to sell their exports in Europe, and, at the same time, imports from Europe became more expensive for U.S. buyers. Consequently, net exports to

Europe strengthened. Exchange rates, in turn, are influenced by many factors, including changes in real GDP, inflation, and interest rates. The complex interaction between net exports and other economic variables will be explored in several coming chapters.

EQUILIBRIUM IN THE CIRCULAR FLOW

In Chapter 2, we introduced the concept of market equilibrium. The market for any single good, say chicken, is said to be in equilibrium when the amount buyers plan to purchase equals the amount that producers supply for sale. When the market for chicken is in equilibrium, there will be no tendency for accumulation or decrease of inventories and no immediate pressure for market participants to change their plans.

Now we will see how the concept of equilibrium can be extended to the circular flow of income and expenditure. To say that total planned expenditures (consumption plus planned investment plus government purchases plus net exports) equal GDP is the same as to say that total planned purchases will equal total production. In that case there will be no unplanned inventory change for the economy as a whole. If something happens to increase total planned expenditures, the equilibrium will be disrupted. Let's see how this process works out as the economy expands and contracts over the business cycle.

An Expansion of Planned Expenditure

Suppose that the circular flow is initially in equilibrium with total planned expenditure exactly equal to GDP. Since goods are being produced at just the rate they are being sold, the level of inventories remains constant from one month to the next. Now suppose that something happens to disturb this equilibrium. For example, suppose that development of new energy-efficient technologies inspires an upturn in investment expenditure as firms replace obsolete energy-wasting equipment.

As equipment makers increase their output of goods to satisfy the increased investment demand, they will take on more workers. The wage component of national income will increase. Profits of equipment makers are also likely to increase, further adding to the expansion of national income.

From our earlier discussion we know that when incomes rise, households will increase their consumption expenditure. So far there has been no change in the output of consumer goods. When consumption expenditure begins to increase with no change in production of consumer goods, the first effect will be an unplanned decrease in inventories of consumer goods. Only then, when makers of consumer goods see inventories falling, will they modify their production plans to meet the new demand. As they do so, they, too, will need to hire new workers, and incomes will rise further.

In this way, the original economic stimulus, which began in the industrial equipment sector, spreads through the economy. GDP and domestic income continue to rise, but not without limit. Because workers spend only a part of their increased income (according to the principle of the marginal propensity to consume), each round of the cycle of more-production-more-wages-more-spending is smaller than the previous one. Before long, GDP reaches a new equilibrium where production and planned expenditure balance, and there are no further unplanned changes in inventories.

Recall that the whole process began with an assumed increase in planned investment. By the time the new equilibrium is reached, the total change in GDP will be greater than the original increase in planned investment because it will also include production of additional consumer goods. The principle that an initial change in planned expenditure changes equilibrium GDP by a greater amount is known as the multiplier effect.

A Contraction of Planned Expenditure

The same process operates in reverse if equilibrium is disturbed by a decrease in some category of planned expenditure. For example, suppose a crisis in the Mexican economy reduces U.S. exports to that country. The first effect will be that U.S. makers of export goods will find inventories rising because Mexican importers are not buying what they planned before the crisis. To bring inventories in line with reduced sales, makers of export goods cut their output. Workers are laid off or work shorter hours, and their incomes fall. As a result, they cut back on consumption expenditures, following the principle of the marginal propensity to consume. When this happens, makers of consumer goods find their inventories also unexpectedly increasing. They, too, cut back on output, and incomes of their workers fall.

As this process continues, GDP and domestic income decrease. They do not decrease without limit, however. Before long a new equilibrium is reached. In the new equilibrium, real GDP will have decreased by a greater amount than the original change in exports. This is an example of the multiplier effect operating in reverse.

The Multiplier Effect and the Business Cycle

Multiplier effect

The tendency of a given exogenous change in planned expenditure to increase equilibrium GDP by a greater amount.

The **multiplier effect** was one of the key ideas in Keynes' *General Theory*, which was published at the height of the Great Depression. The multiplier was immediately seized on as an explanation for the business cycle.

In its simplified, popularized form, the Keynesian explanation of the Great Depression went something like this: During the 1920s, the U.S. economy entered a boom due to the multiplier effect of huge investment expenditures, especially expansion of automobile production and road building. Then in 1929 came Black Friday and the famous stock market crash. The crash destroyed business confidence, and investment fell again. This time the multiplier effect operated in reverse to produce the Great Depression.

At the same time the multiplier effect seemed to give an explanation of the causes of the Great Depression, it seemed to suggest a cure. What if the government increased its purchases of goods and services by enough to offset the drop in private investment? Wouldn't this send equilibrium GDP back to its original level? This reasoning gave rise to various attempts to spend the country back to prosperity, for example, by hiring thousands of unemployed workers for service in national parks.

Modern macroeconomics makes a place for the multiplier effect and recognizes that there is an element of truth in the simple Keynesian view of the business cycle. However, the simple multiplier theory is seriously incomplete. One shortcoming concerns how prices change over the business cycle. When producers respond to an unexpected decrease in inventories, do they increase real output without changing prices, do they raise prices to take advantage of unexpectedly strong demand, or do they do a little of both? Another problem is that the simple multiplier theory does not consider capacity constraints related to labor inputs, capital, and technology. Does real output respond in the same way to a change in planned expenditure when the economy is operating above its natural level of real output as below it? Still another limitation is that the theory pays too little attention to the role of money and the financial sector. Later chapters will deal with all of these issues in order to give a more complete picture.

SUMMARY

1. **How are households and firms linked by incomes and expenditures?** In order to produce goods and services, firms pay wages and salaries to obtain labor inputs, interest to obtain capital, and rents and royalties to obtain natural resources. If sales exceed costs, firms earn profits. The sum of wages, salaries, interest, rents, royalties, and profits constitute domestic income.

2. **How is expenditure divided into consumption, investment, government purchases, and net ex-** ports? The largest part of domestic income is used to purchase consumer goods and services. Some also is used to buy newly produced capital goods or add to inventories (investment), to pay for goods and services purchased by government, or to buy imported goods. Some expenditure is also made by foreign buyers. The term *net exports* refers to exports minus imports.

3. **What are the relationships between injections and leakages in the circular flow?** Saving, net taxes (tax revenues minus transfer payments), and imports are considered leakages from the cir-

cular flow. Investment, government purchases, and exports and considered injections. The total of leakages must always equal the total of injections, but the individual pairs (saving and investment, net taxes and government purchases, imports and exports) do not need to balance. Any imbalance in the individual pairs is balanced by flows of funds through capital markets.

4. **Why is some investment planned and other unplanned?** *Planned investment* means fixed investment (purchases of newly produced capital goods) plus *planned inventory investment* (changes in inventory made on purpose as part of a business plan). In addition, inventories may change unexpectedly in ways not called for by firms' business plans. These changes are called *unplanned inventory investment*.

5. **How can the concept of equilibrium be applied to the circular flow of income and expenditure?** The *circular flow of income and product* is in equilibrium when total planned expenditure equals GDP. If *planned expenditure* exceeds GDP, so that more goods and services are being bought than are being produced, there will be unplanned decreases in inventories. In reaction, firms will increase output and GDP will tend to rise. If total planned expenditure falls short of GDP, there will be unplanned increases in inventories. In response, firms will tend to increase their output and GDP will rise.

6. **What is the multiplier effect and how is it related to the business cycle?** According to the multiplier effect, a given change in one type of expenditure (say, planned investment) will produce a larger change in equilibrium GDP. The multiplier effect helps explain how relatively small disturbances in expenditure can cause relatively larger changes in GDP over the course of the business cycle.

KEY TERMS

Circular flow of income and product	Leakages
	Saving
Consumption	Planned inventory
Investment	investment
Fixed investment	Unplanned inventory
Inventory investment	investment
Government purchases	Planned investment
of goods and services	Planned expenditure
Government expenditures	Marginal propensity to consume
Transfer payments	Disposable income
Tax revenues	Exogenous
Net taxes	Endogenous
Net exports	Multiplier effect
Injections	

PROBLEMS AND TOPICS FOR DISCUSSION

1. **Your personal expenditures.** What was your income last month (or last year) from all current resources, including wages and salaries plus any interest earned or other investment income? Do not count money that you received as transfer payments, such as government benefits, gifts from family, scholarship grants, etc. How much was your saving? Did you add to your savings or draw down on past savings? How much did you spend on consumer goods or services? Of your spending, approximately how much do you think was spent on imported goods or services purchased while on foreign travel? Identify where the answer to each of these questions appears in the circular flow diagram, Figure 9.1.

2. **Planned versus unplanned inventory changes.** Suppose your school bookstore manager learns from the admissions office that enrollment of students will

rise by 10 percent next year. What planned inventory investments would the bookstore manager make? Suppose that a storm delays 100 students from another university who have visited your campus for a hockey game. While waiting for their bus to leave, they decide, because they have nothing better to do, to browse in your school bookstore and buy some items that catch their eye. How would this affect the store's inventories?

3. **Injections and leakages in the Russian economy.** In recent years, Russia has benefited from high world prices for the large amount of oil it produces for export. As a result, Russia has had positive net exports. Because oil is partly state owned and, where privately owned, heavily taxed, government tax revenues have increased so that the Russian government budget is in surplus. How would these differences between the Russian and U.S. economies affect the direction of the arrows in the circular flow diagram of Figure 9.1? Explain any changes that would need to be made.

4. **Unplanned inventory change and disequilibrium.** Suppose that you read in the news that inventories in retail stores fell last month, to the surprise of analysts. Would interpret this as a sign of equilibrium or disequilibrium in the circular flow? Which do you think would be more likely in the coming months, an increase or a decrease in GDP? Why?

5. **Adjustment to change in planned expenditure.** Starting from a state of equilibrium, trace the effects of each of the following. What happens to inventories? How do firms react? What happens to incomes? To consumption expenditure? To GDP?

   a. Business managers, anticipating future profit opportunities in consumer electronics, increase orders for production equipment in order to prepare for the expected increase in demand.

   b. The federal government reduces income tax rates.

   c. Good harvests in Africa reduce the demand for exports of U.S. farm products.

CASE FOR DISCUSSION

Excerpts from the Annual Report of the President's Council of Economic Advisers, 2005

In 2004, the U.S. economic recovery blossomed into a full-fledged expansion, with strong output growth and steady improvement in the labor market. Real gross domestic product (GDP) grew by 4.4 percent in 2004 for the year as a whole. About 2.2 million new payroll jobs were created during 2004—the largest annual gain since 1999. The unemployment rate fell to 5.4 percent by year's end, below the average of each of the past three decades. Inflation remained moderate, especially excluding volatile energy prices.

The U.S. economy is on a solid footing for sustained growth in the years to come. This is a marked reversal from the economic situation the Nation faced when President Bush came into office. Four years ago, the economy was sliding into recession after the bursting of the high-tech bubble of the 1990s. The economy was then affected by revelations of corporate scandals, slow growth among our major trading partners, and the terrorist attacks of September 11, 2001. Business investment slowed sharply in late 2000 and remained soft for more than two years. The economy lost over 900,000 jobs from December 2000 to September 2001, and then almost another 900,000 jobs in the three months after the 9/11 attacks.

Prompt and decisive policy actions helped to counteract the effects of these adverse shocks to the economy. Substantial tax relief together with expansionary monetary policy provided stimulus to aggregate demand that softened the recession and helped put the economy on the path to recovery. In addition to providing timely short-term stimulus, the President's pro-growth tax policies have improved incentives for work and capital accumulation, thereby fostering an environment conducive to long-term economic growth.

The solid advance in real GDP during 2004 was supported by gains in consumer spending, business fixed investment, and, to a lesser extent, housing investment, inventory accumulation, and government spending. Net exports (exports less imports) held down growth in all four quarters as the trade deficit rose in the third quarter to a record high as a percentage of GDP. Progress toward strengthened economic growth among U.S. trading partners led to an increase in exports, but imports continued to outpace exports as U.S. domestic demand and demand for imported oil remained strong. The economy's strong growth performance came about in the face of higher oil prices, which likely reduced growth somewhat during the year. The Administration expects real GDP to grow 3.5 percent during the four quarters of 2005, in line with the consensus of professional forecasters. This growth is expected to be driven by continued gains in consumer spending, investment growth, and stronger net exports.

QUESTIONS

The following questions may be answered on the basis of information in the main text of the chapter. However, if you have read the appendix, use what you learned there to give additional detail to your answers.

1. According to the report, in early 2001 the economy was in recession because of the bursting of the high-tech bubble, corporate scandals, slow growth in trading partners, and the 9/11 attacks. Explain how each of these factors acts on the elements of planned expenditure to produce a recession.

2. According to the report, the Bush administration's policies have helped to put the country on the road to expansion. What particular policies have done so? Explain how each of these policies acts on the elements of planned expenditure. (Note: Monetary policy will be discussed in detail in later units. For the moment, it is enough to know that "expansionary monetary policy" means "lower interest rates.")

3. What does the report mean in saying that net exports held down the expansion? Do you think it is normal, or unusual, for the net exports component of planned expenditure to decrease during the expansion phase of the business cycle? Explain why.

END NOTES

1. Economists use the term *households* to refer to families who live together and make economic decisions together about issues of work and spending, as well as to individuals living alone who make such decisions independently.

2. The term *trade deficit* as popularly used does not always correspond exactly to our term *net exports*. The next chapter will discuss concepts related to imports, exports, and the balance of payments in more detail.

3. The economy's financial sector, including banks, securities markets, insurance companies, and other institutions will be discussed in more detail in Chapter 11.

4. John Maynard Keynes, *The General Theory of Employment, Interest, and Money* (New York: Harcourt, Brace and World, 1936), 96.

5. To understand this example, it is important to remember that buying the backhoe is a purchase of newly produced capital goods, that is, part of the fixed investment component of planned expenditure. Buying the government bond is a financial investment, a purchase of the right to receive future payments from the government. The bonds are not newly produced capital goods and do not count as part of GDP.

CHAPTER 10

Measuring Economic Activity

After reading this chapter, you will understand:

1. How gross domestic product is officially defined and measured
2. How the measurement of domestic income differs from the measurement of gross domestic product
3. The major types of international transactions
4. How changes in the average level of prices are measured
5. The limitations of official economic statistics

Before reading this chapter, make sure you know the meaning of:

1. Real and nominal values
2. Indexation
3. Transfer payments
4. Domestic income and product

IN THE INTERNET age, government reports of GDP and related data are available, and acted on, instantly throughout the world. For example, in May 2005, when the U.S. Commerce Department reported the U.S. GDP rose by 3.5 percent in the first quarter of that year, faster than the 3.1 percent preliminary data had indicated, German stock market prices immediately rose. Evidently, German investors thought that greater U.S. demand for Audis and BMWs would be good for their economy. But just having instant access to the numbers is not enough. To use the latest data intelligently, you must know what they mean and where they come from. That means not only knowing the theoretical relationships among GDP components, as discussed in the previous chapter, but also how they are actually measured. That is the subject of this chapter.

Together, the data on aggregate economic activity published by the government are known as the **national income accounts**. The economists and statisticians whose job it is to

National income accounts

A set of official government statistics on aggregate economic activity.

make these measurements for the U.S. economy are widely held to be the best such team in the world. Yet, as this chapter will show, they face many problems. There are technical problems posed by sampling errors and survey methods. There are conceptual problems that arise when real-world institutions do not match the theoretical categories of economic models. Finally, there are problems of timeliness. Government decision-makers must sometimes work with preliminary data. For example, the 3.5 percent GDP growth rate reported May 2005 was not only higher than preliminary estimates, but would itself be subject to further revision as more data came in. In July 2005, the first-quarter growth estimate was again revised upward, this time to 3.8 percent. The knowledge that early data are often revised makes it necessary to balance the risks of acting on an inaccurate report against those of delaying action until more information is available.

THE NATIONAL INCOME ACCOUNTS IN NOMINAL TERMS

We begin with an examination of the national income accounts in nominal terms—that is, in terms of the prices at which goods and services are actually sold. Nominal measures do not tell the whole story because they are not adjusted to reflect the effects of inflation, but they provide a starting point. Data are first collected in nominal form, and only after a set of nominal accounts have been assembled can the process of adjusting for price changes begin.

Gross Domestic Product

Gross domestic product (GDP)

The value at current market prices of all final goods and services produced annually in a given country.

Final goods and services

Goods and services that are sold to or ready for sale to parties that will use them for consumption, investment, government purchases, or export.

The most widely publicized number in the national income accounts is gross domestic product. **Gross domestic product (GDP)** is the value at current market prices (that is, the nominal value) of all final goods and services produced annually in a given country.

The term **final goods and services** is a key part of the definition of gross domestic product. GDP attempts to measure the sum of the economic contributions of each firm and industry without missing anything or counting anything twice. To do this, care must be taken to count only goods sold to *final users*—parties that will use them for domestic consumption, government purchases, investment, or export. *Intermediate goods*—those that are purchased for use as inputs in producing other goods or services—are excluded.

Table 10.1 shows why counting both final and intermediate goods would overstate total production. The table traces the process of producing a kitchen table with a retail price of $100. The final stage of production takes place in the furniture plant, but the manufacturer does not do $100 worth of work. Instead, the manufacturer takes $40 worth of lumber, turns it into a table, and then adds $60 in worth of inputs in the form of the labor, capital, and other factors of production used to run the furniture plant. The $40 worth of lumber is an intermediate good; the $60 contribution

TABLE 10.1   VALUE ADDED AND THE USE OF FINAL PRODUCTS IN GDP

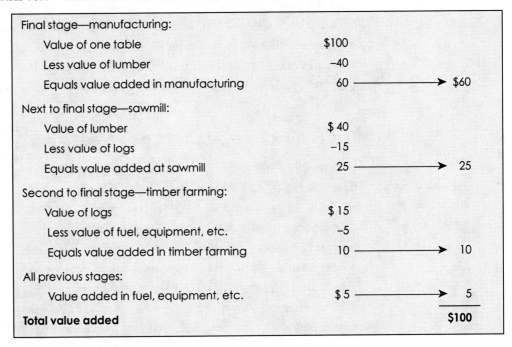

Final stage—manufacturing:		
Value of one table	$100	
Less value of lumber	−40	
Equals value added in manufacturing	60 ——————→	$60
Next to final stage—sawmill:		
Value of lumber	$ 40	
Less value of logs	−15	
Equals value added at sawmill	25 ——————→	25
Second to final stage—timber farming:		
Value of logs	$ 15	
Less value of fuel, equipment, etc.	−5	
Equals value added in timber farming	10 ——————→	10
All previous stages:		
Value added in fuel, equipment, etc.	$ 5 ——————→	5
Total value added		**$100**

This table shows why GDP must include only the value of final goods and services if it is to measure total production without double counting. The value of sales at each stage of production can be divided into the value added at that stage and the value of purchased inputs. The selling price of the final product (a $100 table, in this case) equals the sum of the values added at all stages of production.

Value added

The dollar value of an industry's sales less the value of intermediate goods purchased for use in production.

made by the manufacturer is the **value added** to the product at its final stage. (In practice, other intermediate goods, such as paint and fuel for heating the plant, are used in making the table. To simplify the example we assume that the table is made solely from lumber plus the manufacturer's effort.)

The second section of Table 10.1 shows the next-to-last stage of production: making the lumber. The sawmill buys $15 worth of logs, saws them into lumber that sells for $40, and adds $25 in value as the mill's contribution. The value added at the sawmill stage is $25.

Going still further back, we come to the stage at which the logs were produced. To produce $15 worth of logs, a forest products company bought $5 worth of fuel, equipment, and so on and added $10 in exchange for the effort involved in tending the trees and harvesting the logs. That is an additional $10 of value added.

Clearly, the process of making the table could be traced back indefinitely. The last section of the exhibit sums up the value added at all stages of production prior to timber farming—the fuel and equipment suppliers, their own suppliers, and so on. If production were traced back far enough, every penny could be attributed to the value added to the final product somewhere in the chain of production.

Now compare the first and last lines of the exhibit. Lo and behold, the value of the final good—the table—turns out to be a precise measure of the sum of the values added at each stage of production. This is why only final goods are counted in GDP. Adding together the $100 value of the table, the $40 value of the lumber, the $15 value of the timber, and so on would far overstate the true rate of productive activity (the true total value added) in the economy.

The Expenditure Approach to Measuring GDP

In principle, GDP could be measured by adding together the value of each final good or service sold or by adding up the value added at each stage of production, as shown in Table 10.1. Instead of measuring domestic product directly, however, national income accountants make use of the equality of domestic product and total expenditure. It is easier to gather data on the total amount spent by households, investors, governments, and buyers of exports on final goods produced in the domestic economy than it is to stand at factory gates and count goods as they roll off assembly lines. This method of measuring GDP is known as the *expenditure approach*. Table 10.2 shows how it works, using 2002 data for the U.S. economy.

CONSUMPTION   The first line of Table 10.2 gives total household consumption of both domestically produced and imported goods and services. The national income accounts divide consumption into three categories: durable goods, nondurable goods, and services. In principle, goods that do not wear out within a year, such as cars, furniture, and appliances, are durable, whereas goods that are used up in less than a year, such as soap, food, and gasoline, are nondurable. In practice, however, these categories are somewhat arbitrary. For example, all clothing is considered nondurable, whether the item is a pair of stockings that may last only a few weeks or a wool coat that may last ten years. The remaining category—services—includes everything that is not in the form of a physical object when sold. Examples include haircuts, legal advice, financial services, and education.

All three components of consumption contain some items that bypass the marketplace on their way to consumers. One such item is an estimate of the quantity of food produced and consumed on farms; another is an estimate of the rental value of owner-occupied homes. However, many nonmarket goods and services are not captured in the national income accounts; unpaid childcare and housework are examples.

INVESTMENT   The item termed *gross private domestic investment* is the sum of all purchases of newly produced capital goods (fixed investment) plus changes in business inventories (inventory investment). The fixed-investment component includes both business fixed investment—all new equipment and structures bought by firms—and the value of newly constructed residential housing. In the national income accounts, then, a homeowning household is treated like a small firm. When

TABLE 10.2   NOMINAL GROSS DOMESTIC PRODUCT BY TYPE OF EXPENDITURE, 2002
(Dollars in Billions)

Personal consumption expenditure		$ 8,231.1
Durable goods	$ 995.7	
nondurable goods	2,376.5	
Services	4,859.0	
Plus gross private domestic investment		1,922.4
Fixed investment	1,879.3	
Change in business inventories	43.1	
Plus government purchases of goods and services		2,183.8
Federal	810.0	
State and local	1,373.9	
Plus net exports of goods and services		−609.3
Exports	1,170.2	
Less imports	1,779.6	
Equals gross domestic product (GDP)		$11,728.0
Less capital consumption allowance		−1,406.9
Equals net domestic product (NDP)		$10,321.1

Gross domestic product is estimated using the expenditure approach. This involves adding together the values of expenditures on newly produced final goods and services made by all economic units to get a measure of aggregate economic activity. Net domestic product is derived from gross domestic product by excluding the value of expenditures made to replace worn-out or obsolete capital equipment.

Source: *Economic Report of the President,* 2005, Tables B-1, B-26.

the house is bought, it is counted as an investment. Then, as we saw earlier, the firm's "product"—the rental value of its shelter services—is counted as part of consumption each year.

The gross private domestic investment item does not include investment in structures, software, and equipment made by federal, state, and local governments. These amounted to some $343 billion in 2004, adding about 17 percent to the total. From the point of view of short-run business cycle theory, it makes sense to treat government and private investment differently, since the motives for the investment are different. However, from the point of long-term growth theory, government investment, like private investment, adds to a country's stock of capital and increases future natural real GDP.

GOVERNMENT PURCHASES   The item called "government purchases" in macroeconomic models is titled "Government Consumption Expenditures and Gross Investment" in the official national income accounts. As this formal term implies, the bulk of the government's contribution to GDP at the federal, state, and local levels is treated much like consumption, in that the goods and factor services bought by government are considered to be "used up" as soon as they are purchased. As mentioned in the previous paragraph, about 17 percent of government purchases are investment-type expenditures. Whether consumption or investment, government purchases are valued at cost in the national income accounts. No attempt is made to measure the value added by government, because most government outputs—primary and secondary education, defense services, and police protection, to name a few—are financed by taxes and provided to the public without charge rather than sold. Transfer payments are not included in the expenditure approach to GDP, because they do not represent purchases of newly produced final goods and services.

NET EXPORTS   The last item in the GDP account is *net export*—exports minus imports. In calculating GDP, imports must be subtracted from exports to avoid double counting. Some of the goods bought by consumers, investors, and government and included in their expenditures are not produced in the domestic economy. For example, a consumer might buy a Japanese television set, an insurance company might buy Korean computers for use in its offices, and a city government might buy a Swedish-built police car. The figures for consumption, investment, and government purchases therefore overstate the final use of domestically produced goods and services to the extent that some of those goods and services were produced abroad. To correct for the overstatement in earlier lines in Table 10.2, imports are subtracted from exports at the bottom. Adding total consumption plus total investment plus total government purchases plus exports less imports yields the same sum as would be obtained by adding domestic consumption of domestically produced goods, domestic purchases of domestically produced capital goods, domestic government purchases of domestically produced goods, and total exports.

Gross national product (GNP)

The dollar value at current market prices of all final goods and services produced annually by factors of production owned by residents of a given country, regardless of where those factors are located.

DOMESTIC VERSUS NATIONAL PRODUCT   Gross national product (GNP), is a concept closely related to GDP that was the focus of U.S. government data until the early 1990s. GDP is a geographic concept, measuring economic activity within a country's boundaries. GNP differs from GDP in that it measures the total annual output of factors of production owned by residents of a given country, regardless of where those factors are located. Consider gross domestic and national product for the United States. U.S. gross *national* product includes the contribution to output of U.S. factors of production working abroad, for example, output attributable to capital invested in an English factory by the U.S. stockholders of Ford Motor Company; U.S. gross *domestic* product excludes that output. On the other hand, U.S. gross *domestic* product includes the contribution to output of foreign-owned factors located in the United States—for example, output attributable to capital invested by Honda Motor Company's Japanese stockholders in a factory in Ohio. GDP and GNP normally differ by only a small amount, and GDP has almost entirely replaced GNP in discussions of macroeconomics today.

GROSS VERSUS NET DOMESTIC PRODUCT What makes gross domestic product "gross" is the fact that gross private domestic investment measures total additions to the nation's capital stock without adjusting for losses through wear and tear or obsolescence. For example, it includes the value of new homes and factories built each year without subtracting the value of old homes and factories that are torn down. Gross private domestic investment minus an allowance for depreciation and obsolescence yields net private domestic investment, a measure of the actual net addition to the nation's capital stock each year. Only net investment adds to the capital stock, thereby helping to expand the economy's natural real output over time. The part of gross investment that covers depreciation and obsolescence is needed just to keep the capital stock from shrinking. Although depreciation and obsolescence are hard to measure accurately, national income accountants use an approximate measure called the capital consumption allowance. Gross domestic product minus the capital consumption allowance yields **net domestic product (NDP)**.

Net domestic product (NDP)

Gross domestic product minus an allowance (called the *capital consumption allowance*) that represents the value of capital equipment used up in the production process.

The distinction between domestic and national product applies to the net, as well as the gross, product concepts. Thus, if net receipts of factor income from abroad are added to net domestic product, the result is *net national product (NNP)*.

The Income Approach to Measuring Aggregate Economic Activity

Previously, we looked at the economy in terms of a circular flow of income and product. In principle, aggregate economic activity could be measured by observing the flow at any point as it circulates. In practice, the national income accounts use two points of observation. First, as we have just seen, domestic product is measured by the expenditure approach, which is equivalent to observing the flow of aggregate economic activity at the point at which it enters product markets. Second, measurements are made of the flows of all kinds of income at the point at which they are received by households. This is known as the *income approach* to measuring aggregate economic activity. The result is shown in Table 10.3. Several items in that exhibit deserve comment.

Compensation of employees consists of wages and salaries plus certain *supplements*. The first supplement is employer contributions to social insurance (social security). As the social security tax law is written, employees are legally required to pay only half of the tax; employers must pay the other half. Because both halves contribute to employees' retirement benefits, however, both are counted as part of employee compensation. The supplements line also includes fringe benefits other than social insurance that employers pay for, such as health insurance and private pension plans.

Rental income of persons consists of all income in the form of rent and royalties received by property owners. *Net interest* includes interest income received by households less interest payments made by consumers.

TABLE 10.3   NOMINAL NATIONAL AND DOMESTIC INCOME, 2002
(Dollars in Billions)

Compensation of employees		$6,651.0
Wages and salaries	$ 5,373.4	
Other labor income	1,273.6	
Plus rental income of persons		165.1
Plus net interest		549.5
Plus corporate profits		1,181.6
Plus proprietors' income		902.8
Equals national income		10,339.6
Less receipts of factor income from rest of world		–405.8
Plus payments of factor income to rest of world		361.9
Equals domestic income		10,295.7

National and domestic income is measured using the income approach. This involves adding together the values of all forms of income earned by a country's residents. U.S. national income includes some income received in return for factors of production used abroad, and excludes payments to foreign residents for the use of factors owned by them but located in the United States. Domestic income is derived from national income by subtracting receipts of factor income from the rest of the world and adding factor income paid to the rest of the world.

Source: U.S. Department of Commerce, Bureau of Economic Analysis, National Income and Product Accounts, Tables 1.7.5, May 2005

Corporate profits encompass all income earned by the stockholders of corporations, regardless of whether they actually receive that income. Dividends are the part of corporate income that stockholders actually receive. Another part of corporate profits goes to pay taxes. A third part—undistributed corporate profits—is kept by corporations for use in making investments. In measuring income, corporate profits are also adjusted for changes in inventory values and for capital consumption (depreciation). The final component of income, *proprietors' income,* lumps together all forms of income earned by self-employed professionals and owners of unincorporated business.

National income

The total income earned by a country's residents, including wages, rents, interest payments, and profits.

The total of these items is **national income**, the total income received by a country's residents. The term *national* is appropriate because when net interest and corporate profits are counted, the income approach includes factor income received from abroad by U.S. residents. At the same time, the income approach does not include factor income paid to foreign residents as a result of their investments in the United

States. Following the procedure used in distinguishing between domestic and national product, we can calculate *domestic income,* the income concept that was featured in our discussion of the circular flow in the preceding chapter. Domestic income is equal to national income minus net receipts of factor income from the rest of the world.

RECONCILING THE INCOME AND EXPENDITURE APPROACHES   In the circular flow diagram presented in Chapter 9, domestic income and product are equal by definition. In the actual national income accounts, however, the two fit together less neatly. In addition to the distinctions between gross and net measurements, and between national and domestic measurements, there are two other problems.

One concerns the fact that part of the revenue that firms receive for their products never reaches the suppliers of factor services or the firms' owners. Instead, it is taken by government in the form of so-called *indirect business taxes,* which include sales taxes, excise taxes, and business property taxes. These taxes are treated differently than the corporate profits tax, which is viewed as being earned by owners and then taken from them by the tax collector. Indirect taxes are included in the prices at which goods and services are sold; therefore, they are part of net national product but are not counted as earned in national income.

The other problem is that, in the official accounts, GDP is measured by the expenditure approach using one set of data, and national income is measured by the income approach using a different set of data. No matter how carefully the work is done, there will be some errors and omissions, and therefore the two sets of figures will not quite fit together. The difference between NNP minus indirect business taxes on the one hand, and national income, on the other, is called the *statistical discrepancy.* Most of the time this error is very small—well below 1 percent of GDP.

Neither indirect business taxes nor the statistical discrepancy are of much importance for macroeconomic theory. In coming chapters, our models will continue to treat domestic income and product as equal by definition.

MEASURING INTERNATIONAL LINKAGES

The item "net exports" in the national income accounts gives a glimpse of the linkage between the domestic economy and the rest of the world. These ties have grown much stronger in recent years. In 1960, U.S. exports amounted to only 6 percent of GDP and imports less than 5 percent. By 2004, exports had grown to 9.9 percent of a much larger GDP. Imports grew even more rapidly over the same period, reaching 15.2 percent of GDP. In view of the growing importance of the foreign sector, then, it is worth taking a closer look at the international ties of the U.S. economy.

Any discussion of an economy's balance of international payments is complicated by the fact that thousands of different kinds of international payments are made every day. Payments for the goods and services that are exported and imported come to mind first, but there are many others. Equally important are the long- and short-term loans made to finance imports and exports and the payments made in international markets in connection with purchases or sales of assets, such as securities or real estate. In addition, governments and private individuals make many kinds of transfer payments to residents of other countries, including outright gifts, pension payments, and official foreign aid. Finally, the U.S. Federal Reserve System and foreign central banks engage in many kinds of official transactions. Table 10.4 shows a simplified version of the accounts used to keep track of these international transactions for the United States.

The Current Account

The first section of the international accounts shown in Table 10.4 contains what are called **current account** transactions. These include imports and exports of goods and services, payments of factor income between countries, and international transfer payments. The main items in the current account are as follows:

MERCHANDISE IMPORTS AND EXPORTS   Imports and exports of merchandise (goods) are the most widely publicized items in the international accounts. During much of the nineteenth century the United States was a net importer of merchandise. From 1894 to 1970 it was a net exporter. Since 1970 it has again become largely a net importer. Table 10.4 shows a negative **merchandise balance**. The negative number indicates net merchandise imports.

SERVICES   In addition to trade in merchandise, the United States and other countries carry on a large trade in services. Travel expenditures, airline passenger fares, and other transportation services account for somewhat more than half of these services. Other services include insurance, royalties, and license fees. Certain transactions related to sales of military equipment are included under the heading of services. As the table shows, the United States was a net exporter of services in 2004.

FACTOR INCOME   Earlier, in drawing the distinction between domestic and national product, we noted that U.S. residents receive substantial flows of factor income from U.S. assets located abroad. These are analogous to exports, and enter the current account with a positive sign. At the same time, payments of factor income are made to residents of other countries from foreign-owned assets located in the United States. These are analogous to imports, and enter the current account with a negative sign. The United States received more income from abroad than it paid in 2004.

TRANSFERS   The final item on the current account consists of net transfer receipts. This typically is a negative item in the U.S. international accounts, because

---

Current account

The section of a country's international accounts that consists of imports and exports of goods and services and unilateral transfers.

Merchandise balance

The value of a country's merchandise exports minus the value of its merchandise imports.

TABLE 10.4   U.S. INTERNATIONAL ACCOUNTS FOR 2004
(Dollars in Billions)

Current Account		
1. Merchandise balance		−665.4
2. Exports	807.5	
3. Imports	−1,472.9	
4. Services, net		47.8
5. Exports of services	343.9	
6. Imports of services	−296.1	
7. Net receipts of factor income		30.5
8. Income receipts from abroad	379.5	
9. Income payments to the United States	−349.0	
10. Transfers, net		−80.9
11. Current account balance (lines 1 + 4 + 7 + 10)		−668.0
Capital and Financial Account		
12. Net change in U.S. assets abroad		−855.5
(− indicates increase in U.S. assets abroad,		
that is, a capital outflow)		
13. U.S. private assets	−859.5	
14. U.S. official reserve assets	2.8	
15. Other U.S. government assets	1.2	
16. Net change in foreign assets in the United States		1,440.1
(+ indicates increase in foreign assets in the United		
States, that is, a capital inflow)		
17. Foreign official assets	394.7	
18. Other foreign assets	1,045.4	
19. Capital account transactions, net		-1.6
20. Capital account balance (lines 12 + 16 + 19)		583.0
21. Statistical discrepancy		85.1
(sum of current and capital account balances		
with sign reversed)		

This table gives details of U.S. international transactions for 2004. The first section shows current account transactions, consisting of imports and exports of goods and services, together with international flows of factor income and transfer payments. The second section shows capital and financial account transactions, consisting of international borrowing and lending, securities transactions, direct investment, and official reserve transactions. If all amounts were measured completely and accurately, the current account and capital account balances would be equal and opposite in sign. In practice, there is a statistical discrepancy indicating errors and omissions in measurement.

Source: U.S. Department of Commerce, Bureau of Economic Analysis, *U.S. International Transactions Accounts Data*, Table 1, June 2005.

transfers to other countries exceed transfers received from them. This item takes into account both government transfers, such as foreign aid and social security payments to retired workers living abroad, and private transfers, such as private famine relief and church missions.

Current account balance

The value of a country's exports of goods and services minus the value of its imports of goods and services plus its net transfer receipts from foreign sources.

CURRENT ACCOUNT BALANCE When merchandise trade, services, factor income, and net transfers are combined, the result is the country's **current account balance**. Table 10.4 shows a current account deficit for the United States for 2004. The last year in which the country experienced a current account surplus was 1981.

Although the official name of this item is the current account balance, the term is not always used in news reports. Sometimes the term "balance of payments" is used and sometimes the term "balance of trade." To add to the confusion, the term "balance of trade" is sometimes used in news reports to refer to the merchandise balance. Setting aside certain methodological differences between the balance of payments accounts and the national income accounts, all in all, the current account balance is the closest thing to the item "net exports" that appears our macroeconomic models.

The Capital and Financial Account

Current account transactions are not the only ones that take place among residents of different countries. The international lending and borrowing and international sales and purchases of assets mentioned in an earlier chapter also account for an enormous volume of daily transactions. A U.S. company, for example, might obtain a short-term loan from a London bank to finance the purchase of a shipload of beer for import to the United States. The Brazilian government might get a long-term loan from Citibank of New York to help finance a hydroelectric project. A U.S. millionaire might open an account in a Swiss bank. A Japanese automaker might buy a piece of land in Tennessee on which to build a new plant. All of these transactions are recorded in the capital and financial account section of Table 10.4. In this book, we will use the shorter term "financial account" to refer to this section.[1]

Financial inflow

Purchases of domestic assets by foreign buyers and borrowing from foreign lenders ; also often called capital inflows.

Financial outflow

Purchases of foreign assets by domestic residents or loans by domestic lenders to foreign borrowers; also often called capital outflows.

Purchases of U.S. assets by foreigners and borrowing from foreign financial intermediaries by U.S. firms and individuals create flows of funds into the United States that are termed **financial inflows**. Purchases of foreign assets by U.S. residents or loans by U.S. financial intermediaries to foreigners create flows of funds out of the United States that are termed **financial outflows**.

Table 10.4 lists several types of capital and financial account transactions. Changes in U.S. private assets include direct investments (such as construction of foreign plants by U.S. firms) and purchases of foreign securities. Changes in U.S. official reserve assets include foreign currency and other foreign assets acquired by the

Federal Reserve System and the U.S. Treasury. Changes in other U.S. government assets relate to short- and long-term credits and other assets by government agencies other than the Federal Reserve System and U.S. Treasury. Changes in official foreign assets in the United States involve purchases of U.S. government securities by foreign central banks. Direct investment in the United States and private purchases of U.S. securities by foreign buyers are included under the heading "other foreign assets in the United States." Finally, the "capital account" in the narrow sense in which the term is officially used, is a small item that refers to transactions in nonfinancial assets such as ownership of patents and copyrights, and also includes private and governmental debt forgiveness and defaults on debt.

Relationship of the Accounts

Financial account transactions are logically related to the current account surplus or deficit. If the United States runs a current account deficit, its earnings from the sales of exports will not be enough to pay for all of its imports. Additional funds for financing imports can be obtained through net financial inflows, that is, through U.S. borrowing from abroad that exceeds U.S. lending to foreigners or through sales of U.S. assets to foreigners that exceed purchases of assets abroad. This is the case for the U.S. international transactions shown in Table 10.4. On the other hand, a country with a current account surplus can use its extra import earnings to make net loans to foreign borrowers or net purchases of foreign assets. This would result in a negative balance on the financial account. Countries that are big exporters and have surpluses of funds to invest abroad are in this position. For example, in 2004, Russia and Japan had large net financial outflows.

In principle, the balances of the current and financial accounts should be equal and opposite in sign. If there is a current account surplus of $100 billion (entered with a plus sign in the accounts), there should be a net financial outflow of $100 billion (entered with a minus sign in the accounts). The reason for this symmetry is that the two account components taken together include all the sources and uses of the funds that change hands in international transactions. Every dollar used in international transactions must have a source; thus, when the sources (+) and the uses (−) are added together, the sum should be zero.

In practice, however, government statisticians always miss some items when they tally up imports, exports, and financial flows. As a result, the numbers do not quite add up. The international accounts use the same term to refer to this quantity as is used for the similar quantity in the domestic accounts—*statistical discrepancy*. Much of the discrepancy is believed to reflect unrecorded financial flows, for example, investments made in the United States by residents of other countries, but never officially reported. Part of it also reflects a tendency for U.S. exports, especially to Canada, to be reported less fully than U.S. imports.

MEASURING REAL INCOME AND THE PRICE LEVEL

Between 1979 and 2004, the U.S. gross domestic product, measured in nominal terms, rose from $2.6 trillion to $11.7 trillion. To anyone living through those years, however, it is clear that even though nominal GDP more than doubled, the real output of goods and services did not. Much of the increase in the dollar value of GDP reflected an increase in the prices at which goods and services were sold. To understand what really happened to output in those years, then, we must adjust the growth of nominal GDP to account for inflation.

Real Gross Domestic Product and the Deflator

To adjust nominal GDP for the effects of inflation, we need a measure of the change in the average prices of goods and services. The most broadly based measure of price changes for the U.S. economy is the **GDP deflator**. The appendix to this chapter explains how it is calculated. For now, we will simply define the GDP deflator as a weighted average of the prices of all the final goods and services that make up GDP.

GDP deflator

A weighted average of the prices of all final goods and services produced in the economy.

Base year

The year that is chosen as a basis for comparison in calculating a price index or price level.

BASE YEAR   When we speak of price changes, the first question that comes to mind is: change from what? We can answer this question by choosing a convenient **base year** as a benchmark against which to measure change. The U.S. Department of Commerce currently uses 2000 as a base year for calculating the GDP deflator. The government uses two methods of calculating the GDP deflator: fixed and chained. Here, we will focus on the first method of computing GDP using fixed, or "constant," dollars.

The base year can be used in one of two ways in stating a weighted average of prices. One way is to let the base year value equal 1.0. A statement of average prices relative to a base year value of 1.0 is called a statement of the **price level**; for example, the 2004 price level, relative to the 2000 base year, was 1.082. The other way is to let the base year value equal 100. A statement of average prices relative to a base year value of 100 is known as a **price index**. Thus, using 2000 as a base year we could say that the 2002 price index was 108.2. The price level and price index are two different ways of stating the same information. In news reports the index form is used most frequently, whereas in building economic models the price level form is more convenient.

Price level

A weighted average of the prices of goods and services expressed in relation to a base year value of 1.0.

Price index

A weighted average of the prices of goods and services expressed in relation to a base year value of 100.

To convert nominal GDP for any year to real GDP stated in constant 2000 dollars, we simply divide nominal GDP by the price level for that year. For convenience, we can refer to the year for which we are making the adjustment as the current year. In equation form, then, the rule for adjustment can be stated as follows:

Current-year real GDP = Current-year nominal GDP/Current-year price level.

For example, 2004 nominal GDP was $11,728 billion. Dividing this by the current year GDP deflator of 1.0822 gives the 2004 real GDP, stated in constant 2000 dollars, of

$10,837 billion. If one looks at a year earlier than the base year, the price level has a value less than one. For example, the GDP deflator for 1980, using the 2000 base year, was .54. This indicates that the price level almost doubled over the two decades from 1980 to 2000. Nominal GDP in 1980 was $2,789 billion. Dividing this by .54 gives a value for 1980 real GDP of $5,164 billion. Comparing the various data, we see that while nominal GDP increased about four times from 1980 to 2004, real GDP approximately doubled.

THE CONSUMER PRICE INDEX   Although the GDP deflator is the most broadly based price index for the U.S. economy, it is not the best-known one. That honor belongs to the consumer price index. Rather than taking into account the prices of all final goods and services produced in the economy, as the GDP deflator does, the **consumer price index (CPI)** considers only the goods and services that make up the "market basket" purchased by a typical urban household. For example, the CPI market basket includes cars, but not railway locomotives.

The CPI currently uses the period 1982–1984 rather than a single year as its base year. The appendix to this chapter explains how the CPI is calculated.

The CPI plays a key role in the economy partly because it is widely used to index wages, government transfers, and many other payments. As explained in Chapter 8, indexation of a payment means automatically adjusting it on a regular schedule for changes in the price index involved. Millions of workers whose contracts include *cost-of-living-adjustment* (COLA) clauses receive automatic raises as a result of increases in the CPI.

Producer Price Indexes

Another widely publicized set of price indexes consists of **producer price indexes**. These are price averages for three classes of goods that are traded among business firms. The most widely publicized is the producer price index for *finished goods*—investment goods sold to businesses plus other goods that are ready for final use but have not yet been sold to consumers, for example, wholesale sales of clothing to clothing stores. Other producer price indexes cover intermediate goods and crude materials ready for further processing. The producer price indexes currently use a base year of 1982. Because producer price indexes measure prices at early stages in the production process, they are often studied for hints of trends in consumer prices. They are also frequently used to index payments that firms agree to make to one another.

Table 10.5 shows data for the GDP deflator, the consumer price index, and the producer price index for finished goods. To make comparison easier, the CPI and PPI figures have been restated using the same 2000 base year as the GDP deflator. As can be seen from the table, although the indexes tend to move in the same direction, the amount of inflation recorded by the various indexes differs. This is not surprising, inasmuch as they are based on different baskets of goods and services.

Consumer price index (CPI)

A price index based on the market basket of goods and services purchased by a typical urban household.

Producer price index (PPI)

A price index based on a sample of goods and services bought by business firms.

TABLE 10.5   U.S. PRICE INDEXES, 1980–2004

Year	GDP deflator	CPI	PPI
1980	54.043	47.9	63.8
1981	59.119	52.8	69.6
1982	62.726	56.0	72.5
1983	65.207	57.8	73.6
1984	67.655	60.3	75.1
1985	69.713	62.5	75.9
1986	71.250	63.6	74.8
1987	73.196	66.0	76.4
1988	75.694	68.7	78.3
1989	78.556	72.0	82.3
1990	81.590	75.9	86.4
1991	84.444	79.1	88.2
1992	86.385	81.5	89.3
1993	88.381	83.9	90.4
1994	90.259	86.1	90.9
1995	92.106	88.5	92.7
1996	93.852	91.1	95.1
1997	95.414	93.2	95.5
1998	96.472	94.7	94.7
1999	97.868	96.7	96.4
2000	100.000	100.0	100.0
2001	102.399	102.8	102.0
2002	104.092	104.5	100.7
2003	105.998	106.9	103.8
2004	108.220	109.7	107.6

This table compares the trends of the GDP deflator, the consumer price index, and the producer price index for finished goods from 1980 to 2004 for the United States. For ease of comparison, all three indexes have been restated to use the same base year, 2000.

Source: *Economic Report of the President*, 2005, Tables B-3, B-60, B-65.

How Good are the National Income Accounts?

This chapter began by stressing the importance of the national income accounts to economics and warning that they are less than perfect. Now that we have surveyed the main components of the nominal and real national income accounts, it is time to try to answer the question of how good those accounts are. We will focus on four possible problem areas: the accuracy and timeliness of the data, the underground sector of the economy, bias in price indexes, and the nonmaterial aspects of the standard of living.

ACCURACY AND TIMELINESS　Government decision makers pay close attention to national income accounting data to get an indication of economic trends as they unfold. Unfortunately, however, there is a trade-off between the timeliness and the accuracy of data. For example, in July 2003, the U.S. Department of Commerce released an "advance" estimate of second-quarter real GDP growth equal to 2.4 percent. Later in August 2003, that estimate was revised to 3.1 percent, then again in September to 3.3 percent. Although this revision was unusually large, some observers think that cuts in the budgets of statistical agencies, combined with demands to speed the release of data, are making the problems of accuracy and timeliness worse. In later chapters we will see that lags in the availability of accurate data on GDP, inflation, and other economic quantities have major implications for policy makers' ability to tune economic policy to fit events as they unfold.

THE UNDERGROUND ECONOMY　The economic activity that is measured in the national income accounts constitutes the observed sector of the economy. But a vast amount of production, consumption, and investment is never officially measured. This unobserved sector includes activities ranging from teenage baby-sitting to multimillion-dollar drug and gambling rings to the multibillion-dollar value of cooking, cleaning, and child care performed in the home. The national income accounts attempt to consider this unobserved sector when they include estimates of the rental value of owner-occupied housing and the value of food produced and consumed on farms. Those items are only the tip of the iceberg, however. The bulk of the unobserved sector is missing from the official accounts. Although no one knows exactly how big this sector is, some parts of it are known to be enormous.

Some have estimated that organized crime produces some $150 billion a year in illegal goods and services in the form of drugs, gambling, pornography, and so on. If this estimate is correct, it makes organized crime the second-largest industry in the United States after the oil industry. However, organized crime is probably not the largest sector of the so-called underground economy. The unreported income of businesses and self-employed people may add as much as $250 billion. This includes cash income that goes unreported for tax purposes (for example, a concert pianist giving occasional piano lessons) and barter transactions that involve no cash at all (for example, the pianist gets her teeth straightened in exchange for giving piano lessons to her orthodontist's child).

But even if the U.S. underground economy amounts to as much as 10 percent of officially measured GDP, that proportion is moderate by world standards. The French underground economy is thought to equal one-third of that country's GDP; in Italy, the figure may be 40 percent; and in many third world countries, the official GDP data bear only the haziest relationship to what is actually going on in the economy.

PRICE INDEX BIASES A third problem with the official statistics is that of price index biases. The accuracy with which changes in price levels are measured became a matter of growing concern as inflation increased in the late 1970s and indexing and automatic cost-of-living adjustments became more widespread. If the official price indexes are found to understate inflation, policy makers should perhaps make a greater effort to restore price stability. On the other hand, if price indexes overstate inflation, contracts that provide automatic adjustments for inflation may be too generous.

The problem of price index biases has been closely studied, and the results are far from reassuring. The consumer price index has been criticized for two built-in biases that have caused it to overstate inflation: substitution bias and quality bias.

Substitution Bias The first reason that the consumer price index tends to overstate the true rate of increase in the cost of living is the so-called substitution bias. As the appendix to this chapter explains, the CPI is a weighted average of the prices of goods that are typically purchased by urban consumers. Because the weights used to calculate the index remain constant, they always reflect patterns of consumption at some point in the past. However, because patterns change over time, the weights typically are not those of the most recent year being observed.

If changes in buying patterns were random, an obsolete set of weights would cause only random errors, not an upward bias, in the CPI. The bias results from the fact that consumer demand is influenced by changes in relative prices. As time passes, consumers tend to buy less of the goods whose prices have risen most and more of those whose prices have lagged behind the average or have actually fallen. Thus, the CPI tends to overstate the increase in the cost of living because it assigns unrealistically large weights to products whose prices have increased but that are consumed in relatively smaller amounts than formerly. For example, large increases in gasoline prices in the 1970s eventually led consumers to purchase more fuel-efficient cars, and thus to consume less gasoline, and the same may be starting to happen again in our own time. During such a period, the weight given to gasoline is too high. The market basket on which the CPI is based is periodically adjusted to reflect such changes, but the adjustments are not frequent enough to remove the bias altogether.

Quality Bias A second source of bias in the consumer price index is the failure to adjust product prices for changes in quality. It would be highly misleading, for example, to say that a 2004 model car costs three times as much as a 1984 model without considering the fact that the 2004 model gets better gas mileage, can be driven longer between tune-ups, and is much safer than the 1984 model. In terms of dollars per unit of transportation service, the newer model clearly would be less than three times as expensive.

For automobiles, computers, and a few other major goods, the Bureau of Labor Statistics does try to make quality adjustments. The importance of the effort can be seen in the case of electronic equipment ranging from calculators to mainframe computers. As recently as the late 1960s, it cost over $1,000 to buy a desk-size electro-mechanical calculator that would add, subtract, multiply, and divide. Today half of that sum will buy a basic personal computer, and a calculator equivalent to the 1960 model can be purchased for less than $5. A study of changes in computer quality led to large adjustments in price indexes since the 1980s. However, domestic income accountants do not have the resources to make such detailed studies of all items that enter into GDP.

Taken together, the substitution bias and quality bias are substantial. At one time they may have added 1 to 1$\frac{1}{2}$ percent per year to the stated rate of inflation as measured by the CPI. Recent changes in methodology are thought to have reduced the bias, but it is still probably in the range of $\frac{1}{2}$ to 1 percent per year.

NONMATERIAL SOURCES OF WELFARE   The final problem with GDP is that it measures only material sources of welfare (which, after all, is all it tries to do). Sometimes per capita GDP is used as an indication of living standards, but when one is comparing living standards over time and across countries, nonmaterial sources of welfare are important, too.

One key nonmaterial component of the standard of living is the quality of the environment. This not only varies widely from one place to another but has changed greatly over time. Today's problems of acid rain, toxic wastes, and nuclear radiation are "bads" that, in principle, should be subtracted from GDP just as "goods" are added to it. In the same spirit, Robert Repetto of the World Resources Institute in Washington, D.C., recommends that depletion of such natural resources as oil fields and tropical forests should be subtracted along with the capital consumption allowance in calculating net domestic product. For countries such as Indonesia and Brazil, which have used huge quantities of natural resources to fuel their growth, the effect of this adjustment could cut measured rates of economic growth nearly in half.

A second nonmaterial source of welfare is the state of human health. By broad measures, especially life expectancy, standards of health in the United States appear to be improving. For example, since World War II the life expectancy of a typical 45-year-old American has increased from 72 years to 77, and a 65-year-old American can now expect to live to the age of 81. This increase clearly improves human welfare even for people who add nothing to measured GDP after they retire from their jobs. If the improvement in health could be measured, it would add to the growth of U.S. GDP. On the other hand, such an adjustment would make the economic picture look even bleaker in a country like Russia, where health indicators such as life expectancy and infant mortality have gotten worse in recent years.

The list of nonmaterial sources of welfare is endless. How important are satisfying work, friendship, social justice, economic equality, and freedom? Everyone knows of people who have been willing to give up income and wealth in pursuit of these things. Yet they must remain unmeasured.

For all of these reasons, then, GDP cannot be used as a measure of the true level of human welfare and can be used only with the greatest caution even for comparisons of material welfare in different times and places.

≈

SUMMARY

1. **How is gross domestic product officially defined and measured?** Two domestic product concepts are featured in the official accounts of the United States. *Gross domestic product (GDP)* is defined as the value at current market prices of all *final goods and services* produced annually in a given country. *Gross national product* is the product produced by a country's factors of production, regardless of what country they are located in. *Net domestic product* is derived from GDP by subtracting a capital consumption allowance that reflects the value of capital goods worn out during the year.

2. **How does the measurement of domestic income differ from the measurement of gross domestic product?** *Domestic income* is the sum of wages and supplements, rental income of persons, corporate profits, and proprietors' income earned in a country. In principle, domestic income and gross domestic product should be equal, but in the official accounts, they differ because of the capital consumption allowance, indirect business taxes, and a statistical discrepancy that results from the use of different data sources for income and product measurements.

3. **What are the major types of international transactions?** Many types of transactions appear in the nation's international accounts. Exports less im-

ports of goods constitute the *merchandise balance*. Adding net exports of services yields net exports of goods and services. Adding net international transfers (normally a negative number for the United States) yields the most widely publicized balance-of-payments measure, the *current account balance*. In addition, the international accounts record financial inflows and outflows resulting from private financial transactions and official reserve transactions by the Federal Reserve and foreign central banks.

4. **How are changes in the average level of prices measured?** The *GDP deflator* is the most broadly based measure of the *price level*. It can be viewed as a weighted average of the prices of all final goods and services that go into GDP. The *consumer price index (CPI)* includes only the market basket of goods purchased by a typical urban household. The *producer price index (PPI)* is based on goods that are typically bought and sold by business firms.

5. **What are the limitations of official economic statistics?** The national income statistics of the United States are considered to be among the best in the world. However, they have some limitations. Potential problem areas include timeliness of data, the unobserved sector of the economy, price index biases, and nonmaterial aspects of the standard of living.

KEY TERMS

National income
  accounts
Gross domestic product
  (GDP)
Final goods and services
Value added
Gross national product
  (GNP)
Net domestic product
  (NDP)
National income
Current account
Merchandise balance

Current account balance
Financial account
Financial inflow
Financial outflow
GDP deflator
Base year
Price level
Price index
Consumer price index
  (CPI)
Producer price index
  (PPI)

PROBLEMS AND TOPICS FOR DISCUSSION

1. **Updating the national income accounts.** Data on national income accounts and international transactions for the United States are available from several sources on the Internet. Two of the easiest to use are the tables attached to each year's *Economic Report of the President* (http://www.gpoaccess.gov/eop) and those given by the Commerce Department's Bureau of Economic Analysis (http://www.bea.gov) Using one of these sources, update the tables in this chapter to the most recent year or quarter. If you do not live in the United States, a Web search for national income accounts for your home country will very likely lead to to similar data. Be aware, however, that although the basic principles of national income accounting apply to all countries, there are often noticeable differences in terminology, presentation, and methods of data collection.

2. **Inventory in the national income accounts.** Suppose that a firm sells $10,000 worth of shoes that it has held in inventory for several years. What happens to GDP as a result? Which of its components are affected, and how?

3. **International accounts.** Following the pattern in Table 10.4, show how the international accounts might look for a year in which there was a $50 billion surplus on current account, no official reserve transactions, and no statistical discrepancy. What would the capital and financial account balance have to be?

4. **The current account deficit.** "A current account deficit is a very healthy thing. If we can get foreigners to give us real goods and services and talk them into taking pieces of paper in return, why should we want anything different?" Do you agree or disagree with this statement? Discuss.

5. **Real and nominal quantities.** In 1982 to 1984, the base period used for the consumer price index, the average earnings of construction workers were $442.74 per week. By 1989 the earnings of construction workers had reached $506.72 per week, but the consumer price index had risen to 124.0. What were construction workers' real earnings in 1989 stated in 1982–1984 dollars?

6. **Changes in prices and qualities.** Try to find a mail-order catalog that is at least ten years old; also find a recent catalog. Compare the ads for various items. By how much has the price of each item gone up? What changes in quality have occurred? Assuming that you could buy at list price from either the new catalog or the old one, which items would you buy from the old one and which from the new one?

CASE FOR DISCUSSION

Laid-Off Steel Workers Join the Underground Economy

HOMESTEAD, PA.—A half-dozen men lounge on metal folding chairs outside a storefront on Ann Street, sweating in the muggy afternoon air and talking baseball. A pay phone rings inside, and a young man runs to answer it. Moments later, he speeds off in a long, beat-up sedan.

The man is about to cheat the government. He and the other men drive people around town for a fee, but they don't pay any taxes on the fares they receive. What's more, they don't see why they should.

Most of the men used to work at the sprawling Homestead Works a half block away. Now that the steel mill has closed, their car service allows them to make a living. "It ain't bothering anyone. It ain't stealing," says Earl Jones, who was laid off last December after 36 years at the mill. How much does he make? "Ain't saying," he replies with a smile.

The men are part of a vast underground economy made up of people who work "off the books" for cash. From the tired mill towns of the Midwest to the oil patches dotting the Southwest, the underground thrives. In communities that have suddenly lost a major employer, it helps those who were laid off make ends meet, and it helps keep towns like Homestead alive.

The number of Homestead residents with off-the-books livelihoods began to increase in the early 1980s when USX Corporation's Homestead Works, which employed about 15,000 at its peak, started to lay off workers in droves. The mill's few remaining workers lost their jobs early in 1986. For most residents here, where only half the people have their high-school diplomas, the mill was all there was.

After they were laid off, many older workers retired and some of the younger ones withdrew their savings and migrated south, chasing dreams of work in more prosperous states. But many others stayed, bound by their unmarketable homes, their families, or a strong sense of community. Unable to find legitimate jobs, they have parlayed their handyman skills underground.

One former mill worker says that half the people he knows are working off the books. For the most part, they are intensely proud people who hang the American flag from their neat front porches on holidays and respect the law, believing strongly in right and wrong. They definitely don't like the underground's seamy side—thefts and drugs. But their changed circumstances have altered the way many of them think.

"You tell me. Your kids go to bed crying at night because they're hungry. Is 'off the books' going to bother you?" asks a former steelworker.

In the fall of 2003, President Bush repealed trade legislation that would have protected steel manufacturers from international competition. While this move was very unpopular in states that still have high employment in steel manufacturing, it was lauded in states that rely on steel to produce finished goods.

Source: Clare Ansberry, "Laid-Off Steelworkers Find That Tax Evasion Helps Make Ends Meet," *The Wall Street Journal*, October 1, 1986, 1. Reprinted by permission of *The Wall Street Journal*, © Dow Jones & Company, Inc., 1986. All Rights Reserved Worldwide.

QUESTIONS

1. What are the advantages of working "off the books" from the viewpoint of the people involved?
2. How might the failure to measure off-the-books activity affect economic policy decisions?
3. How might off-the-books work affect the statistical discrepancy in the national income accounts?

END NOTES

1. As in the case of the current account, one needs to be careful with the terminology used in the official accounts, in discussion of economic theory, and in news reports. The official name of this section of the accounts is "The Capital and Financial Account," but hardly anyone uses this long title. Instead, both in news reports and theoretical discussions, this whole section of the account is often called the "capital account." This is especially confusing, since in the official terminology, "capital account" refers only to one relatively small line in the capital and financial account section. Alternatively, some writers refer to the whole section as the "financial account." This practice, which will be followed in this book, seems preferable since the "financial" part of the "capital and financial" account is far more important than the "capital" part narrowly defined. The same principles apply to inflows and outflows. In this book we use the terms "financial inflow" and "financial outflow," but many other writers use the terms "capital inflow" and "capital outflow."

Appendix to Chapter 10:
COMPUTATION OF PRICE INDEXES

This appendix provides further information on the GDP deflator and consumer price index. Knowing these details will make it easier to see the differences between the two indexes and to understand the source of the substitution bias, which affects each one differently.

The GDP Deflator for a Simple Economy

A much simpler economy than that of the United States will serve to illustrate the computation of price indexes. Table 10A.1 shows price and quantity data for two years for an economy in which only three goods are produced: movies, apples, and shirts. The exhibit shows that nominal GDP grew from $1,000 in 1996 to $1,700 in 2002. But what do these figures indicate? Do they mean that people really had more of the things they wanted in 2002 than in 1996? More precisely, do they mean that people had 1.7 times as much? These questions cannot be easily answered by looking at the exhibit in its present form.

A line-by-line comparison of the two years shows that the figures on nominal product do not tell the whole story. Clearly, prices went up sharply between 1996 and 2002. Movies and apples cost more than one and a half times what they used to, and shirts nearly that much. The amounts of goods produced have also changed. Twice as many movies and shirts were produced in 2002 as in 1996, but only half as many apples.

If we wish to know how much better off people were in 2002 than in 1996, we need a way to separate the quantity changes that have taken place from the price changes. One way to do this is to ask how much the total value of output would have changed from 1996 to 2002 if prices had not changed. This approach gives the results shown in Table 10A.2. There we see

TABLE 10A.1   NOMINAL GDP FOR A SIMPLE ECONOMY

1996	Quantity	Price	Value
Movies	50	$ 5.00	$ 250
Apples	1,000	.60	600
Shirts	10	15.00	150
1996 nominal GDP			$ 1,000
2002			
Movies	100	$ 8.00	$ 800
Apples	500	.80	400
Shirts	20	25.00	500
2002 nominal GDP			$1,700

In this simple economy in which only three goods are produced, nominal domestic product grew from $1,000 in 1996 to $1,700 in 2002. But because prices also went up during that time, people did not really have 1.7 times as many goods in 2002 as they did in 1996.

TABLE 10A.2   NOMINAL AND REAL GDP FOR A SIMPLE ECONOMY

Good	2002 Quantity	2002 Price	Value of 2000 Quantity at 1996 Price	1996 Price	Value of 2002 Quantity at 1996 Price
Movies	100	$8.00	800	$ 5.00	$ 500
Apples	500	.80	400	.60	300
Shirts	20	25.00	500	15.00	300
Totals			$1,700		$1,100

2002 nominal GDP = $1,700; 2002 real GDP = $1,100

This table shows how the figures from Table 10A.1 can be adjusted to take changing prices into account. The 2002 quantities are multiplied by 1996 prices to get the value of 2002 GDP that would have existed had prices not changed. The total of 2002 quantities valued at 1996 prices is a measure of real GDP for 2002 stated in constant 1996 dollars. The implicit GDP deflator for 2002, calculated as the ratio of 2002 nominal GDP to 1996 real GDP, has a value of 154.5.

that the 2002 output of 100 movies, 500 apples, and 20 shirts, which had a value of $1,700 in terms of the prices at which the goods were actually sold, would have had a value of only $1,100 in terms of the prices that prevailed in 1996. The $1,100 thus is a measure of real GDP for 2002. It is this measure that we should compare with the 1996 GDP of $1,000 if we want to know what really happened to output between the two years. Instead of having 170 percent as much output in 2002 as in 1996, as indicated by the change in nominal GDP from $1,000 to $1,700, the people in this simple economy really had only about 110 percent as much, as indicated by the change in real GDP from $1,000 to $1,000.

Now we know how to compute real and nominal GDP for 2002 directly from price and quantity data without using a price index to convert nominal values into real values. But although we have not explicitly used a price index, we have created one implicitly. This implicit index, or implicit GDP deflator, is the ratio of current-year nominal GDP to current-year real GDP times 100, as expressed in index form by the following formula:

$$\text{GDP delator} = \frac{\text{Current-year output valued at current-year prices}}{\text{Current-year output valued at base-year prices}} \times 100.$$

Applying the formula to the data in Tables 10A.1 and 10A.2 gives a value of 154.5 for the deflator.

The Consumer Price Index for a Simple Economy

The consumer price index differs from the GDP deflator in two ways. First, as mentioned in Chapter 10, it takes into account only the prices of goods and services consumed by a typical urban household. Second, it is calculated according to a formula that uses base-year rather than current-year quantities. The first difference does not matter for this simple economy in which all goods are consumer goods, but the second does, as Table 10A.3 shows.

TABLE 10A.3   A CONSUMER PRICE INDEX FOR A SIMPLE ECONOMY

Good	1996 Quantity	1996 Price	Value of 1996 Quantity at 2002 Price	2002 Price	Value of 1996 Quantity at 2002 Price
Movies	50	$5.00	250	$8.00	$ 400
Apples	1,000	.60	600	.80	800
Shirts	10	15.00	150	25.00	250
Totals			$1,000		$1,450

$$\text{CPI} = \frac{\$1,450}{\$1,000} \times 100 = 145.0$$

The consumer price index can be calculated as the base-year market basket of goods valued at current-year prices divided by the base-year market basket valued at base-year prices multiplied by 100. This table shows how such an index can be calculated for a simple economy. The 1996 output cost $1,000 at the prices at which it was actually sold. Had it been sold at 2002 prices, it would have cost $1,450. Thus, the CPI for 2002 is 145.0.

To calculate the CPI for this economy, instead of asking how much current-year output would have cost at base-year prices, we begin by asking how much base-year output would have cost at current-year prices. We then calculate the index as the ratio of the two different valuations of base-year quantities:

$$\text{Consumer price index} = \frac{\text{Base-year market basket valued at current-year prices}}{\text{Base-year market basket valued at base-year prices}} \times 100.$$

The CPI is calculated using base-year quantities partly because data on current prices are easier to collect than data on current output. This index, therefore, can be announced each month with little delay.

Comparing the CPI and the GDP Deflator

As Table 10A.3 shows, the CPI for 2002 in our simple economy had a value of 145.0, whereas the GDP deflator for 2002 was 154.5. Both indexes were calculated using the same data, and both used 1996 as a base year. Which, if either, is the true measure of the change in prices between the two years?

The answer is that neither the CPI nor the GDP deflator is the only correct measure of change in the price level; instead, each answers a different question. The GDP deflator answers the question, "How much more did the 2002 output cost at the prices at which it was actually sold than it would have cost had it been sold at 1996 prices?" The CPI, in contrast, answers the question, "How much more would the 1996 output have cost had it been sold at 2002 prices instead of at 1996 prices?"

A close look at the data shows why the answers to the two questions differ. In 1996, lots of apples and few shirts were produced compared with 2002. Yet between the two years the price of apples increased 33 percent whereas the price of shirts increased 67 percent. Because the CPI uses base-year quantities, it gives a heavy weight to apples, which showed the smallest relative price increase, and a lower weight to shirts, which showed only a larger price increase. In contrast, the GDP deflator uses current-year quantities, thereby decreasing the importance of apples and increasing that of shirts.

In actuality, because people will tend to substitute purchases away from items with faster growth in prices, the CPI tends to have an upward substitution bias relative to the GDP deflator. However, that does not make the GDP deflator a true measure of change in the cost of living. It could just as easily be said that the GDP deflator has a downward substitution bias relative to the CPI or that each has an opposite bias from some "true" price index. As yet there is no foolproof way to calculate the true cost-of-living index, although some interesting attempts have been made. A discussion of these more complex types of price indexes would take us far beyond the scope of this book. However, the basic types of price indexes covered here are the ones that are most commonly used for policy-making purposes.

CHAPTER 11

Money and the Banking System

After reading this chapter, you will understand:

1. What money is and what it does
2. How the stock of money in the economy is measured
3. How the quantity of money is related to other key macroeconomic variables
4. The structure of the U.S. banking system
5. How the safety and stability of the banking system are maintained

Before reading this chapter, make sure you know the meaning of:

1. Circular flow of income and expenditure
2. Financial markets
3. Price level

I F WE THINK of the circular flow of income and expenditure as a giant system of pipes connected by pumps and valves, then we can think of money as the fluid that moves through the pipes. In this chapter, money moves to the center of the stage.

We will begin by giving a formal definition of money and explaining how it is measured. Next we will explore the banking system. In the United States, the banking system consists of commercial banks and thrift institutions. Both of these are private businesses that deal with businesses and consumers. Formally, we refer to them as depository institutions. When there is no danger of confusion, we will follow the common practice of referring to depository institutions of all kinds simply as "banks." Like other countries, the United States also has a central bank, which is a government agency that regulates the banking system and carries out monetary policy. In the United States, the central bank is called the Federal Reserve System, or just "the Fed," for short. We will explore the role of the central bank in considerable detail in this and following chapters.

MONEY: WHAT IT IS AND WHAT IT DOES

Money

An asset that serves as a means of payment, a store of purchasing power, and a unit of account.

Money is best defined in terms of what it does: It serves as a means of payment, a store of purchasing power, and a unit of account. Regardless of its name —U.S. dollars, Japanese yen, or the European euro—the monies of all countries function in all three ways.

The Functions of Money

As a means of payment, money reduces the costs of carrying out transactions. Using money avoids the complexities of barter. Imagine a market in which farmers meet to trade produce of various kinds. Apples will get you peppers, cauliflower will get you beets, and turnips will get you garlic. But what if you want garlic and have only potatoes? What you need is a universal means of exchange—one that all sellers will accept because they know that others will also accept it; one that is in limited supply so that you know its exchange value will remain constant; and one that is easily recognized and hard to counterfeit. In times past, gold and silver coins served these purposes. In a modern economy, coins and paper currency serve for many small transactions while transfers of funds among bank deposits by debit card, computer transfer, check, and other means are used for bigger business deals.

As a store of purchasing power, money makes it possible to arrange economic activities in a convenient manner over time. Income-producing activities and spending decisions need not occur simultaneously. Instead, we can accept money as payment for our work and keep the money handy until we want to spend it. The U.S. dollar is a good store of purchasing power—so good, in fact, that billions of dollars of U.S. currency are held by citizens of other countries who trust it more than their own currencies.

Finally, as a unit of account money makes it possible to measure and record economic stocks and flows. A household's needs for food, shelter, and clothing can be expressed in dollar terms. The nation's output of movies, apples, and airplanes can be added together in dollar terms. Without money as a unit of account, private and public economic planning would be virtually impossible.

Money as a Liquid Asset

Anything of value can serve as a store of purchasing power if it can be sold and the proceeds can be used to buy something else. Money, however, has two important traits that no other asset has to the same extent. One is that money itself can be used as a means of payment without first having to be exchanged for something else. A house, a corporate bond, or a steel mill may have great value, but they can rarely be traded without first being exchanged for an equivalent amount of money. The other trait is that money can neither gain nor lose in nominal value; this is necessarily so, because money is the unit of account in which nominal values are stated. Thus, a house, a bond, or a steel mill may be worth more or fewer dollars next year than this year, but the nominal value of a dollar is always a dollar—no more and no less.

An asset that can be used as or readily converted into a means of payment and is protected against gain or loss in nominal value is said to have **liquidity**. No other asset is as liquid as money. In fact, a comparison of the definitions of money and liquidity suggests that any perfectly liquid asset is, by definition, a form of money.

Measuring the Stock of Money

For purposes of economic theory and policy, we need to know not only what money is but also how it can be measured. In all modern economies the stock of money is controlled by government. As we will see, if government fails to supply enough money, real output and employment will decrease, at least temporarily. On the other hand, flooding the economy with too much money causes inflation. Because the money stock cannot be controlled if it cannot be measured, the problem of measurement is an important one.

CURRENCY AND TRANSACTION DEPOSITS[1] We begin with a rather restrictive definition that views money as consisting of just two highly liquid types of assets: currency and transaction deposits. **Currency** includes coins and paper money. **Transaction deposits**—popularly known as *checking accounts*—are deposits from which money can be withdrawn by check or electronic transfer without advance notice and used to make payments.

Although in times past, private banks used to issue their own bank notes, in a modern economy, currency is issued by the government. In the United States, currency consists of the familiar Federal Reserve notes, which are issued in denominations of $1, $2, $5, $10, $20, $50, and $100, and of coins minted by the Department of the Treasury. Coins and paper money were formerly backed by precious metals. Until 1934, the U.S. government issued both gold coins and paper currency that could be exchanged for gold on demand; silver coins and silver-backed paper money survived until the mid-1960s. Today, coins and paper money are simply tokens whose value is based on the public's faith in their usefulness as means of paying for goods and services.

Transaction deposits are available in a number of forms. One major type of transaction deposit is the demand deposit. By law, demand deposits cannot pay interest, but banks compensate *demand-deposit* customers with various services. Until the mid-1970s, demand deposits were the only kind of transaction deposit available in the United States and were offered only by commercial banks. They have since been joined by a variety of interest-bearing checkable deposits available to consumers through commercial banks and thrift institutions.

As Table 11.1 shows, in mid-2005 demand deposits made up roughly half of the total transaction deposits, with all other checkable deposits accounting for the other

Liquidity

An asset's ability to be used directly as a means of payment, or to be readily converted into one, while retaining a fixed nominal value.

Currency

Coins and paper money.

Transaction deposit

A deposit from which funds can be freely withdrawn by check or electronic transfer to make payments to third parties.

TABLE 11.1 COMPONENTS OF THE U.S. MONEY STOCK, JUNE 2005
(BILLIONS OF DOLLARS, SEASONALLY ADJUSTED)

Currency		$708.2
+ Travelers checks		$7.5
+ Transactions deposits		$645.7
Demand deposits	$325.8	
Other checkable deposits	$319.9	
= M1		**$1,361.4**
+ Savings deposits (including MMDAs)	$3,537.3	
+ Small-denomination time deposits	$892.8	
+ Retail money market fund shares	$697.6	
= M2		**$6,489.1**

This table breaks down the U.S. money supply into its components as of November 2002. It gives two of the most commonly used money supply measures. M1 is the total of currency and transaction deposits; M2 includes M1 plus other highly liquid assets.

Source: Board of Governors of the Federal Reserve System, H.6 Statistical Release, June 16, 2005.

half. Currency, travelers checks, and all forms of transaction deposits totaled $1,361.4 billion. The sum of currency and transaction deposits is known as **M1**.

Some readers may find it odd that credit cards are not included in the monetary aggregates. After all, from the consumer's point of view, paying for a purchase with a credit card is a close substitute for paying by cash or check. *Applying Economic Ideas 11.1* discusses the nature of credit cards and explains why they do not figure in the measurement of the nation's money stock.

THE BROADLY DEFINED MONEY STOCK The rationale behind the narrow definition of the money stock, M1, is that almost all transactions are made with either currency or transaction deposits. However, if one chooses to focus on the function of money as a store of value rather than as a means of payment, there are a number of other assets that are almost as liquid as the components of M1 and serve as close substitutes for them.

Shares in money market mutual funds are one example. A *money market mutual fund* is a financial intermediary that sells shares to the public. The proceeds of these sales are used to buy short-term, fixed-interest securities such as Treasury bills. Almost all the interest earned on securities bought by the fund is passed along to shareholders. (The fund charges a small fee for its services.) Shareholders can redeem their shares in a number of ways—by writing checks on the fund (usually in amounts above a minimum of $500), by telephone transfer, or by transfer to another fund.[2] Because the proceeds from sales of shares are invested in very safe short-term assets, a money market mutual fund is able to promise its shareholders a fixed nominal value of $1 per share, although the interest paid on the shares varies with market rates. Except for the mini-

M1

A measure of the money supply that includes currency and transaction deposits.

APPLYING ECONOMIC IDEAS 11.1

"PLASTIC MONEY"

Recent innovations in banking have streamlined how people make payments and have reduced their reliance on using paper currency. For instance, instead of writing a check as a means of payment, individuals can use a debit card or a credit card. Many people wonder how this "plastic money"—the MasterCards, VISA cards, and other bank cards that so many people carry these days—fits into M1 and M2. Just what role do these cards play in the payments system?

Credit cards, the most common type of plastic money, are not really a form of money at all. What sets credit cards apart from currency, bank deposits, and other forms of money is the fact that they are not a store of value. Instead, they are documents that make it easy for their holders to obtain a loan.

When you go into a store, present your credit card, and walk out with a can of tennis balls, you have not yet paid for your purchase. What you have done is borrow from the bank that issued the card. At the same time, you have instructed the bank to turn over the proceeds of the loan to the store. Later the bank will do so by crediting the amount to the store's account. This will pay for the tennis balls. Still later you will send money to the bank to pay off the balance on your credit card account.

Another common form of plastic money is a *debit card*. A debit card directly withdraws money from the payer's bank account and deposits these funds into the receiver's account. The funds are verified electronically, which substantially reduces the time and cost needed to clear a check. Similarly, many students in colleges today can use their student identification card as a stored-value card, or "smart card." Stored-value cards are much like debit cards except that they generally draw on funds stored with the card's administrator (such as the college/university issuing student I.D. cards) rather than in a bank account. Because stored-value and debit cards draw on funds the cardholder has deposited (in a checking or school account), the deposited funds are considered money.

Many businesses operating on the internet accept not only credit card payments but also electronic cash and electronic checks. These are much like their paper counterparts, cash and checks, except the transactions take place electronically over the internet.

The obvious drawback to electronic money is that it increases the likelihood of fraud. It is more difficult to verify the person's identity without photo identification or other personal information. Also, businesses using electronic money gain access to additional personal information not usually provided when using paper cash or checks.

---

mum-amount requirement on checks, then, money market mutual fund balances are almost as liquid as those of ordinary transaction accounts. Money market funds grew rapidly in the late 1970s and early 1980s, when market interest rates rose while rates paid by banks and thrifts were limited by federal regulations. In recent years, when interest rates have been lower, money market funds have lost some of their popularity.

Banks and thrifts also offer a number of other accounts that serve as reasonably liquid stores of purchasing power. **Savings deposits** are a familiar example. Although checks cannot be written on these deposits, they are fully protected against loss in nominal value and can be redeemed at any time. In addition to conventional savings deposits, since late 1982 banks and thrifts have been allowed to compete with money market mutual funds by offering so-called *money market deposit accounts (MMDAs)*. These accounts have limited checking privileges and offer higher interest rates than the transaction accounts included in M1. Their volume grew very rapidly after their introduction. As Table 11.1 shows, savings deposits and MMDAs together totaled $3,537.3 billion in June 2005.

Savings deposit

A deposit at a bank that can be fully redeemed at any time, but from which checks cannot be written.

Time deposit

A deposit at a bank or thrift institution from which funds can be withdrawn without payment of a penalty only at the end of an agreed-upon period.

M2

A measure of the money supply that includes M1 plus retail money market mutual fund shares, money market deposit accounts, and saving deposits.

Banks and thrifts also offer **time deposits**. In the case of small-denomination time deposits (up to $100,000), funds typically must be left on deposit for a fixed period, ranging from less than a month to many years, in order to earn the full interest rate, and they normally cannot be transferred to another person before maturity. This feature makes them less liquid than savings deposits or MMDAs, but in return they usually pay a higher interest rate. They, too, are protected against loss of nominal value.

Retail money market mutual fund shares, MMDAs, savings deposits, and small-denomination time deposits are added to M1 to create a measure of the money supply known as **M2**. As Table 11.1 shows, M2 amounted to $6,489.1 billion in June 2005.

Besides M1 and M2, there are other, still broader measures. M3 includes such items as large-denomination time deposits ($100,000 and up) and other liquid assets.

Why Money Matters

In presenting alternative measures of the money stock, we might seem to have wandered rather far afield from our main macroeconomic themes of real output growth, price stability, and employment. In fact, however, these key variables are closely related to money. Much of the remainder of this book will be devoted to showing why this is so, but a preliminary overview can be given here.

Equation of exchange

An equation that shows the relationship among the money stock (M), the income velocity of money (V), the price level (P), and real domestic product (y); written as MV = Py.

Velocity (income velocity of money)

The ratio of nominal domestic income to the money stock; a measure of the average number of times each dollar of the money stock is used each year for income-producing purposes.

THE EQUATION OF EXCHANGE   The relationship between money and other key variables can be stated in the form of the following equation, which is termed the **equation of exchange**:

$$MV = Py$$

where M stands for a measure of the money stock, P for the price level, and y for real GDP. The remaining variable, V, stands for **velocity** or, more fully, the **income velocity of money**. Velocity can be thought of as the average number of times each dollar of the money stock is spent each year for income-producing transactions. It can also be thought of as the ratio of nominal GDP to the money stock.[3] For example, if a country had a money stock of $200 billion and a real GDP of $1,000 billion, velocity would be 5, indicating that each dollar of the money stock changed hands about 5 times a year for purchases of final goods and services.

The equation of exchange shows that any change in the money stock must affect the price level, real output, velocity, or some combination of these variables. Thus, control over the money stock gives the government a powerful policy instrument with which to influence key macroeconomic variables. Later chapters will show in detail the means by which policymakers can influence the money stock. They will also discuss the effects of changes in the money stock on other variables.

WHICH "M" IS BEST?   As we have seen, there are various measures of the money stock. All of these measures are determined by establishing a cutoff point along a range of financial assets with varying degrees of liquidity, from currency at one end to long-term securities at the other. No hard-and-fast answer can be given to the question of which M is "best" without also asking, "Best for what?"

As mentioned earlier, the basic idea of M1 is to measure the money stock available for use as a means of payment. However, it does not do this perfectly. On the one hand, some consumers use interest-bearing transaction accounts primarily as a store of purchasing power. This savings motive is reflected in the fact that some of these accounts have a low *turnover rate*—that is, the ratio of the volume of transactions per year to the average balance is low. On the other hand, as we have seen, money market mutual funds have limited checking features that allow them to serve as means of payment. These assets are not included in M1 partly because they have even lower turnover rates, but they are still used for some transactions. Thus, M1 is far from perfect as a measure of means-of-payment money.

Similar problems plague M2, which is intended to measure the stock of money as a short-term, highly liquid store of purchasing power. M2 includes items such as savings and small-denomination time deposits, which have fixed nominal values despite their low turnover rates. But the cutoff line between M2 and M3—for example, the $100,000 cutoff for time deposits—is arbitrary.

For purposes of macroeconomic modeling and policy, the best money stock measure would be the one with the most predictable velocity and, hence, the most predictable relationship to the variables lying on the right-hand side of the equation of exchange—that is, real output and the price level. For many years economists were confident that M1, whatever its imperfections, was the best available measure in this regard. In the 1980s, as banking institutions and ways of doing business changed, M1 began to lose its close relationship to other economic variables, and M2 became a better measure. In this book, unless we specify otherwise, the term *money* can be understood to refer to M2.

THE BANKING SYSTEM

As Table 11.1 shows, just 20 percent of U.S. M2 consists of currency issued by government plus balances in money market mutual funds. Most of the other components of M2—transaction deposits, savings deposits, and small-denomination time deposits— are issued by commercial banks and thrifts. Because the bulk of the money stock is issued by depository institutions, we need to understand their structure and operations in order to understand monetary theory and policy.

Depository institutions

Financial intermediaries, including commercial banks and thrift institutions, that accept deposits from the public.

Types of Depository Institutions

There are four principal types of **depository institutions** in the United States. They differ in the types of loans and deposits in which they specialize, although their operations increasingly overlap.

Commercial banks

Financial intermediaries that provide a broad range of banking services, including accepting demand deposits and making commercial loans.

Thrift institutions (thrifts)

A group of financial intermediaries that operate much like commercial banks; they include savings and loan associations, savings banks, and credit unions.

Balance sheet

A financial statement showing what a firm or household owns and what it owes.

Assets

All the things that the firm or household owns or to which it holds a legal claim.

Liabilities

All the legal claims against a firm by nonowners or against a household by nonmembers.

Net worth

The firm's or household's assets minus its liabilities.

The largest group of depository institutions is **commercial banks**. These usually include the word *bank* in their names. One of their specialties is making commercial loans—that is, loans to businesses, frequently short term. They also make consumer loans and home mortgage loans. Until the 1970s, commercial banks were the only institutions that could offer checking accounts, and they still hold the bulk of transaction deposits. They also raise funds by offering savings and time deposits and other financial instruments. Large commercial banks provide many services, such as wire transfers and international banking facilities, to business customers.

As we have already noted, other depository institutions are known as **thrifts**. *Savings and loan associations* (also known as *savings and loans* or *S&Ls*) specialize in home mortgage lending, although they also make other real estate loans, consumer loans, and a limited number of commercial loans. Household savings and time deposits have traditionally been their main source of funds, but today they also offer fully checkable deposits as well as MMDAs with limited checking privileges. Although they may not use the word *bank* in their names, some savings and loan associations shape their operations to resemble those of commercial banks as closely as regulations permit.

Mutual savings banks are a type of depository institution that emerged in the nineteenth century to serve the needs of working-class households needing a depository for their small amounts of savings. Some still have names that reflect these origins, such as "Dime Savings Bank." Mutual savings banks offer the same range of deposits as savings and loan associations, but they tend to offer more diversified types of loans.

Credit unions are small financial intermediaries organized as cooperative enterprises by employee groups, union members, or certain other groups with shared work or community ties. They specialize in small consumer loans, although a few also make mortgage loans. They offer both transaction and savings deposits.

Since the mid-1970s, the traditional distinctions among these four types of institutions have eroded. Today, both from the viewpoint of the consumer and in macroeconomic terms, there is no real difference between a transaction deposit in a commercial bank and one in a thrift institution. That is why we can use the terms *bank* and *banking system* to refer to all depository institutions except when there is a particular reason to single out one type of institution.

The Banking Balance Sheet

The operations of a commercial bank can best be understood by reference to its balance sheet. A firm's or household's **balance sheet** is a financial statement showing what it owns and what it owes, or, to use more technical language, its *assets, liabilities,* and *net worth.* **Assets,** which are listed on the left-hand side of the balance sheet, are all the things that the firm or household owns or to which it holds a legal claim. **Liabilities,** which are listed on the right-hand side of the balance sheet, are all the legal claims against a firm by nonowners or against a household by nonmembers. **Net worth,** also listed on the right-hand side of the balance sheet, is equal to the firm's or household's assets minus its liabilities. In a business firm, net worth represents the owners' claims against the business. *Equity* is another term that is often used to refer to net worth. In banking circles net worth is often referred to as *capital*.

The balance sheet gets its name from the fact that the totals of the two sides always balance. This follows from the definition of net worth. Because net worth is defined as assets minus liabilities, liabilities plus net worth must equal assets. In equation form, this basic rule of accounting reads as follows:

$$\text{Assets} = \text{Liabilities} + \text{Net worth}$$

Table 11.2 shows a total balance sheet for U.S. commercial banks. Balance sheet items for thrift institutions would differ in amount, but the concepts involved would be the same.

ASSETS   On the assets side of the balance sheet, the first line lists the noninterest-bearing deposits that banks maintain with the Federal Reserve System, as well as vault cash, which is currency that banks keep in their own vaults. Deposits at the Fed plus vault cash constitute a bank's reserves. Historically, banks held **reserves** of cash or deposits that could be quickly converted into cash because at any moment some depositors might want to withdraw their funds. Today the minimum level of reserves is not left to the judgment of banks; rather, federal regulations require banks to hold reserves equal to a certain percentage of transaction deposits. The Federal Reserve's power to regulate the level of reserves in the banking system is a major tool of monetary policy. Other cash assets, also included in line one of the balance sheet and sometimes known as secondary reserves, give banks the liquidity to meet unexpected needs.

Reserves

Cash in bank vaults and banks' noninterest-bearing deposits with the Federal Reserve System.

TABLE 11.2   TOTAL BALANCE SHEET FOR U.S. COMMERCIAL BANKS, JUNE 2003 (BILLIONS OF DOLLARS)

Assets		Liabilities	
Reserves and cash items	$374.1	Transaction deposits	$665.7
Securities	$2,074.3	Nontransaction deposits	$4,875.6
Loans	$5,126.2	Bank borrowing	$1,608.5
Other assets	$881.6	Other liabilities	$581.7
Total assets	$8,456.2	Total liabilities	$7,731.5
		Net worth	$724.7
		Total liabilities plus net worth	$8,456.2

This table shows the total balance sheet for all U.S. commercial banks as of December 10, 2003. Assets of banks include noninterest-bearing reserves and interest-bearing loans and securities. Liabilities include deposits of all kinds and other borrowings. Net worth equals assets minus liabilities. The balance sheets of thrift institutions would show the same basic categories but would differ in details.

Source: Board of Governors of the Federal Reserve System, H.8 Statistical Release, June 17, 2005.

The next two items on the assets side of the balance sheet show the banks' main income-earning assets. The largest item is loans made to firms and households. In addition, commercial banks hold a substantial quantity of securities, including securities issued by federal, state, and local governments. The final item on this side includes some smaller income-earning items plus the value of the banks' buildings and equipment.

LIABILITIES   The first two items on the liabilities side of the banks' balance sheet are various kinds of deposits. They are liabilities because they represent funds to which depositors hold a legal claim. Funds that banks have borrowed are also liabilities. A small portion of these are borrowed from the Federal Reserve and the rest from private sources. Because the banks' total liabilities are less than their assets, they have a positive net worth. This sum represents the claim of the banks' owners against the banks' assets.

The Central Bank

Central bank

A government agency responsible for regulating a country's banking system and carrying out monetary policy.

We have already mentioned the Federal Reserve System, or the *Fed*, as it is known in financial circles. The Fed is the central banking system of the United States. Like the **central banks** of all countries, it provides banking services to private banks and to other parts of the government. It is one of the chief regulators and supervisors of the banking system. Its responsibility for monetary policy makes it a major partner with Congress and the executive branch in macroeconomic policy making.

The Fed was established in 1913 as an independent agency of the federal government and therefore is not under the direction of the executive branch. It is subordinate to Congress, but Congress does not intervene in its day-to-day decision making. The reason for making the Fed independent was to prevent the U.S. Treasury Department from using monetary policy for political purposes. In practice, however, the Fed's monetary actions are coordinated with the Treasury's fiscal actions. The chair of the Fed's Board of Governors is in frequent contact with the secretary of the Treasury, the chair of the President's Council of Economic Advisers, and the director of the Office of Management and Budget. By law, the Fed also presents a formal report on monetary policy to Congress twice a year. It also explains how its monetary policy objectives are related to economic conditions and to the economic goals set by the administration and Congress.

FEDERAL RESERVE BANKS   Most countries have a single, unified central bank (the Bank of England, the Bank of Japan, and so on), but the Federal Reserve System differs in some ways from this pattern. Because regional interests played a strong political role in founding the Federal Reserve System, it is composed of 12 Federal Reserve district banks, each of which serves a particular district of the country. The cities in which Federal Reserve Banks are located are Boston, New York, Philadelphia, Cleveland, Richmond, Atlanta, Chicago, St. Louis, Minneapolis, Kansas City, Dallas, and San Francisco. An additional 25 cities, including Seattle, Denver, Cincinnati, Miami, and others, have branches of the Federal Reserve Bank in their district. The only similar multi-part central banking system in the world is the European Central Bank, which consists of a central office that oversees and coordinates the work of the central banks of the 12 European countries that share the euro as their currency.

Each Federal Reserve bank is a separate unit chartered by the federal government. Its stockholders are commercial banks that are members of the Federal Reserve System. Although Federal Reserve banks issue stock to their members, they are not typical private firms in that they are neither operated for profit nor ultimately controlled by their stockholders. The Federal Reserve banks earn income from their holdings of federal securities and, since 1981, from charges for services provided to banks and thrift institutions. Each year the Fed district banks return all their income, minus operating costs, to the Treasury.

Each bank is managed by a nine-member board. Six of those members are selected by the member banks; the other three are appointed by the Fed's Board of Governors. Each board sets the policies of its own bank under the supervision of the Board of Governors. The Board of Governors also approves the appointments of each Reserve bank's top officers.

The Federal Reserve banks perform a number of important functions in the banking system. These include operating a wire system for electronic funds transfers, clearing checks, handling reserve deposits, and making loans to depository institutions. They issue paper currency in the form of Federal Reserve notes and supply Treasury coins. Several of the reserve banks are known for their strong research departments. Together with other federal agencies, they play an important role in supervising the safety and soundness of private banks. Finally, they provide banking services to the Treasury.

THE BOARD OF GOVERNORS   The head of the Federal Reserve System is its Board of Governors. The Board, which supervises the 12 Federal Reserve banks, is comprised of seven members who are appointed by the president and confirmed by the Senate. Each governor serves a single 14-year term, with one term expiring every other year. The president appoints one of the board members to serve as chair for a four-year term.

The Board of Governors has the power to approve changes in the interest rate on loans made to banks and thrifts by the Fed district banks. It also sets, within limits determined by law, the minimum level of reserves that banks and thrifts are required to hold relative to certain deposits. The Board supervises and regulates many types of banking institutions, including state-chartered member banks, bank holding companies, and U.S. offices of foreign banks. It also approves bank mergers and implements consumer credit regulations.

THE FEDERAL OPEN MARKET COMMITTEE   Authority over purchases and sales of government securities held by the Fed—its most important monetary policy tool—rests with the Federal Open Market Committee (FOMC). The FOMC is made up of the seven members of the Board of Governors plus five district bank presidents. The president of the Federal Reserve Bank of New York is a permanent member; the remaining four seats rotate among the other 11 district banks. The committee meets eight times a year (and also confers by telephone) to set a general strategy for monetary policy. Committee decisions regarding changes in the Fed's holdings of securities are carried out through the open market trading desk at the Federal Reserve Bank of New York.

MEMBER AND NONMEMBER BANKS Approximately two-fifths of the 8,621 commercial banks in the United States belong to the Federal Reserve System. National banks must be members; state-chartered banks may join if they meet certain requirements. The member banks serve as stockholders of their district Federal Reserve Bank. Until 1980, member banks enjoyed certain privileges and received free services from the Fed, but in return they were subject to generally stricter regulation than nonmember banks.

In 1980 Congress passed the Depository Institutions Deregulation and Monetary Control Act, which did away with many of the distinctions between member and nonmember banks and between commercial banks and thrift institutions. As a result, since 1980 member banks, nonmember commercial banks, savings and loans, savings banks, and credit unions have all been subject to more uniform reserve requirements. In return for tighter regulation of reserves, thrift institutions won the right to compete more directly with commercial banks in making certain types of loans and offering transaction accounts. Nonmember depository institutions achieved access to Fed services such as check clearing, wire transfers, and loans on the same terms as member banks. In 1982 small depository institutions were exempted from reserve requirements. Thus, as a result of the Monetary Control Act, the distinction between banks and thrift institutions became less important.

THE FED'S BALANCE SHEET Table 11.3 shows a balance sheet for the Federal Reserve System. Government securities are by far the Fed's largest asset. These security holdings play a key role in the Fed's control of the money stock. Loans to banks and thrifts are small compared with other assets, but they are listed separately because they are important for policy purposes. Normally these loans are made to depository institutions on a short-term basis to enable them to meet their reserve requirements. However, in special circumstances longer-term loans are made to banks and thrifts that are experiencing a seasonal need for funds or are having financial difficulties. Other assets include some denominated in foreign currencies; these are important in carrying out the Fed's functions in the international monetary system.

Federal Reserve notes, which account for almost all of the nation's stock of currency, are the Fed's largest liability. These are followed by the reserves deposited with the Fed by banks and thrifts. Other liabilities include deposits of the Treasury and of foreign central banks. Because the Fed's assets exceed its liabilities, it has a positive net worth.

TABLE 11.3   CONSOLIDATED BALANCE SHEET OF THE FEDERAL RESERVE BANKS, DECEMBER 17, 2003 (BILLIONS OF DOLLARS)

Assets		Liabilities	
Securities	$787.9	Fed notes in circulation	$759.6
Loans to banks	$0.2	Bank's reserve balances	$10.2
Other assets	$49.7	Other liabilities plus net worth	$68.0
Total assets	$837.8	Total liabilities plus net worth	$837.8

The Federal Reserve banks have liabilities to the general public in the form of Federal Reserve notes and to banks and thrifts in the form of reserve deposits. The Fed's main assets are government securities. Loans to banks with which to meet reserve requirements are small, but they are a key aspect of banking and monetary policy.

Source: Board of Governors of the Federal Reserve System, H.4.1 Statistical Release, June 17, 2005.

ENSURING THE SAFETY AND STABILITY OF THE BANKING SYSTEM

Banks play a vital role in our economy, yet we often take them for granted until they experience problems. Unfortunately, parts of the U.S. banking system have experienced serious problems from time to time, most recently in the 1980s. Although there has been no system-wide threat to the U.S. banking system since that time, individual banks have, from time to time, run into trouble. This section looks at the sources of these failures and also at the policies used by government to ensure that the problems of individual institutions do not threaten the safety and stability of the banking system as a whole.

Risks of Banking

Banks earn a profit by lending the proceeds from the deposits they receive or by using the proceeds to buy securities at interest rates higher than those they pay to depositors. Banks have been earning profits in this way for hundreds of years, but there are some well-known risks involved.

One is *credit risk*, that is, the risk of loan losses. What happens if a bank makes a loan to a customer who is unable to repay it? When a loan goes bad, the bank's net worth is reduced by an equal amount. (In balance-sheet terms, writing off the bad loan is a reduction in assets. Liabilities—that is, deposits and borrowing—do not change. Therefore, net worth, which equals assets minus liabilities, must fall.) If loan losses are too great, the bank's net worth may fall below zero. At that point the bank will no longer have enough assets to pay off all of its depositors and other creditors. A bank whose liabilities exceed its assets is said to be *insolvent* and usually must cease doing business.

A second risk that banks face is *insufficient liquidity,* that is, having insufficient liquid assets to cover withdrawals. When a depositor withdraws funds from a bank, the bank pays partly by drawing on the reserves it holds on deposit with the Fed or as vault cash and partly by drawing on other liquid assets that it holds for this purpose. Under normal conditions, new deposits approximately offset withdrawals, and the bank does not need to draw on its less liquid assets, such as loans and long-term securities, to cover withdrawals. If an unexpected wave of withdrawals occurs, however, the bank may use up all of its liquid assets. It will then have to convert some of its less liquid assets into cash. This may not be easy, especially if the wave of withdrawals takes place when business conditions are unfavorable, requiring the bank to sell the assets at less than the value at which they are entered on the bank's books. For example, a bank might have paid $1,000,000 for bonds issued by a state government agency. Later, because of unfavorable market conditions, it might have to sell them for just $800,000. Sales of assets at less than book value have an effect on the balance sheet similar to that of loan losses: In accordance with the basic equation of accounting, the reduction in the value of assets causes an equal reduction of the bank's net worth. If net worth falls below zero, the bank becomes insolvent.

Whether the bank's troubles begin with loan losses or with insufficient liquidity, there is a danger that they may trigger a run on the bank. A *run* is a situation in which depositors begin to withdraw their funds because they fear that the bank may become insolvent. Because large withdrawals force the bank to sell assets at less than their book values, depositors' fears become self-fulfilling and the bank fails.

In the worst possible case, the whole banking system, not just one bank, could get into trouble. If many banks faced loan losses or runs at the same time, they could not help one another with temporary loans of reserves. If large banks failed, smaller banks, which keep deposits in the large ones or make other loans to them, might be brought down, too. If many banks simultaneously tried to meet deposit outflows by selling their holdings of securities, the market price of the securities might fall, adding to their losses. A general bank crisis, in which the stability of the whole system would be threatened, could ensue.

Policies to Ensure Safety and Soundness

During the nineteenth century, a number of bank crises were touched off by recessions. As a result, both state and federal governments experimented with policies designed to ensure the safety and soundness of the banking system. Out of these efforts has evolved a system that is based on three basic tools: bank supervision and regulation, loans to troubled banks, and deposit insurance.

SUPERVISION AND REGULATION Bank examinations are the oldest tool for ensuring the safety and soundness of the banking system. These examinations, conducted by state or federal officials, are intended to ensure that banks do not make unduly risky loans, that they value their assets honestly, that they maintain an adequate level of net worth, and that they have competent management. Honest bookkeeping, prudent lending, and adequate net worth help banks to survive business downturns without becoming insolvent. A variety of federal and state agencies—including the Federal Reserve, the Federal Deposit Insurance Corporation (FDIC), and the Office of the Comptroller of the Currency (part of the Treasury) or OCC for short—share responsibility for supervision and regulation.

Supervision and regulation do not always ensure sound banking practices. Examinations do not always spot danger signals. Sometimes examiners are deceived by fraudulent operators of banks and thrifts; in other cases they do no better than bank managers in spotting bad loans or other risk factors. And sometimes the standards that examiners are asked to enforce are themselves too weak. In an attempt to improve the safety and stability of the banking system, standards have been tightened in several ways since the U.S. banking crises of the 1980s.

LENDER OF LAST RESORT   Bank examinations, introduced more than a century ago, were not by themselves enough to prevent banking panics. In 1907 an especially severe panic took place, eventually leading to the establishment of the Federal Reserve System in 1913. Among other duties, the Fed has the power to aid the banking system in times of trouble by acting as a lender of last resort. For example, when the stock market experienced a record 22.6 percent loss on October 19, 1987, the Fed quickly announced that it stood ready to lend extra funds to any banks that needed additional cash because of customers' stock market losses. As discussed in *Economics in the News 11.1*, the Fed played an essential role in maintaining the soundness of the U.S. banking system following the 9/11 terrorist attacks in 2001.

Loans by the Fed to troubled institutions are useful primarily as a device to help fundamentally sound and solvent banks during temporary periods of insufficient liquidity. They cannot solve the problems of banks and thrifts that have fallen into insolvency because of imprudent management practices leading to massive loan losses.

DEPOSIT INSURANCE   Even with its power as a lender of last resort, the Fed failed to prevent a major bank panic in 1933, during the Great Depression. In 1934, in response to that crisis, Congress established the Federal Deposit Insurance Corporation (FDIC). Since the Monetary Control Act of 1980, all deposits are insured up to $100,000 per account (and even more in special cases.)

The idea of deposit insurance is to short-circuit runs on banks. If deposits are insured, depositors need not run to the bank to withdraw their funds; even if the bank fails, the government will pay them their money or arrange for the transfer of their deposits to a solvent bank. Also, if runs can be avoided, the problems of one or a few banks will not touch off a panic that threatens the whole system. Depository institutions are supposed to bear the cost of deposit insurance through premiums charged by the insurance funds. However, in recent years, premiums have fallen short of costs and taxpayers have had to cover the insurance funds' losses.

⮞ **ECONOMICS IN THE NEWS 11.1**

9/11: THE FED AS A LENDER OF LAST RESORT

The September 11, 2001 attacks on the World Trade Center in New York and the Pentagon in Washington, D.C. caused severe disruptions in the financial system that left banks short on funds. The Fed's actions during the crisis highlight its importance not only as a lender of last resort, but as a central authority in the payments system.

At 11:45 A.M., just three hours after the attacks, the Federal Reserve issued the following press statement: "The Federal Reserve System is open and operating. The discount window is available to meet liquidity needs." The discount window refers to a "window" where banks may go to take out loans from the Fed. Today, loan disbursements are made electronically through this "discount window." In addition, the Federal Reserve's staff contacted banks in the days surrounding the attacks to promote borrowing from the Fed as banks faced difficulty in honoring payments and extending lines of credit to their customers.

A series of events prevented timely payments both in the business and banking sectors. The physical damage to communications, computers, and general operations in New York slowed payments dramatically. The Federal Aviation Administration (FAA) halted air traffic, preventing the delivery of checks to banks by air. As a result, the volume of interbank transfers, essential in the bank payments system, fell 43% between September 10 and 11, 2001.

The Federal Reserve System responded by acting in its original role as a lender of last resort, providing large sums in the form of loans to the banking system. Between September 5 and September 12, Fed loans to banks increased from $195 million to $45.6 billion. As the president of the Federal Reserve Bank of St. Louis, William Poole, stated: "In the absence of Fed intervention, we would have seen a cascade of defaults as firms due funds that were not arriving would be unable to meet their obligations."

Sources: Kristin Van Gaasbeck, "Circling the Wagons: The Fed's Response to 9/11," presented at the *Western Economics Association International 78th Annual Meeting*, Denver, CO, July 12, 2003; William Poole, "The Role of Government in U.S. Capital Markets," lecture presented at the Institute of Governmental Affairs, University of California, Davis, October 18, 2001.

One problem with deposit insurance is that it could encourage banks to take on excessive risk, since they know their depositors are insured by the government. The savings and loans (S&L) crisis of the 1980s offers a perfect example of this problem. Deposit insurance encouraged some banks and thrifts to take undue risks with their depositors' money; the depositors did not object, knowing that the federal government would bail them out if the institution failed. Losses at savings and loans associations were so large that the Federal Savings and Loan Insurance Corporation (FSLIC), the deposit insurance fund for S&L and mutual savings banks at the time, itself was forced into insolvency. Since 1989, the FDIC has provided deposit insurance for S&Ls and mutual savings banks.

International Banking

Bank failures in one country have severe consequences for that country's trading partners. For this reason, in 1987 several countries attempted to establish a set of standard requirements for the international banking system. The resulting Basel Accord imposed regulations to help prevent banks from declaring bankruptcy. The Basel Accord guidelines also make recommendations regarding bank balance sheet management. In practice, the accord proved difficult to enforce because of varying accounting definitions and loopholes in the agreement. At the present time, a modified set of international standards, known as Basel II, is in the process of being implemented. It is too early to know whether the new standards will prevent the recurrence of crises like those described in *Economics in the News 11.2*.

As we have seen, in the U.S. banking system, the Federal Reserve acts as a lender of last resort. Most other central banks have similar powers that allow them to support their countries' private banks during times of crises. However, sometimes a country's central bank itself runs short of liquidity. In such cases, the International Monetary Fund (IMF) has the power to make emergency loans to central banks. For example, the IMF used this power to provide loans to Korea and the Philippines during the East Asian financial crisis of 1997.

 ECONOMICS IN THE NEWS 11.2
GLOBAL BANKING CRISES

The international banking system's stability has become increasingly important but it is difficult to maintain. The table below highlights recent international banking crises and reports the estimated losses attributed to bank failures. For each country, the cost as a share of the economy's Gross Domestic Product (GDP) is reported. As the table shows, the U.S. banking crises of the 1980s, although very expensive, were not the worst when their cost is measured as a percentage of GDP.

The Basel Accord of 1987, and its successor Basel II, represent one effort to prevent banking crises around the world. The IMF's ability to provide support for central banks is another weapon. However, as long as the regulatory system of some countries remains weak, and as long as some banks undertake excessive risks, it is unlikely that banking crises will disappear entirely from the international economy.

COST OF INTERNATIONAL BANKING CRISES (1980–PRESENT)

Country	Dates	Estimated Cost as a % of GDP
Argentina	1980–82	55%
Indonesia	1997–2002	50–55%
Thailand	1997–2002	42%
Cote d'Ivoire	1988–1991	25%
Mexico	1995–2002	15%
Japan	1990s	12%
Hungary	1991–1995	10%
Russia	1998–1999	5–7%
United States	1984–1991	3%
Turkey	1982–1985	2.5%
New Zealand	1987–1990	1%

Source: Daniela Klingebiel and Luc Laewan, eds., "Managing the Real and Fiscal Effects of Banking Crises," World Bank Discussion Paper No. 428 (Washington: World Bank, 2002).

SUMMARY

1. **What is money, and what does it do?** *Money* is an asset that serves as a means of payment, a store of purchasing power, and a unit of account. Because money can be used as a means of payment and has a fixed nominal value, it is said to be *liquid*.

2. **How is the stock of money in the economy measured?** A narrow measure of the money stock, *M1,* includes *currency* (coins and paper money) plus *transaction deposits* (deposits on which checks can be freely written). A broader and more widely used measure, *M2,* includes the components of M1 plus money market mutual fund shares, money market deposit accounts, *savings deposits,* small-denomination *time deposits,* and certain other liquid assets.

3. **How is the quantity of money related to other key macroeconomic variables?** The relationship between money and other economic variables can be stated as the *equation of exchange:* $MV = Py$, in which M stands for the money stock, V for *velocity*, P for the price level, and y for real domestic product.

4. **What is the structure of the U.S. banking system?** The U.S. banking system consists of four types of *depository institutions*. The most important are commercial banks, which specialize in commercial loans and transaction deposits. In addition, there are three types of *thrift institutions*: savings and loan associations, savings banks, and credit unions. The Federal Reserve System is the nation's central bank. It provides services to depository institutions, holds much of their required *reserves*, and, together with other federal agencies, regulates the banking system.

5. **How are the safety and stability of the banking system maintained?** Banks fail if they become insolvent—that is, if their assets fall below the level of their liabilities. This may happen because of loan losses or because deposit withdrawals have exhausted liquid assets. The government has three principal tools for ensuring the safety and soundness of the banking system: supervision and regulation; loans to banks and thrifts experiencing liquidity problems; and deposit insurance.

KEY TERMS

Money	Depository institutions
Liquidity	Commercial banks
Currency	Thrift institutions
Transaction deposit	(thrifts)
M1	Balance sheet
Savings deposit	Assets
Time deposit	Liabilities
M2	Net worth
Equation of exchange	Reserves
Velocity (income	Central bank
velocity of money)	

PROBLEMS AND TOPICS FOR DISCUSSION

1. **The functions of money.** Money serves three functions: as a means of payment, a store of purchasing power, and a unit of account. How does inflation undermine each of these functions?

2. **Barter in the modern economy.** For most purposes, money lowers the cost of making transactions relative to barter—the direct exchange of one good or service for another. However, barter has not disappeared, even in an advanced economy such as that of the United States. Can you give an example of the use of barter in the U.S. economy today? Why is barter used instead of money in this case?

3. **Plastic money.** Do you use any credit cards? Does their use reduce the amount of money you need? Which forms of money do you need less of because you have a credit card? How do credit cards differ from debit cards?

4. **The banking balance sheet.** The National Information Center is a database with banking information maintained by the Federal Reserve System. You can download balance sheet information at http://www.ffiec.gov/nic/. Do an institution search for your bank or thrift and download the balance sheet information for this institution. How does this balance sheet compare with that of all commercial banks as given in Table 11.2? *Bonus question:* Obtain the balance sheets of a bank and a thrift and compare them.

5. **Current monetary data.** Every Thursday the Federal Reserve reports certain key data on money and the banking system. These reports are available from the Board of Governors of the Federal Reserve System *H.6 Statistical Release*. Obtain the most recent H.6 release online at http://www.federalreserve.gov/releases/ and answer the following questions:

   a. What items are included in M2 that are not included in M1? What was the total of such items in the most recent month for which data are reported? Which of these money measures grew most quickly in the most recent month for which data are reported?

   b. Demand and other transaction deposits at these banks account for about what percentage of M1? What percentage of M1 is held in the form of currency and travelers checks?

6. **Recent bank failures.** The FDIC maintains a list of recently failed banks online at http://www.fdic.gov/bank/. Go to this list and download the information for a recently failed bank. Why did the institution fail? How did federal authorities respond to the failure?

CASE FOR DISCUSSION

Makeshift Money in the French Colonial Period

The following letter was written by de Meulle, governor of the French province of Quebec in September 1685:

My Lord—

I have found myself this year in great straits with regard to the subsistence of the soldiers. You did not provide for funds, My Lord, until January last. I have, notwithstanding, kept them in provisions until September, which makes eight full months. I have drawn from my own funds and from those of my friends, all I have been able to get, but at last finding them without means to render me further assistance, and not knowing to what saint to pay my vows, money being extremely scarce, having distributed considerable sums on every side for the pay of the soldiers, it occurred to me to issue, instead of money, notes on [playing] cards, which I have had cut in quarters. I send you My Lord, the three kinds, one is for four francs, another for forty sols, and the third for fifteen sols, because with these three kinds, I was able to make their exact pay for one month. I have issued an ordinance by which I have obliged all the inhabitants to receive this money in payments, and to give it circulation, at the same time pledging myself, in my own name, to redeem the said notes. No person has refused them, and so good has been the effect that by this means the troops have lived as usual. There were some merchants who, privately, had offered me money at the local rate on condition that I would repay them in money at the local rate in France, to which I could not consent as the King would have lost a third; that is, for 10,000 he would have paid 40,000 livres; thus personally, by my credit and by my management, I have saved His Majesty 13,000 livres.

[Signed] de Meulle
Quebec, 24th September, 1685

Source: From *Canadian Currency, Exchange and Finance During the French Period,* vol. 1, ed. Adam Shortt (New York: Burt Franklin, Research Source Works Series no. 235, 1968).

QUESTIONS

1. What indication do you find that the playing-card notes issued by the governor served as a means of payment? Why were they accepted as such?
2. What indicates that the notes served as a store of value? What made them acceptable as such?
3. Did the invention of playing-card money change the unit of account in the local economy?

END NOTES

1. The definitions for M1, M2 and related measures of the money stock given here are those used in the United States. Other countries use definitions that are similar but not identical. Before using monetary data from another country, check the web site of that country's central bank for the exact definitions.
2. Money market mutual funds, which compete with banks and thrifts for household savings, make every effort to make their services as convenient as those of their competitors. They provide statements, checkbooks, deposit slips, and so on that closely resemble those used by banks and thrifts. Technically, however, their liabilities are shares in the fund's portfolio of assets, not deposits. Therefore, money market mutual funds are not considered to be depository institutions. Only retail, or consumer, money market mutual funds are included in M2—those owned by corporations are not.
3. This can be demonstrated as follows: First, the right-hand side of the equation, the price level times real domestic product, can be replaced by y, standing for nominal domestic product. Next, both sides of the equation can be divided by M to give $V - y/M$.

CHAPTER 12

Central Banking and Monetary Policy

After reading this chapter, you will understand:

1. How banks create money
2. What limits the size of the money stock
3. What instruments are available to the central bank for controlling the money stock
4. The activities that the central bank undertakes in the international sphere

Before reading this chapter, make sure you know the meaning of:

1. M1, M2
2. Balance sheets
3. Central bank
4. Federal Reserve System
5. Bank reserves
6. Current account and financial account transactions in the balance of payments.

THE INFLUENCE OF the central bank on the economy is like that of the moon on the tides—powerful but largely invisible. H. Walter Heller, who was a member of the Fed's policy-making Open Market Committee, once described joining the committee as like being inducted into the Vatican's College of Cardinals. This chapter will show how central banks influence the internal workings of a country's economy and its economic links to the rest of the world.

The chapter begins by explaining how commercial banks and thrifts create money, and what limits their ability to do so. Next we will look at the tools that the Federal Reserve uses to control the money stock for the country as a whole. Finally, we look briefly at how the Fed, and the central banks of other countries, act to influence international financial markets.

HOW BANKS CREATE MONEY

As we saw in Chapter 11, the bulk of the U.S. money supply consists of the liabilities of commercial banks and thrift institutions. In this section we will see how these institutions create money on the basis of reserves supplied by the Federal Reserve System.

A Simplified Banking System

As we have done in building models of other parts of the economy, we will begin with a simplified situation and add details later. Our simplified banking system is as follows:

1. The system consists of ten identical banks.
2. The banks' only assets are loans and reserve deposits at the Fed; there is no vault cash.
3. The banks' only liabilities are demand deposits; their net worth is zero.
4. Demand deposits are the only form of money in the banking system.
5. The system is regulated by a simplified Federal Reserve System that has the power to set uniform reserve requirements on all deposits.
6. The Fed's only assets are government securities, and its only liabilities are the reserve deposits of member banks. Banks do not borrow reserves from the Fed.

Simplified as it is, this 10-bank system can show us a great deal about the mechanics of money creation in the U.S. banking system.

RESERVES: REQUIRED AND EXCESS   The Federal Reserve System sets a minimum percentage of certain categories of deposits that each bank or thrift must hold as reserve deposits with the Fed or as vault cash. These are called **required reserves**. The ratio of required reserves to total deposits is the **required-reserve ratio**. If the bank holds more than the minimum amount of required reserves, the balance is known as **excess reserves**. In equation form, the relationships among required reserves, excess reserves, deposits, and the required-reserve ratio can be stated as follows:

$$\text{Required reserves} = \text{Deposits} \times \text{Required-reserve ratio}$$

and

$$\text{Excess reserves} = \text{Total reserves} - \text{Required reserves}$$

For our simplified banking system, we will assume a required-reserve ratio of 10 percent on all deposits.

BALANCE SHEET EQUILIBRIUM   As profit-seeking firms, banks want to earn all the interest they can; thus, they normally keep excess reserves to a minimum in order to make as many loans or buy as many securities as possible. The situation in which required reserves equal total reserves represents a state of equilibrium. Although in

Required reserves

The minimum amount of reserves that the Fed requires depository institutions to hold.

Required-reserve ratio

Required reserves stated as a percentage of the deposits to which reserve requirements apply.

Excess reserves

Total reserves minus required reserves.

practice, banks do not maintain reserves exactly at their equilibrium level at all times, in our simplified banking system we will assume that they quickly bring their excess reserves back to zero following any disturbance.

Mechanics of Money Creation

Now we are ready to examine the mechanics of money creation in our simplified banking system. As the following example will show, money creation is governed by the required-reserve ratio, the amount of reserves supplied, and banks' efforts to maximize their profits.

INITIAL BALANCE SHEETS   Assume that each bank in the system starts out with a balance sheet that looks like this:

Initial Balance Sheet of a Representative Bank			
Assets		**Liabilities**	
Reserves	$ 10,000	Demand deposits	$100,000
Required	$10,000		
Excess	0		
Loans	90,000		
Total assets	$100,000	Total liabilities	$100,000

Also assume that the Fed's initial balance sheet looks like this:

The Fed			
Assets		**Liabilities**	
U.S. government securities	$100,000	Reserve deposits	$100,000

Starting from this point, we will look at the effects of an injection of reserves into the banking system. Each bank receives new reserves every time a customer deposits funds that were withdrawn from another bank. However, this does not increase the reserves in the banking system as a whole. For total reserves to be increased, new reserves must come from outside the system. The chief source of new reserves is the Fed.

    Suppose that the Fed decides to increase the amount of reserves available to the banking system by $10,000. It usually does this by adding to its holdings of government securities, buying such securities from a securities dealer. Such an action is called an **open market operation** (in this case, an open market purchase) because the Fed, acting through the Federal Reserve Bank of New York, goes to the securities market and bids against other buyers to purchase the securities. Suppose the Fed buys $10,000 in securities from a dealer and pays for them through a wire transfer to

Open market operation

A purchase (sale) by the Fed of government securities from (to) the public.

the dealer's bank, which we will call Albany National Bank.[1] The *wire transfer* is an electronic instruction made through the Fed's computer network that credits Albany National Bank's reserve account at the Fed with $10,000 and simultaneously directs the bank to credit the same amount to the dealer's demand-deposit account.

At this point the Fed's initial goal of injecting $10,000 of new reserves into the system has been achieved. The balance sheets of the Fed and Albany National Bank now look like this (changes from the previous balance sheet are shown in parentheses):

The Fed			
Assets		**Liabilities**	
U.S. government securities	$110,000 (+10,000)	Reserve deposits	$100,000 (+10,000)

Albany National Bank			
Assets		**Liabilities**	
Reserves	$ 20,000 (+10,000)	Demand deposits	$110,000 (+10,000)
Required	$11,000 (+1,000)		
Excess	9,000 (+9,000)		
Loans	90,000		
Total assets	$110,000 (+10,000)	Total liabilities	$110,000 (+10,000)

LENDING OUT THE EXCESS RESERVES   Note how the $10,000 in new reserves at Albany National Bank is divided between required and excess reserves. Deposits have gone up by $10,000, meaning that the bank must hold $1,000 more in required reserves. The other $9,000 in new reserves need not be held against deposits and hence is listed as excess reserves. Albany National Bank is no longer in equilibrium; it can increase its profits by lending out the excess reserves.

Of course, in order to make a loan the bank must find a borrower. Suppose that on the morning on which Albany gets its new reserves James Anderson walks in and applies for a $9,000 auto loan. The loan is granted and the $9,000 is credited to Anderson's checking account balance. (If Anderson had no checking account at Albany, he could ask the bank to pay him the proceeds of the loan in the form of a check or even currency. In that case, some of the intermediate steps in the following process would differ, but the end result would be the same.) At the moment at which the loan is completed—but before Anderson pays for the car—Albany National Bank's balance sheet looks like this:

Albany National Bank				
Assets			**Liabilities**	
Reserves		$ 20,000	Demand deposits	$119,000
Required	$11,900			
	(+900)			
Excess	8,100			
	(−9000)			
Loans		99,000		
		(+9,000)		
Total assets		$119,000	Total liabilities	$119,000
		(+9,000)		(+9,000)

CHECKING AWAY THE LOAN PROCEEDS   In crediting Anderson's account with $9,000, Albany National Bank has created a new $9,000 asset (the loan) matched by a new $9,000 liability (the deposit). Because of the new deposit, its required reserves have risen by $900. At this point Albany still has $8,100 in excess reserves. Why, then, does it not use those reserves to make yet another loan?

The reason the bank cannot safely make new loans greater than the original amount added to its excess reserves is that it knows Anderson will not leave the $9,000 sitting in his account; instead, he will write a check to pay for his new car. Let's see what happens when he does so.

We will call the dealer who sells the car Joyce Barnard and assume that she keeps her checking account at Bethel National Bank. When Barnard deposits Anderson's Albany National Bank check in her Bethel account, Bethel sends it to the Fed for clearance. *Clearing the check* simply means that the Fed credits $9,000 to Bethel's reserve account and subtracts $9,000 from Albany's reserve account. The Fed then puts the check in the mail so that Albany can forward it to Anderson for his records. When all these transactions have taken place, the two banks' balance sheets look like this:

Albany National Bank				
Assets			**Liabilities**	
Reserves		$ 11,000	Demand deposits	$110,000
		(−9,000)		(−9,000)
Required	$11,000			
	(−900)			
Excess	0			
	(−8,100)			
Loans		99,000		
Total assets		$110,000	Total liabilities	$110,000
		(−9,000)		(−9,000)

Bethel National Bank				
Assets			**Liabilities**	
Reserves		$ 19,000	Demand deposits	$109,000
		(+9,000)		(+9,000)
Required	$10,900			
	(+900)			
Excess	8,100			
	(+8,100)			
Loans		99,000		
Total assets		$109,000	Total liabilities	$109,000
		(+9,000)		(+9,000)

A careful look at these balance sheets reveals two important things. First, we clearly see why Albany National Bank could not safely lend out more than its initial $9,000 of excess reserves. It knew that the $9,000 deposit it created by writing the loan to Anderson would not stay on its books for long. As soon as the check cleared, $9,000 of deposits and reserves would be lost (unless the car dealer also kept an account at Albany). Only $900 loss in deposits (10 percent of the total change in deposits) could be taken from required reserves; it needed the $8,100 of excess reserves to make up the difference.

Second, we see that Albany's loss is Bethel's gain. Albany lost $9,000 in reserves ($900 required and $8,100 excess) when the check was written and cleared, and Bethel gained exactly the same amounts. The check-clearing process thus has left the banking system's total reserves unchanged.

KEEPING THE EXPANSION GOING WITH ANOTHER LOAN   The clearing of Anderson's check put Albany National Bank back in equilibrium, with $10,000 more in total assets and $10,000 more in liabilities than it started with. But now Bethel is out of equilibrium, with $8,100 in excess reserves. The logical thing for Bethel to do is to make a loan of its own using its excess reserves. (We now know that the proceeds of this loan will be checked away quickly, so we will skip the intermediate balance sheet.) After Bethel's borrower has written a check for $8,100, which is deposited in, say, Cooperstown National Bank, Bethel's and Cooperstown's balance sheets looks like the diagrams on the top of the next page.

FURTHER ROUNDS IN THE EXPANSION OF DEPOSITS   We need not go through all the rounds of the expansion process in detail, because a clear pattern has emerged. The initial open market purchase of securities by the Fed injected $10,000 of new reserves into the system. The first bank to receive the funds kept $1,000 (10 percent) as required reserves and lent out the remaining $9,000. When the loan proceeds were checked away, they became $9,000 in new deposits and reserves for a second bank, which kept $900 (10 percent) and lent out the remaining $8,100. The next

Bethel National Bank				
Assets			**Liabilities**	
Reserves		$ 10,900	Demand deposits	$109,000
		(−8,100)		
Required	$10,900			
	(unchanged)			
Excess	0			
	(−8,100)			
Loans		98,100		
		(+8,100)		
Total assets		$109,000	Total liabilities	$109,000

Cooperstown National Bank				
Assets			**Liabilities**	
Reserves		$ 18,100	Demand deposits	$108,100
		(+8,100)		(+8,100)
Required	$10,810			
	(+810)			
Excess	7,290			
	(+7,290)			
Loans		90,000		
Total assets		$108,100	Total liabilities	$108,100
		(+8,100)		(+8,100)

bank, in turn, would be able to lend out $7,290, the next one $6,561, and so on round after round. The loans create new deposits at each round; therefore, the money supply, made up entirely of deposits, expands by $10,000 + $9,000 + $8,100 + $7,290 + $6,561, and so on. In the end, the whole process creates $100,000 in new deposits.

To summarize the process of deposit expansion, let's compare the beginning and final balance sheets for the ten-bank system as a whole. Initially the balance sheet looked like this:

Initial Balance Sheet of a Representative Bank				
Assets			**Liabilities**	
Reserves		$ 100,000	Demand deposits	$1,000,000
Required	$100,000			
Excess	0			
Loans		900,000		
Total assets		$1,000,000	Total liabilities	$1,000,000

After the injection of $10,000 in new reserves, the combined balance sheet for the ten banks looks like this:

Final Balance Sheet for the 10-Bank System				
Assets			**Liabilities**	
Reserves		$ 110,000	Demand deposits	$1,100,000
		(+10,000)		(+100,000)
Required	$110,000			
	(+10,000)			
Excess	0			
Loans		990,000		
		(+90,000)		
Total assets		$1,100,000	Total liabilities	$1,100,000
		(+100,000)		(+100,000)

We see, then, that the expansion of deposits continues until excess reserves have disappeared. By the time the new reserves have become fully absorbed, total demand deposits will have expanded by $100,000. On the assets side of the balance sheet, this $100,000 of new liabilities will be offset by $10,000 in new required reserves and $90,000 in new loans.

Contraction of Money Supply

When the Fed withdraws reserves from the banking system, the whole process works in reverse. For example, assume that all the banks are back in the initial position in the last example and that the Fed decides to withdraw, say, $1,000 in reserves. It can do this by making an open market sale of $1,000 of securities from its portfolio. Now suppose that the securities are bought by a dealer who pays for them with a wire transfer from an account at Denver National Bank. To complete the transfer, the Fed deducts $1,000 from Denver's reserve account. At that point Denver's balance sheet looks like this:

Denver National Bank				
Assets			**Liabilities**	
Reserves		$ 9,000	Demand deposits	$99,000
		(−9,000)		(−1,000)
Required	$9,900			
	(−100)			
Excess	−900			
	(−900)			
		90,000		
Total assets		$99,000	Total liabilities	$99,000
		(−1,000)		(−1,000)

The loss of $1,000 in deposits when the dealer bought the security reduced required reserves by only $100, whereas Denver's total reserves fell by $1,000 when the Fed completed the transaction. This leaves the bank with negative excess reserves—that is, a $900 reserve deficiency—that it must attempt to correct. In our simplified banking system, Denver must make up the deficiency by reducing its loans. It therefore leaves the next $900 it receives in loan payments in its reserve account. (We assume that if the bank did not have the reserve deficiency, it would make new loans as old ones were paid off, keeping its total loan holdings steady.) In the real world, a bank with a reserve deficiency has a number of other options. One is to sell other assets, such as government securities. Another is to borrow reserves from a bank that has excess reserves. Still another is to borrow from the Fed itself. We will return to these options later.

When Denver National Bank reduces its loan holdings to make up its reserve deficiency, it drains reserves from some other bank in the system. For example, suppose that Maria Espinosa writes a check on Englewood National Bank to pay off $900 that she borrowed from Denver. At the moment when the wire transfer is complete, the balance sheets of the Denver and Englewood banks will look like this:

Denver National Bank				
Assets			**Liabilities**	
Reserves		$ 9,900	Demand deposits	$99,000
		(+900)		
Required	$9,900			
	(unchanged)			
Excess	0			
	(+900)			
Loans		89,100		
		(−900)		
Total assets		$99,000	Total liabilities	$99,000

Englewood National Bank				
Assets			**Liabilities**	
Reserves		$ 9,100	Demand deposits	$99,100
		(−900)		(−900)
Required	$9,910			
	(−90)			
Excess	−810			
	(−810)			
Loans		90,000		
Total assets		$99,100	Total liabilities	$99,100
		(−900)		(−900)

At this point, then, Denver has made up its reserve deficiency, but $810 of it has been passed along to Englewood. Now it is Englewood's turn to reduce its loan holdings. Using an $810 loan repayment that it has received from some other bank, Englewood will build up its reserves by the required amount, but a $729 deficiency will appear somewhere else. The contraction process will continue until deposits in the banking system as a whole have been reduced by $10,000—10 times the original loss of reserves that resulted from the Fed's open market security sale.

The Money Multiplier for the Simplified Banking System

As these examples have shown, the total amount of demand deposits that the banking system can hold depends on the total amount of reserves supplied by the Fed and on the required-reserve ratio. In equation form, with rr standing for the required-reserve ratio, the relationship is as follows:

$$\text{Total demand deposits} = (1/\text{rr}) \times \text{Total reserves}$$

Thus, when total reserves were $100,000, the total money stock (consisting entirely of demand deposits in our example) was $1 million. When the Fed injected $10,000 of new reserves into the system, bringing total reserves to $110,000, the money stock rose by $100,000, to $1.1 million. When the Fed withdrew $1,000 of reserves through an open market sale, reducing total reserves to $99,000, the money stock fell by $10,000, to $990,000.

Money multiplier

The ratio of the equilibrium money stock to the banking system's total reserves.

The term 1/rr in the equation just given is called the **money multiplier** and is the ratio of the equilibrium money stock to total reserves. In our simplified banking system, in which the required-reserve ratio was 10 percent, the value of the money multiplier was 10. Each injection or withdrawal of reserves by the Fed thus increases or decreases the money stock by ten times the change in reserves.

THE INSTRUMENTS OF MONETARY POLICY

As we learned in Chapter 11, the Fed, like the central banks of other countries, has a major role in providing services to the banking system and in ensuring its safety and stability. Our discussion of money creation here shows that central banks have another power, namely, the power to control the money stock. Now that we know how money is created, we can examine the policy instruments that the Fed and other central banks use to control the money stock.

Open Market Operations

The preceding section illustrated the most important of the policy instruments that the Fed uses to control the money stock: open market operations. If the Fed wants to expand the money stock, it instructs the Open Market Trading Desk at the Federal Reserve Bank of New York to buy government securities.

This may mean making an outright purchase of securities, but more frequently the Fed buys the securities subject to a *repurchase agreement*. In such an arrangement a dealer selling the securities to the Fed agrees to buy them back at a later date. Open market operations involving repurchase agreements have only a temporary effect on bank reserves; reserves return to their initial level as soon as the "repurchase" part of the agreement is carried out. Such actions are used to make relatively small day-to-day adjustments in bank reserves.

Whichever form the purchase takes, the Fed pays for the securities by means of a wire transfer that adds funds to the reserves of the seller's bank. Because these are newly created reserves and not just a transfer of reserves from one bank to another, they add to the banking system's total reserves. Further, each dollar of reserves added to the banking system permits the volume of deposits subject to reserves to expand by several dollars. The amount of the expansion—the number of dollars added to the money stock per dollar of added reserves—is determined by the money multiplier. In the real world, however, the factors determining the value of the money multiplier are more complex than in the simplified system discussed in the preceding section.

If the Fed wants to decrease the money stock, it reverses this process: It instructs the Trading Desk to carry out an open market sale of securities, either outright or subject to a repurchase agreement. When a dealer buys securities from the Fed and pays for them with a wire transfer of funds from its deposit at a commercial bank, reserves will be drained from the banking system. The money supply will contract by an amount equal to the money multiplier times the size of the open market sale.

Although open market operations are the most frequently used tool for controlling the money stock, they are not the only one. If we remove some of the simplifying assumptions used so far in this chapter, we can see how these other tools work.

The Discount Rate

In our simplified banking system, banks can acquire new reserves only by attracting additional deposits. In practice, however, banks and thrifts that want additional reserves either to meet the Fed's requirements or to expand their loans have another option: borrowing reserves.

One possibility is to borrow reserves from another bank. The market in which banks make short-term loans of reserves to other banks is known as the **federal funds market**. The interest rate charged on such loans is called the **federal funds rate**. Transactions in this market, in which the usual loan term is 24 hours, total billions of dollars per day. The Fed indicates its policy stance through setting a target for the federal funds rate, the **federal funds rate target**. The Fed's policy-making body, the Federal Open Market Committee (FOMC), is responsible for making decisions regarding this target.

Federal funds market

A market in which banks lend reserves to one another for periods as short as 24 hours.

Federal funds rate

The interest rate on overnight loans of reserves from one bank to another.

Federal funds rate target

The Fed's target for the federal funds rate, announced by the Federal Open Market Committee (FOMC).

Funds that banks borrow from one another through the federal funds market have no effect on total bank reserves; this type of borrowing just moves reserves around from one bank to another. Funds that commercial banks borrow directly from the Fed through the so-called **discount window** are another story, however.

Banks borrow from the Fed in two kinds of situations. Most often they borrow for short periods to adjust their reserves when unexpected withdrawals have left them with less than the required amount of reserves. These banks are not in danger of insolvency, but are temporarily short on reserves. Banks with healthy balance sheets qualify for primary credit, and are charged the **discount rate**. To discourage banks from borrowing too often or too much through the discount window, the Fed sets the discount rate above the federal funds rate target. Typically, the discount rate is one percentage point above the federal funds rate.

In addition to primary credit, the Fed sometimes makes loans to troubled banks to give them time to get their affairs in order. Since these banks are less likely to be able to repay the Fed, they must pay a higher interest rate, above the discount rate. Typically, the interest rate is one-half of a percentage point above the discount rate charged on primary credit loans.

The discount rate is a second policy instrument for controlling the money supply, although a less powerful one than open market operations. If the Fed wants to encourage more discount borrowing, it lowers the discount rate. As the discount rate falls relative to the federal funds rate, the cost of discount borrowing falls relative to the cost of borrowing from other banks and the volume of discount borrowing expands. However, because of the administrative pressures that the Fed uses to discourage excessive discount borrowing, there is a limit to how much discount borrowing banks will want to undertake. If the Fed wants to reduce borrowing from the discount window, it raises the discount rate.

Changes in Required-Reserve Ratios

Changes in required-reserve ratios are a third potential policy instrument that the Fed can use to control the money supply. Earlier in the chapter we showed that the total volume of demand deposits in a simplified banking system is determined by the formula

$$\text{Total demand deposits} = (1/rr) \times \text{Total reserves}$$

where rr stands for the required-reserve ratio. Similar but somewhat more complex formulas apply to the relationship between required-reserve ratios and all of the elements of M1 and M2 in the actual U.S. banking system. Thus, a reduction in required-reserve ratios will increase the money stock that can be created on the basis of a given quantity of reserves, and an increase in the ratios will decrease the money stock for a given quantity of reserves.

Discount window

The department through which the Federal Reserve lends reserves to banks.

Discount rate

The interest rate charged by the Fed on loans of reserves to banks.

Although changes in required-reserve ratios have never been used for day-to-day control over the money supply, there have been times in the past when the Fed changed the ratios when it wanted to make a strong move toward expansion or contraction of the money supply. For example, in late 1990, the Fed eliminated a 3 percent reserve requirement on nonpersonal saving and time deposits. In April 1992, it reduced the required reserve ratio on transaction deposits from 12 percent to 10 percent. These changes were made, in part, to speed recovery from the 1990–1991 recession, although they also reflected a belief that lower reserve requirements would reduce bank's cost, encourage bank lending, and strengthen the role of banks in the financial system. More recently, the Fed has not used the reserve requirement as an instrument to control the money supply, because it poses difficulties in bank balance sheet management.

Other Factors Affecting the Money Multiplier and Reserves

In our simplified banking system, the money multiplier is a constant and the Fed has full control over bank reserves. In practice, however, the situation is more complex; both the money multiplier and reserves can vary for reasons beyond the Fed's control.

Consider, for example, the multiplier for the most important monetary aggregate, M2. M2 includes both transaction deposits, on which reserves are required, and saving and time deposits, on which no reserves are required. The total amount of M2 that banks can create per dollar of reserves (that is, the M2 multiplier) thus depends, among other things, on the relative amounts of reservable and nonreservable deposits that banks' customers decide to hold. If people decide to move their funds from transactions deposits to savings or time deposits, the M2 multiplier rises. If they move them from savings and time deposits to transactions deposits, the M2 multiplier falls.

Total reserves in the banking system can also be affected by choices made by bank customers. In our simplified banking system, reserve deposits at the Fed were the only form of reserves. In the real world, however, part of reserves are held in the form of vault cash. If bank customers decide to withdraw larger than normal amounts of currency from their accounts, as they typically do at Christmas time and during summer vacations, total bank reserves fall. If bank customers reduce their holdings of currency, reserves rise.

Such changes in reserves and the money multiplier make the Fed's job more difficult. When reserves or the money multiplier unexpectedly increase, the Fed must offset the increase with open market sales of securities or a rise in the discount rate. When reserves or the money multiplier fall, the Fed must buy securities on the open market or lower the discount rate. Such offsetting actions allow the Fed to maintain fairly close control over the money stock, but the control is not as direct or precise as in our simplified banking system.

CENTRAL BANKING IN THE INTERNATIONAL ECONOMY

The preceding section of this chapter looked at three instruments of monetary policy—open market operations, changes in the discount rate, and changes in reserve ratios—all of which operate entirely within the domestic economy. In this section we turn to a fourth instrument of monetary policy—operations in the foreign-exchange market, in which U.S. dollars, Japanese yen, European euros, British pounds, and the currencies of other countries are exchanged for one another. In this section, we take a preliminary look at the mechanics of the central bank activities in the **foreign-exchange market** and the relationship between those activities and domestic monetary policy. Succeeding chapters add details relating exchange rates to the balance of payments, interest rates, inflation, and economic growth.

Like its fellow central banks in other countries, the Fed has the right to use foreign-exchange market transactions as an instrument of monetary policy. However, for a variety of reasons, the Fed has not used this instrument as actively in recent years as have central banks abroad. Keep in mind as you read this section that although foreign-exchange market operations are a minor instrument of monetary policy for the Fed, they are a very important instrument, often the most important, for many other central banks.

Foreign-exchange market

A market in which the currency of one country is traded for that of another.

The Structure of the Foreign-Exchange Market

As a traveler you may have had occasion to exchange U.S. dollars for Canadian dollars, Mexican pesos, or the currency of some other country. This trading in paper currencies is a small corner of the largest set of markets in the world—the foreign-exchange market, in which hundreds of billions of dollars are traded each day. Such trading reflects the fact that virtually every international transaction in goods, services, or financial assets is preceded by the exchange of one currency for another.

Large transactions in the foreign-exchange market, like large domestic transactions, are conducted with transaction deposits in commercial banks. A key role is played by large banks in the world's money centers—London, Zurich, Tokyo, and other cities—which are known as *trading banks*. These banks have branches all over the world and accept deposits denominated in many different currencies.

Suppose that Bloomingdale's department store in New York needs to buy euros to purchase Italian goods. Italy is one of twelve countries in Europe that use the euro as their currency. Bloomingdale's can ask a commercial bank where it maintains a deposit, say, Citibank, to debit its dollar-denominated account and credit a deposit of equal value to an account in Rome, Italy, denominated in euros that it can use to pay an Italian supplier. Similarly, if a German pension fund wants to buy U.S. Treasury bills, it can exchange a deposit denominated in euros at a German or U.S. bank for a deposit denominated in dollars and use those dollars to buy the Treasury bills. The banks make a profit on these transactions by charging an *asked* price for the currency they sell that is slightly higher than the *bid* price they pay for the currency they buy.

Supply and Demand in the Foreign-Exchange Market

What determines the number of euros that a customer gets in exchange for its dollars? Why, on a given day, is the exchange rate 0.80 euros per dollar rather than 1.20 or 1? The answer is that the rate depends on supply and demand. Here, we will consider a simplified illustration of the foreign-exchange market in which dollars are exchanged for euros.

Current account transactions include imports and exports of goods and services and international transfer payments, and *financial account transactions* involve international purchases and sales of assets and international borrowing and lending. Both play a role in determining the supply and demand for dollars in the foreign-exchange market.

In the example given earlier, a U.S. department store wanted to buy Italian leather shoes. To buy the leather shoes, it must first buy euros. An importer of goods or services to the United States enters the foreign-exchange market as a *supplier* of dollars. The supply curve for dollars shown in Figure 12.1 combines the transactions of all importers. In this diagram the supply curve has a positive slope, indicating that an increase in the exchange rate of the dollar relative to the euro (meaning that more euro can be bought per dollar) will increase the number of dollars supplied.[2]

On the other side of the market, a Spanish grocery chain that wishes to buy wheat exported from the United States must buy U.S. dollars to carry out the transaction. A buyer of U.S. exports enters the foreign-exchange market as a *demander* of dollars. The demand curve shown in Figure 12.1 includes the demand for dollars of all European buyers of U.S. exports.

In addition to current account transactions, U.S. and European firms and individuals carry out numerous financial account transactions. For example, a German pension fund that wishes to buy U.S. Treasury bills must first buy dollars to use in paying for those securities. A *financial inflow* to the United States thus is associated with a demand for dollars above and beyond the demand arising from current account transactions. What about a *financial outflow,* such as a purchase of foreign securities by a U.S. buyer? Such a transaction represents a source of dollars supplied to the foreign-exchange market in addition to the supply of dollars needed to buy exports of U.S. goods and services. To simplify, it is often useful to subtract financial outflows from financial inflows, and focus only on *net* financial flows. The United States has experienced a net financial inflow each year for more than a decade, so financial transactions represent, on balance, an additional source of demand for dollars.

PRICES IN THE FOREIGN-EXCHANGE MARKET   Foreign-exchange rates—the prices of currencies in terms of other currencies, as determined by supply and

FIGURE 12.1 THE FOREIGN-EXCHANGE MARKET FOR DOLLARS AND EURO

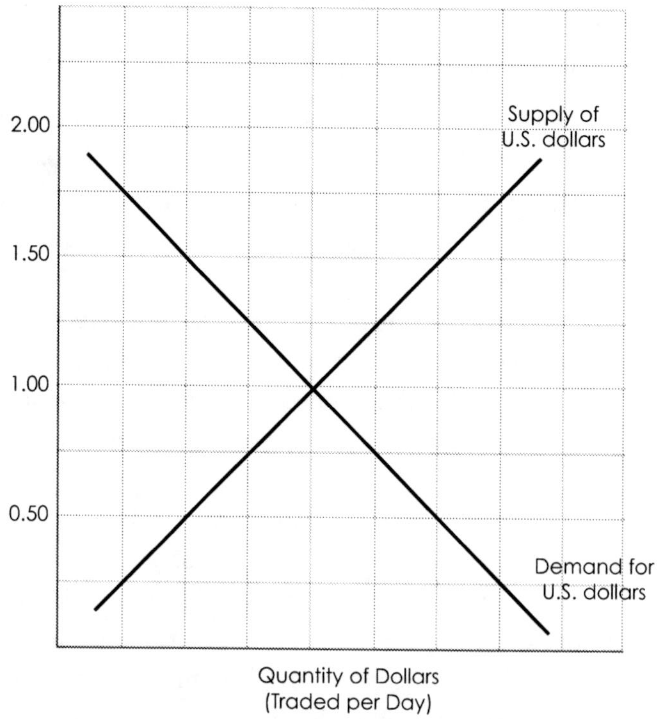

This diagram represents the foreign-exchange market in which U.S. dollars are exchanged for European euros and euros are exchanged for dollars. The exchange rate is expressed as the number of euros required to purchase one U.S. dollar. The supply curve of dollars reflects the activities of U.S. importers of European goods and services. They sell dollars to obtain the euros they need in order to buy Italian leather shoes, German automobiles, and so on. The demand curve for dollars reflects the activities of European buyers of exports from the United States. They use euros to buy the dollars they need to buy Boeing aircraft, American wheat, and other goods. The demand curve also includes the effects of net financial inflows to the United States. For example, a German pension fund that wants to buy U.S. government bonds first needs to exchange euros for dollars to use in purchasing the bonds.

Appreciate

A currency is said to appreciate if its value increases relative to the currency of another country.

Depreciate

A currency is said to depreciate if its value decreases relative to the currency of another country.

demand—are published daily in financial newspapers and on the Internet. Figure 12.2 shows a representative selection of foreign-exchange rate quotations for a typical day. Most currencies are quoted in terms of units of foreign currency per dollar, as in our supply and demand diagrams. A few currencies are commonly quoted in U.S. dollars per unit of foreign currency (Australian dollar, British pound, euro), as in Figure 12.2.

As supply and demand conditions change, exchange rates also change, as shown by the difference between the rates for successive entries in Figure 12.2. If a currency gets stronger, it is said to **appreciate**. For example, in Figure 12.2 we see that in April 2005, one U.S. dollar would buy 35.5 Thai baht, whereas in May, it would buy 35.8 baht. The dollar appreciated relative to the baht over that period. If a currency gets weaker, it is said to **depreciate**. For example, in April 2005, a dollar would buy 11.1

FIGURE 12.2   FOREIGN-EXCHANGE RATES (DAILY RATES FOR WEEK ENDING NOVEMBER 21, 2003)

Country	Monetary Unit	May, 2005	April, 2005	March, 2005	May, 2004
* Australia	dollar	0.7663	0.7738	0.7848	0.7039
Brazil	real	2.4554	2.576	2.7061	3.1023
Canada	dollar	1.2555	1.2359	1.216	1.3789
China, P.R.	yuan	8.2764	8.2765	8.2765	8.2771
Denmark	krone	5.8628	5.7554	5.6488	6.2021
* EMU Members	euro	1.2697	1.2943	1.3185	1.2000
Hong Kong	dollar	7.7914	7.7984	7.7994	7.7971
India	rupee	43.4100	43.6400	43.5900	45.1800
Japan	yen	106.6000	107.1900	105.2500	112.2000
Malaysia	ringgit	3.8000	3.8000	3.8000	3.8000
Mexico	peso	10.9760	11.1120	11.1550	11.5200
* New Zealand	dollar	0.7191	0.7209	0.7300	0.6151
Norway	krone	6.3656	6.3147	6.2116	6.8428
Singapore	dollar	1.6507	1.6511	1.6308	1.7124
South Africa	rand	6.3267	6.1469	6.0328	6.7996
South Korea	won	1001.8400	1010.0700	1007.7800	1177.8800
Sri Lanka	rupee	99.7910	99.6710	99.3900	98.9290
Sweden	krona	7.2382	7.0814	6.8954	7.6097
Switzerland	franc	1.2172	1.1954	1.1756	1.2839
Taiwan	dollar	31.2650	31.4800	31.1060	33.4440
Thailand	baht	39.8000	39.5210	38.5940	40.5600
* United Kingdom	pound	1.8559	1.8961	1.9043	1.7860
Venezuela	bolivar	2144.6000	2144.6000	2124.6500	1919.7600

This table shows the exchange rate of the U.S. dollar relative to a number of foreign currencies. In most cases, the exchange rate is shown as units of foreign currency per dollar, for example, 10.9 Mexican pesos per dollar. In a few cases, marked by a star (*), the exchange rate is shown as dollars per unit of foreign currency, e.g., 1,26 dollars per euro. Exchange rates vary according to supply and demand conditions. If a currency strengthens, it is said to appreciate. If it weakens, it is said to depreciate.

* U.S. dollars per unit of foreign currency

Source: Board of Governors of the Federal Reserve System, H.5 Statistical Release, June 1, 2005.

Mexican pesos, whereas in May it would buy only 10.9 pesos. The dollar depreciated relative to the baht over this period.[3]

A number of factors can cause an appreciation or depreciation . For example, suppose we look at the market where U.S. dollars are exchanged for Mexican pesos. A recession in the the U.S. economy would decrease the demand for all sorts of goods, including goods imported from Mexico. Reduced sales of dollars by U.S. importers to acquire the pesos needed to purchase those goods would cause the supply curve for dollars to shift to the left, as shown in Part (a) of Figure 12.3. The shift of the supply curve changes the equilibrium exchange rate from 10 pesos per

FIGURE 12.3 **THE FOREIGN-EXCHANGE MARKET FOR DOLLARS AND MEXICAN PESOS**

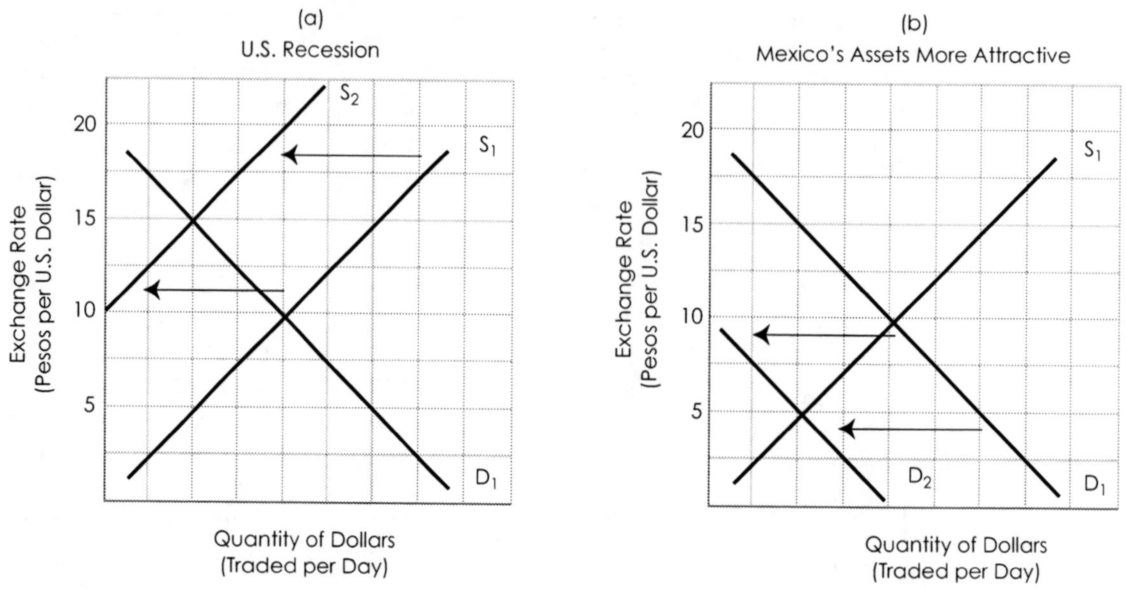

(a)
U.S. Recession

(b)
Mexico's Assets More Attractive

This diagram represents the foreign-exchange market in which U.S. dollars are exchanged for Mexican pesos and pesos are exchanged for U.S. dollars. The exchange rate is expressed as the number of pesos required to purchase one U.S. dollar. The supply curve of dollars reflects the activities of U.S. importers of Mexican goods and services. Therefore, as shown in part (a), when the U.S. economy goes into a recession, U.S. importers will buy fewer goods and services from Mexican businesses. This leads to a decrease in supply of U.S. dollars because American importers do not need to exchange as many U.S. dollars for pesos. The result is an increase in the exchange rate from 10 pesos to 15 pesos per U.S. dollar. A change in market conditions may also start in the financial sector. Part (b) shows the result of a change in market conditions that makes Mexican assets more attractive to U.S. buyers.

dollar to 15 pesos per dollar—an appreciation of the dollar and a depreciation of the peso.

An increase in any condition making Mexican assets more attractive to U.S. buyers would decrease net financial inflows to the United States (or increase net financial outflows, if there was an outflow to begin with). In Part (b) of Figure 12.3, such a reduced financial inflow is shown as a leftward shift in the demand curve for dollars. Possible causes might include an increase in Mexican interest rates or a change in Mexican tax laws that improved the Mexican investment climate. The leftward shift of the demand curve changes the equilibrium exchange rate from 10 pesos per dollar to 5 pesos per dollar—a depreciation of the dollar and an appreciation of the peso.

These are only a few of the factors that can affect supply and demand in the foreign-exchange market. Changes in exchange rates have an important effect on the prices of goods and services in international trade. *Economics in the News 12.1* discusses what happened when the U.S. dollar lost value relative to the euro in the early 2000s, and how this affected Europeans' travel to the United States.

Central Bank Intervention in the Foreign-Exchange Market

Exchange rates are not mere numbers; they have major impacts on the economy. For example, if the value of the dollar rises relative to that of the yen, as it did during the first half of the 1980s, more yen can be bought for a dollar. Japanese goods thus become relatively inexpensive for U.S. consumers. Imports from Japan increase, and U.S. firms competing with those imports face possibly devastating competition. At the same time, U.S. goods and services become relatively more expensive to Japanese

ECONOMICS IN THE NEWS 12.1
WHERE TO SPEND VACATION?

DECEMBER 22, 2003—For 21-year-old Yannick Stolk, a trip to the United States from her hometown near Antwerp, Belgium, was too big an expense.

Until now.

The euro has risen nearly 19 percent against the U.S. dollar this year, and European tourists like Yannick are cashing in on the dream trip that has suddenly become, well, 19 percent cheaper.

At American cruise operator Royal Caribbean Cruise Ltd., European bookings for 2004 are up 120 percent from last year, and 40 percent of those bookings are for U.S. destinations such as Miami and the U.S. Virgin Islands. "The price sensitivity is definitely working to our advantage," said Gary Burton, senior vice president of marketing at Royal Caribbean.

International visitors' contribution to the U.S. economy this year is estimated at $65.8 billion, with the projection for next year at $69.4 billion, according to the Travel Industry Association of America. "Forty-five percent of that money comes from European travelers," Cathy Keefe, TIA spokeswoman, told Reuters.

The British pound also reached a five-year high against the U.S. dollar last Thursday, prompting Britons to hop on planes to New York in order to pick up the designer items on their Christmas lists. "All the designer products are so much cheaper in the U.S. now. New York is an absolute hotspot for Christmas shopping, so they get an international holiday, plus they save money on their shopping at the same time," said Jessica Potter, spokeswoman at ebooker.com, a British online travel agency that handles reservations for flights, hotels, and car rentals. "Bookings are significantly up this year, and flight availability has become difficult for us to find," said Potter, who visited the U.S. for a shopping spree herself. "Levis and Reebok—they are so much cheaper there now!" she said.

The euro has risen 50 percent from its lowest point three years ago, making the United States and all its tourist attractions a better value for Europeans. "The only reason I'm here is that it's cheaper," said Marc Stolk, Yannick's father, after a day of hiking and biking around the Everglades in Florida. "I've been wanting to come for a while, but when it was one euro to one dollar, it was too expensive."

But with one euro now translating to $1.24, the number of Europeans visiting the United States is on a climb from the 9.4 million European visitors last year, according to the Orlando/Orange County Visitors Bureau. Of the top 25 tourism generating countries, Sweden and the United Kingdom are expected to gain the biggest market share in the United States in 2003, according to the Travel Industry Association. The Stolks stayed at the Everglades Youth Hostel in Florida City, where 90 percent of the guests are European, and holiday bookings are up 30 percent from last year, the owner of the hostel told Reuters.

"Historically, the strength of foreign currency has always favored travel to the U.S.," said Jose Estorino, senior vice president of marketing at the Orlando/Orange County Convention and Visitor's Bureau, which is investing $1.7 million in an upcoming marketing campaign in the United Kingdom. The campaign, which is scheduled to launch just after Christmas, will include direct mail at targeted households, advertisements on television, in newspapers, in the tunnels of the underground transportation system, and on buses. "We expect the economic impact of the campaign to be $225 million in the next year," Estorino said.

In the meantime, Marc Stolk said he is enjoying his affordable holiday. "And if the euro keeps going up, I'll come back to see California."

Source: Jui Chakravorty, "Euro Vacationers Find America Affordable," *Reuters*, December 22, 2003.

buyers, not because the price in dollars has gone up, but because it now takes more yen to buy those dollars. U.S. exporters thus experience a decline in demand for their products when the value of the dollar rises relative to that of the yen.

When the dollar falls in value relative to the yen, as it did after February 1985, these effects are reversed. More dollars must be spent to import a given quantity of Japanese goods. The price that U.S. consumers pay for imports rises, and U.S. firms face less competition than before. U.S. exporters benefit from a fall in the value of the dollar, because Japanese buyers now find it easier to buy their products.

Because exchange rates affect the welfare of consumers and firms, their level is a matter of concern for policymakers. Consequently, central banks may intervene in the foreign-exchange market in an attempt to stabilize exchange rates by offsetting marker pressures that tend to raise or lower the exchange values of their currencies. As mentioned earlier, central banks in many foreign countries are very active in foreign exchange markets, while the Fed has rarely intervened in recent years. The relatively infrequent foreign-currency operations of the U.S. government are directed by the Treasury, which has overall responsibility for the management of international financial policy, in close cooperation with the Federal Open Market Committee. They are carried out by the Fed through its foreign trading desk in New York.

Figure 12.4 shows how the Fed could act to affect the exchange rate of the dollar relative to the Japanese yen, if asked to do so by the Treasury. Suppose, for example, that equilibrium has been established at an exchange rate of 125 yen to the dollar, as shown by point E_1 in Figure 12.4. Firms and consumers have adjusted to this exchange rate, and the Treasury would like to avoid a sudden change. However, the U.S. economy now begins to expand strongly, shifting the dollar supply curve to the right, from S_1 to S_2. If no action were taken, a new equilibrium will be established at an exchange rate of 100 yen to the dollar—point E_2 in the exhibit. What could the Fed do to stabilize the exchange rate at 125 yen?

MECHANICS OF INTERVENTION   If it wanted to support the price of the dollar relative to the yen, the Treasury would instruct the Fed to intervene in a way that would increase the quantity of dollars demanded. The mechanics of such an action would be similar to those of an open market operation. What makes intervention possible is the fact that on the assets side of its balance sheet the Fed holds foreign securities along with its holdings of U.S. government securities; these include yen-denominated securities issued by the Japanese government.

To resist downward pressure on the exchange rate, the Fed first would sell some yen-denominated securities to a securities dealer in Tokyo. It would receive payment in the form of a yen-denominated transaction deposit at the Bank of Japan, that country's central bank. The Bank of Japan acts as the Fed's agent in this transaction. To acquire dollars the Fed sells the yen-denominated deposit to a Tokyo branch of one of the New York trading banks. The bank would pay for the yen deposit by drawing

FIGURE 12.4   EFFECTS OF INTERVENTION IN THE FOREIGN-EXCHANGE MARKET

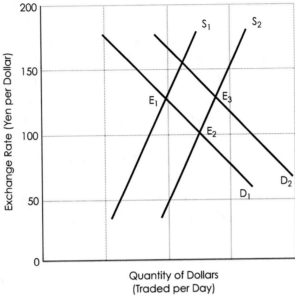

The Federal Reserve can intervene in the foreign-exchange market to resist changes in currency values. In this case, the exchange rate is initially in equilibrium at a rate of 125 yen per dollar. Expansion of the U.S. economy increases U.S. demand for imports from Japan, thus increasing the supply of dollars and shifting the supply curve to the right, from S_1 to S_2. By itself, this shift would move the equilibrium exchange rate to 100 yen per dollar. However, the Fed intervenes by purchasing dollars with yen. This has the effect of shifting the demand curve for dollars to the right, thereby preventing a decrease in the exchange rate.

on the reserves of dollars it had on deposit with the Fed in the United States. The end result of this series of transactions would be a purchase of dollars by the Fed whose effect is to increase the demand for dollars. It would shift the demand curve to the right, from D_1 to D_2. A new equilibrium would be established at E_3, where the exchange rate is unchanged because supply and demand have increased equally.

If at another time the Fed wanted to counter upward pressure on the value of the dollar, it would have to reverse these transactions. In that case it would buy a yen-denominated deposit from the New York trading bank and pay for it with a wire transfer crediting the appropriate number of dollars to the bank's reserve account at the Fed. The Fed would then use the yen deposit to buy Japanese government securities for its portfolio. This set of trades would tend to nudge down the value of the dollar in the foreign-exchange market.

EFFECTS ON THE DOMESTIC MONEY STOCK   Foreign-exchange market intervention as described in the preceding section would affect the U.S. banking system's reserves at the same time that they influenced the dollar's exchange value. If the Fed were to buy foreign currencies in order to push down the value of the dollar and invest the funds in foreign government securities, it would increase the U.S. banking system's reserves in exactly the same way that it does when it buys U.S. government securities on the open market. If it were to sell foreign currencies obtained by reducing holdings of foreign government securities in order to support the value of the dollar, bank reserves would be depleted just as they are when the Fed conducts an open market sale of U.S. government securities. Thus, the Fed's actions in the exchange market potentially affect bank reserves and domestic monetary policy.

On the relatively rare occasions when the Fed does act in the foreign-exchange markets, it routinely acts to offset the effects of its foreign-exchange activities on domestic bank reserves by engaging in a special type of open market operation known as **sterilization**. To *sterilize* a sale of foreign currencies, which tends to decrease U.S. bank reserves, the Fed simultaneously makes an equal open market purchase of U.S. government securities. The open market purchase restores total reserves to their previous value. To sterilize a purchase of foreign currencies, which tends to increase bank reserves, the Fed carries out an offsetting domestic open market sale. The central banks of many other countries also use sterilization to limit the impact of foreign-exchange market operations on the domestic money supply. However, not all do so.

In concluding this section, it is worth emphasizing that foreign-exchange markets and exchange rates are very important to the Fed's decision making even though it does not often intervene to affect them and even though it uses sterilization when it does. The reason is that any decisions the Fed makes about domestic monetary policy affect domestic interest rates, real output, and the price level, and those changes in turn influence the value of the dollar via their effects on supply and demand in the foreign-exchange market. At the same time, movements in exchange rates that have their origin elsewhere in the world have far-reaching effects on the U.S. domestic economy. For these reasons, the Fed must take developments in the foreign-exchange market into account in determining domestic monetary policy. One rarely reads a newspaper article related to domestic monetary policy that does not also discuss effects on the international value of the dollar or a story on the value of the dollar that does not end by discussing U.S. monetary policy and interest rates.

Sterilization

A monetary operation by a central bank intended to offset the effect on the domestic money stock of intervention in the foreign exchange market.

SUMMARY

1. **How do banks create money?** Banks can make loans whenever their *reserves* exceed the minimum amount of *required reserves* set by the Fed. When a bank makes a loan, it credits the proceeds to the borrower's transaction account. When the borrower spends this newly created money, the recipient deposits it in another bank, which in turn can use its excess reserves to make another loan. In this way, each dollar of new reserves that the banking system receives becomes the basis for a multiple expansion of deposits.

2. **Why is the size of the money stock limited by the quantity of bank reserves?** Banks can create money only to the extent that they have *excess reserves*. The total quantity of deposits that the banking system can create is thus limited by the total quantity of reserves available and the *required-reserve ratio*. In a simplified banking system, the number of dollars of deposits that can be created for each dollar of reserves equals 1/rr, where rr is the required-reserve ratio. The ratio 1/rr is the *money multiplier* for the simplified banking system.

3. **What instruments are available to the Fed for controlling the money stock?** *Open market operations,* in which the Fed affects the banking system's reserves through purchases or sales of government securities, are the Fed's principal instrument of monetary control. An open market purchase injects reserves into the banking system and allows the money stock to expand; an open market sale drains reserves and causes the money stock to contract. Changes in the discount rate charged by the Fed on loans of reserves to banks are a second instrument of monetary control. An increase in the *discount rate* reduces the quantity of reserves borrowed. This absorbs excess reserves and thus tends to cause the money stock to contract. Lowering the discount rate encourages borrowing of reserves and thus tends to allow the money stock to expand. Changes in required-reserve ratios are a third means of controlling the money stock. A decrease in the required-reserve ratio creates excess reserves and allows the money stock to expand; an increase in the ratio causes the money stock to contract.

4. **How well can the money stock be controlled?** The Fed is able to control the money stock reasonably closely through the use of open market operations and changes in the discount rate. However, its control is not perfect; unpredicted variations in the money multiplier or in total reserves can cause unexpected changes in the money stock.

5. **What activities does the Fed undertake in the international sphere?** Central banks can intervene in the *foreign-exchange market* to counteract upward or downward pressure on their currencies relative to those of other countries. For example, although the Fed is less active in foreign exchange markets than many other central banks, if asked to do so by the Treasury, it can lower the exchange value of the dollar by selling dollars and buying foreign currencies; and it can raise the value of the dollar by buying dollars and selling foreign currencies. Intervention in the foreign-exchange market can potentially affect the U.S. banking system's reserves and, hence, the domestic money stock. These effects on the domestic money stock are routinely avoided

because the Fed offsets the reserve impact of its interventions through domestic open market operations, a practice known as *sterilization*. However, sterilization does not completely break the linkage between domestic and international monetary and financial developments. The Fed intervenes in foreign exchange markets relatively infrequently, but this instrument of monetary policy is much more important for the central banks of some other countries.

KEY TERMS

Required reserves	Discount window
Required-reserve ratio	Discount rate
Excess reserves	Foreign-exchange
Open market operation	market
Money multiplier	Appreciation
Federal funds market	Depreciation
Federal funds rate	Sterilization
Federal funds rate target	

PROBLEMS AND TOPICS FOR DISCUSSION

1. **Multiple expansion of deposits.** Rework the deposit expansion examples in this chapter on the basis of the following assumptions:
   a. An injection of $5,000 in reserves via an open market purchase
   b. An injection of $20,000 in reserves with a 20 percent rather than 10 percent required-reserve ratio
   c. Withdrawal of $500 in reserves via an open market sale

2. **Currency and the money stock.** Use a balance sheet approach to trace the effects of a withdrawal of $1,000 in currency from a bank.

Assume that reserves are initially held half in the form of vault cash and half in the form of reserves on deposit with the Fed. Also assume that after the initial currency withdrawal there are no further changes in currency holdings by the public.

3. **The federal funds rate and the discount rate.** *The Federal Reserve Bulletin*, published monthly by the Fed, gives the values of the discount and federal funds rates and data for total and borrowed reserves. What has happened to the difference between these rates recently? Has the discount rate been changed? What has happened to the volume of borrowed reserves? Have they moved in the direction you would expect given the behavior of interest rates?

4. **The foreign-exchange market.** Find the most recent foreign-exchange quotations from the Board of Governors, *H.5 Statistical Release*, available at http://www.federalreserve.gov/releases/. How has the value of the dollar changed relative to other major currencies compared with the data given in Figure 12.2?

CASE FOR DISCUSSION

Is the Chinese Yuan Too Weak?

One of the most dramatic events in the global economy in recent decades has been the rise of China as an export powerhouse. China has many advantages that have contributed to its export success. It has low wage rates and an enormous pool of workers willing to acquire industrial skills. It has a high savings rate, resulting in high investment. And it has a government that actively encourages export-oriented businesses. By 2005, these advantages had combined to bring the U.S. trade deficit with China to a level of $160 billion, the largest bilateral deficit with any country.

One controversial aspect of China's export push concerns the role of the Chinese central bank in regard to the Chinese currency, the yuan. The Chinese central bank intervenes aggressively to influence the value of the value of the yuan. Until mid-2005, it held the yuan closely to a value of about 8.3 yuan per dollar. Without intervention, the yuan would quickly appreciate. Such an appreciation would increase the cost of Chinese goods to U.S. buyers and would make it easier for U.S. firms to export to China.

Many U.S. politicians, eager to help exporters in their home districts, wanted to see an appreciation of the yuan. President George W. Bush spoke out in favor of such a policy change. A bill was introduced in the U.S. Congress to put pressure on China to allow the yuan to "float" to a stronger value. Finally, on July 21, 2005, China's central bank governor Zhou Xiaochuan gave into pressure and announced a change in policy. Despite the announced change, many observers were disappointed that the yuan initially appreciated by only about 2 percent. They took this as evidence that the Chinese central bank was still intervening behind the scenes to limit change in the exchange rate.

Some U.S. economists noted that a change in Chinese policy would not be beneficial to the U.S. economy in all ways. They pointed out that in order to keep the yuan at 8 to the dollar, the Chinese central bank had become a huge buyers of dollars. Its growing official reserves of dollars were invested in U.S. government bonds, helping to keep U.S. interest rates low. They warned that a change in Chinese policy might lead to a rise in U.S. interest rates that would more than offset the beneficial effect of a decrease in the trade deficit.

In the end, whether a stronger appreciation of the yuan would help or hurt the U.S. economy will be decided only when it happens. Most observers expect that to happen sooner or later, but just when is anyone's guess.

QUESTIONS

1. Explain why a strong yuan leads to large net exports from China to the United States.
2. Draw a supply and demand diagram showing yuan per dollar on the vertical axis. Draw supply and demand curves showing an initial equilibrium exchange rate of 8 yuan per dollar. Next, suppose rapid growth of the U.S. economy increases demand for imports from China. What will happen to the supply and/or demand curves?
3. In your diagram, show a rightward shift of the supply curve, tending to cause an appreciation of the yuan (fewer yuan per dollar). What could the Chinese central bank do to hold the exchange rate at 8 yuan per dollar? Would this require buying or selling dollars for its international reserves of dollars?
4. Based on your understanding of the elements of planned expenditure, what would be the effect on U.S. GDP of a decrease in net imports from China, other things being equal? What would be the effect of an increase in U.S. interest rates? Would these two effects work in the same, or opposite directions? Why?

END NOTES

1. Only one of the nearly 40 primary security dealers is a bank; the remainder are nonbank institutions. For clarity, we assume in this discussion that the Fed does business only with nonbank dealers. Open market operations carried out through a bank dealer have exactly the same final effects, but some of the intermediate steps are different.
2. The slope of the current account supply curve for dollars depends on the price elasticity of demand for European goods imported into the United States. The preliminary conclusions drawn in this section will be restated to apply to a broader variety of circumstances in that chapter.
3. In determining whether a country's currency appreciates or depreciates, be sure to notice whether the currency is quoted in terms of dollars per unit of foreign currency or units of foreign currency per dollar.

CHAPTER 13

Fiscal Policy and Economic Stability

After reading this chapter, you will understand:

1. How fiscal policy—that is, changes in government purchases and net taxes—can be used to fight recession and inflation
2. How government receipts and expenditures are affected by changing economic conditions
3. How the federal budgetary system works and the limitations of that system
4. How the federal budget deficit is measured and why it has grown
5. Whether large federal deficits are a threat to economic stability

Before reading this chapter, make sure you know the meaning of:

1. Fiscal policy
2. Real and nominal interest rates
3. Government purchases
4. Transfer payments
5. Net taxes
6. Expenditure multiplier

THE WORLD OF fiscal policy is one in which economics and politics are tightly mixed, as events of the past few years have shown. One of the first actions of U.S. President George W. Bush after taking office in 2001 was to propose broad cuts in federal income taxes. The tax cuts were justified on the grounds that they would stimulate the economy and speed recovery of the U.S. economy from recession. Soon the terrorist attacks of September 11, 2001 led to further changes in fiscal policy in the form of greatly increased spending as the U.S. government fought wars in Afghanistan and Iraq. By 2003, the economy was expanding rapidly, but unemployment was still higher than usual for that stage of the economic recovery. To position themselves more favorably for the upcoming 2004 elections, the president and Republicans in Congress agreed to extend the 2001 tax cuts, making many of them permanent. Such interactions of political and economic motivations could be illustrated with fiscal policy decisions in almost any country or time period.

In this chapter, we use the models developed earlier to explore the economics of fiscal policy, including such topics as defense spending, the federal budget deficit, and the national debt. We will also look at the political process behind fiscal policy decisions. Finally, we will look at the economic and political debate over the budget deficit and the national debt.

THE THEORY OF FISCAL POLICY

As long ago as the 1930s, John Maynard Keynes and his followers proposed increases in government purchases as an antidote to the Great Depression. The arguments given at that time for using fiscal policy to stimulate economic expansion remain relevant to the **fiscal policy** debate in the United States today. Consequently, a discussion of how fiscal policy can be used as a tool for combating economic contractions makes a suitable starting point for the chapter.

Fiscal policy

Policy that is concerned with government purchases, taxes, and transfer payments.

Using Government Purchases to Combat a Contraction

Figure 13.1 uses the aggregate supply and demand model to show how fiscal policy can be used to combat an economic contraction. In that figure, the economy has fallen into recession at point E_1, where the aggregate supply curve, AS_1, meets aggregate demand curve AD_1. There real domestic product is $500 billion below its natural level of $2,000 billion, and, as a result, unemployment is above its natural rate. According to the model, in the long run the expected and actual levels of input prices would gradually adjust to this level of demand. Real output would eventually return to its natural level as the aggregate supply curve shifted downward and the economy slid down and to the right along AD_1. But would the return to normalcy occur fast enough? Or would the reluctance of firms to lower their prices and the unwillingness of workers to accept lower nominal wages make the adjustment slow and painful?

As Keynes once said, "in the long run, we are all dead." Suppose that the president and Congress, impatient with the economy's natural speed of adjustment, want to do something about the recession now. The problem is insufficient aggregate demand. Given the position of the aggregate supply curve, the aggregate demand curve needs to be shifted from AD_1 to AD_2 in order to bring real output back to its natural level at E_2. How can this be done?

IDENTIFYING THE SPENDING GAP   Although real domestic product is only $500 billion below its natural level, the horizontal gap between AD_1 and AD_2 is

FIGURE 13.1   USING FISCAL POLICY TO COMBAT AN ECONOMIC CONTRACTION

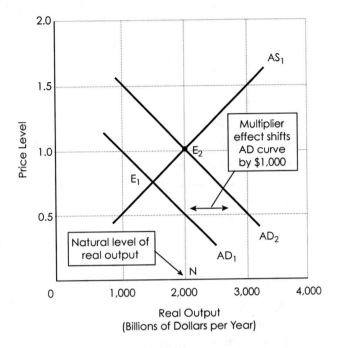

In this figure, the economy has fallen into recession at E_1. To reach the natural level of real output at E_2 without waiting for a downward shift of the aggregate supply curve, the aggregate demand curve must be shifted to the right by $1,000 billion, from AD_1 to AD_2. This can be done by increasing real government purchases and taking advantage of the multiplier effect. Given an expenditure multiplier of 4, a $250 billion increase in government purchases will bring about the required $1,000 billion shift in the aggregate demand curve. However, because the price level rises, equilibrium real domestic product does not increase by the full $1,000 billion by which the aggregate demand curve shifts. The same shift can be accomplished with a cut in net taxes, but the multiplier effect of a tax cut will be smaller than that of an increase in government purchases.

$1,000 billion, as shown by the arrow in Figure 13.1. This means that the equilibrium level of real planned expenditure at any given price level falls short of what is needed by $1,000 billion. If policy makers can fill that gap, they can shift the aggregate demand curve to the position AD_2 and bring real output to its natural level.

Of course, the gap might be filled even if policy makers did nothing. Exports might pick up; business managers might become more optimistic and increase planned investment; a rise in consumer confidence might spur consumption. But instead of waiting and hoping, policy makers could turn to the element of planned expenditure that is most directly under their control: government purchases. It is not hard to think of things that the government could spend money on—a new postal sorting station here, a stretch of interstate highway there, new vehicles for park rangers somewhere else. But just how much spending for new government purchases is needed?

USING THE MULTIPLIER EFFECT   To move the aggregate demand curve to the right by $1,000 billion, it is not necessary to increase government purchases by that amount. The reason is that each dollar of new government purchases is amplified by the multiplier effect. Spending $1 on a federal highway project boosts the income of construction workers, who then spend more on, say, groceries, clothing, and cats. Their spending raises the incomes of grocers, textile workers, and autoworkers, who in turn consume more. As the multiplier effect cascades through the economy, each $1 of new government purchases stimulates more than $1 of additional planned expenditure.

Suppose that the value of the expenditure multiplier is 4. This means that $1 of government purchases will raise the equilibrium level of planned expenditure at a given price level by $4. (This calculation takes into account both the initial increase in government purchases and the induced increases in consumption expenditure.) Therefore, it will take $250 billion of additional government purchases to shift the aggregate demand curve to the right by $1,000 billion.[1]

CHANGING PRICES AND AGGREGATE DEMAND   As the aggregate demand curve shifts from AD_1 to AD_2, the economy moves up and to the right along the aggregate supply curve. In the process, the increase in prices affects real planned expenditure in ways that partially offset the multiplier effect of the original increase in government purchases. There are four reasons why a change in the price level will affect real planned expenditure:

1. Real consumption is restrained by the fact that the real value of nominal money balances falls as the price level rises.
2. Real planned investment is moderated by the higher interest rates associated with a higher price level.
3. The parts of government budgets that are set in nominal terms will command fewer real goods and services as the price level rises.
4. Real net exports will fall because domestic prices will rise relative to prices abroad.

These effects are built into the slope of the aggregate demand curve. They do not cause the aggregate demand curve to shift away from its new position at AD_2. Instead, they cause the economy to move up to point E_2 on AD_2. There equilibrium planned expenditure is $2,000 billion, which is only $500 billion greater than at E_1, despite the fact that the aggregate demand curve has shifted to the right by $1,000 billion.

In short, because a rise in the price level tends to lower every type of planned expenditure, the equilibrium level of real domestic product rises by less than the expenditure multiplier times the initial change in real government purchases.

Using a Change in Taxes or Transfer Payments to Combat a Contraction

Government purchases are only one side of the fiscal policy equation. The other side consists of net taxes. The term *net taxes* means tax revenues collected by government minus transfer payments made by government to individuals. A tax cut or an increase in transfer payments operates in the economy via its effect on consumption.

Let us return to point E_1 in Figure 13.1 and see how a change in net taxes can be used to combat the contraction. As before, the problem is to shift the aggregate demand curve to the right by $1,000 billion. Suppose that in an attempt to stimulate the economy Congress votes a $100 billion increase in real social security benefits while leaving taxes unchanged. This amounts to a $100 billion cut in real net taxes. How does it affect aggregate demand?

To begin with, the action raises the real disposable incomes of social security recipients by $100 billion. If the marginal propensity to consume is, say, 75, they raise their consumption by $75 billion. The increase in consumer spending by social security recipients for groceries, cars, and the like boosts the incomes of grocers, autoworkers, and others by $75 billion; they, in turn, increase their consumption expenditures by $56,250,000,000; and so on.

We see, then, that a cut in net taxes, like an increase in government purchases, touches off an expansionary multiplier process. This is true whether the reduction in net taxes takes the form of a cut in taxes paid to government or an increase in transfer payments made by government. However, there is an important difference in the first-round impact of the two policy changes. A $100 billion increase in government purchases is itself a $100 billion *direct* addition to aggregate demand. However, a $100 billion tax cut or increase in transfer payments is not in itself a direct addition to aggregate demand, because it does not represent a decision by government to buy any newly produced goods and services. Therefore, the only effect of the cut in net taxes is the induced increases in consumption expenditures. For that reason, a cut in net taxes has a multiplier effect that is somewhat smaller than the effect of an equal increase in planned expenditure.

Suppose, for example, that the multiplier for a reduction in net taxes is 3, rather than the multiplier of 4 for government purchases. We can now return to Figure 13.1 and see how much of a cut in real net taxes is needed to bring the economy out of its recession. The required shift in the aggregate demand curve is $1,000 billion, so $333 billion in tax cuts or transfer payment increases are needed to shift the aggregate demand curve to the right by $1,000 billion. In response to this shift, real output rises by $500 billion, taking into account the effects of a rising price level on the various components of real planned expenditure.

An important qualification is in order, however. The preceding analysis suggests that, on a dollar-for-dollar basis, changes in net taxes are only slightly less effective than changes in government purchases in influencing the level of aggregate demand. But in reaching this conclusion, we have assumed that households will spend the same fraction of an additional dollar received through tax cuts as they will of an additional dollar in earned income. As *Applying Economics Ideas 13.1* indicates, some economists think that this may not be the case. If they are correct, tax changes would be a less effective fiscal policy tool than the simple multiplier model suggests.

≈ APPLYING ECONOMIC IDEAS 13.1

DO TAX CHANGES REALLY AFFECT AGGREGATE DEMAND?

The **net tax multiplier** correctly predicts the effect of tax changes on equilibrium aggregate demand only if people treat a dollar of added disposable income received through a tax cut the same way they treat a dollar received from any other source: dividing it between saving and consumption according to the marginal propensity to consume. However, recent U.S. experience suggests that in practice saving is affected more strongly and consumption less strongly by tax changes than by other changes in disposable income.

The accompanying chart shows personal saving and total personal tax payments at all levels of government as a percentage of personal income since 1960. Tax cuts, such as the tax rebate of 1975, appear to produce an offsetting jump in saving; as a result, they add little to consumption. Likewise, tax increases, such as the tax surcharge of 1968 and the one-time increase in tax payments in April 1987, produce a jump in tax payments but an offsetting drop in saving. This implies a smaller net tax multiplier than would otherwise be expected. If a tax change were fully offset by a change in saving, it would have no multiplier effect at all. In practice, econometric studies indicate that tax changes are partly but not wholly offset by changes in saving.

Economists differ in the reasons they give for the relatively small impact of tax cuts on consumption. One far-reaching hypothesis has been put forth by Robert J. Barro of Harvard University. Barro points out that today's tax cut has implications for tomorrow's fiscal policy. If the government cuts taxes today and does not cut spending, it will have to increase its borrowing in order to cover the resulting deficit. In the future, then, taxes will have to be raised to repay this borrowing, or at least to pay interest on it. If households think ahead, Barro says, they will react to a tax cut today by increasing their saving. Income from assets that they buy with the added savings will allow them to afford the higher future taxes needed to cover today's government borrowing. To protect themselves fully against the higher future taxes, they must save 100 percent of today's tax cut. Attributing the idea to the nineteenth-century British economist David Ricardo, Barro refers to it as the "Ricardian" view of taxation.

Other economists are skeptical of the Ricardian view. They doubt that consumers are so farsighted as to adjust their saving to offset the future effects of today's tax cuts in full. They see a simpler explanation for the tendency of tax changes to be offset by changes in saving: the fact that consumers tend to save a higher percentage of temporary changes in income than of permanent changes. Some tax changes have been explicitly labeled as temporary, such as the income tax surcharge of 1968 and the tax rebate of 1975. There was also a temporary bulge in tax revenues in the second quarter of 1987. This reflected heavy realization of capital gains in late 1986 in anticipation of higher capital gains tax rates, which were scheduled to go into effect in 1987. As the chart shows, these tax changes were almost fully offset by changes in saving, at least in the short run. Even tax changes that are said to be permanent may at first be treated as if they were temporary. Only after enough time has passed for consumers to adjust to the tax changes will these changes affect consumption in proportion to the full long-run marginal propensity to consume.

A bigger puzzle is the steady decline in personal savings since 1992. Until 2001, there were only minor changes in the tax code, so the percentage of income that consumers had to pay in taxes remained steady. Exceptional U.S. growth during much of the 1990s can explain the growth in personal income taxes. When people earn more income, they may have to pay a larger percentage of their income

---

Net tax multiplier

The ratio of an induced change in real aggregate demand to a given change in real net taxes.

Fiscal Policy and Inflation

In previous sections we have seen how fiscal policy can be used to speed up recovery from a contraction. Now we will see that fiscal policy can also play a part in fighting inflation or, for that matter, causing inflation if used irresponsibly.

COUNTERACTING PROJECTED INFLATION Consider the situation shown in Figure 13.2. The economy has been in equilibrium for some time at E_1, where real output is at its natural level. As the federal budget for the coming year is being pre-

DO TAX CHANGES REALLY AFFECT AGGREGATE DEMAND?, continued

in taxes. This leaves the trends in U.S. savings unresolved. Falling personal savings could be unrelated to fiscal policy and driven by some other factor, such as increased access to credit based on rising home prices, which permits households to borrow more.

On the diagram, we see a sharp drop in personal income taxes after the Bush tax cuts mentioned at the beginning of this chapter. If consumers viewed the tax cut as temporary, they should increase their personal savings. From the graph, we see that personal savings rose slightly between 2001 and 2002, but then resumed their downward trend despite a continued fall in the tax burden. This behavior appears to run contrary to the idea of Ricardian equivalence.

Source: Economic Report of the President, 2005, Table B-30.

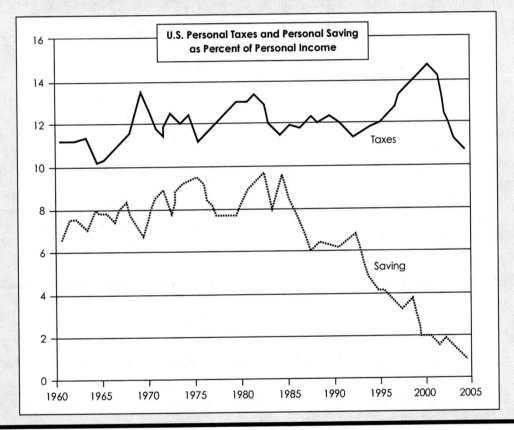

pared, forecasters warn of the possibility of inflation. The threat stems from a projected growth in the private components of aggregate demand—a surge in export demand, a boom in consumer spending, or an increase in planned investment. If something is not done, the forecasters say, the aggregate demand curve for the coming year will shift rightward to AD_2. That will drive the economy up and to the right along aggregate supply curve AS_1, to E_2.

The result will be an increase in the price level from P_1 to P_2. But inflation will not stop there. The rise in the prices of final goods will, in time, cause firms to raise

FIGURE 13.2 FISCAL POLICY AND INFLATION

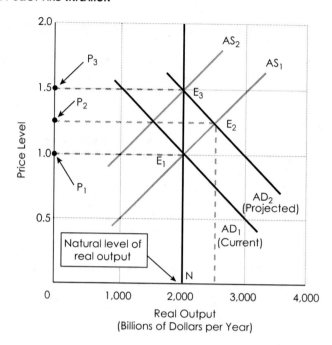

Initially the economy is at E_1. Forecasts show that if no policy changes are made, increases in real private planned expenditure will shift the aggregate demand curve from AD_1 to AD_2, causing the price level to rise as the economy moves to a short-run equilibrium at E_2. In the long run, assuming nothing is done about aggregate demand, the price level would rise still more as the aggregate supply curve shifted upward and the economy moved toward a new long-run equilibrium at E_3. To prevent an increase in the price level, government purchases can be cut or net taxes increased to offset the projected change in private planned expenditure, thus restoring the aggregate demand curve to position AD_1.

their expectations regarding wages and other input prices. As a result, the short-run aggregate supply curve will shift upward to AS_2. As real output falls back to its natural level, the price level will continue to rise until it reaches a new long-run equilibrium at P_3.

Restrictive fiscal policy is one way of warding off the inflation threat. The federal budget for the coming year can be written in such a way as to combine cuts in government purchases and increases in net taxes that will offset the projected increases in private aggregate demand. Suppose that the multiplier is 4, as in our earlier examples. For each $100 by which aggregate demand is projected to shift beyond the level needed to reach the natural level of real output, government purchases can be cut by $25 or net taxes increased by enough to produce the same shift in aggregate demand. The right combination of cuts in government purchases, cuts in transfer payments, and increases in taxes will hold the aggregate demand curve in the desired position at AD_1.

EXPANSIONARY FISCAL POLICY AS A SOURCE OF INFLATION   In the preceding example, federal policy makers are the "good guys," crafting a sensible budget designed to restrain inflation. That is the role we would hope for them to play. However, the same diagram could be used to tell a different story.

In this scenario the economy is in equilibrium at E_1 and forecasters expect it to stay there. However, there is an election coming up. Members of Congress would like to please the voters by boosting federal benefits, cutting taxes, and initiating public works projects. The president, who is also up for reelection, would like to conduct the coming campaign in an atmosphere of rising real output and falling unemployment. Seeing their common interests, Congress and the president craft a strongly expansionary budget for the upcoming election year. When the expansionary budget first goes into effect, the economy moves from E_1 to E_2 in Figure 13.2. As hoped, real output expands and unemployment falls, with only a moderate increase in the price level. Voters are pleased, and everyone is reelected.

The next year, however, wages and other input prices begin to rise. As firms adjust their expectations to the new circumstances, not only does inflation of final goods prices continue but real output falls and the unemployment rate rises. The hangover from the election party sets in.

Automatic Fiscal Policy

The type of fiscal policy discussed so far—changes in the laws regarding government purchases, taxes, and transfer payments designed to increase or decrease aggregate demand—is known as **discretionary fiscal policy**. In practice, however, the levels of government purchases and net taxes can change even if no discretionary changes are made in the laws governing them. The reason is that many tax and spending laws are written in such a way that the levels of fiscal policy variables change automatically as economic conditions vary. Such changes in government purchases or net taxes, which are known as **automatic fiscal policy**, are most closely associated with changes in real output, the price level, and interest rates.

CHANGES IN REAL OUTPUT   The level of real output is important because it affects both tax revenues and outlays. An increase in real output increases real revenues from all major tax sources, including income taxes, social security payroll taxes, taxes on corporate profits, and sales taxes. At the same time, an increase in real output cuts real government outlays for transfer payments. This occurs largely because increases in real output are associated with decreases in the unemployment rate. Taking both effects together, an increase in real domestic product tends to reduce the federal budget deficit in both real and nominal terms.

CHANGES IN THE PRICE LEVEL   An increase in the price level affects both sides of the federal budget. With real output held constant, an increase in the price level

Discretionary fiscal policy
_____
Changes in the laws regarding government purchases and net taxes.

Automatic fiscal policy
_____
Changes in government purchases or net taxes that are caused by changes in economic conditions given unchanged tax and spending laws.

tends to increase federal tax receipts in nominal terms. At the same time, an increase in the price level tends to increase nominal expenditures. This is partly because most major transfer programs are now indexed so that they can be adjusted for changes in the cost of living and partly because inflation raises the prices of the goods and services that government buys. However, as pointed out before, some elements of government expenditures are fixed in nominal terms. This means that the increase in nominal expenditures will tend to be less than proportional to the increase in the price level.

On balance, nominal taxes rise more than nominal expenditures when the price level increases. Thus, an increase in the price level, other things being equal, reduces the deficit in both real and nominal terms.

CHANGES IN INTEREST RATES   An increase in nominal interest rates raises the nominal cost of financing the national debt. This is only slightly offset by increases in nominal government interest income. Therefore, on balance, an increase in nominal interest rates shifts the budget toward deficit in both nominal and real terms.

AUTOMATIC STABILIZATION   We have seen that when the economy expands real output rises, the price level rises, and unemployment falls. Each of these effects tends to move the government budget toward surplus in real terms, that is, to increase receipts, depress outlays, or both. Whichever side of the budget we look at, then, automatic fiscal policy operates so as to restrain aggregate demand during an expansion. By the same token, when the economy slows down, the growth rate of real output drops and unemployment rises. The inflation rate slows even if the contraction is not severe enough to cause the price level actually to fall. Thus, during a contraction the real budget swings toward deficit.

Because automatic fiscal policy operates to offset changes in other elements of planned expenditure, such budget components as income taxes and unemployment benefits are known as **automatic stabilizers**. These mechanisms serve to moderate the economy's response to changes in consumption, private planned investment, and net exports.

Automatic stabilizers
_____

Those elements of automatic fiscal policy that move the federal budget toward deficit during an economic contraction and toward surplus during an expansion.

THE BUDGET PROCESS

Our discussion of fiscal policy would be incomplete without at least a brief discussion of how federal officials actually go about making tax and spending decisions. In practice, the decision-making process for fiscal policy often has little to do with the theory of discretionary policy that we have just discussed. Herbert Stein, a former chairman of the Council of Economic Advisers, once wrote that "We have no long-run budget policy—no policy for the size of deficits and for the rate of growth of the public debt over a period of years." Each year, according to Stein, the president and Congress make short-term budgetary decisions that are wholly inconsistent with their declared long-run goals, hoping "that something will happen or be done before the long-run arises, but not yet."[2]

The Federal Budgetary System

In discussing the theory of fiscal policy, it is convenient to refer to unnamed "policy makers" who manipulate taxes, transfers, and government purchases. In practice, however, no single agency is responsible for fiscal policy. Budgetary authority is divided between the executive branch, headed by the president, and Congress. Also, budgetary policy must serve many goals, ranging from national security and social equity to simple political ambition, as well as price stability, full employment, and economic growth.

THE BUDGETARY PROCESS   A brief look at the federal budgetary process will indicate where the formal authority for fiscal policy lies. The U.S. government operates on a **fiscal year** that runs from October through September. For example, fiscal 2006 runs from October 1, 2005, through September 30, 2006. About 18 months before the beginning of a fiscal year, the executive branch begins preparing the budget. The Office of Management and Budget (OMB) takes the lead in this process. It receives advice from the Council of Economic Advisers (CEA) and the Department of the Treasury. After an outline of the budget has been drawn up, it is sent to the various departments and agencies. Within the executive branch, a period of bargaining ensues in which the Pentagon argues for more defense spending, the Department of Transportation for more highway funds, and so on. During this process the OMB is supposed to act as a restraining force, keeping macroeconomic goals in mind.

By January—nine months before the fiscal year starts—the president must submit the budget to Congress. After the budget has been submitted, Congress assumes the lead in the budgetary process. Its committees and subcommittees look at the president's proposals for the programs and agencies under their jurisdiction. The Congressional Budget Office (CBO) employs a staff of professionals who advise the committees on economic matters, in somewhat the same way that the OMB and CEA advise the president. In May the House and Senate are expected to pass a first budget resolution that sets forth overall spending targets and revenue goals.

Bargaining among committees, between the House and the Senate, and between Congress and the executive branch continues throughout the summer. During this period committees prepare specific spending and tax laws; these are supposed to be guided by the May resolution. Finally, in September, Congress is supposed to pass a second budget resolution that sets binding limits on spending and taxes for the fiscal year beginning October 1. Any bills passed earlier that do not fit within these guidelines are expected to be changed accordingly.

LIMITATIONS OF THE BUDGETARY PROCESS   In practice, many things can—and do—go wrong with this process.

Fiscal year

The federal government's budgetary year, which starts on October 1 of the preceding calendar year.

The first and most basic problem is that macroeconomic goals—full employment, price stability, and economic growth—carry little weight in the actual budgetary process. Tax and spending decisions are made in dozens of subcommittees, where they are dominated by interest group pressures, vote trading, and the desire of each member of Congress to help the folks at home.

A second problem is that Congress has not always been willing to follow its own rules. The required budget resolutions often are not passed on time; if they are passed, they are not treated as binding. Sometimes the fiscal year starts without a budget. Then agencies must operate on the basis of "continuing resolutions," meaning that they can go on doing whatever they were doing the year before. In 1995, the government shut down for six days in November when Congress failed to pass appropriations bills. According to a document released by the Clinton administration, the government shutdown cost $700–$800 million, including $400 million to furloughed federal employees who were paid, but did not report to work. The Treasury Department reported another $400 million in lost revenue over the four days that the IRS enforcement divisions were closed. More recently in 2003, lawmakers used the threat of a government shutdown to tack provisions on to the needed appropriations bills that benefit their individual districts and states.

Entitlements
***
Transfer payments governed by long-term laws that are not subject to annual budget review.

Next, there is the problem of so-called mandatory or uncontrollable costs. These include **entitlements**, which are transfer programs governed by long-term laws that are not subject to annual budget review. Examples include social security, military retirement pay, and Medicare. Another major expense that is uncontrollable—for a different reason—is interest on the national debt. Total interest expense is determined by the size of the debt and market interest rates, which, in turn, are beyond the control of fiscal policy. Today well over half of the federal budget is in the "uncontrollable" category. Congress could control most of these costs by passing new laws to replace the current ones, but doing so is not part of the normal budgetary process.

Finally, there are emergency items that cannot be predicted. Modest amounts are included in regular budgets to cover costs of natural disasters such as hurricanes, but some expenses exceed the budgeted emergency allowances. Since 2003, the most glaring example has been spending on the war in Iraq. The Bush administration has not included Iraq war expenditures in its regular budget; instead, it has asked for annual supplemental appropriations to cover the cost of the war. In 2003 through 2005, these totaled nearly $300 billion dollars. In contrast, aside from just one emergency appropriation, the entire cost of the Vietnam war was financed within the normal budget process.

FISCAL POLICY AND THE FEDERAL DEFICIT

The federal budget deficit has remained a concern for federal and state lawmakers since the large U.S. deficits in the 1980s. Indeed, prior to the Great Depression

FIGURE 13.3   FEDERAL GOVERNMENT DEFICIT/SURPLUS (BILLIONS OF DOLLARS, 1962–2004)

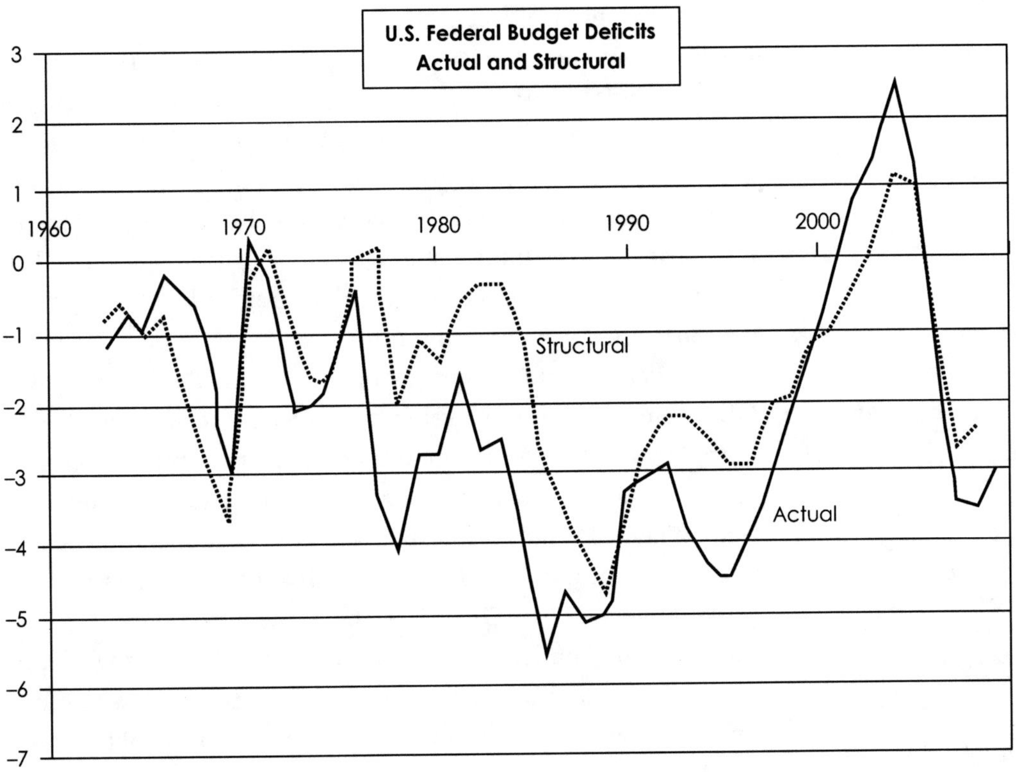

This figure shows two views of the U.S. federal surplus or deficit from 1962 to 2004. The actual surplus or deficit measures the difference between each year's revenues and outlays. The structural deficit is corrected to remove the influence of the business cycle. It can be interpreted as showing what the deficit would have been, given each year's tax and spending laws, if the economy had been at its natural level of GDP in that year.

Source: Congressional Budget Office, *The Economic and Budget Outlook: Fiscal Years 2004–2013*, January 2003, Appendix F, Historical Budget Data, Table 1.

(1929–1933), one of the primary goals of fiscal policy was to balance the budget. We begin this section by examining the origins of the record deficits of recent years, which lie in both discretionary and automatic elements of fiscal policy. We then turn to the controversy over the effects of the deficit on the economy as a whole.

Figure 13.3 gives two views of the U.S. government budget over time. The actual budget deficit measures the difference between each year's revenues and outlays. Deficit is the norm. From 1962 through 1997, there was only one small surplus, in 1969. The deficit hit a record of 5.1 percent of GDP in 1985. The economic boom of the 1990s caused revenues to grow faster than outlays, so that by 1998, the budget achieved a surplus. This lasted for four years until recession, tax cuts, and rising defense spending brought the surpluses to an end.

Automatic Fiscal Policy: The Structural Versus Cyclical Deficit

The second view of deficit separates the impact of changes in discretionary policy decisions from the effect of the business cycle. Policymakers do not determine actual levels of government receipts and expenditures. Rather, they pass laws setting tax rates, formulas for transfer payments, and goals for purchases of goods and services. Given these laws, the actual levels of receipts and expenditures depend on the stage of the business cycle. As we have seen, the budget shifts toward deficit when the economy contracts, as tax collections fall and transfer payments rise. Similarly, during expansions the budget shifts toward surplus. As discussed at the beginning of the chapter, the federal government budget is a combination of discretionary fiscal policy decisions and economic conditions.

Structural budget

The budget surplus or deficit that the federal government would incur given current tax and spending laws and unemployment at its natural rate.

The federal budget surplus or deficit that the federal government would run if GDP were at its natural level in a given year is called the **structural budget**. Changes in the structural budget are interpreted as representing discretionary fiscal policy. The difference between the structural and actual budget is called the **cyclical deficit/surplus**. When GDP falls below its natural rate and unemployment rises above its natural rate, the cyclical deficit becomes positive because the structural budget exceeds the actual budget. When GDP rises above the benchmark, the structural budget is less than the actual budget, causing a cyclical surplus. Changes in the cyclical deficit/surplus reflect changes in taxes and spending that occur automatically as real output, unemployment, and inflation change over the course of the business cycle.

Cyclical deficit/surplus

The difference between the structural budget and the actual federal budget. If the actual budget is above the structural budget, there is a cyclical surplus. Likewise, when the actual budget is below the structural budget, there is a cyclical deficit.

As Figure 13.3 shows, changes in policy, reflected in the structural deficit, account for the greater part of variations in the actual deficit since 1962. In the early 1980s and early 1990s, when real GDP was below its natural level, the cyclical deficit added to substantial structural deficits. The surpluses of the late 1990s were in part structural, due to increase in taxes relative to outlays, and partly cyclical, due to the economic boom. Similarly, the deficits of the early 2000s were in part cyclical, due to the recession of 2001 and its lingering effects in the next few years, and partly structural, due to the tax cuts and spending increases under the Bush administration.

Economic Priorities

As we have indicated, U.S. federal taxes and spending are the joint result of political decisions reached by the executive branch and Congress. For much of the past 40 years, these have represented compromises between the two main U.S. political parties, one of which held the presidency and the other of which controlled at least one branch of Congress. It is hard to judge budget priorities from political rhetoric alone. Both parties like to provide voters with benefits and promise moderate taxes. Both profess to think that deficits are bad, defending the country is good, and providing income security, especially for the elderly, is sacrosanct. To find which of these priorities has dominated, we need to look at the numbers, as given in Figure 13.4.

FIGURE 13.4   REVENUE AND SPENDING TRENDS FOR THE U.S. FEDERAL GOVERNMENT

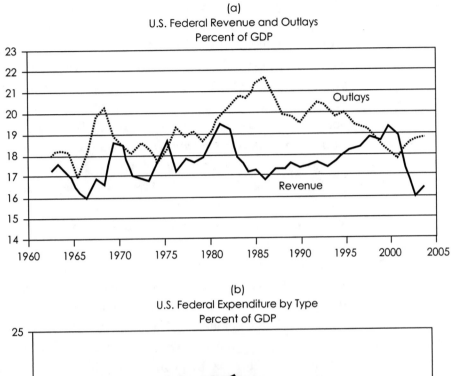

(a)
U.S. Federal Revenue and Outlays
Percent of GDP

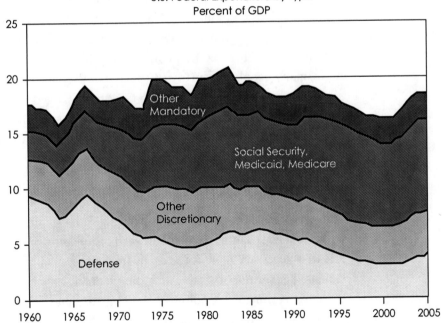

(b)
U.S. Federal Expenditure by Type
Percent of GDP

Part a of this figure shows trends in total outlays and revenues as a percent of GDP. They show that the large deficits of the Reagan and George W. Bush administrations were due not solely to tax cuts, but also to spending increases. Part b shows that over the long term, defense spending has decreased as a percentage of GDP while Social Security, Medicare, and Medicaid have increased markedly. Other components of spending, and the total as a percentage of GDP, have varied from year to year around an approximately flat trend.

Source: Congressional Budget Office, *The Economic and Budget Outlook: Fiscal Years 2006–2015,* January 2005, Appendix F, Historical Budget Data, Tables F-8 and F-10.

Part a of Figure 13.4, which shows separate series for federal revenues and outlays, provides additional insight into the origins of deficits and surpluses. We see that the largest deficits (those of the first Regan administration in the early 1980s and the George W. Bush administration of the early 2000s) were the result of a combination of tax cuts and increased outlays. In both cases, a significant part of the increased outlays were defense expenditures. Periods of narrowing deficits (the late 1980s) and surpluses (the late 1990s) occurred during periods of rapidly expanding GDP. During such periods, the economy as a whole tends to grow faster than federal spending, so budget outlays decrease as a percentage of GDP without being cut in absolute terms. At the same time, tax laws are written in a way that tends to make total tax revenues increase as a percentage of GDP unless there are changes in tax laws.

Part b of Figure 13.4 breaks down total outlays into four categories. As the figure shows, there has been a long-term decrease in defense spending relative to GDP. Although in absolute terms the United States today spends about as much on defense as the entire rest of the world put together, defense spending as a percent of GDP has risen only a little above its post–Cold War low point. By far the greatest increase in federal outlays have come in the "entitlements" categories of Social Security, Medicare, and Medicaid. These outlays reflect the increased size and political influence of older people in the U.S. population. The category "other discretionary" spending includes a great variety of programs, ranging from farm subsidies to road building to space exploration. Considering the frequency with which these spending categories make the news, many people are surprised to see that they account for a relatively small part of all spending. Their share relative to GDP has changed little over time. Much the same can be said for the category "other mandatory" spending, which includes items like unemployment compensation and interest on the federal debt.

International Comparisons

Our perspective on government spending in the United States would be incomplete without at least a brief comparison with other countries. To make such a comparison, it is first necessary to shift the focus from the federal government budget to the consolidated government sector, including federal, state, and local branches. The reason is that government spending in the United States is much less centralized than in countries like France or Japan, so that comparisons of central government spending alone would be misleading. As Figure 13.5a shows, spending on direct federal programs in the United States accounted for about 17 percent of GDP as of 1998, and state and local government spending for about 12 percent of GDP. About a quarter of state and local government spending (accounting for about 3 percent of GDP) was financed by federal grants rather than state and local tax revenues.

Part b of Figure 13.5 compares total government spending in the United States with that in other industrialized countries. Government spending in the United States accounts for a smaller share of GDP than in any of the other countries shown. Only

FIGURE 13.5 **INTERNATIONAL COMPARISONS OF GOVERNMENT SPENDING**

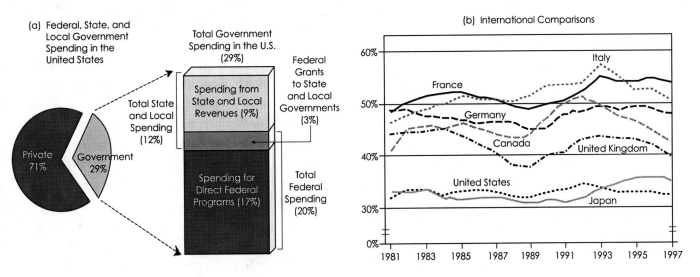

Government spending in the United States is less centralized than in many other countries. As part a shows, direct federal spending on federal programs accounts for just 17 percent of GDP, compared with 29 percent when all levels of government are included. Part b shows that total government spending in the United States accounts for a smaller percentage of GDP than in other high-income countries.

Source: Government Printing Office, GPO Access, Citizen's Guide to the Federal Budget,
http://www.gpoaccess.gov/usbudget /fy00/guide01.html#Chart1-2, Charts 1-1 and 1-2.

Japan comes close in the relatively small size of its government sector. This is especially remarkable when we take into account the fact U.S. defense expenditures account for nearly 4 percent of GDP, compared to 1 to 2 percent in the other countries shown.

The Deficit as a Policy Issue

In recent years, as federal red ink has reached record levels, the deficit has gained prominence as a policy issue. Ordinary people questioned in public opinion polls, joined by many professional economists, look on the deficit with foreboding. Can the government go on spending beyond its means forever? Does the deficit place a drag on economic growth? Does it represent a burden on future generations? We will see that there are sound reasons to be concerned. Before examining those reasons, however, we will look at the differing views of economists on the issue.

Reasons Not to Worry About the Deficit

Economists who argue that the federal deficit is not so great a problem begin by making a series of numerical adjustments, which suggest that the federal deficit is not really as large as it seems. We will look at four of these adjustments here.

ADJUSTING FOR THE STATE AND LOCAL SURPLUS　The first adjustment is based on the notion that it is not the federal deficit that matters but the combined deficit or surplus of federal, state, and local governments. Although the federal government has been in deficit for all but 4 years since 1970, state and local governments have been in surplus in all but four of those years. The state and local surpluses represent a flow of saving into financial markets that can be used to finance private investment and the federal deficit. For example, when the federal budget deficit hit a record $190 billion in 1986, state and local governments offset more than 10% of that with a $21 billion surplus. However, this argument does not seem to apply to the current round of deficits. In 2002 and 2003, as the federal budget again recorded record deficits, combined state and local government budgets were in deficit also.

ADJUSTING FOR THE CYCLICAL COMPONENT　When one assesses the impact of fiscal policy on the economy, one should also adjust the federal deficit to remove its cyclical component. The reason is that the cyclical component reflects the state of the economy rather than discretionary policy decisions. Data on the actual and structural deficits were shown earlier in Figure 13.3. For example, in 2004, when the actual deficit was 3.5 percent of GDP, the structural deficit was just 2.4 percent of GDP. It is often argued that the cyclical component of the deficit (1.1 percent of GDP in 2004) is beneficial since it reflects automatic stabilizers that help to moderate the business cycle.

ADJUSTING FOR INFLATION　A third adjustment is needed to take the effects of inflation into account. Each year inflation erodes the real value of the federal debt held by the public. For example, if the nominal value of federal debt in the hands of private investors were $1 trillion and the inflation rate were 4 percent, private investors would have to buy almost $40 billion in newly issued government securities just to keep the real value of the total debt constant. This part of the deficit, it is argued, puts no real burden on the rest of the economy because, in real terms, it simply returns investors to the same position they started from. In recent years, as the rate of inflation has fallen, this adjustment is less significant, but it still works to reduce the economic impact of the deficit.

THE DEFICIT AND PRIVATE SAVING　Some economists offer another, rather different reason not to worry about the deficit. This is based on Robert Barro's argument, mentioned in *Applying Economic Ideas 13.1*, that changes in taxes tend to be fully offset by changes in private saving. If this is true, the public would respond to a tax cut by increasing saving by just the amount needed to buy the extra securities the Treasury would have to sell in order to finance the added deficit. Likewise, a tax increase made to reduce the deficit would decrease saving by the same amount, leaving no additional resources with which to finance private investment. However, the data presented earlier in the chapter suggest that this argument, too, is weaker in the case of recent deficits than in earlier years.

Reasons to Worry About the Deficit

Despite the arguments just given, many economists—probably the majority—still worry about current and projected federal budget deficits. Let's look at some of their concerns.

EFFECTS ON INVESTMENT   Earlier in the chapter we saw that when the Treasury borrows to finance a deficit, it adds to total demand for the limited funds made available by private domestic saving, thereby pushing up interest rates. Private borrowers are then crowded out of financial markets. The reduction in private investment is a burden on the economy that slows economic growth and reduces the living standards of future generations. In the early 2000s, as federal budget deficits grew, interest rates remained surprisingly low. As a result, the impact of the deficit on investment was less than it might have been. Whether interest rates will remain low if the budget continues to show a large deficit is a matter of some controversy.

BORROWING FROM ABROAD   In defense of deficits it used to be said that the national debt is something "we owe to ourselves." In other words, taxes collected to repay the debt come out of the pockets of some U.S. citizens but go back into the pockets of others, leaving the country as a whole no poorer. However, federal budget deficits push up interest rates in the United States relative to those in the rest of the world. Attracted by the high rates, foreign buyers purchase many of the securities that the Treasury sells to finance the deficit. In addition, because high interest rates on government securities push up the rates on competing private securities, many private U.S. securities also move into foreign hands.3 Repaying the part of public and private debt owed to foreign investors places a real future burden on the U.S. economy, so the argument that we owe it to ourselves does not apply. As recently as 1993, just 20 percent of the federal debt was owed to foreign investors. Today, the figure is about half.

THE ENLARGED STRUCTURAL DEFICIT   It is widely acknowledged that any cyclical component of a federal deficit is less of a problem than the structural component. What worried many economists in the early 1980s was the way the structural component grew during the 1980s even as the cyclical component fell. The structural deficit was not eliminated until 1999. In the early 2000s, the pattern seems to be repeating itself. By 2004, tax cuts and spending increases not only eliminated the structural surplus (which, arguably, could be seen as a drag on economic growth) but have sent the structural deficit back to levels not seen since the 1980s.

THE DANGER OF AN "EXPLODING" DEFICIT   The growth of the structural deficit calls attention to still another worry: the increase in the part of the deficit associated with interest payments on the debt.

In the explosive-growth scenario, the amount of borrowing needed just to make interest payments on the debt is so great that the debt grows faster than domestic income even if the rest of the budget remains in balance. As the government borrows more and more each year to make interest payments, it adds to the demand for loanable funds in credit markets. This pushes interest rates higher, making it necessary to borrow even more to make the interest payments. Eventually the deficit "explodes" and threatens to swallow the entire domestic income.[4]

As the point of explosive growth approaches, the government is left with only one way out. It begins to "monetize" the deficit, which in effect means that it finances the deficit by creating new money rather than by borrowing. But financing deficits with newly created money is the classic formula for inflation. Thus, monetization of the deficit converts an explosive deficit into explosive inflation.

Is this scenario too farfetched to be a real threat? Not at all. Creating new money to cover the government deficit is the source of the runaway inflations (at annual rates of 1,000 percent per year and more) that devastated such countries as Bolivia, Argentina, Brazil, and Israel in the early 1980s. Today inflation is not running out of control in the United States; in fact, it has slowed dramatically from the double-digit rates of the late 1970s and early 1980s. Nevertheless, many economists think that continuing large federal deficits are a potential danger that cannot be ignored.

SUMMARY

1. **How can fiscal policy be used to fight recession and inflation?** *Fiscal policy* means policy that is related to government purchases and net taxes. If a decrease in private planned expenditure threatens to send the economy into a recession, an increase in government purchases or a cut in net taxes can be used to shift the aggregate demand curve to the right, thereby restoring the economy to its natural level of real output. If an excess of private planned expenditure threatens the economy with inflation, a cut in government purchases or an increase in net taxes can shift the aggregate demand curve to the left, thereby restoring stability.

2. **How are government receipts and expenditures affected by changing economic conditions?** Some changes in government receipts and expenditures reflect *discretionary* changes in the laws that govern fiscal policy. However, changes in the levels of these items can also result *automatically* from changes in economic conditions, including real output, unemployment, and the price level. In general, economic expansion tends to raise receipts and restrain expenditures, thereby moving the budget toward surplus. Contraction tends to lower receipts and raise expenditures, thereby moving the budget toward deficit. These automatic changes in receipts and expenditures damp the economy's response to shifts in private planned expenditure and, hence, are known as *automatic stabilizers*.

3. **How does the federal budgetary system work, and what are the limitations of that system?** In the United States authority for fiscal policy is divided between the president and Congress. Each year the president submits a budget plan, which Congress modifies and enacts into law by the beginning of the *fiscal year* on October 1. In practice, macroeconomic goals play a secondary role to political considerations in setting budget priorities.

4. **How is the federal deficit measured, and why has it grown?** The federal deficit can be divided into a cyclical component and a structural component. The *structural deficit* is the estimated level of the deficit, given current tax and spending laws and unemployment at the natural rate. The *cyclical deficit* is the difference between the actual and structural deficits; it tends to increase during a recession and to decrease during an expansion. If unemployment drops below the natural rate at the peak of an expansion, the cyclical deficit becomes negative (that is, there is a cyclical surplus). During the expansion that followed the 1981–1982 recession, the cyclical component of the deficit declined nearly to zero while the structural component grew dramatically. The actual deficit then ballooned during the 1991–1992 recession. Both the actual and structural budgets went into a surplus during the mid- to late-1990s, only to plummet again in the early 2000s.

5. **Are large federal deficits a threat to economic stability?** Some economists argue that if the federal deficit is adjusted for state and local government surpluses, the cyclical component of the deficit, capital expenditures, and the effects of inflation, it looks somewhat less threatening. Others claim that the deficit crowds out private investment. They are also concerned about borrowing from abroad to finance the deficit and the possibility that explosive growth of the deficit could ultimately cause severe inflation.

KEY TERMS

Fiscal policy

Net tax multiplier

Discretional fiscal policy

Automatic fiscal policy

Automatic stabilizers

Fiscal year

Entitlements

Structural budget

Cyclical deficit/surplus

PROBLEMS AND TOPICS FOR DISCUSSION

1. **Discretionary spending.** Suppose that in response to a foreign crisis, the government increases defense spending by $50 billion. Assuming no other changes in government policy and an expenditure multiplier of 4, how would a defense spending increase of that magnitude affect the economy? On the basis of what you have learned in this chapter, what can you say about whether such an increase in defense spending would help or harm the economy?

2. **Applying the multiplier.** Suppose that real output is at its natural level in the current year but forecasts show that if no action is taken, the aggregate demand curve will shift to the left by $500 billion in the coming year. Assuming a multiplier of 2.5, what change in real government purchases will be needed to keep real output at the natural level?

3. **A balanced budget amendment.** From time to time it has been proposed that a law or constitutional amendment be passed that will force the federal government to balance its budget every year Do you think it would be possible to keep the actual budget deficit at zero each year, or should such an amendment aim only to keep the structural deficit at zero? Discuss.

4. **Foreign governments and the federal debt.** In recent years, the biggest buyers of U.S. government securities used to finance the deficit have been foreign governments, especially those of China and Japan. In what ways do foreign government purchases of U.S. securities make the size of the deficit more of a worry than if they had been sold to U.S. investors instead? In what ways do they make the deficit less of a worry?

CASE FOR DISCUSSION

Did California Spend Its Way into a Fiscal Crisis?

At the end of 2003, California had a projected $38.2 billion state budget deficit. Unlike the federal government, California cannot simply borrow when it experiences a shortfall in receipts. State governments may borrow only if voters approve bond measures on the state ballot. With California's credit rating in jeopardy, voters may be reluctant to approve bonds to finance state deficits.

The media has been quick to blame the California's current budget crisis on excessive spending during the 1990s. A closer examination of the data indicates that state government expenditures have grown at a slower rate since the 1989–1990 fiscal year. Much of the spending growth that occurred in the late 1990s represented the restoration of cuts made during the budget crisis of the early 1990s.

State government spending grew rapidly during 1959–1969 (8.8 percent) and 1969–1979 (6.8 percent), compared with only 1% growth between 1989 and 2002. The biggest growth in spending during the 1989–2002 period was in K–12 education, reflecting California's booming population growth.

This leaves California's governor, Arnold Schwarzenegger, in a difficult position. During his campaign, he promised that he would not raise taxes, nor would he cut funding to education. In fact, making good a campaign promise, he repealed an increase in vehicle registration fees imposed by the previous governor. The California state legislature recently passed Governor Schwarzenegger's request to put a bond measure on the ballot, but this is only a temporary solution to a growing dilemma. The problems facing California's legislature and governors are not unique. As the federal government has reduced its contributions to state and local expenditures (see Table 13.1), states are struggling to cope.

Source: David Carroll, "Did California Spend its Way into a Fiscal Crisis?" California Budget Project, May 2003.

QUESTIONS

1. Does the reduction in vehicle license fees in California count as fiscal policy even though it takes place at the state level? Why or why not?

2. Assuming a multiplier for the economy as a whole of 4, how would GDP be affected by $1 billion in California state budget cuts? By $650 million in California state tax increases?

3. Assume that all states cut spending and raise taxes when recession strikes. Does this make it easier or harder for the economy to recover from recession? What would happen if the federal government followed the same policy?

4. How do recent trends in federal outlays affect state and local budgets? Suppose Congress approves a tax cut, but reduces expenditures paid to state governments by the same amount. If the state government cannot borrow, how will it respond? How will this affect state and national production?

END NOTES

1. This is an approximation in that it assumes that interest rates, planned investment, and exchange rates are unaffected by the fiscal policy change. Chapter 14 will explain how the analysis of fiscal policy needs to be modified to take these factors into effect.

2. Herbert Stein, "After the Ball," *AEI Economist* (December 1984): 2.

3. These effects can also be expressed in terms of concepts that deal with international economic relations: An increase in the federal deficit, other things being equal, tends to move the financial account in the direction of a net financial inflow. This must be offset by a movement of the current account toward deficit. Thus, in an open economy, a federal deficit crowds out net exports as well as domestic investment.

4. The issue of the exploding deficit was raised in Thomas J. Sargent and Neil Wallace, "Some Unpleasant Monetarist Arithmetic," *Federal Reserve Bank of Minneapolis Quarterly Review* (Fall 1981): 1–17. Michael R. Darby refines the argument by showing that the deficit will explode if the real rate of interest (that is, the nominal market rate minus the inflation rate), adjusted for the average tax rate on federal interest payments, exceeds the long-term rate of growth of real GDP. See "Some Pleasant Monetarist Arithmetic," *Federal Reserve Bank of Minneapolis Quarterly Review* (Spring 1984).

CHAPTER 14

An Integrated View of Monetary and Fiscal Policy

After reading this chapter, you will understand:

1. How changes in the money stock affect real output, the price level, and unemployment
2. What is meant by the neutrality of money
3. How fiscal policy affects interest rates and planned investment
4. Keynesian and monetarist views of the Great Depression

Before reading this chapter, make sure you know the meaning of:

1. Elasticity
2. Real and nominal interest rates
3. Natural level of real output
4. Multiplier effect
5. Monetary sector
6. Transmission mechanism

IN CHAPTERS 11 AND 12 we looked at the monetary sector of the economy in isolation. In this chapter we return to the broader themes of inflation, real output, and employment and see how these are shaped by developments in the monetary sector. The goals of high employment, price stability, and economic growth require the president, Congress, and the Federal Reserve to work together. By combining a monetary sector model with the aggregate supply and demand model and the analysis of fiscal policy developed earlier, we will gain a better understanding of why both monetary and fiscal policy play important roles in economic policy, and why the two branches of policy need to be carefully coordinated.

SHORT-RUN EFFECTS OF MONETARY POLICY

The most important mechanism through which monetary policy affects the economy is the channel acting from monetary policy to planned investment via interest rates. Figure 14.1 shows the interest-investment transmission mechanism at work in the short run in response to a one-time expansion in the money stock.

Initially the monetary sector is in equilibrium at point E_1 in part (a) of the figure. The money supply curve is in the position MS_1, and the money demand curve is at MD_1; thus, the equilibrium interest rate is R_1. Part b of the figure shows a planned investment schedule, which gives a graphical view of the interest-rate transmission mechanism. According to the planned-investment schedule in part (b), interest rate R_1 will result in a level of real planned investment indicated by I_1. This level of planned investment is used as a basis for the aggregate demand curve AD_1 in part (c) along with given conditions regarding consumption, government purchases, and net exports. The initial equilibrium point in part (c) is thus e_1, at the intersection of AD_1 and the aggregate supply curve, AS. Equilibrium real output is y_1, and the price level is P_1.

Now assume that the Fed raises its target value for the money stock. This is shown in part (a) of Figure 14.1 as a rightward shift of the money supply curve to the position MS_2. The shift is accomplished by means of an injection of new reserves into the banking system via open market purchases.

As banks compete to put their new reserves to work, the interest rate falls. The falling interest rate lowers the opportunity cost of investment; thus, firms move downward and to the right along the planned-investment schedule shown in part (b). The increase in real planned investment, in turn, causes the aggregate demand curve to shift to the right, as shown in part (c). In response to the boost in demand, real output and the price level both increase and the economy moves upward and to the right along its short-run aggregate supply curve.

As the economy expands, the increase in prices and real output causes nominal domestic income to rise. Bringing the story full circle, the rise in nominal domestic income causes the money demand curve to shift to the right, from MD_1 to MD_2. This limits the fall in the interest rate, but the curve does not shift enough to prevent the interest rate from falling somewhat. The monetary sector comes into equilibrium at point E_2, where the new money supply and demand curves intersect. At the new equilibrium interest rate, R_2, real planned investment is I_2. This level of planned investment, together with the same underlying conditions as before regarding real consumption, government purchases, and net exports, puts the aggregate demand curve in the position AD_2. The new short-run equilibrium for the economy thus is e_2 in part (c), where real domestic product is y_2 and the price level is P_2.

FIGURE 14.1 **SHORT-RUN EFFECTS OF EXPANSIONARY MONETARY POLICY**

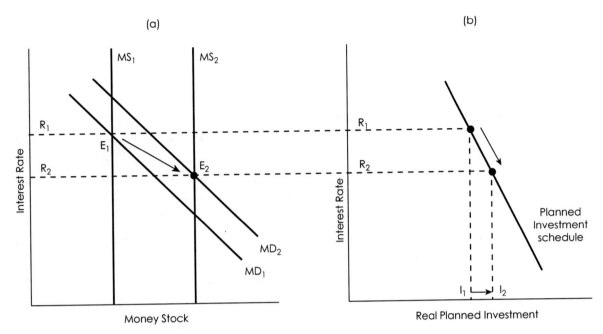

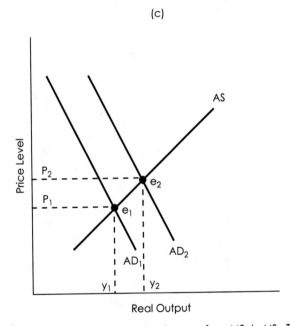

A one-time increase in the money stock shifts the money supply curve from MS_1 to MS_2. The interest rate begins to fall. Real planned investment begins to increase as the economy moves down and to the right along the planned-investment schedule. The increase in planned investment shifts the aggregate demand curve from AD_1 to AD_2, raising real output and the price level. The resulting rise in nominal domestic income shifts the money demand curve to the right from MD_1 to MD_2. This shift is enough to limit the drop in the interest rate but not sufficient to prevent it altogether. In the new short-run equilibrium, the interest rate is lower and real investment, real output, and the price level are all higher than they were initially.

To summarize, expansionary monetary policy has the following effects in the short run:

1.   A reduction in the interest rate

2.   An increase in the level of real output

3.   An increase in the price level

Contractionary policy produces an opposite set of short-run effects, as can also be shown using Figure 14.2. Starting at E_2 in the monetary sector, the Fed lowers its money stock target, shifting the money supply curve to the left. All the arrows are now reversed. A rising interest rate causes a reduction in planned investment. Falling planned investment shifts the aggregate demand curve to the left, causing prices and real output to fall. This, in turn, means that nominal income declines, causing the money demand curve to shift to the left as well, but not enough to prevent some increase in the interest rate. In the new short-run equilibrium, the monetary sector returns to E_1 and the economy as a whole returns to e_1.

FIGURE 14.2   LONG-RUN EFFECTS OF EXPANSIONARY MONETARY POLICY

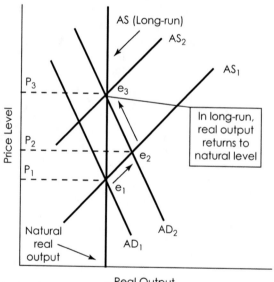

A one-time increase in the money stock causes real output to rise temporarily above its natural level, reaching point e_2. The economy cannot remain at this point indefinitely, however. As expected input prices begin to adjust upward, the aggregate supply curve will shift from AS_1 to AS_2. The economy will move along aggregate demand curve AD_2 until it reaches a new long-run equilibrium at e_3. As it does so, nominal domestic income will continue to rise, pushing interest rates up until they return to their initial level. Thus, in the long run, a one-time increase in the money stock will only induce a proportional increase in the price level and leave real output and the interest rate unchanged. This result is known as the *neutrality of money*.

LONG-RUN EFFECTS AND THE NEUTRALITY OF MONEY

Movements along the short-run curve are based on firms' expectation that input prices will not change immediately in response to a change in aggregate demand. However, a change in the prices of final goods will eventually affect the level of input prices. As the actual and expected values of input prices adjust to changes in the prices of final goods, the short-run aggregate supply curve shifts upward until the economy returns to equilibrium at the natural level of real output.

The economy will undergo such a process of long-run adjustment when the money stock changes and then remains at its new level. This process is shown in Figure 14.2.

As Figure 14.2 shows, expansionary monetary policy lowers interest rates and stimulates aggregate demand. As the aggregate demand curve shifts rightward, from AD_1 to AD_2, the economy moves to a new short-run equilibrium at e_2. Now let us see what happens next.

As the economy moves from e_1 to e_2, the average level of final-goods prices increases. After a time, this causes a change in the expected level of input prices to increase as well. This happens partly because some goods serve as both inputs and final goods and partly because the rise in the price level raises the cost of living, putting upward pressure on wage rates. Once this process begins to affect firms' expectations regarding input prices, the short-run aggregate supply curve begins to shift upward toward the position AS_2. As it does so, the economy moves up and to the left along aggregate demand curve AD_2 until, eventually, it returns to the natural level of real output at e_3. At that point both final-goods prices and input prices have adjusted upward in proportion to the initial increase in the money stock. For example, if the money stock increases by 10 percent, both final-goods prices and input prices will also increase by 10 percent.

We know that the aggregate demand curve is relatively inelastic. Therefore, as the economy moves up and to the left along the curve, the percentage increase in price is greater than the percentage decrease in real output. This, in turn, means that nominal domestic income and product will increase. In the monetary sector, the increase in nominal domestic income will put upward pressure on real interest rates, eventually pushing them all the way back up to the level they were at before expansionary monetary policy was undertaken. Real planned investment, which had increased while interest rates were lower, decreases again as interest rates rise until investment, too, is back where it started.

The preceding analysis shows that a one-time increase in the money stock has the following long-run effects:

1. An increase in the equilibrium levels of both final-goods and input prices in proportion to the change in the money stock

2. No change in the equilibrium level of real output

3. No change in the equilibrium interest rate

**Neutrality
of Money**

The proposition that
in the long run a
one-time change
in the money stock
affects only the
price level and
not real output,
employment,
interest rates, or
real planned
investment.

This set of conclusions is called the principle of the **neutrality of money**. Money is neutral in the sense that one-time changes in its level do not affect the long-run equilibrium values of real variables such as real output, real planned investment, employment, or real interest rates. In the long run, a one-time change in the money stock affects only price levels.

The principle of the neutrality of money has a long history in economics. It was stated clearly by Adam Smith's friend David Hume (see *Who Said It? Who Did It? 14.1*). It can also be stated in terms of the equation of exchange. If the terms are rearranged, the equation of exchange can be written in the form $P = MV/y$. As we know, the value of velocity depends on the interest rate. Because the long-run equilibrium value of the interest rate is not affected by a one-time change in the money stock, velocity, too, will be unaffected by such a change. Thus, the equation just given tells us that if y is held constant at its natural level and V is unchanged, a one-time change in the money stock will produce a proportional change in the price level. For example, a doubling of the money stock has the long-run effect of doubling the price level from P_1 to P_3.

 WHO SAID IT? WHO DID IT? 14.1

DAVID HUME ON THE NEUTRALITY OF MONEY

David Hume was an early member of the classical school of economics, as well as a noted historian and philosopher. Born in 1711, he was a colleague of Adam Smith at Edinburgh University. He much admired Smith's *Wealth of Nations*, which was published in 1776, the year Hume died. Although today Smith's contributions to economics overshadow Hume's, many of Hume's writings are regarded as insightful for his time.

Eighteenth-century economists widely agreed that an increase in the money stock—chiefly gold and silver coins at the time—would raise the price level. Price increases had been observed, for example, when the Spanish began bringing gold back to Europe from the New World. A less settled question was whether an increase in the money stock would also "stimulate industry"—that is, cause real output to increase. Today we would say that the issue concerns whether or not money is "neutral."

On that subject, Hume says that although an increase in the price of goods is a "necessary consequence" of an increase in the stock of gold and silver, "it follows not immedi-

ately." The change in the money stock does not affect all markets at once: "At first, no alteration is perceived; by degrees the price rises, first of one commodity, then of another; till the whole at last reaches a just proportion with the new quantity of [money]." Agreeing with the modern theory that the stimulus to real output during this phase is only temporary, Hume continues: "In my opinion, it is only in this interval or intermediate situation, between the acquisition of money and the rise of prices, that the increasing quantity of gold and silver is favorable to industry." In Hume's view, there is no long-run effect on real output. In the long run, unlike the short run, money is neutral. A one-time change in the quantity of money has a lasting proportional effect on the price level but on nothing else.

Source: David Hume, "Of Money," in his *Writings on Economics*, ed. Eugene Rotwein (Madison: University of Wisconsin Press, 1955). Quotations from Hume are taken from Thomas M. Humphrey, "The Early History of the Phillips Curve," *Economic Review* (September–October 1985).

MONEY AND FISCAL POLICY

In Chapter 13, we examined the effects of fiscal policy on planned expenditure and the equilibrium level of real output. We saw that an increase in government purchases or a decrease in net taxes causes an increase in aggregate demand. Now, in this section, we will put our analysis of fiscal policy together with material from earlier chapters to show how changes in fiscal policy interact with developments in the monetary sector.

The Crowding-out Effect

Figure 14.3 presents the expanded analysis of the effects of fiscal policy, taking the monetary sector into account. Initially the economy is in equilibrium at point e_1 in part (c). Real output is at its natural level, y_1; the price level is at P_1 and stable. The monetary sector, shown in part (a), is in equilibrium at E_1 with an interest rate of R_1. This interest rate results in real planned investment at the level I_1, as shown in part (b). This level of planned investment, together with consumption, government purchases, and net exports, determines the level of total planned expenditure.

Now the government undertakes expansionary fiscal policy in the form of, say, an increase in real government purchases. (A cut in taxes or an increase in transfer payments would have essentially the same effects.) The result is a rightward shift of the aggregate demand curve. The economy begins to expand. The price level and real output both increase as the economy moves up and to the right along the short-run aggregate supply curve.

Next consider the effects on the monetary sector, shown in part (a) of Figure 14.3. Because both prices and real output are increasing, nominal domestic income must also be rising. The money demand curve therefore shifts to the right. With the money supply curve unchanged, interest rates rise. As they do so, firms move up and to the left along the planned-investment schedule shown in part (b). The level of real planned investment begins to fall, partly offsetting the initial expansionary effect of the decrease in government purchases.

Crowding-out effect

The tendency of expansionary fiscal policy to raise the interest rate and thereby cause a decrease in real planned investment.

This tendency for an increase in government purchases to cause a decrease in real private planned investment is known as the **crowding-out effect**. The crowding out of real investment spending limits the expansion of real output. In Figure 14.3 the economy reaches a new short-run equilibrium at point e_2 in part (c), where real output is at y_2 and the price level at P_2. This point corresponds to point E_2 in part (a) of the figure. In the new short-run equilibrium, both the price level and real output are lower than they would be if the indirect effect of government purchases on interest rates and investment had not been taken into account.

In an earlier chapter we discussed the effects of fiscal policy in terms of the multiplier effect. Now we see that because of crowding out, a given increase in government purchases shifts the aggregate demand curve by less than the simple multiplier

FIGURE 14.3   THE CROWDING-OUT EFFECT

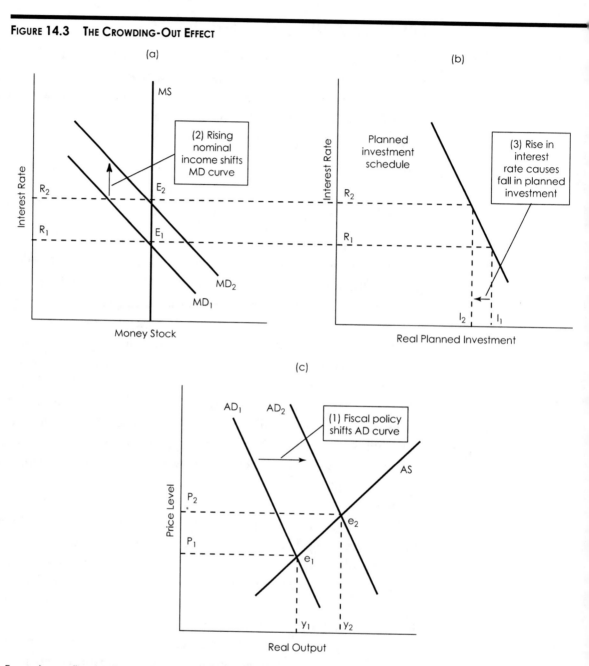

Expansionary fiscal policy shifts the aggregate demand curve to the right from AD_1 to AD_2, as shown in part (c). The resulting increase in nominal domestic income shifts the money demand curve to the right from MD_1 to MD_2, as shown in part (a). As interest rates rise, real planned investment will decrease and the economy will move to the left along the planned-investment schedule shown in part (b). The tendency of expansionary fiscal policy to reduce private planned investment is known as the *crowding-out effect*.

applied to government purchases would imply. Suppose, for example, that the multiplier is 4 and the change in government purchases is $100 billion. Multiplying these two numbers would lead one to expect a $400 billion shift. But in practice the shift is less because the expansionary effect of the increase in government purchases is partially offset by a decrease in private planned investment.[1] What is more, the price increases caused by the shift in aggregate demand push interest rates up still higher and further reduce planned investment.

Fiscal Policy in the Long Run

Fiscal policy is no more able than monetary policy to permanently raise real domestic product above its natural level. Figure 14.4 picks up where Figure 14.3 left off; it shows the long-run effects of expansionary fiscal policy.

Expansionary policy has shifted the aggregate demand curve in part (c) from AD_1 to AD_2, moving the economy to a short-run equilibrium at e_2. Compared with the situation in the initial equilibrium, e_1, real output is above the natural level and the level of final-goods prices has increased. Over time, as the rise in the prices of final goods begins to affect the expected level of input prices, the short-run aggregate supply curve shifts upward. As the economy moves up and to the left along the aggregate demand curve AD_2, prices continue to rise, but real output falls back toward the natural level. A new long-run equilibrium is reached at e_3.

Because the aggregate demand curve is relatively inelastic, nominal domestic income increases in the course of the move from e_2 to e_3. As nominal domestic income rises, the money demand curve must shift farther to the right, from MD_2 to MD_3 in part (a) of Figure 14.4. This causes further crowding out of private planned investment. A continued increase in the interest rate pushes firms farther up and to the left along the planned-investment schedule, as shown in part (b). A new long-run equilibrium is not reached until the expansionary effects of the original fiscal policy action are completely crowded out. The aggregate demand curve remains in its new position, AD_2, but the economy's movement upward and to the left along this curve brings real domestic product all the way back to its natural level.

In one respect, the long-run effects of fiscal policy are similar to those of monetary policy: In both cases there is a higher price level in the new long-run equilibrium but no permanent change in real output. However, there is one important difference. Monetary policy is said to be "neutral" because a one-time increase in the money stock (and perhaps even a lasting change in the rate of money growth) has no long-run effects on any real variables—real output, planned investment, or real interest rates. But fiscal policy is not "neutral" in this sense. Even though expansionary fiscal policy does not change the long-run equilibrium level of real output, it does change the long-run equilibrium values of the real and nominal interest rates and real planned investment.

The Importance of the Fiscal-Monetary Policy Mix

We have now seen that both fiscal and monetary policy can be used to stimulate aggregate demand and encourage economic expansion, but with opposite effects on interest rates and investment. Other things being equal, expansionary monetary

FIGURE 14.4   CROWDING OUT IN THE LONG RUN

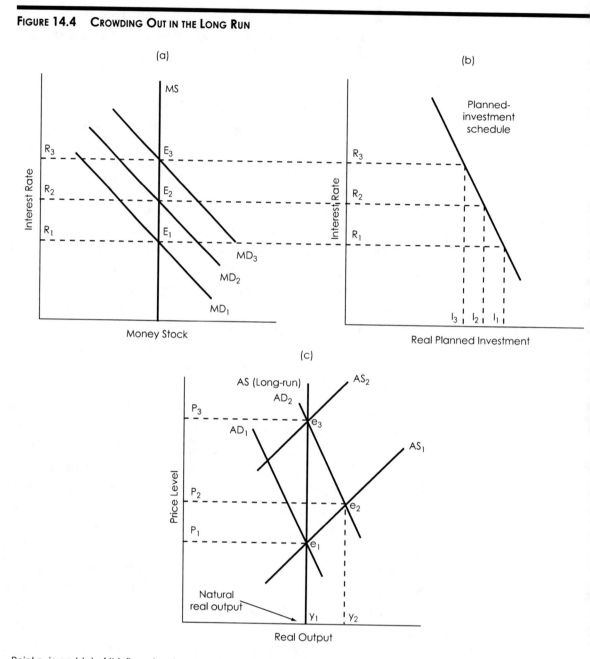

Point e_2 in part (c) of this figure is only a short-run equilibrium. As the aggregate supply curve shifts upward and the economy moves to a new long-run equilibrium at e_3, nominal domestic income continues to rise. The money demand curve shifts farther to the right from MD_2 to MD_3, as shown in part (a). As it does, the economy moves farther to the left along the planned-investment schedule, as shown in part (b). Thus, the crowding-out effect intensifies in the long run as real output returns to its natural level.

policy tends to lower interest rates and encourage planned investment. On the other hand, tax cuts or increases in government purchases, while also stimulating aggregate demand, do so in a way that raises interest rates and reduces private planned investment—the crowding-out effect. All this suggests that in order to maintain the private investment in machinery, technology, and human resources needed for healthy economic growth in the long run, policy makers must carefully balance the mix of fiscal and monetary policy.

Unfortunately, the natural dynamics of democratic politics make it difficult to maintain the needed monetary-fiscal balance. When economic stimulus is needed, both the president and Congress are quick to suggest a fiscal remedy. After all, lower taxes and higher spending on schools, roads, or social benefits are a form of medicine that is always easy to swallow. The difficulty comes when the fiscal remedy has done its work and the economy is growing again. At that point, unless some fiscal restraint is exercised, monetary policy may be called upon to do too much of the work of slowing the growth of aggregate demand to avoid unwanted inflation. If a clash between excessively expansive fiscal policy and severe tightening of monetary policy does develop, interest rates will be forced up, investment will be discouraged, and the nation's long-term economic health will be threatened.

The issue of fiscal-monetary balance assumed particular importance in 2003–2005. Although strong economic growth usually causes the budget deficit to decrease, it failed to do so during the recovery from the 2001 recession—a recovery that was stimulated, in part, by aggressive tax cuts early in the administration of President George W. Bush. *Economics in the News 14.1* summarizes some of the issues facing policy makers at that time.

Monetarism Versus Keynesianism: A Historical Note

One of the key events in the formation of modern macroeconomics was the Great Depression, which affected the United States from 1929 to 1939. In the first four years of the Depression, real output and prices fell by more than a third and the unemployment rate rose to over a quarter of the labor force. Although there had been serious economic contractions many times during the nineteenth century, there had never been a depression of this magnitude and duration. It forced economists to re-examine their theories from the ground up.

John Maynard Keynes, introduced earlier in *Who Said It? Who Did It? 5.1,* was the most influential theorist of the Depression era. Among other things, he had clear views on the relationship between monetary and fiscal policy. Certainly Keynes recognized that monetary policy could affect interest rates, interest rates planned investment, and planned investment GDP. But he thought these effects would be weak. "There are not many people," he wrote, "who will alter their way of living because the rate of interest has fallen from 5 to 4 percent."[2]

Liquidity trap

A situation in which interest rates near zero lead to accumulation of liquid assets instead of stimulating planned investment.

If interest rates had little effect on investment, Keynes thought, investment might remain inadequate to bring the economy to full employment even if nominal interest rates fell near zero, as they can during a severe contraction. Even if the central bank greatly increased bank reserves and the money supply, people would simply accumulate liquid assets rather than using them to finance investment in plants and equipment. Keynes called this situation a **liquidity trap**.

ECONOMICS IN THE NEWS 14.1

DEALING WITH THE DEFICIT

Testifying before Congress in February 2004, Federal Reserve Chairman Alan Greenspan began by noting that "the most recent indicators suggest that the economy is off to a strong start in 2004, and prospects for sustaining the expansion in the period ahead are good." The economy was growing, inflation was low, and the financial health of businesses had improved. However, he went on to warn, "This favorable short-term outlook for the U.S. economy...is playing out against a backdrop of growing concern about the prospects for the federal budget." More specifically, the federal deficit, which had risen to $375 billion in fiscal year 2003 was projected to rise to a record level of over half a trillion dollars in fiscal year 2004.

Where did this enormous deficit come from? Greenspan noted three sources. First, the Iraq war added tens of billions of dollars to military spending. Second, there were increased expenditures on domestic programs, ranging from agricultural subsidies to education. Greenspan attributed these increases in discretionary spending partly to a weakening of fiscal discipline in Congress as a result of the budget surplus years of the 1990s.

Spending was not the whole story, however. The Bush Administration's tax cuts, which for a time had been helpful in stimulating the recovery from the 2001 recession, were now contributing to the growing budget deficit. Greenspan noted that the ratio of federal debt to GDP—a key indicator of long-term fiscal health—had already begun to edge up after falling during the 1990s. This meant a weakening of the starting point from which lawmakers would have to address future fiscal challenges.

The greatest of these challenges, in Greenspan's view, will be the growth in Social Security and Medicare costs as the country prepares for the retirement of the baby-boom generation. He warned "under a range of reasonably plausible assumptions about spending and taxes, we could be in a sit-

uation in the decades ahead in which rapid increases in the unified budget deficit set in motion a dynamic in which large deficits result in ever-growing interest payments that augment deficits in future years. The resulting rise in the federal debt could drain funds away from private capital formation and thus over time slow the growth of living standards." In short, he warned of a looming crowding-out effect on an unprecedented scale.

What could be done? As Greenspan pointed out, the alternatives are not terribly attractive. Social Security and Medicare spending, under current law, are expected to rise from 7 percent of GDP in 2004 to 12 percent in 2030. Covering these outlays with increased taxes would not simply mean reversing the Bush tax cuts, but going beyond this to raise the tax burden to a historic high. Greenspan proposed instead slowing the growth of benefits by a combination of increased retirement age and revision of the formula under which retirees are protected against the effects of inflation. That suggestion, however, set off a storm of protest from all corners of the Washington political establishment, where Social Security cuts are regarded as the "third rail" of politics. But doing nothing and letting the deficit grow would force such a severe tightening of monetary policy that interest rates would rise sharply, threatening investment.

"The dimension of the challenge is enormous," Greenspan said in conclusion. "The one certainty is that the resolution of this situation will require difficult choices and that the future performance of the economy will depend on those choices."

If a liquidity trap made monetary policy powerless during a severe contraction, what could policy makers do to return the economy to full employment? For Keynes and his followers, the answer was clear: An increase in government purchases should be used to fill the gap between the actual and full-employment aggregate demand. Keynes did not think that monetary policy would always be ineffective. After the economy returned to full employment and interest rates rose back to normal levels, and even higher, in times when an overheated economy brought on inflation, monetary policy would play its traditional role. But because of the depression context in which Keynes wrote, the special case of "impotent monetary policy—potent fiscal policy" became the best remembered of his ideas.

After World War II many Keynesian economists forecast a new depression and economic stagnation. They thought that private investment would dry up with the end of wartime government spending. They were wrong: The postwar recovery of the United States and Western Europe was rapid. Central banks in most of the major economies pursued easy monetary policies during those years, and inflation was more widespread than depression. The countries that were able to control inflation did so only by using standard policies of monetary restraint. Economists began to take renewed interest in the role of money in the economy.

The new emphasis on money was strongest among a group of economists led by Milton Friedman (*Who Said It? Who Did It? 14.2*). Friedman's research led him to think that movements in the money supply had a much greater effect on economic events, even under depression conditions, than the early Keynesians had been willing to admit. Because of the emphasis Friedman and his followers placed on monetary policy, their school of thought came to be known as **monetarism**.

Monetarism

A school of economics that emphasizes the importance of changes in the money stock as determinants of changes in real output and the price level.

☙ WHO SAID IT? WHO DID IT? 14.2

MILTON FRIEDMAN AND MONETARISM

In October 1976, Milton Friedman received the Nobel Memorial Prize in economics, becoming the sixth American to win or share that honor. Few people were surprised. Most people wondered why he had had to wait so long. Perhaps it was because Friedman has built his career outside the economics establishment, challenging almost every major doctrine of that profession.

Friedman was born in New York in 1912, the son of immigrant garment workers. He attended Rutgers University, where he came under the influence of Arthur Burns, then a young assistant professor and later chairman of the Federal Reserve Board. From Burns, Friedman learned the importance of empirical work in economics. Statistical testing of all theory and policy prescriptions became a key feature of Friedman's later work. From Rutgers, Friedman went to the University of Chicago for an M.A. and then east again to Columbia University, where he received his Ph.D. in 1946. He returned to Chicago to teach. There he and his colleagues of the "Chicago school" of economics posed a major challenge to the economists of the "eastern establishment."

If one could single out a recurrent theme in Friedman's work it would be his belief that the market economy works—and that it works best when left alone. This can be seen in his best-known work, *A Monetary History of the United States*. Written with Anna Schwartz, this book attacks two major tenets of Keynesian economics: (1) that the market economy is unstable without the guiding hand of government, and (2) that monetary policy was tried and found useless as a cure for the Great Depression. Friedman and Schwartz found both beliefs to be far from the truth. "The Great Depression," Friedman later wrote, "far from being a sign of the inherent instability of the private enterprise system, is a testament to how much harm can be done by mistakes on the part of a few men when they wield vast power over the monetary system of the country."

Friedman strongly favors a hands-off policy by government in almost every area. In his view, the problem is not that government is evil by nature, but that so many policies end up having the opposite of their intended effects: "The social reformers who seek through politics to do nothing but serve the public interest invariably end up serving some private interest that was not part of their intention to serve. They are led by an invisible hand to serve a private interest." Transport regulation, public education, agricultural subsidies, and housing programs are among the many policy areas in which Friedman believes that the government has done more harm than good and for which a free competitive market would do better.

Friedman's research led to a reinterpretation of the Great Depression. In *A Monetary History of the United States,* Friedman and Anna J. Schwartz explained why what began as a fairly ordinary business contraction in the summer of 1929 turned into a four-year downward spiral from which complete recovery took an entire decade.[3] Their analysis focused on the collapse of the banking system and a precipitous decline in the money stock early in the Depression. In the monetarist view, it was not the inherent impotence of monetary policy that caused the Great Depression, but rather the terrible impact on the economy of serious monetary policy errors. If the Fed had used its policy instruments—especially open market purchases of securities—more aggressively, the downturn that began in 1929 might never have been more than a brief cyclical contraction.

The debate between monetarists and Keynesians over monetary versus fiscal policy raged throughout the 1960s and 1970s. Some monetarists went so far as to stand Keynes on his head, insisting that the crowding-out effect would be so strong and complete that fiscal policy would be impotent to affect the economy, so that "only money matters." On the other side, some Keynesians advocated using fiscal policy to fine-tune the economy with a degree of short-term precision that now seems implausible. In recent years, the debate has died out or taken other directions than the oversimplified "monetary versus fiscal policy" issue. Mainstream economic policymakers in all countries today acknowledge the importance of prudent management of both monetary and fiscal policy if the goals of long-term economic growth and stability are to be achieved.

SUMMARY

1. **How do changes in the money stock affect real output, the price level, and unemployment?** An increase in the money stock initially lowers interest rates. The resulting increase in real planned investment shifts the aggregate demand curve to the right. As the economy moves up and to the right along the aggregate supply curve, in the short run real output increases, the price level increases, and the unemployment rate falls. A decrease in the money stock has the opposite effects.

2. **What is meant by the neutrality of money?** An increase in the money stock can cause real output

to rise above its natural level only in the short run. As input prices rise, the economy returns to the natural level of real output at a higher price level than initially. In the new equilibrium the prices of both final goods and inputs will have changed in proportion to the increase in the money stock, but the values of all real variables—interest rates, planned investment, real output, and employment—will be unaffected. This proposition is known as the *neutrality of money.*

3. **How does fiscal policy affect interest rates and planned investment?** Expansionary fiscal policy shifts the aggregate demand curve to the right. Real output and the price level rise in the short run, as

does nominal domestic income. The increase in nominal domestic income shifts the money demand curve to the right, causing both real and nominal interest rates to increase. This rise in interest rates *crowds out* some real planned investment. As the economy returns to a long-run equilibrium at the natural level of real output, a further rise in the price level causes nominal domestic income to rise still higher, putting additional upward pressure on interest rates. Thus, there is a further depressing effect on real investment, and the crowding-out effect intensifies in the long run.

4. **How did Keynesian and monetarist economists view the relationship of monetary to fiscal policy?** Keynes and his early followers thought that the transmission mechanism from money to GDP via interest rates and investment was weak, especially under depression conditions. They thought that the economy would be unable to recover from a depression on its own and that only expansionary fiscal policy could do the job. After World War II, *monetarists,* led by Milton Friedman, argued that monetary policy is important even under depression conditions. They saw the Fed's policy mistakes following the 1929 crash as a major factor in the length and severity of the Depression. The debate over the relative importance of monetary and fiscal policy continued throughout the 1960s and 1970s. Today most economists see proper management of both monetary and fiscal policy as essential to economic stability and prosperity.

5. **What are the effects of fiscal policy in an open economy?** In a closed economy, assuming no change in the saving rate, an increase in the government budget deficit will lead to a change in investment—the crowding-out effect. In an open economy, the economy may compensate for an increase in the budget deficit through an increase in the current account deficit and a correspon-

ding rise in net capital inflows. This appears to have happened in the United States in the 1980s, when the economy experienced "twin deficits"—a federal budget deficit and a current account deficit. When the federal budget balance moved into surplus in the late 1990s, current account deficits continued because of high investment relative to saving in the United States. In the early 2000s, the twin deficits returned.

KEY TERMS

Neutrality of money   Liquidity trap
Crowding-out effect   Monetarism

PROBLEMS AND TOPICS FOR DISCUSSION

1. **Update on current policy.** Using government data sources such as the *Economic Report of the President* (http://www.gpoaccess.gov/eop) or current news sources, determine what has happened to inflation, the unemployment rate, the rate of growth of real GDP, and the federal budget deficit since this chapter was written in mid-2005.

2. **Long-run effects of contractionary monetary policy.** Use a set of diagrams similar to Figures 14.1 and 14.2 to trace the long-run effects of a one-time contraction of the money stock beginning from equilibrium at the natural level of real output.

3. **Effects of a tax increase.** Use a set of diagrams similar to Figure 14.4 to trace the effects of a contractionary fiscal policy such as a tax increase. What happens to real output, unemployment, the price level, interest rates, and real planned investment in the short run and in the long run?

4. **Crowding out and the money supply curve.** Use a set of diagrams similar to Figure 14.3 to investi-

gate how the crowding-out effect is influenced by the shape of the money supply curve. First use a positively sloped curve and then a horizontal curve. Discuss the policy implications of your results.

5. What is the relevance of the fiscal-monetary policy mix to the "twin deficit" phenomenon? What kind of mix is most likely to produce "twin deficits"?

CASE FOR DISCUSSION

Germany's Budget Woes

For decades following World War II, the Germany economy was the engine that pulled the train of European economic growth. Today, the engine is on a sidetrack. The German economy is in its worst slump in half a century, and politicians face a dilemma in deciding how to get things moving again.

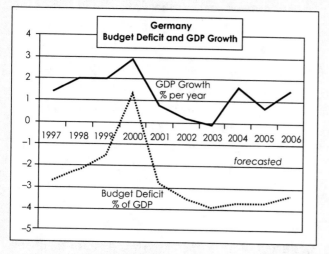

The issue of fiscal-monetary policy mix lies at the heart of the German dilemma. As the chart below shows, since the growth slowdown started, the German government has let its budget deficit increase, from a small surplus in 2000 to a level approaching 4 percent of GDP today. To some extent, the growth of

the deficit reflects cyclical factors—a decline in tax revenues and an increase in jobless benefits as the economy has slumped. But it also reflects a conscious policy decision in Berlin to use tax relief and increased spending to stimulate aggregate demand in order to get growth going again.

Unfortunately, Germany's fiscal policy has run head first into budget rules set by the EU for the 12 member economies of the euro-zone. Those rules state that a country must not run a budget deficit of more than 3 percent of GDP, subject to potentially large fines. Ironically, Germany itself insisted on such strong rules when the euro zone was formed, fearing irresponsible fiscal policy on the part of some of its European neighbors.

Setting a limit for budget deficits would make sense if a country that had hit the limit, but still needed to stimulate aggregate demand, could simply switch its mix away from fiscal policy toward an easing of monetary conditions. But doing so lies beyond the power of the German central bank. Since Germany gave up its beloved mark in favor of the euro, there is no way to ease German monetary conditions without also easing them for the eleven other countries of the euro zone. And the European central bank, so far, has refused to do so.

The reason is inflation. Germany's own inflation is low, expected barely to exceed 1 percent in 2005. As recently as the end of 2003, there were fears of actual deflation. But elsewhere in the euro zone things are different. Several other EU countries, including Greece, Spain, Portugal, and Italy, have inflation rates that are above the 2 percent target set by the European Central Bank. Any shift toward more expansionary monetary policy for the benefit of Germany would quickly spill over into those countries and push them even higher above the inflation ceiling.

Is there a way out? Not an easy one. In 2005, Germany, together with France, another high-deficit euro-zone member, reached an uneasy compromise with EU policymakers that will let them continue to violate the deficit ceiling without invoking the feared penalties. But there will be no monetary bale-out, and prospects for German growth in 2005 and 2006 don't look any brighter than in the preceding three years. In the long run, structural reforms of labor markets and tax law may make the German economy flexible enough to start growing again while meeting EU macroeconomic targets. But don't expect that to happen any time soon. For the foreseeable future, the tension between fiscal policy, set at the level of country governments, and monetary policy, set for the euro zone as a whole, will surely continue.

QUESTIONS

1. In the days when Germany had its own currency, the mark, how would a switch toward smaller deficits and faster growth of the money stock have affected interest rates? Investment? Aggregate demand? GDP?

2. Some economists think a uniform deficit limit of 3 percent of GDP for all euro zone countries is unrealistic. They say the limit should be higher for countries that are in recession. Explain how an alternative "full employment deficit limit" might be defined and implemented.

3. In the United States, the Fed sets monetary policy for the whole country, but each state has a substantial role in determining taxes and government spending. In what ways do you think the situation of an individual state that grows slower than the U.S. national average is similar to that of Germany within the EU? In what ways does it differ? Discuss.

END NOTES

1. In an earlier chapter we assumed, as a working approximation, that the change in government purchases times the expenditure multiplier would equal the horizontal shift in the aggregate demand curve. Now we can see why this was only an approximation: There would be some crowding out even if the economy moved horizontally to the right on the aggregate supply and demand diagram with the price level unchanged. Even with no change in the price level, there would be some increase in nominal domestic income as a result of the increase in real domestic product. That alone would be enough to shift the money demand curve to the right, although not as far as the shift to MD_2 shown in Figure 14.3. Thus, the interest rate would rise somewhat, and there would be some crowding out of private investment. This fixed-price portion of the crowding-out effect keeps the aggregate demand curve from shifting to the right by the full amount of the change in government purchases times the multiplier. However, the amount of the shift can still be thought of as equal to the change in autonomous expenditure times the expenditure multiplier, provided that the change in autonomous expenditure is interpreted as the increase in government purchases minus the change in planned investment resulting from the fixed-price component of crowding out.

2. John Maynard Keynes, *The General Theory of Employment, Interest, and Money* (New York: Harcourt, Brace, and World, 1936), 94.

3. Milton Friedman and Anna Jacobson Schwartz, *A Monetary History of the United States, 1867–1960* (Princeton, NJ: Princeton University Press, 1963).

PART III

CHAPTER 15

Custom Supplement

Third Edition compiled by members of the GCSU economics faculty:

Dr. J. J. Arias

Dr. Chris Clark

Dr. Ken Farr

Dr. Ben Scafidi

Dr. John Swinton

This chapter contains supplemental information on the following topics:

1. THE ECONOMICS MAJOR AT GEORGIA COLLEGE

The choice of a major is an important life decision; it constitutes a significant step in shaping your future opportunities. According to a recent *USA Today* report, forty percent of workers ages 20–29 say they are in the wrong career. To avoid this situation, you should choose a major that interests you and will provide the power and flexibility to satisfy the current and future needs of employers. Economics is a great choice because it provides career flexibility.

Despite common misconceptions (including those that come from high school classes), economics is not just about money, the stock market or "the economy." It is a behavioral science—the only social science for which a Nobel Prize is awarded. Economics draws upon the traditional liberal arts such as history and philosophy; natural sciences such as mathematics and physics; and social sciences, such as political science, sociology, and psychology. The interdisciplinary nature of economics lies at the heart of a liberal arts university.

The most basic and enduring strength of economics is that it provides a logical, ordered way of analyzing social problems (e.g., poverty, unemployment, crime, economic growth, the effects of government policy, pollution) as well as individual behavior (e.g., the labor-leisure tradeoff, drug addiction, taxes, voting, marriage, consumer behavior, business decisions).

Consider these aspects of our Economics Program:

- **Curriculum Flexibility**—The economics program is the only program in the School of Business that offers B.A. and B.S. degrees. The B.A. program includes 21–24 elective hours, and the B.S. includes 30 elective hours of coursework. This enables students to complete a minor or a double major—within four years of study. (Other programs in the School of Business allow only 6 or 9 non-business elective hours, making it impossible to complete a minor or double major without spending extra time in school.)

- **Respected Degree & Career Flexibility**—Economics graduates have an advantage entering the job market because employers recognize that economics curricula are rigorous and challenging. Unlike some programs, the economics curriculum is not just job training. Instead, we focus on teaching analytical and critical thinking, deductive reasoning, quantitative tools, and communication skills. These skills are sought by employers in all fields. This means economics graduates have flexibility, which is critical in today's world, where it is common to make several job changes during a career.

- **Preparation for Graduate School**—If you're thinking of law school, graduate training in economics, or getting an MBA, an economics degree is excellent preparation. For example, a 2006 study of the Law School Admissions Test reported that economics majors score higher than any other major! In 2006 we introduced a Concentration in Graduate Study Preparation for B.S. students. The concentration prepares students by focusing them on the math tools necessary for graduate study. In recent years, graduates from the Georgia College economics program have been accepted to high-quality Ph.D., law, and MBA programs.

- **Public Economics Concentration**—With four faculty specializing in public economics, we are able to offer a variety of courses that focus on different aspects of government and public policy. Students who are interested in working in business or government, or who are interested in graduate programs in economics, political science, or law, may wish to take the concentration in public economics.

- **ECON Majors Get Paid More!**—On average, economics majors earn more than any other major offered at Georgia College (except nursing and computer science)! See the next page for details.

- *Small Classes*—Our upper-level economics courses usually have fewer than 20 students. Small classes help to facilitate student-professor interaction. Because the economics program is relatively small, economics students often work through their courses in "cohorts," which makes the classroom atmosphere informal and collegial.

- *Senior Seminar*—Our "Senior Seminar" capstone course (ECON 4990) focuses on economic research. During the seminar, students are required to read and present economic research. In addition, each student is required to produce a formal research paper. This capstone course provides a preview of graduate school as it helps to develop the communications and research skills necessary for a successful career in business or research.

- *Student Organizations*—Our best economics students are honored with invitations to join the prestigious Omicron Delta Epsilon, the international honor society in economics. All economics students are invited to join the Econ Club, which sponsors guest speakers, field trips, occasional lunch seminars, and other social activities. Aside from their formal activities, these organizations facilitate informal interaction among economics students and faculty.

- *Faculty*—We have seven full-time Ph.D. economists and two Ph.D. finance professors in the department. Our professors have diverse backgrounds, receiving their doctorates from respected schools like Auburn, Georgia, Kentucky, Purdue, Texas A&M, Texas (Arlington), Virginia, and Wisconsin. This degree of faculty diversity is rare in departments at Georgia College. For students, it means they receive a valuable diversity of perspectives. In terms of research, our faculty are very active, and regularly publish in a variety of peer-reviewed journals.

- *For More Information* … Go to http://economics.gcsu.edu, or talk with your professor. Degree requirement check-sheets are on the department webpage.

Salaries for ECON Majors Are Higher Than Those for Most Other Majors at GCSU!

A recently published study on salaries paid to U.S. college graduates shows that economics majors earn higher salaries, on average, than most other majors offered at Georgia College. Table 1 below shows wage gaps relative to economics majors, for full-time college graduate workers aged 25 to 55. Table 15.1 shows that, for example, business administration majors earn 10.7% *less* than economics majors; political science majors earn 13.4% less. In fact, next to computer science and nursing, economics and math are the highest paid majors, on average, of all the majors offered at Georgia College!

What about students who go on to get an MBA? Table 15.2 illustrates relative wage gaps for those with an MBA, sorted by undergraduate major, compared to economics majors. Again, the data are for workers aged 25 to 55.

**TABLE 15.1   AVERAGE WAGE GAPS (%) COMPARED TO ECONOMICS MAJORS.
(* INDICATES STATISTICAL SIGNIFICANCE)**

Major	Wages Relative to ECON Majors (%)	Major	Wages Relative to ECON Majors (%)
BUSINESS		**ARTS & SCIENCES**	
Accounting	−0.8	Biology	−16.2
Business Admin.	−10.7*	Computer Science	8.5*
Economics	(0.0)	Criminology	−17.7*
Finance	−1.2	English/Journalism	−15.6*
Marketing	−6.9*	Fine Arts	−17.7*
Other Business	−14.0*	Foreign Languages	−16.0*
		History	−18.2*
EDUCATION		Mathematics	2.5
Elementary	−17.7*	Music	−37.3*
Secondary	−23.9*	Political Science	−13.4*
		Philosophy/Theology	−47.6*
HEALTH		Psychology	−18.0*
Nursing	5.2*	Sociology	−18.7*

**TABLE 15.2   AVERAGE WAGE GAPS (%) FOR MBA HOLDERS, BY UNDERGRADUATE MAJOR, COMPARED TO
ECONOMICS MAJORS. (* INDICATES STATISTICAL SIGNIFICANCE)**

Undergraduate Major	Wages Relative to Undergraduate ECON Majors (%)	Undergraduate Major	Wages Relative to Undergraduate ECON Majors (%)
BUSINESS		**ARTS & SCIENCES**	
Accounting	−18.9*	Biology	−22.4*
Business Admin.	−19.8*	Computer Science	−11.8*
Economics	(0.0)	English	−8.8
Finance	−14.5*	History	−29.7*
Marketing	−18.0*	Mathematics	−5.4
Other Business	−19.8*	Political Science	−7.9
		Psychology	−22.6*
		Sociology	−27.6*

* Data are from "The Economic Reward for Studying Economics," by Dan Black, Seth Sanders, and Lowell
Taylor. *Economic Inquiry*, July 2003 (vol. 41, no. 3, pp. 365–377). The article is available online through
Galileo's Pro Quest.

Similarly, among those who get a law degree, economics undergraduate majors
have the highest salaries of any major. So whether you plan on working or pursuing
an MBA or a law degree, getting an economics undergraduate degree pays more!

2. EXCISE TAXES BY STATE

State Excise Tax Rates on Motor Fuel *(January 1, 2007)*

Note: The tax rates listed are fuel excise taxes collected by distributor/supplier/retailers in each state. Aditional taxes may apply to motor carriers. Carrier taxes are coordinated by IFTA.

State	Gasoline Excise Tax[1]	Add'l Tax	Total Tax	Diesel Fuel Excise Tax[1]	Add'l Tax	Total Tax	Gasohol Excise Tax[1]	Add'l Tax	Total Tax	Notes
Alabama[1]	16.0	2.0	18.0	19.0	—	19.0	16.0	2.0	18.0	Inspection fee
Alaska	8.0	—	8.0	8.0	—	8.0	0.0	—	0.0	
Arizona	18.0	—	18.0	18.0	—	18.0	18.0	—	18.0	[3]
Arkansas	21.5	—	22.5	22.5	—	22.5	21.5	—	21.5	
California	18.0	—	18.0	18.0	—	18.0	18.0	—	18.0	Sales tax applicable
Colorado	22.0	—	22.0	20.5	—	20.5	22.0	—	22.0	
Connecticut	25.0	—	25.0	26.0	—	26.0	25.0	—	25.0	
Delaware	23.0	—	23.0	22.0	—	22.0	23.0	—	23.0	Plus 0.5% GRT [5]
Florida[2]	4.0	11.3	15.3	16.8	11.6	28.4	4.0	11.3	15.3	Sales tax added to excise [2]
Georgia	7.5	7.7	15.2	7.5	8.5	16.3	7.5	7.7	15.2	Sales tax added to excise
Hawaii[1]	16.0	—	16.0	16.0	—	16.0	16.0	—	16.0	Sales tax applicable
Idaho	25.0	—	25.0	25.0	—	25.0	22.5	—	22.5	[7]
Illinois[1]	19.0	1.1	20.1	21.5	1.1	22.6	19.0	1.1	20.1	Sales tax add., envir. & LUST fee [3]
Indiana	18.0	—	18.0	16.0	—	16.0	18.0	—	18.0	Sales tax applicable [3]
Iowa	21.0	—	21.0	22.5	—	22.5	19.0	—	19.0	—
Kansas	24.0	—	24.0	26.0	—	26.0	24.0	—	24.0	—
Kentucky	18.3	1.4	19.7	15.3	1.4	16.7	18.3	1.4	19.7	Environmental fee [4][3]
Louisiana	20.0	—	20.0	20.0	—	20.0	20.0	—	20.0	—
Maine	26.8	—	26.8	27.9	—	27.9	26.8	—	26.8	[5]
Maryland	23.5	—	23.5	24.25	—	24.25	23.5	—	23.5	—
Massachusetts	21.0	—	21.0	21.0	—	21.0	21.0	—	21.0	—
Michigan	19.0	—	19.0	15.0	—	15.0	19.0	—	19.0	Sales tax applicable
Minnesota	20.0	—	20.0	20.0	—	20.0	20.0	—	20.0	—
Mississippi	18.0	.04	18.4	18.0	0.4	18.4	18.0	0.4	18.4	Environmental fee
Missouri	17.0	0.55	17.55	17.0	.55	17.55	17.0	0.55	17.55	Inspection fee
Montana	27.0	—	27.0	27.75	—	27.75	27.0	—	27.0	
Nebraska	27.0	0.9	28.0	27.1	0.3	27.4	27.1	0.9	28.0	Petroleum fee [5]
Nevada[1]	24.0	0.805	24.805	27.0	0.75	27.75	24.0	0.805	24.805	Inspection & cleanup fee
New Hampshire	18.0	1.625	19.625	18.0	1.625	19.625	18.0	1.625	19.625	Oil discharge clean up fee
New Jersey	10.5	4.0	14.5	13.5	4.0	17.50	10.5	4.0	14.5	Petroleum fee
New Mexico	17.0	1.875	18.875	21.0	1.875	22.875	17.0	1.875	18.875	Petroleum loading fee
New York	8.0	16.6	24.6	8.0	14.85	22.85	8.0	16.6	24.6	Sales tax applicable, Petrol tax
North Carolina	29.9	0.25	30.15	26.9	0.25	30.15	26.9	0.25	30.15	[4] Inspection tax
North Dakota	23.0	—	23.0	23.0	—	23.0	23.0	—	23.0	—
Ohio	28.0	—	28.0	28.0	—	28.0	28.0	—	28.0	Plus 3 cents commercial
Oklahoma	16.0	1.0	17.0	13.0	1.0	14.0	16.0	1.0	17.0	Environmental fee
Oregon[1]	24.0	—	24.0	24.0	—	24.0	24.0	—	24.0	—
Pennsylvania	12.0	19.2	31.2	12.0	26.1	38.1	12.0	19.2	31.2	Oil franchise tax
Rhode Island	30.0	1	31.0	30.0	1.0	31.0	30.0	1.0	31.0	LUST tax
South Carolina	16.0	—	16.0	16.0	—	16.0	16.0	—	16.0	—
South Dakota	22.0	—	22.0	22.0	—	22.0	20.0	—	20.0	
Tennessee[1]	20.0	1.4	21.4	17.0	1.4	18.4	20.0	1.4	21.4	Petroleum tax & envir. fee
Texas	20.0	—	20.0	20.0	—	20.0	20.0	—	20.0	—
Utah	24.5	—	24.5	24.5	—	24.5	24.5	—	24.5	
Vermont	19.0	1.0	20.0	25.0	1.0	26.0	19.0	1.0	20.0	Petroleum cleanup fee
Virginia[1]	17.5	—	17.5	16.0	—	16.0	17.5	—	17.5	[6]
Washington[8]	34.0	—	34.0	34.0	—	34.0	34.0	—	34.0	0.5% privilege tax
West Virginia	20.5	11.0	31.5	20.5	11.0	31.5	20.5	11.0	31.5	Sales tax added to excise tax
Wisconsin	29.9	3.0	32.9	29.9	3.0	32.9	29.9	3.0	32.9	[5] Petroleum inspection fee
Wyoming	13.0	1.0	14.0	13.0	1.0	14.0	13.0	1.0	14.0	License tax
Dist. of Columbia	20.0	—	20.0	20.0	—	20.0	20.0	—	20.0	
Federal	18.3	0.1	18.4	24.3	0.1	24.4	13.0	0.1	13.1	[7] LUST tax

SOURCE: Compiled by FTA from various sources (www.taxadmin.org).

[1] Tax rates do not include local option taxes. In AL, 1–3 cents; HI, 8.8 to 18.0 cent; IL, 5 cents in Chicago and 6cents in Cook county (gasoline only); NV, 4.0 to 9.0 cents; OR, 1 to 3 cents; SD and TN, one cent; and VA 2%.

[2] Local taxes for gasoline and gasohol vary from 10.2 cents to 18.2 cents. Plus a 2.07 cent per gallon pollution tax.

[3] Carriers pay an additional surcharge equal to AZ—8 cents, IL—6.3 cents (g) 6.0 cents (d), IN—11 cents, KY—2% (g) 4.7% (d).

[4] Tax rate is based on the average wholesale price and is adjusted quarterly. The actual rates are: KY, 9%; and NC, 17.5¢ + 7%.

[5] Portion of the rate is adjustable based on maintenance costs, sales volume, or inflation.

[6] Large trucks pay an additional 3.5 cents.

[7] Tax rate is reduced by the percentage of ethanol used in blending (reported rate assumes the max. 10% ethanol).

[8] Tax rate scheduled to increase to 36 cents on July 1, 2007.

State Excise Tax Rates on Beer *(January 1, 2007)*

STATE	EXCISE TAX RATES ($ per gallon)	SALES TAXES APPLIED	OTHER TAXES
Alabama	$0.53	Yes	$0.52/gallon local tax
Alaska	1.07	NA	$0.35/gallon small breweries
Arizona	0.16	Yes	
Arkansas	0.23	Yes	under 3.2%—$0.16/gallon; $0.008/gallon and 3% off- 10% on-premise tax
California	0.20	Yes	
Colorado	0.08	Yes	
Connecticut	0.19	Yes	
Delaware	0.16	NA	
Florida	0.48	Yes	2.67¢/12 ounces on-premise retail tax
Georgia	0.48	Yes	$0.53/gallon local tax
Hawaii	0.93	Yes	$0.54/gallon draft beer
Idaho	0.15	Yes	over 4%—$0.45/gallon
Illinois	0.185	Yes	$0.16/gallon in Chicago and $0.06/gallon in Cook County
Indiana	0.115	Yes	
Iowa	0.19	Yes	
Kansas	0.18	—	over 3.2%—(8% off- and 10% on-premise), under 3.2%—4.25% sales tax
Kentucky	0.08	Yes*	11% wholesale tax
Lousiana	0.32	Yes	$0.048/gallon local tax
Maine	0.35	Yes	additional 5% on-premise tax
Maryland	0.09	Yes	$0.2333/gallon in Garrett County
Massachusetts	0.11	Yes*	0.57% on private club sales
Michigan	0.20	Yes	
Minnesota	0.15	—	under 3.2%—$0.077/gallon. 9% sales tax
Mississippi	0.43	Yes	
Missouri	0.06	Yes	
Montana	0.14	NA	
Nebraska	0.31	Yes	
Nevada	0.16	Yes	
New Hampshire	0.30	NA	
New Jersey	0.12	Yes	
New Mexico	0.41	Yes	
New York	0.11	Yes	$0.12/gallon in New York City
North Carolina	0.53	Yes	
North Dakota	0.16	—	7% state sales tax, bulk beer $0.08/gallon
Ohio	0.18	Yes	
Oklahoma	0.40	Yes	under 3.2%—$0.36/gallon; 13.5% on-premise
Oregon	0.08	NA	
Pennsylvania	0.08	Yes	
Rhode Island	0.10	Yes	$0.04/case whoesale tax
South Carolina	0.77	Yes	
South Dakota	0.28	Yes	
Tennessee	0.14	Yes	17% wholesale tax
Texas	0.19	Yes	over 4%—$0.198/gallon, 14% on-premise and $0.05/drink on airline sales
Utah	0.41	Yes	over 3.2%—sold through state store
Vermont	0.265	No	
Virginia	0.26	Yes	
Washington	0.261	Yes	
West Virginia	0.18	Yes	
Wisconsin	0.06	Yes	
Wyoming	0.02	Yes	
Dist. of Columbia	0.09	Yes	8% off- and 10% on-premise sales tax
U.S. Median	**$0.188**		

SOURCE: Compiled by FTA from various sources (www.taxadmin.org).

* Sales tax is applied to on-premise sales only.

State Excise Tax Rates on Wine *(January 1, 2007)*

STATE	EXCISE TAX RATES ($ per gallon)	SALES TAXES APPLIED	OTHER TAXES
Alabama	$1.70	Yes	over 14%—sold through state store
Alaska	2.50	NA	
Arizona	0.84	Yes	
Arkansas	0.75	Yes	under 5%—$0.25/gallon; $0.05/case; and 3% off- and 10% on-premise
California	0.20	Yes	sparkling wine—$0.30/gallon
Colorado	0.32	Yes	
Connecticut	0.60	Yes	over 21% and sparkling wine—$1.50/gallon
Delaware	0.97	NA	
Florida	2.25	Yes	over 17.259%—$3.00/gallon, sparkling wine $3.50/gallon 6.67¢/4 ounces on-premise retail tax
Georgia	1.51	Yes	over 14%—$2.54/gallon; $0.83/gallon local tax
Hawaii	1.38	Yes	sparkling wine—$2.12/gallon and wine coolers—$0.85/gallon
Idaho	0.45	Yes	
Illinois	0.73	Yes	over 20%—$4.50/gallon; $0.246/gallon in Chicao and ($0.16–$0.30)/gallon in Cook County
Indiana	0.47	Yes	ove 21%—$2.68/galloin
Iowa	1.75	Yes	under 5%—$0.19/gallon
Kansas	0.30	No	over 14%—$0.75/gallon; 8% off- and 10% on-premise
Kentucky	0.50	Yes*	11% wholesale
Lousiana	0.11	Yes	14% to 24%—$0.23/gallon, over 24% and sparkling wine—$1.59/gallon
Maine	0.60	Yes	over 15.5%—sold through state stores, sparkling wine—$1.25/gallon; additional 5% on-premise sales tax
Maryland	0.40	Yes	
Massachusetts	0.55	Yes*	sparkling wine—$0.70/gallon
Michigan	0.51	Yes	over 16%—$0.76/gallon
Minnesota	0.30	—	14% to 21% - $0.95/gallon, under 24% and sparkling wine—$1.82/gallon; over 24%—$3.52/gallon; $0.01/bottle (except miniatures) and 9% sales tax
Mississippi	0.35	Yes	over 14% and sparkling wine—sold through the state
Missouri	0.30	Yes	
Montana	1.06	NA	over 15%—sold through state stores
Nebraska	0.95	Yes	
Nevada	0.70	Yes	14% to 22%—$1.30/gallon, over 22%—$3.60/gallon
New Hampshire	see footnote[1]	NA	
New Jersey	0.70	Yes	
New Mexico	1.70	Yes	over 14%—$5.68/gallon
New York	0.19	Yes	
North Carolina	0.79	Yes	over 17%—$0.91/gallon
North Dakota	0.50	—	over 17%—$0.60/gallon, sparkling wine—$1.00/gallon; 7% state sales tax
Ohio	0.30	Yes	over 14%—$0.98/gallon, vermouth—$1.08/gallon and sparkling wine—$1.48/gallon
Oklahoma	0.72	Yes	over 14%—$1.40/gallon, sparkling wine—$2.08/gallon; 13.5% on-premise
Oregon	0.67	NA	over 14%—$0.77/gallon
Pennsylvania	see footnote[1]	Yes	
Rhode Island	0.60	YeYess	sparkling wine—$0.75/gallon
South Carolina	0.90	Yes	$0.18/gallon additional tax
South Dakota	0.93	Yes	14% to 20%—$1.45/gallon, over 21% and sparkling wine—$2.07/gallon; 2% wholesale tax
Tennessee	1.21	Yes	$0.15/case and 15% on-premise
Texas	0.20	Yes	over 14%—$0.408/gallon and sparkling wine—$0.516/gallon; 14% on-premise and $0.05/drink on airline sales
Utah	see footnote[1]	Yes	
Vermont	0.55	Yes	over 15%—sold through state store, 10% on-premise sales tax
Virginia	1.51	Yes	under 4%—$0.2565/gallon and over 14%—sold through state store
Washington	0.87	Yes	over 14%—$1.72/gallon
West Virginia	1.00	Yes	5% local tax
Wisconsin	0.25	Yes	over 14%—$0.45/gallon
Wyoming	see footnote[1]	Yes	
Dist. of Columbia	0.30		8% off- and 10% on-premise sales tax, over 14%—$0.40/gallon and sparkling wine—$0.45/gallon
U.S. Median	**0.69**		

SOURCE: Compiled by FTA from various sources (www.taxadmin.org).

* Sales tax is applied to on-premise sales only.

[1] All wine sales are through state stores. Revenue in these states is generated from various taxes, fees, and net profits.

State Excise Tax Rates on Liquor *(January 1, 2007)*

STATE	EXCISE TAX RATES ($ per gallon)	SALES TAXES APPLIED	OTHER TAXES
Alabama	see footnote [1]	Yes	
Alaska	$12.80	NA	under 21%—$2.50/gallon
Arizona	3.00	Yes	
Arkansas	2.50	Yes	under 5%—$0.50/gallon, under 21%—$1.00/gallon; $0.20/case and 3% off- 14% on-premise retail taxes
California	3.30	Yes	over 50%—$6.60/gallon
Colorado	2.28	Yes	
Connecticut	4.50	Yes	under 7%—$2.05/gallon
Delaware	5.46	NA	under 25%—$3.64/gallon
Florida	6.50	Yes	under 17.259%—$2.25/gallon, over 55.780%—$9.53/gallon 6.67¢/ounce on-premise retail tax
Georgia	3.79	Yes	$0.83/gallon local tax
Hawaii	5.98	Yes	
Idaho	see footnote [1]	Yes	
Illinois	4.50	Yes	under 20%—$0.73/gallon; $1.845/gallon in Chicago and $2.00/gallon in Cook County
Indiana	2.68	Yes	unde 15%—$0.47/gallon
Iowa	see footnote [1]	Yes	
Kansas	2.50	No	8% off- and 10% on-premise retail tax
Kentucky	1.2	Yes*	under 6%—$0.25/gallon; $0.05/case and 11% wholesale tax
Lousiana	2.50	Yes	under 6%—$0.32/gallon
Maine	see footnote [1]	Yes	
Maryland	1.50	Yes	
Massachusetts	4.05	Yes*	under 15%—$1.10/gallon, over 50% alcohol—$4.05/proof gallon; 9.57% on private club sales
Michigan	see footnote [1]	Yes	
Minnesota	5.03	—	$0.01/bottle (except miniatures) and 9% sales tax
Mississippi	see footnote [1]	Yes	
Missouri	2.00	Yes	
Montana	see footnote [1]	NA	
Nebraska	3.75	Yes	
Nevada	3.60	Yes	under 14%—$0.70/gallon and under 21%—$1.30/gallon
New Hampshire	see footnote [1]	NA	
New Jersey	4.40	Yes	
New Mexico	6.06	Yes	
New York	6.44	Yes	not more than 24%—$2.54/gallon; $1.00/gallon New York City
North Carolina	see footnote [1]	Yes*	
North Dakota	2.50	—	7% state sales tax
Ohio	see footnote [1]	Yes	
Oklahoma	5.56	Yes	13.5% on-premise
Oregon	see footnote [1]	NA	
Pennsylvania	see footnote [1]	Yes	
Rhode Island	3.75	Yes	
South Carolina	2.72	Yes	$5.36case amd 9% surtax
South Dakota	3.93	Yes	under 14%—$0.93/gallon, 2% wholesale tax
Tennessee	4.40	Yes	$0.15/case and 15% on-premise; under 7%—$1.21/gallon
Texas	2.40	Yes	14% on-premise and $0.05/drink on airline sales
Utah	see footnote [1]	Yes	
Vermont	see footnote [1]	No	10% on-premise sales tax
Virginia	see footnote [1]	Yes	
Washington	see footnote [1]	Yes*	
West Virginia	see footnote [1]	Yes	
Wisconsin	3.25	Yes	
Wyoming	see footnote [1]	Yes	
Dist. of Columbia	1.50	Yes	8% off- and 10% on-premise sales tax
U.S. Median	**$3.75**		

SOURCE: Compiled by FTA from various sources (www.taxadmin.org).

* Sales tax is applied to on-premise sales only.

[1] In 18 states, the government directly controls the sales of distilled spirits. Revenue in these states is generated from various taxes, fees and net liquor profits.

State Excise Tax Rates on Cigarettes *(January 1, 2007)*

STATE	TAX RATE (¢ per pack	RANK	STATE	TAX RATE (¢ per pack)	RANK
Alabama (1)	42.5	40	Nebraska	64	31
Alaska (3)	180	7	Nevada	80	26
Arizona	200	4	New Hampshire	80	26
Arkansas	59	33	New Jersey	257.5	1
California	87	24	New Mexico	91	23
Colorado	84	25	New York (1)	150	13
Connecticut	151	11	North Carolina	35	44
Delaware	55	36	North Dakota	44	39
Florida	33.9	45	Ohio	125	16
Georgia	37	41	Oklahoma	103	19
Hawaii (3)	160	10	Oregon	118	18
Idaho	57	34	Pennsylvania	135	15
Illinois	98	22	Rhode Island	246	2
Indiana	55.5	35	South Carolina	7	51
Iowa	36	42	South Dakota	53	38
Kansas	79	28	Tennessee (1) (2)	20	48
Kentucky (2)	30	46	Texas	141	14
Louisiana	36	42	Utah	69.5	30
Maine	200	4	Vermont	179	8
Maryland	100	20	Virginia (1)	30	46
Massachusetts	151	11	Washington	202.5	3
Michigan	200	4	West Virginia	55	36
Minnesota (4)	123	17	Wisconsin	77	29
Mississippi	18	49	Wyoming	60	32
Missouri (1)	17	50	Dist. of Columbia	100	20
Montana	170	9	**U.S. Median**	**80.0**	

SOURCE: Compiled by FTA from various sources (www.taxadmin.org).

(1) Counties and cities may impose an additional tax on a pack of cigarettes in AL, 1¢ to 6¢; IL, 10¢ to 15¢; MO, 4¢ to 7¢; NYC $1.50; TN, 1¢; and VA, 2¢ to 15¢.
(2) Dealers pay an additional enforcement and administrative fee of 0.1¢ per pack in KY and 0.05¢ in TN.
(3) Tax rate is scheduled to increase to $2.00 per pack on July 1, 2007 in AK and to $2.00 on Sept. 30, 2007 in HI.
(4) Plus an additional 25.5 cent sales tax is added to the wholesale price of a tax stamp (total $1.485).

3. COMMON MISCONCEPTIONS ABOUT GLOBALIZATION AND TRADE

Perhaps the only issue on which economists of all stripes are nearly unanimous is international trade. Free international trade is the best policy, whatever other countries are doing. Here we summarize some common myths about trade and globalization.

Trade Deficits

It is difficult to read business news or watch TV economic news without hearing alarming news about the U.S. trade deficit. Lou Dobbs of CNN bashes trade daily on his show. Recently, CNN reported that our deficit with China had grown to a record level in August. Apparently, many people believe a trade deficit is "bad" because they think it represents an outflow of either money or jobs from the country running the deficit. Or maybe it's just because "deficit" sounds bad. But this view ignores half of what is going on in trade. For example, U.S. manufacturing industries have been declining for decades. You often hear about Ford, GM, or textile plant closings. But what you don't hear about are new businesses and industries that flourish. These do not get attention from the media because they are not seemingly obviously related to international trade. Empirical studies show that international trade does not have an effect on overall employment in a country, but it does affect the allocation of jobs among industries in a country. So while trade may harm particular industries (those competing with imports), overall the benefits to consumers and exporting industries outweigh the costs to import-competing industries. Trade deficits are nothing to worry about, and trade surpluses are no reason to be happy.

Fair or Free Trade?

Economists are staunch advocates of international trade, and oppose artificial trade barriers such as import quotas and tariffs. This is because trade leads to economic efficiency, which is maximizing the mutual gains from voluntary exchange. Another consideration is liberty or economic freedom. If two parties agree on a mutually beneficial arrangement, they should be free from interference by third parties, including national governments. In contrast, advocates of 'fair trade' are focused on the equity implications of international trade. Some fair traders want to moderate or reform the market to protect the vulnerable, while others are socialists who are fundamentally opposed to the very notion of free markets.

Despite these different perspectives, there is some important common ground. Both free and fair traders agree that wealthy nations should stop protecting and subsidizing their farmers and commodity producers at the expense of poor farmers and producers in other countries. The refusal of wealthy nations to lower these trade barriers is the main reason the most recent round of World Trade Organization negotiations has collapsed.

Sweatshops

In the late 1990s and early 2000s, "sweatshops" in low-wage countries became a big concern for many Americans. It seems unethical that wealthy U.S. companies go to low-wage countries and apparently take advantage of the cheap foreign labor. Aside from low wages, workers are often subject to long hours and poor working conditions. Unfortunately, while we might all be sympathetic with this view, it ignores the key issue: the welfare of the poor. If we were to disallow American or other rich country companies from building factories in low-wage countries, the only result is to remove the poor workers' best opportunity. After all, why would a worker accept a job in a "sweat-shop" if she had other, better opportunities for work? While it may be worthwhile to chide or encourage U.S. companies to offer even higher wages and better working conditions, limiting the ability to build new factories and hire workers in low-wage countries can only harm the people we all agree need help.

The Outsourcing Scare

"Outsourcing" was the "downsizing" of the last presidential election. (Any bets on the phrase for 2008?) It referred to firms hiring foreign residents for service jobs. In the past, white-collar, service workers have been immune from the international competition faced by their blue-collar, manufacturing counterparts due to the difficulty of trading services across nations. This all changed with the installation of fiber-optic cables, connecting the U. S. with other countries. The top countries for outsourcing include Ireland, Canada, India and Iceland. It is important to stress that the economic benefits of specialization and trade are no less true for services than manufacturing. Proportionally speaking, outsourcing is overstated since less than two percent of all service sector jobs are done overseas. It is also important to realize that other countries outsource their jobs to the U.S. Both the outflow and inflow of service jobs are part of reallocating our resources—in this case labor—to their most valued uses.

4. THE HIGH COSTS OF PROTECTIONISM

The average cost of protecting an American job is $231,289, according statistics on 20 protected industries. The total cost to U.S. consumers is estimated at $100 billion annually, or over $300 per person per year. Aside from higher prices of the protected goods, import restrictions also cause higher prices in "downstream" industries (industries that use the protected products as input resources).

Estimated jobs saved, total costs, and cost per job saved are presented in Table 15.3 on the following page. These data are reproduced from the Dallas Fed's 2002 *Annual Report*.

5. PUBLIC GOODS AND EXTERNALITIES

Economic theory provides a good proscription for the efficient allocation of resources when certain circumstances hold true. In a well functioning market all goods and services that have value to society have a price that reflect both their value to society and the cost of providing them to society. When ownership of valuable resources is clearly defined and defended the owners of resources have an incentive to put those resources to their highest valued use. Sometimes, however, markets do not function properly. When the prerequisites of a well functioning market do not exist, markets will not bestow the highest possible value of resource use on society. The study of

TABLE 15.3

	Protected industry	Jobs saved (in millions)	Total cost	Annual cost per job saved
1	Benzenoid chemicals	216	$297	$1,376,435
2	Luggage	226	290	1,285,078
3	Softwood lumber	605	632	1,044,271
4	Sugar	2261	1868	826,104
5	Polyethylene resins	298	242	812,928
6	Dairy products	2378	1630	685,323
7	Frozen concentrated orange juice	609	387	635,103
8	Ball bearings	146	88	603,368
9	Maritime services	4411	2522	571,668
10	Ceramic tiles	347	191	551,367
11	Machine tools	1556	746	479,452
12	Ceramic articles	418	140	335,876
13	Women's handbags	773	204	263,535
14	Canned tuna	390	100	257,640
15	Glassware	1477	366	247,889
16	Apparel and textiles	168,786	33,629	199,241
17	Peanuts	397	74	187,223
18	Rubber footwear	1701	286	168,312
19	Women's non-athletic footwear	3702	518	139,800
20	Costume jewelry	1067	142	132,870
	Total	**191,764**	**$44,352 (million)**	
	Average (weighted)			**$231,289**

(Excerpt from the Dallas Fed *Annual Report 2002*, p. 19)

market failures helps economists predict when markets will not function to their highest potential and provide policy proscriptions to help fix the markets.

Market Failure and Property

Clearly defined property rights require two things: Property must be excludable and rival in consumption. Excludability is easily understood. It is the property that ownership allows a person to determine who will and who will not enjoy the benefits of a resource. For example, ownership of a car implies that the owner can drive the car and the owner can prevent other people from driving the car. If someone tries to drive the car without permission the police have an obligation to attempt to apprehend the person and charge him with grand theft auto. Another facet of ownership is that the owner can transfer the benefits to another person. The owner may sell the car to another driver who will now have the right to drive the car to the exclusion of others. Not all goods are excludable. Ownership is not always clearly defined. No individual owns a rainbow. Therefore, any can enjoy a rainbow without fear of official retribution. No individual owns the fish in International waters. Therefore, anyone can catch and consume fish that swim in international waters. (Some countries do have restrictions on what you can offload at a dock—effectively restricting the harvest of some fish by anglers of particular countries.)

Rivalry is a little more difficult to understand. Rivalry implies that a good or service enjoyed by one person no longer exists for another person to enjoy. Consider a peanut butter and jelly sandwich. If a person eats a peanut butter and jelly sandwich, the sandwich no longer exists (at least not in its same useful state). The act of consumption removed the benefits of the good. A counter example exists with the rainbow. If one person sees a rainbow, the rainbow still exists in its same state and is available for others to enjoy. The rainbow is non-rival.

Together, excludability and rivalry define how well a market will efficiently allocate resources. Both characteristics can be thought of on a continuum. The lack of either characteristic can lead to market failure.

Non-excludability

When a good is non-excludable people tend to overuse the good. The example of fish on international waters is instructive. If a person must pay to acquire a good, the person will use it until the marginal benefit of its use is equal to the marginal cost of its acquisition. But any good that is free of charge will be consumed until it provides no additional benefit. In the case of the oceanic fish, the problem goes much deeper. Not only is there an incentive to consume more fish, there is no incentive to save fish for tomorrow. Any fish left behind are available to the next angler. Therefore, there is no benefit to preservation. Resources that are non-excludable are often called open access resources. Other common names include race resources or common property resources. When such a circumstance exists there is a need for regulation. Governments can limit access to the resource by requiring licensing or limiting the amount of the resource that anyone can use.

Goods that are non-rival in consumption pose a different problem. Once a person produces such a good, multiple people can consume the good. If the good is excludable the problem is surmountable. An example is a concert. Many people can enjoy the same concert. By owning a concert hall, a promoter can exclude those people who do not have a ticket. But when a non-rival good is also non-excludable, the invisible hand cannot allocate resources properly. A common example is a lighthouse. The owner of a lighthouse cannot turn the lighthouse on for those who pay for its benefits and turn it off again for those who do not pay for its benefits. Once a lighthouse is on, it is on for everyone. Goods that are both non-rival and non-excludable are called public goods. Entrepreneurs have little incentive to produce public goods for two reasons: First, because the good is non-excludable, the entrepreneur cannot limit who has access to the good. Second, because the good is non-rival, multiple people can enjoy the same good simultaneously. Therefore, the entrepreneur cannot extract the full benefits the good provides. Public goods will be underprovided by the private market. Government can step in and directly provide public goods.

Third-party Effects

Many people are familiar with consumption decisions that have spill-over affects that contain characteristics of non-rivalry and non-excludability. When one person makes electricity by burning coal, other people downwind breathe the soot that results from the burning coal. The people whose health is damaged did not buy the soot. The person who made the electricity did not pay for the use of air to transport his soot away from the plant. The use of air is an open-access good. Similar examples include the noise of a neighbor's late-night party keeping you awake or the congestion of a freeway making you late for work. Examples of positive spill-over effects exist as well. The bees of the beekeeper pollinate the trees of the peach grower without additional compensation. In each of the above examples a harm or benefit is bestowed upon someone who did not participate in a market. The problem is that the harm or effect is not priced. Therefore, the invisible hand cannot affect it. One potential solution is for government to place a tax on any activity that causes a spillover effect. If electricity makers have to pay for any harm their soot causes they are likely to reduce their use of the air until the marginal cost of reducing soot is equal to the price they pay per unit of soot they emit. Similarly, the government could subsidize those people who produce positive spill-over effect to encourage more of the activity. If bee keepers receive a fee for the pollination services their bees produce they will be likely to keep more bees.

6. PRODUCTION THEORY

Here we model the firm in a perfectly competitive market. We include an examination of profit maximizing and loss minimizing behavior, as well as a discussion of economic profits and losses and how they cause entry into and exit from a particular industry.

We build on this theory by using the same tools to analyze the monopolist's profit maximizing behavior in terms of Quantity produced and the profit maximizing Price. This discussion also explores briefly other market structures characterized by market power: oligopoly and monopolistic competition.

Short-run Costs:

➤ We develop a simple model of production costs for the firm, assuming only two inputs, K (capital) and L (labor). We'll look at a short run model in which some inputs (K) are fixed and others (L) are variable.

   ✦ "Fixed inputs," resulting in fixed costs, remain constant in the short run, regardless of the level of output.

      ▪ These would include rent for factory, machinery, etc.

- We assume K is the only fixed input.
  - ✦ "Variable inputs," resulting in variable costs, change in the direction that output changes.
    - These would include inputs like raw materials, shipping costs, labor, etc.
    - We assume L is the variable input.
  - ✦ Total cost is the sum of fixed costs and variable costs: TC = FC + VC

➤ The firm's decision about how much to produce depends, in part, on the costs of production.
  - ✦ A "labor productivity curve" illustrates the additional output produced by adding labor to a fixed amount of capital.
    - Note that at some point additional units of labor may actually decrease output. This is due to diminishing marginal productivity.

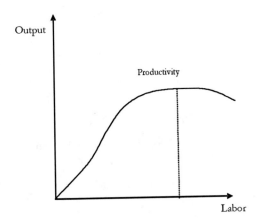

  - ✦ To determine how much it costs to produce an additional unit of output (assuming Labor is our only variable input and Capital is fixed) all we need do is determine how much labor is required to produce one more unit and multiply by the wage rate (w).
    - Total Variable Cost: TVC = w × L
  - ✦ The fixed costs are represented with a horizontal curve, since these don't vary with output. It is the cost per unit of Capita (r—often referred to as the rental rate of capital) times the amount of capital being employed:
    - Total Fixed Cost: TFC = r × K
  - ✦ The total cost curve, then, represents the sum of the fixed and variable costs for each unit.
    - TC = TFC + TVC

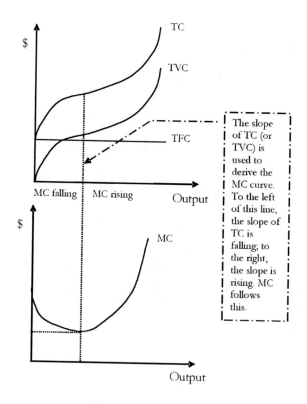

➤ The firm makes its decisions about whether to remain in business and how much to produce, based on the average and marginal cost information, in comparison to the market price for its product.

✦ Marginal cost (MC) is change in total cost for a one-unit change in output: $MC = \Delta TC/\Delta Q$

▪ Generally we consider a 1-unit change in output but marginal cost can be measured over other ranges of output as well.

✦ The MC curve is derived from the total variable cost curve. In the figure above, you can see that MC falls when the slope of TVC is decreasing; MC rises when the slope of TVC is increasing.

✦ $AC = TC/Q = AFC + AVC$

▪ $AFC = TFC/Q$

▪ $AVC = TVC/Q$

▪ As an exercise, derive these curves.

Maximizing Profit

➤ Maximizing profit requires a comparison of costs with revenues.

✦ We consider firms that are "price takers." These firms produce in industries where the market (market Supply and Demand together) determines price.

- For example, if you produce corn and want to sell it in a commodities market, you can get the market price and no more. The firm has no "market power."

  ∞ Marginal Revenue: MR = ΔTR/ΔQ

  ∞ The price taking firm's MR = market price (P).

➤ *Profit Maximization Rule:* To maximize profit, the firm wants to sell any output it can produce as long as MR > MC; that is, they will continue selling as long as the benefit outweighs the cost. So they produce up to the point at which MR = MC.

  ✦ If there is a level of output (Q) where MR=MC the profit maximizing firm will produce *exactly* at that point.

  ✦ If there is no Q for which MR = MC, then the firm should produce at the last Q where MR > MC, and not produce any units for which MC > MR.

➤ Since the firm must sell for the market price (P = MR also equal to average revenue, AR), we can illustrate profit-maximizing behavior, as in the figure below.

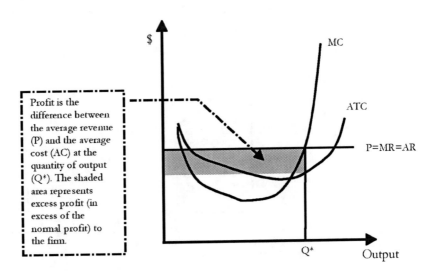

Profit is the difference between the average revenue (P) and the average cost (AC) at the quantity of output (Q*). The shaded area represents excess profit (in excess of the normal profit) to the firm.

  ✦ We show the firm's total profit as the difference between average revenue and average cost.

    - Average Revenue: AR = TR/Q = P, when all units are sold at the same P.

    - Therefore, Profit = Q × (P − AC). This is illustrated in the figure above as the shaded rectangle.

  ✦ In a competitive market, firms are attracted to profit. If there is a profit firms will enter the market. Market supply will shift to the right and price will fall. This will occur until P = MR = AR falls to the lowest point on the ATC curve—the point where ATC is equal to MC.

  ✦ A firm that is at the breakeven point (no economic profit, no loss) is shown in the next figure.

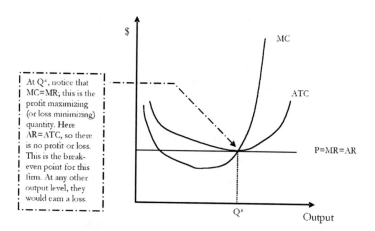

At Q*, notice that MC=MR; this is the profit maximizing (or loss minimizing) quantity. Here AR=ATC, so there is no profit or loss. This is the break-even point for this firm. At any other output level, they would earn a loss.

✦ Note: A firm making no economic profit is still covering all opportunity costs. The owner can do no better in another industry (and if opportunity costs are substantial, may be doing quite well financially).

✦ In the figure below, the same firm illustrated immediately above chooses to produce at Q1. Their loss is the shaded area.

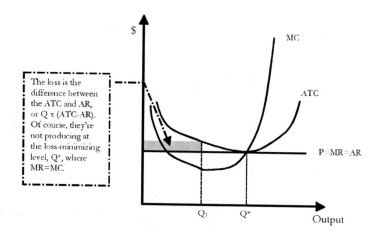

The loss is the difference between the ATC and AR, or Q x (ATC-AR). Of course, they're not producing at the loss-minimizing level, Q*, where MR=MC.

✦ In the next figure, another firm is earning a loss.

▪ Is there any other quantity that would be better?

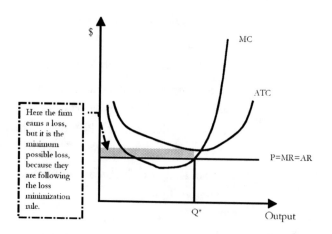

Here the firm earns a loss, but it is the minimum possible loss, because they are following the loss minimization rule.

➤ Short-run shut down point: A firm decides to shut down if the price per unit cannot even cover the variable costs of production:

  ✦ A firm should shut down if at P = MC, P < AVC. We can illustrate this, as below.

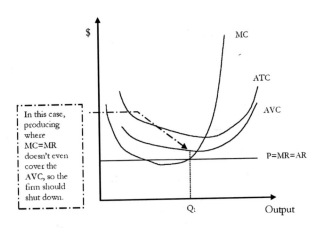

  ✦ Even in the case where the firm shuts down, it must still pay its fixed costs. But this is better than producing and losing additional money on each unit produced (shown by the difference between P and variable cost).

➤ Shutting down occurs in the short run. In the long run, a firm would exit the industry and produce something else instead.

  ✦ The opposite of "exit" is new firms entering the industry ("entry"). This occurs when there are economic profits in the industry.

Types of Markets

➤ Market structure refers to the types of goods offered, and the number of firms offering them.

  ✦ In the above discussion we assumed perfectly competitive markets. These are markets with homogeneous (identical) goods, many producers, many buyers, no barriers to entry and perfect information about products and prices so that no individual producer has any market power (i.e., no one can affect market price; if one seller raises price 1¢, sales fall to zero).

  ✦ The opposite extreme is a monopoly. This is a single firm that produces a product with no close substitutes. Because the monopolist is the only supplier of the good, it can set the market price where it wants (but still faces a market demand so the quantity sold is determined by consumers at the price the monopolist sets).

  ✦ Monopolistic competition is an industry with many firms and differentiated products, and firms have a slight ability to affect price. (Sales don't fall to zero if they raise price a bit.)

✦ Closer to a monopoly is the oligopoly market structure. Here there are few firms and the product may be differentiated. At least one of the firms in this market can affect price.

Perfect Competition

➤ Firms in competitive markets are price takers.

   ✦ They can sell as much as they want at the market price (Pe), but none at any price above Pe.

   ✦ The product is homogeneous.

   ✦ Since their products and prices are the same, firms do not advertise in competitive markets.

   ✦ Entry and exit are free of barriers.

➤ Although the market demand curve has a negative slope, each firm in the industry faces a flat demand curve (perfectly elastic demand).

   ✦ This means that they can sell as much as they want at the market equilibrium price. But if they raise their price even 1¢, their sales fall to zero.

   ✦ Then the firm's demand curve is flat, at the Pe.

➤ The firm's supply curve is found along its MC curve (above the minimum of the AVC curve).

   ✦ Recall that each firm produces up to the point at which P = MC in order to maximize profit. Also recall that a supply curve indicates the quantities a firm is willing to produce/sell at each P.

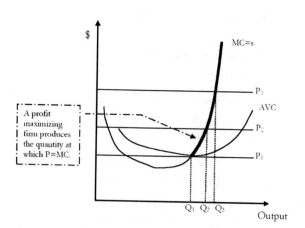

   ✦ Summing all firms' individual supply curves (s), yields the market supply curve (S).

➤ Since economic profits will attract entry into the industry (→ S↑) , and losses will cause exit from the industry (→ S↓), then in the absence of other supply changes or changes in demand, in the long-run, the market will look like the figure below.

✦ The figure shows an initial price above the long-run equilibrium. The expectation of economic profits encourages market entry. This causes an increase in supply, P falls, and eventually all firms in the market earn a normal profit.

✦ The long-run equilibrium shows market Qe = 25. Suppose there are 5 identical firms, each producing 5 units of output.

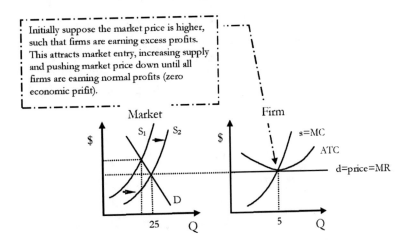

➤ This model of a perfectly competitive market is a benchmark for comparison.

✦ Commodity markets function this way, as do stock markets. But markets for other goods are usually not perfectly competitive.

Sources of Monopoly

➤ Monopolies are single sellers of goods/services for which there are no close substitutes.

✦ Since they're the only sellers, it means they are price makers, rather than price takers. That is, they can control market price.

➤ The main reason monopolies exist, or continue to exist, is that there are barriers to entry. This means that it would be prohibitively costly for new firms to enter the industry.

✦ Even when there are only potential entrants, monopolies might act more like competitive firms.

➤ What are the types of monopoly?

✦ A legal monopoly is enforced by the government. A good example here is the Post Office.

- Why do they advertise and sponsor sporting events, etc., if they're a monopoly?

◆ Monopoly "by possession" means that the firm owns all or most of the resources necessary to produce a particular good or service.

- Examples of these are difficult to find, mainly because you can usually find some type of substitute good.

◆ A natural monopoly is an industry/firm that has decreasing long run average costs throughout the demand for the product.

- In this case, it is less costly to have a single firm producing, rather than two or more firms.

- Examples typically include utilities (power, water, cable TV, phone, etc.), but now only the physical lines are the "natural monopoly" part of these businesses.

  • Power and phone lines can be owned by one firm, but used by a number of carriers.

◆ All firms that have market power, including monopolists, have negative-sloped demand curves. This means the firms can affect market prices. They are price "makers" not takers.

The Profit Maximizing Monopoly

➤ Since the monopolist enjoys barriers to entry to its industry, it can raise price and earn excess profits without attracting new entrants.

➤ To determine the profit maximizing quantity and price, we need to introduce the monopolist's marginal revenue curve.

◆ The monopolist has a negative-sloped demand curve. But the marginal revenue curve is steeper than the demand curve.

◆ In order to increase the quantity of sales, the price must be lowered. But the same price is charged to all consumers. So if price falls, there is less revenue from each sale, but more sales. So when price is lowered to get more sales, the marginal revenue from the additional sale is not equal to the price. It's actually lower.

◆ Like all profit maximizing firms, the monopolist wants to produce up to the point at which MR = MC. This is shown in the following figure.

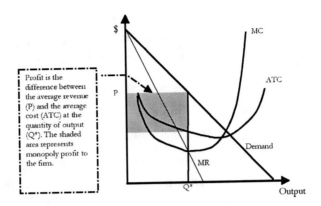

Profit is the difference between the average revenue (P) and the average cost (ATC) at the quantity of output (Q*). The shaded area represents monopoly profit to the firm.

Antitrust and Regulation

➤ If you compare the monopolist's profit maximizing output to the "socially efficient" output level, you'll find the monopolists is smaller.

   ✦ Recall that the competitive market output is allocatively efficient. It's found where MC = MB (where the firm's supply or MC curve crosses the demand curve).

➤ The Federal Trade Commission (est. 1914) is charged with administering the government's antitrust laws, which are designed to prevent businesses from engaging in "anticompetitive" activities, i.e., those that reduce competition in the market.

   ✦ Ideally, these laws and their enforcement would be geared at making consumers better off. But often, firms make complaints against each other so that they can enjoy higher prices or greater market share.

   ✦ A specific example is regulated pricing for monopolies (called rate of return regulation). For example, average cost pricing might be imposed.

      ▪ This results in a greater than monopoly output, but still it's less than the competitive output.

      ▪ One potential problem is that there is no incentive for the monopolist to control costs. Thus, the policy might not be great for the consumers, in terms of getting less expensive goods.

Oligopoly and Monopolistic Competition

➤ Now we have outlined the two extreme forms of market structure. Perfect competition and monopoly are two benchmarks. In between these two extremes are two others with market power, but less than the monopolist.

- ✦ Oligopoly and monopolistic competition are market structures that also have negative sloped demand curves, but theirs are flatter than the monopolist's, which means they are less able to control prices than the monopolist is.

➤ An oligopolistic market is one with relatively few firms.

- ✦ One or more of the firms produces a significant proportion of total industry output.

- ✦ The product may be homogeneous or differentiated.

- ✦ For example, the car industry is an oligopoly.

➤ Monopolistic competition means lots of firms.

- ✦ Products are generally differentiated.

➤ The oligopoly and monopolistically competitive firms attempt to increase demand for their firms through advertising. Recall that there was no need for the monopolist to advertise.

- ✦ If you can stress product differentiation, that should help.

➤ Price discrimination is charging different prices to different customers, when the cost of producing the good is the same for the different customers.

- ✦ Examples include airline tickets, movie theaters (kids, adults, seniors pay different prices), and college tuition (in-state and out-of-state).

- ✦ Firms would like to be able to do this—to charge the maximum price each individual is willing to pay. But this is difficult to do in practice, because firms do not know what a person's demand curve looks like.

- ✦ Car dealers attempt to price discriminate, for example. They ask you questions about your career, how much you'd "like to pay," whether you've looked at other cars or at online sources, etc., to make some determination of how strong your demand is.

7. U.S. MACROECONOMIC DATA

Variable/Year	2000	2001	2002	2003	2004	2005	2006	2007*	2008*
Nominal GDP (billions $)	9,817.0	10,128.0	10,469.0	10,960.0	11,686.0	12,434.0	13,195.0		
GDP Price Deflator (2000=100)	100.0	102.4	104.2	106.4	109.5	113.0	116.6		
Real GDP (billions $)	9,817.0	9,890.0	10,049.0	10,301.0	10,672.0	11,004.0	11,317.0		
CPI (1982–84=100)	172.2	177.0	179.9	184.0	188.9	195.3	201.6		
Unemployment Rate (%)	4.0	4.7	5.8	6.0	5.5	5.1	4.6		

SOURCE: Federal Reserve Bank of Dallas (www.dallasfed.org)

* You may fill-in these cells once the data are available.

8. PRESENT AND FUTURE VALUE

Suppose you could choose between receiving a new flat screen TV today, and receiving the same TV one month from now. Unless you have unusual preferences, you would choose receiving the TV today. In general, we prefer present consumption over future consumption because we discount the future. *How much* we should discount the future is determined by the interest rate and the present value formula. The relationship between present and future value is often referred to as "the time value of money," but it is important to keep in mind that it is what we do with the money (e.g. consumption or investment) that really matters.

One of the easiest ways to see this relationship is to imagine you are putting money into a savings account at your local bank. If you put $100 into the account now, you would like to know how much money you will have in one, two and three or more years. This initial $100 is referred to as the principle, and the extra income earned on the principle are interest payments. We normally assume there is *compound* interest, meaning that the interest earned each period is applied to the principle and the interest income from all previous periods. If the bank calculates and pays compound interest on an annual basis, we can use the following formula:

$$FV_t = PV(1 + r)^t, \qquad (1)$$

where FV_t is the future value in t years, PV is the present value and r is the interest rate (or yield) per annum. In this case the present value is $100. If the annual interest rate is 5% then r is expressed as a decimal so that the value of the deposit after one, two and three years will be (rounding to the nearest cent),

Year One: $FV_1 = PV(1 + r) = \$100(1.05) = \$105$

Year Two: $FV_2 = PV(1 + r)^2 = \$100(1.05)^2 = \$110.25$

Year Three: $FV_3 = PV(1 + r)^3 = \$100(1.05)^3 = \$115.76.$

In general, to find the future value in t periods, multiply the present value by $(1 + r)$ to the t power. One can also think of r as a growth rate for any variable which grows at a constant rate.

Up to this point, compounding has occurred in discreet periods. Continuous compounding is essentially making the compounding periods infinitely small, so that interest is compounding continuously. In order to calculate future value when using continuous compounding the following equation must be used.

$$FV_t = PVe^{rt} \qquad (2)$$

We can do a simple example using the concept of retirement savings. Assume you save $2,000 for retirement your first year out of college when you are 22 years old and you plan to retire when you are 65 years old (t = 43). Let's try this with interest rates of 5% and 10%.

5% interest rate: $FV_t = PVe^{rt} = 2{,}000e^{(.05*43)} = \$17{,}169.72$

10% interest rate: $FV_t = PVe^{rt} = 2{,}000e^{(.10*43)} = \$147{,}399.59$

The \$2,000 you saved as a 22 year old will be worth \$17,170 if it earns 5% interest and the \$2,000 would be worth \$147,400 if you can earn 10%. It's no wonder Albert Einstein supposedly said,"The most powerful force in the universe is compound interest."

Most people can easily grasp the idea of a present value growing through time to become a future value. What comes less easily for some is the intuition behind discounting a future value to arrive at a present value. For any future value we can rearrange formula (1) to calculate a present value,

$$PV = \frac{FV_t}{(1 + r)^t}. \tag{3}$$

For example, if the interest rate is 7%, what is the present value of receiving \$150 in ten years? We simply plug the appropriate values into the present value formula to get,

$$PV = \frac{\$150}{(1.07)^{10}} = \$76.25.$$

The present value formula answers the following question: How much would I need to save now in order to have \$150 in ten years? Based on an annual compound interest rate of 7%, the answer is \$76.25. As an exercise, you can calculate the present value when the interest rate is 10%. Your answer should confirm that the present value is inversely related to the interest rate.

Present value is a useful way to compare different dollar amounts in different time periods. Again you have two options: receiving \$200 in two years (option A) and \$250 in three years (option B). Which is better? To answer the question we use the market interest rate to convert both options into present value. If the interest rate is 10%, the present values are,

$$PV_A = \frac{\$200}{(1.1)^2} = \frac{\$200}{1.21} = \$165.29.$$

$$PV_B = \frac{\$250}{(1.1)^3} = \frac{\$250}{1.331} = \$187.83.$$

so option B is better. Since the present values will change with different interest rates, we cannot say that option B is always better; only that it is better with an interest rate of 10%. [Exercise: find the interest rate in which someone is indifferent between the two options.]

9. FEDERAL INCOME TAX

The marginal tax rates apply to "taxable income," which is gross income minus exemptions and deductions. (See below for more info on these for 2007.)

Here we show the tax tables for single taxpayers. There are different tables for married couples and single heads of household.

Marginal Tax Rates

2001

Taxable Income	Marginal Tax Rate
$ 0 – 27,050	15.0%
$ 27,050 – 65,550	27.5%
$ 65,550 – 136,750	30.5%
$ 136,750 – 297,350	35.5%
$297,350 and above	39.1%

Example: If your taxable income had been $80,000 in 2001, your tax would be ...

$$(\$27,050 \times 0.15) + ([\$65,550 - 27,050] \times 0.275) + ([80,000 - 65,550) \times 0.305$$

$$= \quad 4057.50 \quad + \quad 10,587.50 \quad + \quad 4,407.25$$

$$= \$19,052.25$$

In this case the *average tax rate* is the tax paid/taxable income, or 23.8%.

2007

Taxable Income	Marginal Tax Rate	Tax Amount
$ 0 – 7,825	10%	10% of amount
$ 7,825 – 31,850	15%	$782.50 + 15% of amt. over $7,825
$ 31,850 – 77,100	25%	$4,386.225 + 25% of amt. over $31,850
$ 77,100 – 160,850	28%	$15,698.75 + 28% of amt. over $77,100
$ 160,850 – 349,700	33%	$39,148.75 + 33% of amt. over $128,500
$349,700 and above	35%	$101,469.25 + 35% of amt. over $349,700

Example: If your taxable income had been $80,000 in 2007, your tax would be ...

$$\$15,698.75 + ([80,000 - 77,100] \times 0.28) = \$16,510.75$$

Here the *average tax rate* is 20.6%.

The personal and dependent exemption is $3,400 for 2007. The standard deduction is $5,350 (single).

Both of these are typically adjusted for inflation each year.

10. FEDERAL RECEIPTS AND OUTLAYS, BY MAJOR CATEGORY, AND SURPLUS OR DEFICIT, FISCAL YEARS 1980–2007

Year	Receipts (on-budget and off-budget)					Outlays (on-budget and off-budget)										Surplus or deficit (-) (on-budget and off-budget)
	Total	Individual income taxes	Corp. income taxes	Soc. Ins. and ret. Receipts	Other	Total	National defense		Intl. affairs	Health	Medicare	Income security	Social security	Net interest	Other	
							Total	Def. Dept, military								
1980	517.1	244.1	64.6	157.8	50.6	590.9	134.0	130.9	12.7	23.2	32.1	86.6	118.5	52.5	131.3	-73.8
1981	599.3	285.9	61.1	182.7	69.5	678.2	157.5	153.9	13.1	26.9	39.1	100.3	139.6	68.8	133.0	-79.0
1982	617.8	297.7	49.2	201.5	69.3	745.7	185.3	180.7	12.3	27.4	46.6	108.2	156.0	85.0	125.0	-128.0
1983	600.6	288.9	37.0	209.0	65.6	808.4	209.9	204.4	11.8	28.6	52.6	123.0	170.7	89.8	121.8	-207.8
1984	666.5	298.4	56.9	239.4	71.8	851.9	227.4	220.9	15.9	30.4	57.5	113.4	178.2	111.1	117.9	-185.4
1985	734.1	334.5	61.3	265.2	73.1	946.4	252.7	245.1	16.2	33.5	65.8	129.0	188.6	129.5	131.0	-212.3
1986	769.2	349.0	63.1	283.9	73.2	990.4	273.4	265.4	14.2	35.9	70.2	120.6	198.8	136.0	141.4	-221.2
1987	854.4	392.6	83.9	303.3	74.6	1,004.1	282.0	273.9	11.6	40.0	75.1	124.1	207.4	138.6	125.3	-149.7
1988	909.3	401.2	94.5	334.3	79.3	1,064.5	290.4	281.9	10.5	44.5	78.9	130.4	219.3	151.8	138.8	-149.7
1989	991.2	445.7	103.3	359.4	82.8	1,143.8	303.6	294.8	9.6	48.4	85.0	137.4	232.5	169.0	158.4	-152.6
1990	1,032.1	466.9	93.5	380.0	91.7	1,253.1	299.3	289.7	13.8	57.7	98.1	148.7	248.6	184.3	202.6	-221.0
1991	1,055.1	467.8	98.1	396.0	93.2	1,324.3	273.3	262.3	15.9	71.2	104.5	172.5	269.0	194.4	223.6	-269.2
1992	1,091.3	476.0	100.3	413.7	101.4	1,381.6	298.4	286.8	16.1	89.5	119.0	199.6	287.6	199.3	172.2	-290.3
1993	1,154.5	509.7	117.5	428.3	99.0	1,409.5	291.1	278.5	17.2	99.4	130.6	210.0	304.6	198.7	158.0	-255.1
1994	1,258.7	543.1	140.4	461.5	113.8	1,461.9	281.6	268.6	17.1	107.1	144.7	217.2	319.6	202.9	171.7	-203.2
1995	1,351.9	590.2	157.0	484.5	120.2	1,515.9	272.1	259.4	16.4	115.4	159.9	223.8	335.8	232.1	160.3	-164.0
1996	1,453.2	656.4	171.8	509.4	115.5	1,560.6	265.8	253.1	13.5	119.4	174.2	229.7	349.7	241.1	167.3	-107.4
1997	1,579.4	737.5	182.3	539.4	120.3	1,601.3	270.5	258.3	15.2	123.8	190.0	235.0	365.3	244.0	157.4	-21.9
1998	1,722.0	828.6	188.7	571.8	132.9	1,652.7	268.5	256.1	13.1	131.4	192.8	237.8	379.2	241.1	188.8	69.3
1999	1,827.6	879.5	184.7	611.8	151.7	1,702.0	274.9	261.3	15.2	141.1	190.4	242.5	390.0	229.8	218.1	125.6
2000	2,025.5	1,004.5	207.3	652.9	160.9	1,789.2	294.5	281.2	17.2	154.5	197.1	253.7	409.4	222.9	239.8	236.2
2001	1,991.4	994.3	151.1	694.0	152.0	1,863.2	304.9	290.3	16.5	172.3	217.4	269.8	433.0	206.2	243.3	128.2
2002	1,853.4	858.3	148.0	700.8	146.2	2,011.2	348.6	332.0	22.4	196.5	230.9	312.7	456.0	170.9	273.2	-157.8
2003	1,782.5	793.7	131.8	713.0	144.1	2,160.1	404.9	387.3	21.2	219.6	249.4	334.6	474.7	153.1	302.6	-377.6
2004	1,880.3	809.0	189.4	733.4	148.5	2,293.0	455.9	436.5	26.9	240.1	269.4	333.1	495.5	160.2	311.9	-412.7
2005	2,153.9	927.2	278.3	794.1	154.2	2,472.2	495.3	474.2	34.6	250.6	298.6	345.8	523.3	184.0	339.9	-318.3
2006	2,285.5	997.6	277.1	841.1	169.7	2,708.7	535.9	512.1	34.8	268.8	343.0	360.6	554.7	220.1	390.8	-423.2
2007	2,415.9	1,096.4	260.6	884.1	174.8	2,770.1	527.4	504.9	33.3	280.9	392.0	367.2	585.9	247.3	336.0	-354.2

2006 and 2007 are estimates. Note.—All are in billions of dollars for fiscal years. (Source: Table B-80 from 2006 Economic Report of the President.)

11. AGGREGATE DEMAND AND AGGREGATE SUPPLY

As you probably remember, the performance of any macroeconomy will vary over time. We observe the effects of these fluctuations as changes in output (as measured by GDP), employment, and inflation rates. Through the years GDP in the United States has grown at an average rate of approximately 3 percent, but unfortunately it can, and does, vary considerably over time. During recessionary periods GDP actually declines, which means that fewer goods and services are produced. In this section we introduce the Aggregate Demand (AD)/Aggregate Supply (AS) model to help explain and understand the workings of the macroeconomy and what leads to changes in its performance. Additionally, the model is useful to explain the impacts of fiscal and monetary policy on macroeconomic performance. Fiscal policy revolves around government's spending and taxing powers to achieve economic goals while monetary policy involves control of the money supply to accomplish economic goals. The goals most commonly sought by fiscal and monetary policy are healthy rates of growth for GDP, high employment, and stable prices. Once the model is developed your professor will illustrate the impact of various policy prescriptions on the macroeconomy.

Aggregate Demand:

We begin by developing the concept of Aggregate Demand (AD). Recall that GDP represents the aggregate output of an economy over a specified period of time, normally one year. One way to calculate GDP is by summing expenditures made by individuals on domestically produced final goods and services. The sum of these expenditures represents the aggregate demand for final goods and services produced in the domestic economy. It is common to group these expenditures into four major areas for study. They are (1) purchases by domestic households known as personal consumption expenditures (C), (2) purchases by businesses known as investment expenditures (I), (3) purchases by governments (G) and (4) foreign purchases, commonly referred to as net exports (NX). This is represented mathematically as AD = C + I + G + NX. A number of different causal economic variables affect each of these spending components. One such variable is the price level where its impact on aggregate purchases is illustrated in Figure 15.1. In this graph, AD is drawn downward sloping illustrating that when the price level (the price level is measured on the vertical axis by a general price index such as the GDP deflator) is relatively higher, the aggregate purchases of goods and services (measured on the horizontal axis as Y) is lower and visa versa. At point A in Figure 15.1 the price level is P_1 and the aggregate purchases

FIGURE 15.1

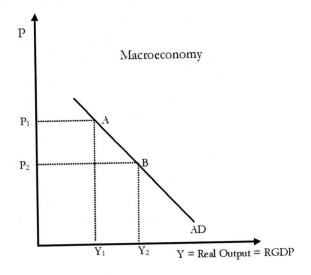

of goods and services is Y_1, while at a relatively lower price level P_2 the aggregate purchases of goods and services is higher as illustrated by Y_2.

Three primary factors cause this inverse relationship between the price level and aggregate purchases. The first (the wealth effect) is that as the price level declines, *ceteris paribus*, the purchasing power of assets, particularly money, increases. For example, a given amount of money in a checking account will purchase more goods and services if, on average, the costs of those products purchased decline. The opposite occurs when prices rise. The second reason the AD curve is drawn downward sloping is due to the impact that changes in the price level have on interest rates (the interest rate effect). When prices fall, *ceteris paribus*, individuals need less money for day-to-day expenditures, like buying groceries and paying for someone to mow their lawn. Assuming the money supply remains constant, as the need for money decreases people have more to save in interest-earning assets like savings accounts and bonds. This means more funds available to the loanable funds market, which leads eventually to lower interest rates. Lower interest rates lead, for example, to more purchases by households (C) on items normally purchased with borrowed money and more purchases by businesses on new plant and equipment (I). The opposite is true when the price level rises. The final reason for drawing the AD curve downward sloping is the effect that price level changes have on the purchases of domestically produced goods and services by people throughout the world (the net export effect). For example, if the price level declines in the United States, *ceteris paribus*, goods and services produced here become relatively cheaper than the same products produced in other countries. This fact provides an incentive for foreigners to buy more products produced in the United States (greater exports) and an incentive for domestic buyers to buy fewer foreign produced goods and services (fewer imports). The net effect is an increase in net exports (exports minus imports) which increases domestic aggregate purchases. Again, the opposite is true when prices rise in the United States relative to the rest of the world. To summarize, the three effects just discussed, which are caused by price level changes, alter aggregate purchases of goods and services and are illustrated by movement along a given downward sloping AD curve.

As mentioned earlier, the spending components of aggregate demand may be affected by changes in a number of causal economic variables in addition to the price level (examples include the money supply, tax rates, expectations of households and businesses, and government spending). When an economic factor, other than the price level, causes changes in spending its impact is to shift aggregate demand. The easiest way to visualize and understand what this means is to look at Figure 15.2. Assume the price level is constant at P_1 (any price level will do) and now allow the expectations of households and businesses to become more optimistic. This change will result in these two groups spending more on goods and services at any price level. The reason is because members of the household sector feel better about the future and consider their jobs secure while members of the business sector believe

FIGURE 15.2

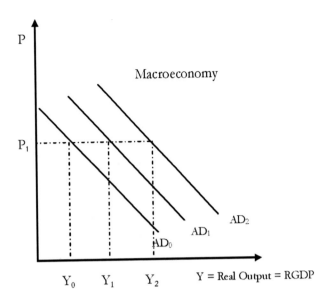

people will buy more from them in the future hence they are more willing to invest in their business. Such an occurrence will result in greater purchases (an increase in aggregate demand) at any price level. In Figure 15.2, this is illustrated as a shift in the aggregate demand curve from AD_0 to AD_1. Another example would be a recession enveloping an important trading partner of the United States. The recession would result in a decline in income for members of the affected economy resulting in fewer purchases of goods and services, including those produced in the United States. Such an occurrence (a decline in NX) would result in a reduction in the aggregate demand for domestically produced goods and services. This possibility is illustrated in the figure as a shift in the aggregate demand curve from AD_2 to AD_1. Any factor that affects one of spending components of aggregate demand, other than the price level, will cause a shift in the aggregate demand curve to the right or left. The macroeconomic effects of these shifts will be discussed shortly.

Aggregate Supply:

We now introduce the concept of aggregate supply (AS), which focuses on the aggregate output of goods and services produced in an economy. As with aggregate demand (AD), there are many causal factors that affect production decisions of businesses. Additionally, the period of time under consideration influences business production decisions. Because of this, we discuss AS in both the short-run (a period of time when some economic factors cannot be changed) and the long run (a period of time sufficient for businesses to fully adjust to a change in a causal economic factor).

FIGURE 15.3

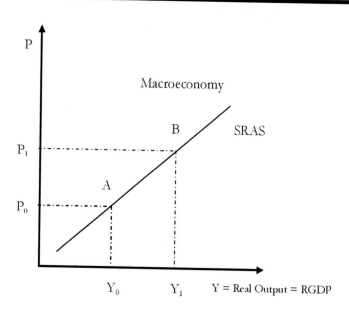

Short-run Aggregate Supply:

Short-run aggregate supply (SRAS) is illustrated in Figure 15.3 as an upward sloping curve.

This shows that as the price level increases in the short-run, *ceteris paribus*, businesses respond by increasing production. For example, when the price level is P_0 firms produce output Y_0 shown at point A and when the price level rises to P_1 firms respond by increasing production to Y_1 shown at point B. The reason for this relationship in the short-run is due to how businesses and resource owners plan for the future. Decisions made today result in many production costs remaining fixed for a set period of time. For example, when negotiating a labor contract a primary concern is to protect wage earners from the effects of rising prices. Expectations regarding the future price level will be incorporated into wage increases when negotiating a labor contract. After the contract is signed, wages become fixed to the firm during the remainder of the contract period. A similar situation would also exist for many other inputs used in the production process. This means that when individuals agree to contacts today, which are influenced by expected future prices, production costs remain relatively fixed during the contract period.

If future prices deviate from those widely anticipated, firm profits will change thus altering the incentives faced by firms that then lead to changes in aggregate production levels. For example, assume individuals expect price level P_0 to exist in the future. This means firms and resource owners will negotiate contracts based on this expectation of future prices. If this price level actually exists, firms will produce output Y_0 as shown in Figure 15.3. However, if the actual price level turns of to be P_1, the aggregate production of firms will be output Y_1 in the short-run rather than Y_0. This is due to the fact that the price level is higher than expected and given that some input costs are fixed by contract, profits of firms will increase providing the incentive to increase aggregate production above Y_0. The opposite would occur if the actual price level falls below expectations leading firms to produce less than expected.

Long-run Aggregate Supply:

One aspect of the long-run is that contracts are no longer fixed since they can eventually be renegotiated. If the price level is different than expected when contracts were originally signed, they will be renegotiated including this new information. The ultimate result of this is that aggregate production will not be affected by price level changes in the long-run. The main factors that determine aggregate production in the long-run are resource availability, the level of technology, and the economy's institutional structure. The long-run aggregate supply (LRAS) is illustrated in Figure 15.4 as a vertical line. This is conceptually similar to an economy's production possibilities, which defines the maximum production of goods and services given full-employment and efficient use of resources. Economists traditionally refer to this aggregate production level as the potential output of an economy (Y_p)—the output the economy can produced on a sustained basis with full and efficient utilization of economic resources. Potential output is produced when the actual price level is equal to the expected price level.

FIGURE 15.4

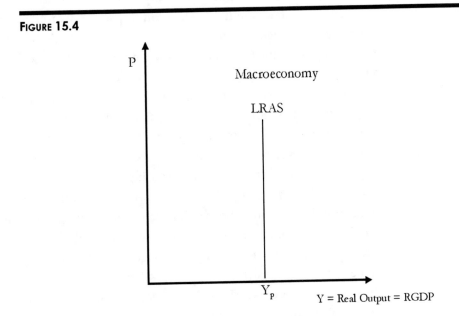

FIGURE 15.5

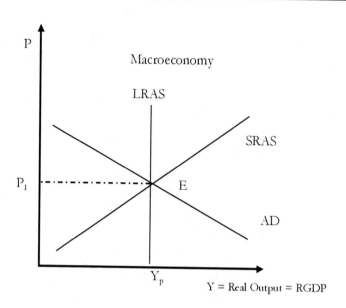

Equilibrium in the Macroeconomy:

Equilibrium in this context refers to where the economy settles after it has had time to adjust to causal economy events. Additionally, we should mention that there will be an equilibrium for the short-run and one for the long-run as you will soon see. The concept of equilibrium in the macroeconomy is illustrated in Figure 15.5 at point E where the price level is P_1 and the aggregate output is Y_p. This is an example of a long-run equilibrium for the macroeconomy since AD equals SRAS and the economy is producing its potential output. The economy will remain there until some causal economic factor changes sending the economy in search of another equilibrium. As the macroeconomy adjusts towards a new equilibrium we observe changes in aggregate output (GDP), employment, and the price level.

To illustrate this process further refer to Figure 15.6 and assume the macroeconomy is currently in long-run equilibrium at point E_0. Now assume that AD unexpectedly increases from AD_0 to AD_1. The unexpected rise in aggregate demand will result in the price level increasing from P_0 to P_1. Since P_1 is a price level higher than expected, firm profits will rise thus causing output to expand from Y_p to Y_1. Point E_1 in the figure is an example of a short-run macroeconomic equilibrium. The movement from E_0 to E_1 are observed in the economy as increases in GDP, employment, and the level of prices. However, these outcomes will not persist since, as mentioned earlier, contracts will eventually be renegotiated that incorporate expectations of the higher price level. As this happens, production costs rise thus leading to a leftward shift of the SRAS curve. This shift illustrates that the increased costs of production cause lower profits (at all possible price levels) and lead firms to reduce aggregate production. This process will continue until a new equilibrium, this time a long-run

FIGURE 15.6

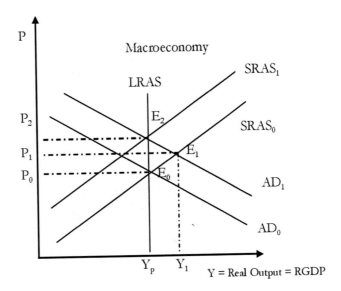

equilibrium, is achieved at point E_2 where the new aggregate demand curve (AD_1) is equal to the new short-run aggregate supply curve ($SRAS_1$) and LRAS. At this point the price level has risen to P_2 and aggregate output falls back to potential output (Y_p). Specific examples of factors that change aggregate demand and their impact on the economy will be discussed and illustrated by your professor.

GLOSSARY

Accommodating policy Expansionary monetary or fiscal policy used to increase aggregate demand in order to moderate the effects of a supply shock on real output.

Aggregate demand Total real planned expenditure.

Aggregate demand curve A graph showing the relationship between aggregate demand and the aggregate price level.

Aggregate supply Total real output of final goods and services (real GDP).

Aggregate supply curve A graph showing the relationship between real output (real domestic product) and the average price level of final goods.

Appreciate A currency is said to appreciate if its value increases relative to the currency of another country.

Assets All the things that the firm or household owns or to which it holds a legal claim.

Automatic fiscal policy Changes in government purchases or net taxes that are caused by changes in economic conditions given unchanged tax and spending laws.

Automatic stabilizers Those elements of automatic fiscal policy that move the federal budget toward deficit during an economic contraction and toward surplus during an expansion.

Autonomous In the context of the income-expenditure model, refers to an expenditure that is independent of the level of real domestic income.

Autonomous consumption The part of total real consumption expenditure that is independent of the level of real disposable income; for any given consumption schedule, real autonomous consumption equals the level of real consumption associated with zero real disposable income.

Autonomous net taxes Taxes or transfer payments that do not vary with the level of domestic income.

Average propensity to consume   Total consumption for any income level divided by total disposable income.

Balance sheet   A financial statement showing what a firm or household owns and what it owes.

Base year   The year that is chosen as a basis for comparison in calculating a price index or price level.

Bond   A certificate that represents a promise, in return for borrowed funds, to repay the loan over a period of years, with interest, according to an agreed-upon schedule.

Business cycle   A pattern of irregular but repeated expansion and contraction of aggregate economic activity.

Capital   All means of production that are created by people, including tools, industrial equipment, and structures.

Capital account   The section of a country's international accounts that consists of purchases and sales of assets and international borrowing and lending.

Capital account net demand curve   A graph that shows the net demand for a country's currency that results at various exchange rates from capital account transactions.

Capital inflows   Net borrowing from foreign financial intermediaries and net funds received from sales of real or financial assets to foreign buyers.

Capital outflows   Net lending to foreign borrowers and net funds used to purchase real or financial assets from foreign sellers.

Central bank   A government agency responsible for regulating a country's banking system and carrying out monetary policy.

Change in demand   A change in the quantity of a good that buyers are willing and able to purchase that results from a change in some condition other than the price of that good; shown by a shift in the demand curve.

Change in quantity demanded   A change in the quantity of a good that buyers are willing and able to purchase that results from a change in the good's price, other things being equal; shown by a movement from one point to another along a demand curve.

Change in quantity supplied   A change in the quantity of a good that suppliers are willing and able to sell that results from a change in the good's price, other things being equal; shown by a movement along a supply curve.

Change in supply   A change in the quantity of a good that suppliers are willing and able to sell that results from a change in some condition other than the good's price; shown by a shift in the supply curve.

Circular flow of income and product   The flow of goods and services between households and firms, balanced by the flow of payments made in exchange for goods and services.

Closed economy   An economy that has no links to the rest of the world.

Commercial banks Financial intermediaries that provide a broad range of banking services, including accepting demand deposits and making commercial loans.

Common stock A certificate of shared ownership in a corporation that gives the owner a vote in the selection of the firm's management and the right to a share in its profits.

Comparative advantage The ability to produce a good or service at a relatively lower opportunity cost than someone else.

Complementary goods A pair of goods for which an increase in the price of one results in a decrease in demand for the other.

Conditional forecast A prediction of future economic events in the form "If A, then B, other things being equal."

Consumer Price Index (CPI) An average of the prices of a market basket of goods and services purchased by a typical urban household.

Consumption All purchases of goods and services by households for the purpose of immediate use.

Consumption schedule (consumption function) A graph that shows how real consumption expenditure varies as real disposable income changes, other things being equal.

Cost-push inflation Inflation that is caused by an upward shift in the aggregate supply curve while the aggregate demand curve remains fixed or shifts upward more slowly.

Cross-elasticity of demand The ratio of the percentage change in the quantity of a good demanded to a given percentage change in the price of some other good, other things being equal.

Crowding-out effect The tendency of expansionary fiscal policy to raise the interest rate and thereby cause a decrease in real planned investment.

Currency Coins and paper money.

Current account The section of a country's international accounts that consists of imports and exports of goods and services and unilateral transfers.

Current account balance The value of a country's exports of goods and services minus the value of its imports of goods and services plus its net transfer receipts from foreign sources.

Cyclical deficit/surplus The difference between the structural budget and the actual federal budget. If the actual budget is above the structural budget, there is a cyclical surplus. Likewise, when the actual budget is below the structural budget, there is a cyclical deficit.

Cyclical unemployment The difference between the observed rate of unemployment at a given point in the business cycle and the natural rate of unemployment.

Demand The willingness and ability of buyers to purchase goods.

Demand curve A graphical representation of the relationship between the price of a good and the quantity of that good that buyers demand.

Demand-pull inflation   Inflation caused by an upward shift of the aggregate demand curve while the aggregate supply curve remains fixed or shifts upward at no more than an equal rate.

Depository institutions   Financial intermediaries, including commercial banks and thrift institutions, that accept deposits from the public.

Depreciate   A currency is said to depreciate if its value decreases relative to the currency of another country.

Direct relationship   A relationship between two variables in which an increase in the value of one variable is associated with an increase in the value of the other.

Discount rate   The interest rate charged by the Fed on loans of reserves to banks.

Discount window   The department through which the Federal Reserve lends reserves to banks.

Discouraged worker   A person who would work if a suitable job were available but has given up looking for such a job.

Discretionary fiscal policy   Changes in the laws regarding government purchases and net taxes.

Disposable personal income (disposable income)   Income minus taxes.

Domestic income   The total income of all types, including wages, rents, interest payments, and profits, paid in return for factors of production used in producing domestic product.

Domestic product   The total value of all goods and services produced annually in a given country.

Econometrics   The statistical analysis of empirical economic data.

Economic efficiency   A state of affairs in which it is impossible to make any change that satisfies one person's wants more fully without causing some other person's wants to be satisfied less fully.

Economics   The social science that seeks to understand the choices people make in using scarce resources to meet their wants.

Efficiency in distribution   A situation in which it is not possible, by redistributing existing supplies of goods, to satisfy one person's wants more fully without causing some other person's wants to be satisfied less fully.

Efficiency in production   A situation in which it is not possible, given available knowledge and productive resources, to produce more of one good without forgoing the opportunity to produce some of another good.

Elastic demand   A situation in which quantity demanded changes by a larger percentage than price, so that total revenue increases as price decreases.

Elasticity   A measure of the response of one variable to a change in another, stated as a ratio of the percentage change in one variable to the associated percentage change in another variable.

Empirical   Based on experience or observation.

Employed   A term used to refer to a person who is working at least 1 hour a week for pay or at least 15 hours per week as an unpaid worker in a family business.

Employment-population ratio   The percentage of the noninstitutional adult population that is employed.

Endogenous   Term applied to any variable that is determined by other variables included in an economic model.

Entitlements   Transfer payments governed by long-term laws that are not subject to annual budget review.

Entrepreneurship   The process of looking for new possibilities—making use of new ways of doing things, being alert to new opportunities, and overcoming old limits.

Equation of exchange   An equation that shows the relationship among the money stock (M), the income velocity of money (V), the price level (P), and real domestic product (y); written as MV = Py.

Equilibrium   A condition in which buyers' and sellers' plans exactly mesh in the marketplace, so that the quantity supplied exactly equals the quantity demanded at a given price.

Excess quantity demanded (shortage)   A condition in which the quantity of a good demanded at a given price exceeds the quantity supplied.

Excess quantity supplied (surplus)   A condition in which the quantity of a good supplied at a given price exceeds the quantity demanded.

Excess reserves   Total reserves minus required reserves.

Exchange controls   Restrictions on the freedom of firms and individuals to exchange the domestic currency for foreign currencies at market rates.

Exchange-rate based stabilization policy   A policy that uses the exchange rate as the principle operating target for macroeconomic policy.

Exogenous   Term applied to any variable that is determined by non-economic considerations, or by economic considerations that lie outside the scope of a given model.

Expenditure multiplier   The ratio of the resultant shift in real aggregate demand to an initial shift in one of the components of aggregate demand.

Factors of production   The basic inputs of labor, capital, and natural resources used in producing all goods and services.

Federal funds market   A market in which banks lend reserves to one another for periods as short as 24 hours.

Federal funds rate   The interest rate on overnight loans of reserves from one bank to another.

Federal funds target   The Fed's target for the federal funds rate, announced by the Federal Open Market Committee (FOMC).

Final goods and services   Goods and services that are sold to or ready for sale to parties that will use them for consumption, investment, government purchases, or export.

Financial inflow   Purchases of domestic assets by foreign buyers and borrowing from foreign lenders; also often called *capital inflows*.

Financial intermediaries   A group of firms, including banks, insurance companies, pension funds, and mutual funds, that gather funds from net savers and lend them to net borrowers.

Financial markets   A set of market institutions whose function is to channel the flow of funds from net savers to net borrowers.

Financial outflow   Purchases of foreign assets by domestic residents or loans by domestic lenders to foreign borrowers; also often called *capital outflows*.

Fiscal policy   Policy that is concerned with government purchases, taxes, and transfer payments.

Fiscal year   The federal government's budgetary year, which starts on October 1 of the preceding calendar year.

Fixed investment   Purchases of newly produced capital goods.

Flow   A process that occurs continuously through time, measured in units per time period.

Foreign-exchange market   A market in which the currency of one country is traded for that of another.

Frictional unemployment   The portion of unemployment that is accounted for by the short periods of unemployment needed for matching jobs with job seekers.

GDP deflator   A weighted average of the prices of all final goods and services produced in the economy.

Government expenditures   Government purchases of goods and services plus transfer payments.

Government purchases of goods and services (government purchases)   Purchases of goods by all levels of government plus purchases of services from contractors and wages of government employees.

Gross domestic product (GDP)   The value at current market prices of all final goods and services produced annually in a given country.

Gross national product (GNP) The dollar value at current market prices of all final goods and services produced annually by factors of production owned by residents of a given country, regardless of where those factors are located.

Growth recession A situation in which real output grows, but not quickly enough to keep unemployment from rising.

Hierarchy A way of achieving coordination in which individual actions are guided by instructions from a central authority.

Hyperinflation Very rapid inflation.

Income elasticity of demand The ratio of the percentage change in the quantity of a good demanded to a given percentage change in consumer incomes, other things being equal.

Income-expenditure model A model in which the equilibrium level of real domestic income is determined by treating real planned expenditure and real domestic product as functions of the level of real domestic income.

Income-product line A graph showing the level of real domestic product (aggregate supply) associated with each level of real domestic income.

Inconvertibility (of a currency) A situation in which a country's currency can be exchanged for foreign currency only through a government agency or with a government permit.

Indexation A policy of automatically adjusting a value or payment in proportion to changes in the average price level.

Inelastic demand A situation in which quantity demanded changes by a smaller percentage than price, so that total revenue decreases as price decreases.

Inferior good A good for which an increase in consumer incomes results in a decrease in demand.

Inflation A sustained increase in the average level of prices of all goods and services.

Inflationary recession An episode in which real output falls toward or below its natural level and unemployment rises toward or above its natural rate while rapid inflation continues.

Inflation targeting A strategy for price stability in which policy makers adopt an explicit target range for the rate of inflation over an intermediate time horizon.

Injections The government purchase, investment, and net export components of the circular flow.

Inside lag The delay between the time a policy change is needed and the time a decision is made.

Inventory A stock of a finished good awaiting sale or use.

Inventory investment   Changes in stocks of finished goods ready for sale, raw materials, and partially completed goods in process of production.

Inverse relationship   A relationship between two variables in which an increase in the value of one variable is associated with a decrease in the value of the other.

Investment   The sum of fixed investment and inventory investment.

Labor   The contributions to production made by people working with their minds and muscles.

Labor force   The sum of all individuals who are employed and all individuals who are unemployed.

Labor productivity   A measure of how much workers produce in a given period of time, usually measured as output per hour of work.

Law of demand   The principle that an inverse relationship exists between the price of a good and the quantity of that good that buyers demand, other things being equal.

Leakages   The saving, net tax, and import components of the circular flow.

Liabilities   All the legal claims against a firm by nonowners or against a household by nonmembers.

Liquidity   An asset's ability to be used directly as a means of payment, or to be readily converted into one, while retaining a fixed nominal value.

Liquidity trap   A situation in which interest rates near zero lead to accumulation of liquid assets instead of stimulating planned investment.

M1   A measure of the money supply that includes currency and transaction deposits.

M2   A measure of the money supply that include M1 plus retail money market mutual fund shares, money market deposit accounts, and saving deposits.

Macroeconomics   The branch of economics that studies large-scale economic phenomena, particularly inflation, unemployment, and economic growth.

Marginal propensity to consume   The proportion of each added dollar of real disposable income that households devote to consumption.

Marginal propensity to import   The percentage of each added dollar of real disposable income that is devoted to real consumption of imported goods and services.

Marginal tax rate   The percentage of each added dollar of real domestic income that must be paid in taxes.

Market   Any arrangement people have for trading with one another.

Merchandise balance   The value of a country's merchandise exports minus the value of its merchandise imports.

Microeconomics   The branch of economics that studies the choices of individuals, including households, business firms, and government agencies.

Model   A synonym for theory; in economics, often applied to theories that are stated in graphical or mathematical form.

Monetarism   A school of economics that emphasizes the importance of changes in the money stock as determinants of changes in real output and the price level.

Money   An asset that serves as a means of payment, a store of purchasing power, and a unit of account.

Money multiplier   The ratio of the equilibrium money stock to the banking system's total reserves.

Multiplier effect   The tendency of a given exogenous change in planned expenditure to increase equilibrium GDP by a greater amount.

National income   The total income earned by a country's residents, including wages, rents, interest payments, and profits.

National income accounts   A set of official government statistics on aggregate economic activity.

Natural level of real output   The trend of real GDP growth over time, also known as potential real output.

Natural rate of unemployment   The sum of frictional and structural unemployment; the rate of unemployment that persists when the economy is experiencing neither accelerating nor decelerating inflation.

Natural resources   Anything that can be used as a productive input in its natural state, such as farmland, building sites, forests, and mineral deposits.

Negative slope   A slope having a value less than zero.

Net domestic product (NDP)   Gross domestic product minus an allowance (called the *capital consumption allowance*) that represents the value of capital equipment used up in the production process.

Net exports   Exports minus imports of goods and services.

Net taxes   Tax revenue minus transfer payments.

Net tax multiplier   The ratio of an induced change in real aggregate demand to a given change in real net taxes.

Net worth   The firm's or household's assets minus its liabilities.

Neutrality of Money   The proposition that in the long run a one-time change in the money stock affects only the price level and not real output, employment, interest rates, or real planned investment.

Nominal   In economics, a term that refers to data that have not been adjusted for the effects of inflation.

Nominal exchange rate   The exchange rate expressed in the usual way: in terms of current units of foreign currency per current dollar.

Nominal interest rate   The interest rate expressed in the usual way: in terms of current dollars without adjustment for inflation.

Normal good   A good for which an increase in consumer incomes results in an increase in demand.

Normative economics   The area of economics that is devoted to judgments about whether economic policies or conditions are good or bad.

Okun's law   A rule of thumb according to which each 2 percent by which real output rises above (or falls below) its natural level results in an unemployment rate one percentage point below (or above) the natural rate.

Open economy   An economy that is linked to the outside world by imports, exports, and financial transactions.

Open market operation   A purchase (sale) by the Fed of government securities from (to) the public.

Operating target   A financial variable for which the Fed sets a short-term target, which it then uses as a guide in the day-to-day conduct of open market operations.

Opportunity cost   The cost of a good or service measured in terms of the forgone opportunity to pursue the best possible alternative activity with the same time or resources.

Outside lag   The delay between the time a policy decision is made and the time the policy change has its main effect on the economy.

Perfectly elastic demand   A situation in which the demand curve is a horizontal line.

Perfectly inelastic demand   A situation in which the demand curve is a vertical line.

Personal income   The total income received by households, including earned income and transfer payments.

Phillips curve   A graph showing the relationship between the inflation rate and the unemployment rate, other things being equal.

Planned expenditure   The sum of consumption, government purchases, net exports, and planned investment.

Planned-expenditure schedule   A graph showing the level of total real planned expenditure associated with each level of real domestic income.

Planned inventory investment   Changes in the level of inventory made on purpose, as part of a firm's business plan.

Planned investment   The sum of fixed investment and planned inventory investment.

Planned investment schedule   A graph showing the relationship between the total quantity of real planned investment expenditure and the real interest rate.

Positive economics   The area of economics that is concerned with facts and the relationships among them.

Positive slope   A slope having a value greater than zero.

Price elasticity of demand   The ratio of the percentage change in the quantity of a good demanded to a given percentage change in its price, other things being equal.

Price elasticity of supply   The ratio of the percentage change in the quantity of a good supplied to a given percentage change in its price, other things being equal.

Price index   A weighted average of the prices of goods and services expressed in relation to a base year value of 100.

Price level   A weighted average of the prices of goods and services expressed in relation to a base year value of 1.0.

Price stability   A situation in which the rate of inflation is low enough so that it is not a significant factor in business and individual decision making.

Producer price index (PPI)   A price index based on a sample of goods and services bought by business firms.

Production possibility frontier   A graph that shows possible combinations of goods that can be produced by an economy given available knowledge and factors of production.

Purchasing power parity   A situation in which a given sum of money will buy the same market basket of goods and services when converted from one currency to another at prevailing exchange rates.

Real   In economics, a term that refers to data that have been adjusted for the effects of inflation.

Real exchange rate   The nominal exchange rate adjusted for changes in the price levels of both countries relative to a chosen base year.

Real interest rate   The nominal interest rate minus the rate of inflation.

Realized expenditure   The sum of all planned and unplanned expenditures.

Realized investment   The sum of planned and unplanned investment.

Real output   A synonym for real gross domestic product.

Recession   A cyclical economic contraction that lasts six months or more.

Required-reserve ratio   Required reserves stated as a percentage of the deposits to which reserve requirements apply.

Required reserves   The minimum amount of reserves that the Fed requires depository institutions to hold.

Reserves Cash in bank vaults and banks' non-interest-bearing deposits with the Federal Reserve System.

Revenue Price times quantity sold.

Saving The part of household income that is not used to buy goods and services or to pay taxes.

Savings deposit A deposit at a bank that can be fully redeemed at any time, but from which checks cannot be written.

Scarcity A situation in which there is not enough of a resource to meet all of everyone's wants.

Securities A collective term for common stocks, bonds, and other financial instruments.

Slope For a straight line, the ratio of the change in the y value to the change in the x value between any two points on the line.

Spontaneous order A way of achieving coordination in which individuals adjust their actions in response to cues from their immediate environment.

Sterilization A monetary operation by a central bank intended to offset the effect on the domestic money stock of intervention in the foreign exchange market.

Stock A quantity that exists at a given point in time, measured in terms of units only.

Structural budget The budget surplus or deficit that the federal government would incur given current tax and spending laws and unemployment at its natural rate.

Structural budget deficit The deficit that would prevail in any year given that year's tax and spending laws, assuming real GDP to be at its natural level.

Structural unemployment The portion of unemployment that is accounted for by people who are out of work for long periods because their skills do not match those required for available jobs.

Substitute goods A pair of goods for which an increase in the price of one causes an increase in demand for the other.

Supply The willingness and ability of sellers to provide goods for sale in a market.

Supply curve A graphical representation of the relationship between the price of a good and the quantity of that good that sellers are willing to supply.

Supply shock An event, such as an increase in the price of imported oil, a crop failure, or a natural disaster, that raises input prices for all or most firms and pushes up workers' costs of living.

Tangent A straight line that touches a curve at a given point without intersecting it.

Tax incidence The distribution of the economic burden of a tax.

Tax revenue The total value of all taxes collected by government.

Theory A representation of the way in which facts are related to one another.

Thrift institutions (thrifts) A group of financial intermediaries that operate much like commercial banks; they include savings and loan associations, savings banks, and credit unions.

Time deposit A deposit at a bank or thrift institution from which funds can be withdrawn without payment of a penalty only at the end of an agreed-upon period.

Total Factor Productivity A measurement of improvements in technology and organization that allow increases in the output produced by given quantities of labor and capital.

Transaction deposit A deposit from which funds can be freely withdrawn by check or electronic transfer to make payments to third parties.

Transfer payments Payments by government to individuals not made in return for services currently performed, for example, unemployment conpensation and pensions.

Transmission mechanism The set of channels through which monetary policy affects planned expenditure.

Unemployed A term used to refer to a person who is not employed but is actively looking for work.

Unemployment rate The percentage of the labor force that is unemployed.

Unit elastic demand A situation in which price and quantity demanded change by the same percentage, so that total revenue remains unchanged as price changes.

Unplanned inventory investment Changes in the level of inventory arising from a difference between planned and actual sales.

Value added The dollar value of an industry's sales less the value of intermediate goods purchased for use in production.

Velocity (income velocity of money) The ratio of nominal domestic income to the money stock; a measure of the average number of times each dollar of the money stock is used each year for income-producing purposes.

Printed in the United States
94999LV00002BA/75-338/A